ENVIRONMENTAL LAW HANDBOOK

Third Edition

Prepared by
Goodsill Anderson Quinn & Stifel LLP

Editor
Lisa Woods Munger

Contributing Author
Lisa A. Bail

Government Institutes
A Division of ABS Group Inc.
Rockville, Maryland

Government Institutes, a Division of ABS Group Inc.
4 Research Place, Rockville, Maryland 20850, USA
Phone: (301) 921-2300
Fax: (301) 921-0373
Email: giinfo@govinst.com
Internet: http://www.govinst.com

Published October 2000.

04 03 02 01 00 5 4 3 2 1

ISBN: 0-86587-713-0

Printed in the United States of America

SUMMARY OF CONTENTS

CHAPTER 1: STATE ENVIRONMENTAL AGENCIES AND STATE ENVIRONMENTAL POLICY 1

CHAPTER 2: AIR POLLUTION CONTROL 12

CHAPTER 3: WATER POLLUTION CONTROL 73

CHAPTER 4: SAFE DRINKING WATER 128

CHAPTER 5: SOLID WASTE MANAGEMENT 150

CHAPTER 6: HAZARDOUS WASTE MANAGEMENT 194

CHAPTER 7: UNDERGROUND STORAGE TANKS 238

CHAPTER 8: HAWAII ENVIRONMENTAL RESPONSE LAW AND HAWAII EMERGENCY PLANNING AND COMMUNITY RIGHT-TO-KNOW ACT 279

CHAPTER 9: RELEASE REPORTING PROVISIONS 323

CHAPTER 10: ENVIRONMENTAL IMPACT STATEMENTS 335

CHAPTER 11: ADDITIONAL ENVIRONMENTAL LAWS 368

CHAPTER 12: HAWAII ENVIRONMENTAL COMMON LAW 421

CHAPTER 13: ADMINISTRATIVE PROCEDURE AND JUDICIAL REVIEW 436

CHAPTER 14: WATER USE 455

TABLE OF CONTENTS

CHAPTER 1: STATE ENVIRONMENTAL AGENCIES AND STATE ENVIRONMENTAL POLICY

1.0 INTRODUCTION 1

2.0 STATE ENVIRONMENTAL POLICY 2

3.0 DEPARTMENT OF HEALTH 3
- 3.1 HAZARD EVALUATION AND EMERGENCY RESPONSE OFFICE 4
- 3.2 ENVIRONMENTAL PLANNING OFFICE 5
- 3.3 ENVIRONMENTAL RESOURCES OFFICE 6
- 3.4 CLEAN AIR BRANCH 6
- 3.5 CLEAN WATER BRANCH 6
- 3.6 SAFE DRINKING WATER BRANCH 7
- 3.7 SOLID AND HAZARDOUS WASTE BRANCH 7
- 3.8 WASTEWATER BRANCH 8
- 3.9 OFFICE OF ENVIRONMENTAL QUALITY CONTROL 8
- 3.10 ENVIRONMENTAL COUNCIL 9

4.0 DEPARTMENT OF THE ATTORNEY GENERAL 9

5.0 DEPARTMENT OF AGRICULTURE 10

6.0 DEPARTMENT OF LAND AND NATURAL RESOURCES 10

7.0 COUNTY OFFICIALS 11

CHAPTER 2: AIR POLLUTION CONTROL

1.0 INTRODUCTION 12

2.0 RELATIONSHIP TO THE FEDERAL CLEAN AIR ACT 13

3.0 AMBIENT AIR QUALITY STANDARDS AND THE AIR POLLUTION CONTROL LAW 16
- 3.1 DISTRICT ATTAINMENT PLANS 17
  - 3.1.1 AREA CLASSIFICATION 17
  - 3.1.2 NAAQS ATTAINMENT PLANS 18

4.0 OTHER STATEWIDE AIR POLLUTION PROVISIONS 20
4.1 VISIBLE EMISSIONS 21
4.2 OPEN BURNING 21
4.2.1 AGRICULTURAL BURNING 21
4.2.2 NON-AGRICULTURAL BURNING 23

5.0 PERMITTING OF SOURCES 23
5.1 COVERED SOURCE AND NONCOVERED SOURCE PERMITS 24
5.1.1 COVERED SOURCE PERMIT 25
5.1.2 NONCOVERED SOURCE PERMIT 25

5.2 TRANSITION PERIOD 26
5.3 PERMIT APPLICATION 28
5.3.1 COMPLIANCE PLAN 30

5.4 PERMIT TERM AND CONTENT 30
5.5 TYPES OF PERMITS 31
5.5.1 TEMPORARY PERMIT 32
5.5.2 GENERAL PERMIT 33
5.5.3 ADMINISTRATIVE PERMIT 34
5.5.4 APPLICATIONS FOR MODIFICATIONS 34
5.5.5 PERMIT RENEWAL 36

5.6 PERMIT FEES 37
5.6.1 APPLICATION FEES 37
5.6.2 ANNUAL FEES 38

5.7 PUBLIC PARTICIPATION 40
5.8 PUBLIC ACCESS TO INFORMATION 41
5.9 PERMIT ACTION 42
5.10 REPORTING REQUIREMENTS 43

6.0 EQUIPMENT SHUTDOWN AND FAILURE 44

7.0 PREVENTION OF SIGNIFICANT DETERIORATION OF AIR QUALITY 45
7.1 PSD EXEMPTIONS 45
7.2 AMBIENT AIR INCREMENTS AND CEILINGS 46
7.3 CONTROL TECHNOLOGY REVIEW 47
7.4 PSD AIR QUALITY AND ADDITIONAL IMPACT ANALYSIS 47
7.5 DISPERSION TECHNIQUES 49

8.0 OTHER EMISSION CONTROL REGULATIONS 50
8.1 EMERGENCY AIR POLLUTION CONTROLS 50
8.2 HAZARDOUS AIR POLLUTANTS 51
8.2.1 MACT AND EQUIVALENT MACT STANDARDS 52

9.0 MUNICIPAL WASTE COMBUSTORS 53

10.0 OZONE LAYER PROTECTION 54

11.0 VARIANCES FROM AIR POLLUTION STANDARDS 55
11.1 TYPES OF VARIANCES 55
11.2 VARIANCE CONDITIONS 56
11.3 VARIANCE PROCEDURE 56

12.0 EMISSIONS TRADING 56

13.0 ENFORCEMENT MECHANISM FOR AIR POLLUTION CONTROL 57
13.1 ADMINISTRATIVE PENALTIES 57
13.2 CIVIL PENALTIES 57
13.3 CRIMINAL PENALTIES 62
13.4 PROCEDURE AND DEFENSES 63
13.5 MISCELLANEOUS ENFORCEMENT PROVISIONS 65

14.0 ASBESTOS AND LEAD 66
14.1 ASBESTOS AND LEAD EMISSION CONTROL 67
14.2 VARIANCE FROM ASBESTOS OR LEAD BASED PAINT HAZARDS STANDARDS 68
14.3 ENFORCEMENT OF THE ASBESTOS LAW 69
14.4 PENALTIES UNDER THE ASBESTOS LAW 71

CHAPTER 3: WATER POLLUTION CONTROL

1.0 INTRODUCTION 73

2.0 RELATIONSHIP TO THE FEDERAL CLEAN WATER ACT 73

3.0 STATE POLICIES AND PROGRAMS 74
3.1 MAINTAINING THE HIGH QUALITY OF STATE WATERS 75
3.2 WATER QUALITY MONITORING PROGRAM 76
3.3 CLASSIFICATION OF STATE WATERS AND WATER USES 77

4.0 REGULATION OF WASTE DISCHARGES TO WATER 81
4.1 NPDES PROGRAM 81
4.1.1 PERMIT APPLICATION 82

4.1.2 PERMIT PROCEDURE 83
4.1.3 PERMIT STANDARDS 86
4.1.4 WASTE DISCHARGE REPORTS AND REQUIREMENTS 87
4.1.5 SCHEDULE OF COMPLIANCE 88

4.2 WATER QUALITY CERTIFICATION 89
4.2.1 WAIVERS 93

4.3 WATER QUALITY CRITERIA 94
4.3.1 USES AND SPECIFIC CRITERIA 94
4.3.2 ZONES OF MIXING 96

4.4 WETLAND MANAGEMENT 98

4.5 NONPOINT SOURCE POLLUTION MANAGEMENT 100
4.6 STORMWATER REGULATIONS 103
4.7 REGULATION OF RECLAIMED WATER AND SEWAGE SLUDGE 107
4.8 REGULATION OF GRAY WATER 108
4.9 VARIANCES 109
4.9.1 CONDITIONS 109
4.9.2 PROCEDURES 110

5.0 REGULATION OF DISCHARGES TO PUBLICLY OWNED TREATMENT WORKS 111

6.0 WASTE DISCHARGES 114
6.1 REPORTING OF DISCHARGES 115

7.0 ENFORCEMENT OF DISCHARGE LIMITATIONS 115
7.1 INVESTIGATORY POWERS AND CONFIDENTIAL INFORMATION 115
7.2 ADMINISTRATIVE AND CIVIL PENALTIES 116
7.3 CRIMINAL PENALTIES 120
7.4 RECORD KEEPING AND MONITORING REQUIREMENTS 122
7.5 CITIZEN SUITS 124
7.6 ENFORCEMENT OF INDUSTRIAL WASTEWATER DISCHARGE PERMITS 125
7.7 MISCELLANEOUS ENFORCEMENT PROVISIONS 126

CHAPTER 4: SAFE DRINKING WATER

1.0 INTRODUCTION 128

2.0 RELATIONSHIP TO FEDERAL SAFE DRINKING WATER ACT 129

2.1 SOURCE WATER ASSESSMENT PROGRAM 130

3.0 STATE PRIMARY DRINKING WATER REGULATIONS 131
3.1 FILTRATION AND DISINFECTION REQUIREMENTS 133
3.2 VARIANCES AND EXEMPTIONS 134

4.0 NOTIFICATION REQUIREMENTS 135
4.1 NOTIFICATION PROCEDURE 135
4.2 CONSUMER CONFIDENCE REPORTS 136

5.0 STATE INTERIM ACTION LEVELS 137

6.0 EMERGENCY PLAN FOR SAFE DRINKING WATER 137

7.0 CROSS-CONNECTION AND BACKFLOW CONTROL 138

8.0 UNDERGROUND INJECTION CONTROL PROGRAM 139
8.1 UNDERGROUND INJECTION CONTROL STANDARDS 140
8.2 INJECTION WELL PERMITS 142
8.3 UIC PROGRAM ENFORCEMENT AND PENALTIES 144

9.0 CERTIFICATION OF DRINKING WATER TREATMENT PLANT OPERATORS 144

10.0 WELLHEAD PROTECTION PROGRAM 146

11.0 DRINKING WATER TREATMENT REVOLVING LOAN FUND 147

12.0 ENFORCEMENT MECHANISMS 147

CHAPTER 5: SOLID WASTE MANAGEMENT

1.0 INTRODUCTION 150

2.0 RELATIONSHIP TO FEDERAL LAW 151

3.0 DEFINITION OF SOLID WASTE 152
3.1 GENERAL RESPONSIBILITIES 152

4.0 PERMITS 154
4.1 REQUIREMENTS 155
4.2 PERMIT PROCEDURE 155
4.3 VARIANCES 157

5.0 STANDARDS FOR SOLID WASTE DISPOSAL FACILITIES 159
5.1 STANDARDS FOR MUNICIPAL SOLID WASTE LANDFILLS 159
5.1.1 MUNICIPAL SOLID WASTE LANDFILL CRITERIA 160
5.1.2 CLOSURE AND POST-CLOSURE CARE OF MSWLs 162
5.1.3 FINANCIAL ASSURANCE REQUIREMENTS FOR MSWLs 162
5.2 CONSTRUCTION AND DEMOLITION WASTE 163

6.0 STANDARDS FOR RECYCLING FACILITIES 165

7.0 STANDARDS FOR SOLID WASTE INCINERATION 166

8.0 STANDARDS FOR TRANSFER STATIONS 168

9.0 STANDARDS FOR SOLID WASTE SALVAGE FACILITIES 169

10.0 STANDARDS FOR RECLAMATION FACILITIES 169

11.0 STANDARDS FOR REMEDIATION FACILITIES 170

12.0 SPECIAL WASTE MANAGEMENT 171
12.1 PETROLEUM CONTAMINATED SOIL 172
12.2 FOREIGN SOLID WASTE 172

13.0 INTEGRATED SOLID WASTE MANAGEMENT PLAN 173

14.0 RECYCLING 178
14.1 GLASS CONTAINER RECOVERY 178
14.2 RECYCLING OF HOUSEHOLD WASTE 180
14.3 RECYCLING OF SPECIAL WASTES 182
14.3.1 LEAD ACID BATTERIES 182
14.3.2 USED MOTOR VEHICLE TIRES 183
14.3.3 ENFORCEMENT OF SPECIAL WASTE PROVISIONS 186

15.0 INFECTIOUS WASTE MANAGEMENT 186
15.1 TRANSPORTATION AND DISPOSAL OF INFECTIOUS WASTE 188
15.2 INFECTIOUS WASTE MANAGEMENT PLAN AND ENFORCEMENT 189
15.3 INFECTIOUS WASTE TREATMENT AND DISPOSAL FACILITIES 190

16.0 ENFORCEMENT AND PENALTIES 191
16.1 INSPECTIONS 191
16.2 PENALTIES 192
16.3 MISCELLANEOUS ENFORCEMENT PROVISIONS 193

CHAPTER 6: HAZARDOUS WASTE MANAGEMENT

1.0 INTRODUCTION 194

2.0 RELATIONSHIP TO FEDERAL RCRA 195

3.0 REGULATED WASTES 196

4.0 REGULATION OF GENERATORS, TRANSPORTERS, AND HAZARDOUS WASTE FACILITIES 198
- 4.1 GENERATORS 198
  - 4.1.1 MANIFEST SYSTEM 200
  - 4.1.2 OTHER REQUIREMENTS 201
- 4.2 TRANSPORTERS 203
- 4.3 TREATMENT, STORAGE AND DISPOSAL FACILITIES 205
  - 4.3.1 MANIFESTS AND RECORDKEEPING 206
  - 4.3.2 SAFETY MEASURES AND RELEASE RESPONSE 208
  - 4.3.3 OTHER REQUIREMENTS 211
  - 4.3.4 LAND DISPOSAL REGULATIONS 213
  - 4.3.5 RECYCLING AND RECLAMATION 213

5.0 HAZARDOUS WASTE BROKERS 214

6.0 TECHNICAL ASSISTANCE AND PUBLIC EDUCATION PROGRAMS 215

7.0 PERMITS 216

8.0 GUARANTORS 220

9.0 ENFORCEMENT 221
- 9.1 INSPECTIONS 222
- 9.2 CIVIL PENALTIES 222
- 9.3 CRIMINAL PENALTIES 225
- 9.4 RECORD KEEPING REQUIREMENTS AND ADMINISTRATIVE PROCEDURES 226
- 9.5 OTHER ENFORCEMENT PROVISIONS 227

10.0 MANAGEMENT OF USED OIL 228
- 10.1 USED OIL GENERATORS 230
- 10.2 USED OIL TRANSPORTER AND TRANSFER FACILITIES 232
- 10.3 PROCESSORS AND RE-REFINERS 234
- 10.4 USED OIL BURNERS 236

10.5 USED OIL FUEL MARKETERS 237

CHAPTER 7: UNDERGROUND STORAGE TANKS

1.0 INTRODUCTION 238

2.0 RELATIONSHIP TO FEDERAL UST REGULATIONS 239

3.0 USTs AND SUBSTANCES COVERED 240
3.1 WHO IS COVERED BY UST PROVISIONS 240
3.2 LENDER LIABILITY 241
3.3 DEFINITION OF UST 242
3.4 REGULATED SUBSTANCES 243

4.0 UST PERMITTING 243
4.1 VARIANCES 247

5.0 NOTIFICATION REQUIREMENTS 248

6.0 CONSTRUCTION AND MONITORING REQUIREMENTS 249

7.0 UST OPERATION REQUIREMENTS 252

8.0 FINANCIAL RESPONSIBILITY REQUIREMENTS 253

9.0 REPORTING REQUIREMENTS 257

10.0 RESPONSE ACTION 259

11.0 CLOSURE REQUIREMENTS 265

12.0 DEPARTMENT RESPONSE TO PETROLEUM RELEASES 268
12.1 LUST FUND 268
12.2 RESPONSE ACTION 269
12.3 COST RECOVERY 271

13.0 ENFORCEMENT MECHANISMS 271
13.1 FIELD CITATIONS 274
13.2 ADMINISTRATIVE PENALTIES 275
13.3 CIVIL PENALTIES 276

14.0 REPORT SUBMITTAL GUIDELINES 278

15.0 DIRECTORY OF UST SERVICE PROVIDERS 278

CHAPTER 8: HAWAII ENVIRONMENTAL RESPONSE LAW AND HAWAII EMERGENCY PLANNING AND COMMUNITY RIGHT-TO-KNOW ACT

1.0 INTRODUCTION 279

2.0 RELATIONSHIP TO THE FEDERAL SUPERFUND PROGRAM 281

3.0 STATE CONTINGENCY PLAN 281

4.0 DEFINITION OF REGULATED SUBSTANCES 282

5.0 RESPONSIBLE PARTIES AND DEFENSES 283
- 5.1 LENDERS AND INNOCENT LAND PURCHASERS 286

6.0 PROGRAM FUNDING 287

7.0 ROLE OF REVOLVING RESPONSE FUND IN SITE CLEANUP 288

8.0 LIABLE PARTY CLEANUP PARTICIPATION 289

9.0 REPORTABLE QUANTITIES AND REPORTING REQUIREMENTS 290
- 9.1 NOTIFICATION OF RELEASES 292

10.0 CLEANUP PROCESS 295
- 10.1 INITIAL ASSESSMENTS 297
- 10.2 REMOVAL ACTIONS 298
- 10.3 REMEDIAL INVESTIGATIONS AND ACTIONS 299
- 10.4 SITE LISTING AND NO FURTHER ACTION DETERMINATIONS 300
- 10.5 ORDER FROM DEPARTMENT 301

11.0 COST ALLOCATION AND RECOVERY 302
- 11.1 COST RECOVERY 303
- 11.2 REIMBURSEMENT 304
- 11.3 APPORTIONMENT AND CONTRIBUTION 305
- 11.4 *DE MINIMIS* SETTLEMENTS 306

12.0 VOLUNTARY RESPONSE 307

13.0 ADMINISTRATIVE RECORDS 311

14.0 JUDICIAL REVIEW 312

15.0 ENFORCEMENT MECHANISMS 313
15.1 CIVIL PENALTIES 314
15.2 CRIMINAL PENALTIES 315

16.0 CITIZEN SUITS 316

17.0 HAWAII EMERGENCY PLANNING AND COMMUNITY RIGHT-TO-KNOW ACT 317
17.1 HAWAII STATE EMERGENCY RESPONSE COMMISSION 318
17.2 LOCAL EMERGENCY PLANNING COMMITTEE 318
17.3 REPORTING REQUIREMENTS 320
17.4 PENALTIES 322

CHAPTER 9: RELEASE REPORTING PROVISIONS

1.0 INTRODUCTION 323

2.0 RELATIONSHIP TO FEDERAL REPORTING STATUTES 324

3.0 RELEASE REPORTING OF POLLUTANT DISCHARGES INTO HAWAII WATERS 324

4.0 RELEASE REPORTING FOR UNDERGROUND STORAGE TANKS 325

5.0 REPORTING REQUIREMENTS FOR RELEASES OF HAZARDOUS SUBSTANCES 327

6.0 REPORTING REQUIREMENTS FOR THE RELEASE OF EXTREMELY HARZARDOUS SUBSTANCES 332

7.0 RADIATION RELEASE REPORTING REQUIREMENTS 333

CHAPTER 10: ENVIRONMENTAL IMPACT STATEMENTS

1.0 INTRODUCTION 335

2.0 RELATIONSHIP TO THE FEDERAL NEPA 336

3.0 ACTIONS SUBJECT TO HAWAII LAW 338
3.1 EXEMPTIONS 342

4.0 PREPARATION OF THE ENVIRONMENTAL ASSESSMENT 345
4.1 DETERMINATION OF SIGNIFICANCE 347
4.2 SIGNIFICANCE CRITERIA 348

5.0 PREPARATION OF THE ENVIRONMENTAL IMPACT STATEMENT 350
5.1 DRAFT EIS CONTENT REQUIREMENTS 352
5.2 FINAL EIS CONTENT REQUIREMENTS 355
5.3 ACCEPTABILITY 356
5.4 SUPPLEMENTAL EIS 357

6.0 PUBLIC PARTICIPATION 358

7.0 ROLE OF THE ENVIRONMENTAL COUNCIL 359

8.0 APPEALS 361
8.1 ADMINISTRATIVE APPEALS 362
8.2 JUDICIAL REVIEW 362

CHAPTER 11: ADDITIONAL ENVIRONMENTAL LAWS

1.0 DISCLOSURES IN REAL ESTATE TRANSACTIONS 368
1.1 APPLICABILITY OF MANDATORY DISCLOSURE LAW 368
1.2 WRITTEN DISCLOSURE OF REAL PROPERTY STATEMENT 369
1.3 DAMAGES 371

2.0 HAWAII ENVIRONMENTAL DISCLOSURE LAW 372

3.0 HAWAII ENDANGERED SPECIES ACT 374
3.1 DETERMINATION OF ENDANGERED AND THREATENED SPECIES 375
3.2 PROHIBITED ACTIVITIES 375
3.3 PERMITS 376
3.4 CONSERVATION PROGRAMS 377
3.5 LANDOWNER CONSERVATION INCENTIVES 377
3.5.1 HABITAT CONSERVATION PLANS 378
3.5.2 SAFE HARBOR AGREEMENT 380
3.6 ENFORCEMENT MECHANISMS 382

4.0 HAWAII COASTAL ZONE MANAGEMENT LAW 383
4.1 RELATIONSHIP TO THE FEDERAL COASTAL ZONE MANAGEMENT ACT 384
4.2 SPECIAL MANAGEMENT AREAS 385
4.3 PERMITTING FOR DEVELOPMENT 385
4.4 SHORELINE AND SETBACKS 388

4.4.1 DETERMINATION OF SHORELINE 389
4.4.2 SHORELINE SETBACKS AND VARIANCES 389

4.5 ENFORCEMENT OF SETBACKS 391
4.6 PENALTIES 391

5.0 HAWAII PESTICIDES LAW 392
5.1 LICENSING AND SALE OF PESTICIDES 392
5.2 LABELING AND SALE REQUIREMENTS 393
5.3 SEIZURES, "STOP-SALE" AND "REMOVAL FROM SALE" ORDERS 394
5.4 PESTICIDE USE 394
5.5 SPECIAL LOCAL NEED AND EXPERIMENTAL USES 395
5.6 EXEMPTIONS 396
5.7 CANCELLATION OR SUSPENSION OF PESTICIDE USES 397
5.8 PESTICIDE USE REVOLVING FUND 397
5.9 ENFORCEMENT MECHANISMS AND PENALTIES 397

6.0 HISTORIC PRESERVATION AND STATE BURIAL LAWS 399
6.1 STATE BURIALS LAW 400
6.2 PROCEDURAL RULEMAKING 401
6.3 BURIAL SITE IDENTIFICATION 402
6.4 HANDLING OF HUMAN SKELETAL REMAINS 403
6.5 NOTIFICATION OF INADVERTENT DISCOVERY OF BURIAL SITES 404
6.6 JURISDICTION OVER BURIAL SITES 405
6.7 DETERMINATIONS TO PRESERVE IN PLACE OR RELOCATE REMAINS 406
6.8 REMOVAL OF SKELETAL REMAINS OR BURIAL GOODS 407
6.9 BURIAL SITES OF STATE LANDS 408
6.10 ENFORCEMENT AND PENALTIES 408
6.11 APPEALS 410

7.0 RADIATION CONTROL 411
7.1 LICENSING 412
7.2 CONSTRUCTION REQUIREMENTS 414
7.3 TRANSPORTATION 415
7.4 LABELING AND STORAGE REQUIREMENTS 415
7.5 RADIOACTIVE WASTE DISPOSAL 416
7.6 RECORD KEEPING 417
7.7 REPORTING AND NOTIFICATION REQUIREMENTS 418
7.8 INSPECTIONS 420
7.9 ENFORCEMENT 420

CHAPTER 12: HAWAII ENVIRONMENTAL COMMON LAW

1.0 INTRODUCTION 421

2.0 NUISANCE 421

3.0 INTENTIONAL TORTS 424
- 3.1 TRESPASS 424
- 3.2 INFLICTION OF EMOTIONAL DISTRESS 425

4.0 NEGLIGENCE 426

5.0 STRICT LIABILITY 429

6.0 PUNITIVE DAMAGES 430

7.0 REAL PROPERTY TRANSACTIONAL LIABILITY 431
- 7.1 STATUTORY DUTY TO DISCLOSE 431
- 7.2 DISCLOSURE DUTIES OF SELLERS, GENERALLY 432
- 7.3 DISCLOSURE DUTIES OF BROKERS 432

8.0 LENDER LIABILITY 433

9.0 CRIMINAL LIABILITY 434

CHAPTER 13: ADMINISTRATIVE PROCEDURE AND JUDICIAL REVIEW

1.0 ADOPTION OF RULES AND REGULATIONS 436
- 1.1 RULEMAKING PROCEDURE 436
- 1.2 PUBLIC HEARING 438
- 1.3 EMERGENCY RULES 439
- 1.4 VALIDITY OF RULES 440

2.0 DECLARATORY JUDGMENTS AND RULINGS 441

3.0 CONTESTED CASES 442
- 3.1 CONTESTED CASE PROCEDURE 443
- 3.2 ADMINISTRATIVE RECORD 446

4.0 JUDICIAL REVIEW OF CONTESTED CASES 446
- 4.1 STANDARDS OF REVIEW 450
- 4.2 APPEALS 452

5.0 PUBLIC RECORDS 453

CHAPTER 14: WATER USE

1.0 THE STATE WATER CODE 455

2.0 THE HAWAII WATER PLAN 457
2.1 THE WATER RESOURCE PROTECTION AND WATER QUALITY PLANS 459
2.2 AGRICULTURAL WATER USE PLAN 460
2.3 COUNTY WATER USE AND DEVELOPMENT PLANS 461
2.4 WATER QUALITY PLAN 461

3.0 DECLARATION AND CERTIFICATION OF WATER USE 462

4.0 INSTREAM USE PROTECTION PROGRAM 462
4.1 PROCEDURE FOR ESTABLISHING INSTREAM FLOW STANDARDS 463
4.2 PROCEDURE FOR ESTABLISHING INTERIM INSTREAM FLOW STANDARDS 463

5.0 DESIGNATION OF WATER MANAGEMENT AREAS 464
5.1 PETITIONS FOR RESERVATIONS OF WATER IN WATER MANAGEMENT AREAS 467

6.0 DECLARATION OF WATER SHORTAGE 467

7.0 DECLARATION OF WATER EMERGENCY 468

8.0 PERMITS 469
8.1 WATER USE PERMITS 469
8.1.1 PERMIT MODIFICATION 471
8.1.2 PERMIT REVOCATION 471
8.2 STREAM CHANNEL ALTERATION PERMITS 471
8.3 STREAM DIVERSION WORKS PERMITS 473

9.0 WELLS 474
9.1 WELL CONSTRUCTION AND PUMP INSTALLATION PERMITS 475
9.2 WELL COMPLETION REPORTS 477
9.3 REPORTING REQUIREMENTS 477
9.4 ABANDONMENT 477

10.0 ENFORCEMENT 478

11.0 CWRM RULEMAKING PROCEEDINGS 478

12. DISPUTE RESOLUTIONS 479
12.1 CONTESTED CASE HEARINGS 480

13. JUDICIAL REVIEW 482

14.0 COMMON LAW WATER RIGHTS 482
14.1 APPURTENANT RIGHTS 482
14.2 RIPARIAN RIGHTS 483
14.3 CORRELATIVE RIGHTS 483
14.4 PRESCRIPTIVE RIGHTS 484

PREFACE

The **Hawaii Environmental Law Handbook** is intended to provide a general guide to the complex series of statutes and regulations that make up Hawaii's environmental laws. We have included in this third edition the statutes and regulations adopted prior to August 1, 2000. Since the second edition of the Handbook was published in 1996, several statutes have been amended, including the Hawaii Water Pollution Law, the Hawaii Hazardous Waste Law, the Hawaii Environmental Response Law, and the Pesticide Law. In addition, new regulations in the areas of used oil management, underground storage tank regulation, radiation control and burial regulation have been promulgated and rules pertaining to water quality standards, environmental impact statements and air pollution control have been amended. In addition, Hawaii has adopted a new Wetland Policy as well as several new penalty policies used as guidance in connection with the enforcement of environmental laws. This third edition includes those statutory and regulatory changes and additions. Because the Handbook is an overview, and because of anticipated changes to the law and regulations in this area, a reader addressing a specific problem should consult the latest version of the statutes and regulations.

The emphasis in the Handbook is on the provisions of Hawaii environmental law that affect the private sector, including businesses and real property owners. Our continued effort to maintain the Handbook as a succinct, ready overview also dictates some selectivity in the topics covered.

I wish to thank Lisa A. Bail for her substantial commitment to writing this Handbook. I also wish to thank Eva Lapham for her substantial assistance in the preparation of our text for publication. Finally, we wish to thank and acknowledge the contributions of various staff members and branch chiefs at the State of Hawaii, Department of Health who provided information utilized in the preparation of this Handbook.

Lisa Woods Munger

August 2000

ABOUT THE EDITORS AND AUTHORS

LISA WOODS MUNGER

Ms. Munger received her A.B. from the University of California at Los Angeles (Summa Cum Laude, Phi Beta Kappa) and graduated from Harvard Law School, where she was founder and editor-in-chief of the *Harvard Women's Law Journal*. Ms. Munger practiced in Los Angeles for six years with the law firm of McCutchen Black Verleger & Shea concentrating in environmental law before joining Goodsill Anderson Quinn and Stifel in 1985. She continues to concentrate on environmental matters and commercial litigation.

Ms. Munger has expertise in environmental compliance and permitting matters, administrative proceedings and civil litigation. Ms. Munger is a frequent lecturer at seminars on environmental law and civil litigation.

LISA A. BAIL

Ms. Bail received her B.A. with distinction in philosophy from Boston University's College of Liberal Arts (Magna Cum Laude, Phi Beta Kappa) and graduated from Boston University School of Law where she was on the editorial board of the *American Journal of Law and Medicine*. Ms. Bail has practiced with Goodsill Anderson Quinn & Stifel since 1993 and concentrates on environmental matters and commercial litigation.

In the field of environmental law, Ms. Bail represents businesses and landowners in civil litigation, administrative enforcement proceedings, permit assistance, rule making and compliance counseling.

GLOSSARY OF ABBREVIATIONS AND ACRONYMS

BACT	Best Available Control Technology
BLNR	Board of Land and Natural Resources
C&C	City and County of Honolulu
CAA	Clean Air Act
CEMS	Continuous emission monitoring systems
CERCLA	Comprehensive Environmental Response Compensation and Liability Act (Superfund)
CFC	Chlorofluorocarbon
CNPCP	Coastal Nonpoint Pollution Control Program
CWRM	Commission on Water Resource Management
DBEDT	Hawaii Department of Business Economic Development and Tourism
DLNR	Hawaii Department of Land and Natural Resources
DMR	Discharge monitoring report
DOA	Department of Agriculture
DOT	Department of Transportation
EA	Environmental Assessment
EC	Environmental Council, Hawaii Department of Health
EIS	Environmental Impact Statement
EPA	U.S. Environmental Protection Agency
EPO	Environmental Planning Office, Hawaii Department of Health
EPCRA	Federal Emergency Planning and Community Right-to-Know Act
ERL	Hawaii's Environmental Response Law
ERO	Environmental Resources Office, Hawaii Department of Health
FIFRA	Federal Insecticide, Fungicide and Rodenticide Act
FONSI	Finding of no significant impact (negative declaration)
HEER	Office of Hazard Evaluation and Emergency Response, Hawaii Department of Health
HEPCRA	Hawaii Emergency Planning and Community Right-to-Know Act
HSERC	Hawaii State Emergency Response Commission

LAER	Lowest Available Emission Rate
LEPC	Local emergency planning committee
LUST	Leaking underground storage tank
MACT	Maximum achievable control technology
MCL	Maximum contaminant level
MOU	Memorandum of understanding
MSDS	Material safety data sheet
MSWL	Municipal solid waste landfill
MWC	Municipal waste combustor
NAAQS	National Ambient Air Quality Standards
NEPA	National Environmental Policy Act
NESHAP	National Emission Standards for Hazardous Air Pollutants
NGPC	Notice of general permit coverage
NOAA	National Oceanic and Atmospheric Administration
NOV	Notice of Violation
NPDES	National Pollutant Discharge Elimination System
NSPS	New Source Performance Standards
OEQC	Office of Environmental Quality Control, Hawaii Department of Health
OSWM	Office of Solid Waste Management, Hawaii Department of Health
PCB	Polychlorinated biphenyls
PCS	Petroleum contaminated soil
POTW	Publicly owned treatment works
PRP	Potentially responsible party
PSD	Prevention of Significant Deterioration
RBCA	Risk based corrective action
RCRA	Resource Conservation and Recovery Act
SAAQS	State Ambient Air Quality Standards
SCP	State Contingency Plan
SDWA	Safe Drinking Water Act
SIC	Standard Industrial Classification
SIP	State Implementation Plan

SMA	Special management area
SWTR	Surface Water Treatment Rule
TSD facility	Hazardous waste treatment storage and disposal facility
UIC	Underground injection control
USDW	Underground sources of drinking water
UST	Underground storage tank
VOC	Volatile organic compound
VRP	Voluntary Response Program

CHAPTER 1

STATE ENVIRONMENTAL AGENCIES
AND
STATE ENVIRONMENTAL POLICY

1.0 INTRODUCTION

The Hawaii State Department of Health ("Department") is the state agency which is analogous to the United States Environmental Protection Agency ("EPA"). The Department is responsible for implementation and enforcement of the principal state environmental laws, as well as a number of federal laws for which authority has been delegated to the State.

In addition to the Department, several other state agencies have environmental responsibilities. The Department of Agriculture and the Department of Land and Natural Resources are responsible for the implementation and enforcement of several environmental laws and programs. County health officials and police officers are authorized to enforce most environmental laws, and the county planning departments are responsible for the designation of Special Management Areas and shoreline setbacks under the Coastal Zone Management Act. The Attorney General's office represents the State in all environmental matters involving administrative enforcement and litigation. In terms of long range planning, a number of state and county councils are tasked with waste management planning, the development of research and educational programs and planning for emergencies involving releases of hazardous substances.

2.0 STATE ENVIRONMENTAL POLICY

The State's Environmental Policy is codified in the Hawaii Revised Statutes.[1] The Policy serves as a declaration of concerns and goals of environmental protection in a general sense.[2] The stated purpose of the Policy is to

> encourage productive and enjoyable harmony between man and his environment, promote efforts which will prevent or eliminate damage to the environment and biosphere and stimulate the health and welfare of man, and enrich the understanding of the ecological systems and natural resources important to the people of Hawaii.[3]

The State Policy adds another dimension to environmental rights defined in the Hawaii State Constitution:

> Each person has the right to a clean and healthful environment, as defined by laws relating to environmental quality, including control of pollution and conservation, protection and enhancement of natural resources.[4]

The Policy mandates conservation of natural resources by controlling pollution and safeguarding the State's unique natural environmental characteristics to promote conditions where nature and man can exist in productive harmony.[5] In addition to this broadly worded policy statement, specific goals to enhance the quality of life are described in greater detail: the setting of population limits, creating opportunities for Hawaii residents through diverse economic activities, establishing communities with a sense of identity in harmony with the unique natural

---

1 Haw. Rev. Stat. ch. 344 (Michie 1999). All references to the Hawaii Revised Statutes are made to the printed version of the statutes current through the 1999 legislative session, unless otherwise noted. Where appropriate, references to acts passed during the 2000 legislative session have also been added.

2 *See*, *Molokai Homesteaders Coop. Ass'n v. Cobb*, 63 Haw. 453, 642 P.2d 1134 (1981).

3 Haw. Rev. Stat. § 344-1.

4 Hawaii Constitution, art. XII, § 9. For discussion of this constitutional provision, *see*, Robert A. McLaren, Comment, *Environmental Protection Based on State Constitutional Law: A Call for Reinterpretation*, 12 U. Haw. L. Rev. 123 (1990).

5 Haw. Rev. Stat. § 344-3(1).

Hawaiian environment and establishing a personal commitment to reduce the drain on nonrenewable resources.[6]

The State Environmental Policy also establishes ten guidelines which State and county agencies, officers, boards and commissions are to consider in the development of their programs. The guidelines address the following factors and their impact on the environment: population, natural resources, flora and fauna, parks, recreation and open space, economic development, transportation, energy, community life and housing, education and culture, and citizen participation.[7] Although the guidelines are intended to help shape agency programs, they do not mandate the adoption of environmental guidelines by individual agencies to prior to *ad hoc* agency decisions.[8]

3.0 DEPARTMENT OF HEALTH

The Department of Health is one of 18 principal executive departments within the Hawaii State government under the supervision of the Governor. The Department is responsible for the administration of programs designed to protect, preserve and improve the physical and mental health of the people of Hawaii.[9] The Department is headed by the Director of Health ("Director"), who is advised by the Board of Health.[10]

The Director and the members of the Board of Health are appointed by the Governor. The implementation and enforcement of environmental laws are carried out by the Environmental Management Division, which is headed by the Deputy Director of Environmental

---

6 Kent M. Keith, Survey, *Laws Affecting the Development of Ocean Resources in Hawaii*, 4 U. Haw. L. Rev. 227 (1982); Susan M. Komo-Kim, Comment, *Municipal Waste Combustion: A Wasted Investment?*, 12 U. Haw L. Rev. 153 (1990); *Article, Manganese Nodule Process in Hawaii: An Environmental Prospectus*, 14 Haw. B.J. 103 (1978).

7 Haw. Rev. Stat. § 344-4.

8 *Molokai Homesteaders Coop. Ass'n v. Cobb*, 63 Haw. 453, 629 P.2d 1134 (1981).

9 Haw. Rev. Stat. § 26-13.

10 *Id.*

Health ("Deputy Director").[11] The Environmental Management Division implements the programs which monitor and protect coastal water, drinking water, land and air quality. The Division is comprised of five branches: clean air, clean water, safe drinking water, solid and hazardous waste and wastewater.

3.1 HAZARD EVALUATION AND EMERGENCY RESPONSE OFFICE

The Office of Hazard Evaluation and Emergency Response ("HEER") is the "first response" center for the State and reports directly to the Deputy Director. In general, the function of the HEER office is to plan for and respond to hazardous substance, pollutant, contaminant and oil releases to the environment.[12] The HEER office is divided into the following sections: emergency prevention and response, site discovery and assessment, remediation and program development. HEER responds to releases of hazardous substances, evaluates the health and environmental risks of exposure to released substances and coordinates the remediation of releases. HEER acts as the on-scene coordinator in cooperation with other agencies, including the EPA, police, civil defense and fire department. The HEER office also is responsible for implementing response actions under the federal Comprehensive Environmental Response Compensation and Liability Act,[13] the Oil Pollution Act of 1990,[14] the Environmental

---

11 In 1994, the Legislature enacted Act 223, which eliminated various positions in the Executive Branch, including the position of Deputy Director of Environmental Health. *See* Act approved June 22, 1994, ch. 223, 1994 Haw. Sess. Laws 538. Also during the 1994 Legislative Session, legislation which would have created a separate principal executive Department of the Environment was proposed, but failed to pass. In 1995, the position of Deputy Director of Environmental Health within the Department of Health was restored. *See* Act approved June 14, 1995, ch. 162, 1995 Haw. Sess. Laws 265.

12 Hawaii Department of Health, *Report to the Twentieth Legislature in Compliance with Hawaii Revised Statutes Chapters 128D and 128E On the Activities of the Department of Health, Environmental Health Administration, Office of Hazard Evaluation and Emergency Response and Use of the Environmental Response Revolving Fund* at 2 (2000).

13 42 U.S.C. § 9601 *et seq.*

14 33 U.S.C. § 2701 *et seq.*

Response Law[15] and the State Contingency Plan.[16] Finally, the HEER office implements the Hawaii Emergency Planning and Community Right-to-Know Act, which was enacted in 1993.[17]

3.2 ENVIRONMENTAL PLANNING OFFICE

The Environmental Planning Office ("EPO") also reports directly to the Deputy Director, and its responsibilities include environmental risk ranking,[18] long-range planning for surface and groundwater protection, strategic planning for environmental managers and communities, including the establishment of environmental goals and benchmarks, and the promotion of pollution prevention programs. The EPO was instrumental in revising the State Water Quality Standards to include 97 priority pollutants as required under the 1987 amendments to the Clean Water Act.[19] The EPO also developed the State's "Nonpoint Source Pollution Control Program" to manage urban and agricultural runoff.[20] It is involved in watershed management projects and comprehensive state groundwater protection programs.[21]

The EPO was instrumental in the development of the wellhead protection program and receipt of EPA approval for the program.[22] The EPO also participates in legislative coordination on bills affecting the environment. Finally, the EPO manages grants and administers contracts for federally-funded programs within the Environmental Management Division.

---

15 Haw. Rev. Stat. ch. 128D; *see infra* ch. 8 of this Handbook.

16 Haw. Admin. Rules, tit. 11, ch. 451; *see infra* ch. 8 of this Handbook.

17 Haw. Rev. Stat. ch. 128E; *see infra*, ch. 11 of this Handbook.

18 State of Hawaii, Department of Health, *Hawaii Environmental Risk Ranking Study* (Sept. 1992), and *Phase II Final Report: Public Outreach Results* (Oct. 1994).

19 33 U.S.C. § 1251 *et seq.*

20 State of Hawaii, Department of Health, *Environmental Health, Annual Report Supplement, Fiscal Year 1988-1989*, p. 4 (1989).

21 The EPO also assisted in the development of the Geographic Imaging System (GIS) computer program, which is instrumental in mapping groundwater sources as well as wells and underground storage tanks which may impact groundwater. Interview with June Harrigan, Ph.D., Environmental Planning Office (Sept. 5, 1995).

22 State of Hawaii, Department of Health, *Groundwater Protection Program* (May 1995).

3.3 ENVIRONMENTAL RESOURCES OFFICE

The Environmental Resources Office ("ERO") serves as the administrative branch for the Environmental Management Division. The ERO, reporting to the Deputy Director, handles financial and personnel matters for the environmental programs.

3.4 CLEAN AIR BRANCH

The clean air program[23] is handled by the Clean Air Branch. The Branch is divided into four functional sections: asbestos abatement, engineering, monitoring, permitting and enforcement. The Branch is responsible for implementing the covered source and non-covered source permit programs, which are independently funded through the Clean Air Special Fund.[24] In addition to implementing and enforcing the statewide air pollution control program, the Branch has certain duties under the Toxic Substances Control Act[25] and the Asbestos Hazard Emergency Response Act[26] for identification, evaluation and control of asbestos containing materials in public and private schools. The Branch is also charged with enforcement of the Ozone Layer Protection Law.[27]

3.5 CLEAN WATER BRANCH

The Clean Water Branch implements and enforces the statewide water pollution control program[28] which includes permitting, compliance monitoring, inspection, investigation of complaints and ambient water quality monitoring. The National Pollutant Discharge Elimination System permit program is administered by the Branch to monitor and control point source

---

23 *See infra* ch. 2 of this Handbook.

24 Haw. Rev. Stat. § 342B-32. The Clean Air Special Fund is funded by covered and noncovered source permit application fees and annual emission fees. This fund is to be used solely for the development, support and administration of the air permit program.

25 15 U.S.C. §§ 2601-2629.

26 15 U.S.C. §§ 2641 *et seq.*

27 Haw. Rev. Stat. ch. 342C.

28 *See infra* ch. 3 of this Handbook.

pollution and stormwater discharges. A regulatory program for the control of nonpoint source pollution is currently under development at the Branch. The Branch also administers the Clean Water Act, Section 401 Water Quality Certification Program[29] for those federally permitted activities which may result in discharges to navigable waters of the State.

3.6 SAFE DRINKING WATER BRANCH

The Safe Drinking Water Branch establishes state drinking water standards and conducts extensive testing of Hawaii's drinking water through the public water supply supervision program.[30] The Branch tests for a variety of chemical and bacterial compounds pursuant to federal law and for an additional thirty-four chemicals which are not regulated under federal law. The Branch also conducts testing of water from rain catchment systems for the presence of lead and copper. The Underground Injection Control Program is a permit program implemented by the Branch to protect the state aquifers from potential contamination from underground injection wells. The Branch is also vested with monitoring responsibilities for the groundwater protection program.

3.7 SOLID AND HAZARDOUS WASTE BRANCH

The Solid and Hazardous Waste Branch is responsible for implementing and enforcing the following programs: hazardous waste, underground storage tanks, leaking underground storage tanks and integrated solid waste management. Solid waste management includes the regulation of petroleum contaminated soil, lead acid batteries, motor vehicle tires and infectious medical waste. The Integrated Solid Waste Management Law, enacted in 1991, focuses on source reduction and reuse, energy recovery and recycling, and established the Office of Solid Waste Management.[31] The Office is responsible for monitoring all solid waste management facilities pursuant to its rules, which were revised and adopted in December 1993.[32]

---

29 Clean Water Act § 401, 33 U.S.C. § 1341.

30 *See infra* ch. 4 of this Handbook.

31 *See infra* ch. 5 of this Handbook.

32 Haw. Admin. Rules, tit. 11, ch. 58.1.

The hazardous waste statute was amended during the 1991 and 1992 Legislative Sessions to more fully conform to EPA's requirements for state authorization,[33] and hazardous waste regulations were adopted in May 1994 and amended in 1999.[34]

The underground storage tank program administers the federal regulations, and the Branch has developed state underground storage tank rules.[35] The leaking underground storage tank program is funded by the national Leaking Underground Storage Tank Trust Fund and enables the State to complete corrective action on certain petroleum contaminated sites.

3.8 WASTEWATER BRANCH

The Wastewater Branch manages the construction grant and state revolving fund loan programs for wastewater treatment projects and provides a wastewater operation training program for wastewater treatment plant operators. The Branch regulates all wastewater systems, including public and private systems, throughout the State.[36] The Branch also regulates the handling of wastewater sludge and effluent, including development of the effluent reuse guidelines.

3.9 OFFICE OF ENVIRONMENTAL QUALITY CONTROL

The Office of Environmental Quality Control ("OEQC") serves the Governor in an advisory capacity on matters relating to environmental quality control.[37] The OEQC is headed by a single director appointed by the Governor. The OEQC director assists state agencies in the coordination of environmental quality matters, organizes public education environmental

---

33 *See infra* ch. 6 of this Handbook.

34 Haw. Admin. Rules, tit. 11, chs. 260 to 266, 268, 270, 271, 279 and 280.

35 *See infra* ch. 7 of this Handbook.

36 *See* Haw. Rev. Stat. ch. 340F; Haw. Admin. Rules chs. 61 to 62. This Handbook will not address wastewater regulation or programs.

37 Haw. Rev. Stat. § 341-3(a).

programs, and assists in research. In addition, the director provides recommendations on legislation and administrative rules, and offers assistance to industry, agencies and the public.[38]

The OEQC administers the Environmental Impact Statement Program[39] for both government and private actions. The OEQC acts as a liaison between applicants and the reviewing agency. It also handles the Environmental Impact Statement notice requirements. The OEQC serves as the filing office and enforcement agency for disclosure statements filed pursuant to the Hawaii Environmental Disclosure Law.[40]

3.10 ENVIRONMENTAL COUNCIL

The Environmental Council ("EC") consists of a maximum of fifteen persons appointed by the Governor. The EC selects its own chairperson. The members represent business, education and other environmentally pertinent professions.[41] The EC fills a liaison position between the general public and the director of the Office of Environmental Quality Control. The EC may call public hearings to solicit information and is required to submit an annual report summarizing environmental developments during the year, with recommendations, to the Legislature, the Governor and the public.[42] Finally, the EC is designated to hear appeals from the nonacceptance of environmental impact statements.[43]

4.0 DEPARTMENT OF THE ATTORNEY GENERAL

The Department of the Attorney General is responsible for providing legal services to the State, including the furnishing of legal opinions, representing the State in all civil actions to

38 *Id.* § 341-4.

39 *See infra* ch. 10 of this Handbook.

40 *See infra* ch. 11 of this Handbook.

41 Haw. Rev. Stat. § 341-3(c).

42 *Id.* § 341-6. *See, e.g.*, The Environmental Council and the Office of Environmental Quality Control, *Environmental Report Card, 1999.*

43 *See infra* ch. 10 of this Handbook.

which the State is a party, prosecuting cases involving violations of state laws and acting otherwise as provided by common law.[44] The Department of Attorney General also assists the Department of Health in the drafting of proposed legislation, administrative rules, and in matters involving the Hawaii Legislature. Within the Department of the Attorney General, the Regulatory Division handles civil and criminal matters involving violations of state environmental laws.

5.0 DEPARTMENT OF AGRICULTURE

The Department of Agriculture is a principal executive department headed by the Board of Agriculture.[45] The Department is responsible for the conservation, development and utilization of agricultural resources in the State of Hawaii. The duties of the Department include the adoption and enforcement of administrative rules on the grading and labeling of agricultural products. The Hawaii Pesticides Law[46] is implemented and enforced by the Department of Agriculture.

6.0 DEPARTMENT OF LAND AND NATURAL RESOURCES

The Department of Land and Natural Resources is a principal executive department headed by the Board of Land and Natural Resources, whose members are appointed by the Governor.[47] The Department of Land and Natural Resources is charged with the management and administration of public lands and all water and coastal areas of the State, including wildlife resources and aquatic life.

The Department of Land and Natural Resources serves as the implementing agency for the Conservation of Aquatic Life, Wildlife and Land Plants Law (Hawaii Endangered Species

---

44 Haw. Rev. Stat. § 26-7.

45 *Id.* § 26-16.

46 *See infra* ch. 11 of this Handbook.

47 Haw. Rev. Stat. § 26-15.

Law).[48] The Board of Land and Natural Resources is responsible for the determination of shorelines and for handling appeals of shoreline determinations under the Coastal Zone Management Law.[49]

7.0 COUNTY OFFICIALS

The county planning commission serves an important role in the implementation of the Coastal Zone Management Law.[50] The county planning commission is responsible for enforcement of the shoreline setback lines and for the implementation and operation of the Special Management Area Use Permit program. Each county is required to establish at least one Local Emergency Planning Committee pursuant to the Hawaii Emergency Planning and Community Right-to-Know Act.[51] Each Committee consists of members of county agencies, media, and the public who are tasked with the preparation of a local emergency response plan for the release of hazardous substances. Certain counties have also established household hazardous waste collection and/or used oil recycling programs.

County health officials and county police officers are charged with enforcement of a number of environmental laws. Although they are authorized to enforce most environmental statutes, county officials and officers have generally deferred enforcement to the State.

---

48 *See infra* ch. 11 of this Handbook.

49 *Id.*

50 *Id.*

51 *See infra* ch. 8 of this Handbook.

CHAPTER 2

AIR POLLUTION CONTROL

1.0 INTRODUCTION

This chapter addresses the regulation of sources of air pollutants in Hawaii.[1] In 1992, the Hawaii Legislature enacted Act 240 to repeal the previous Air Pollution Control Law and establish statutory authority more consistent with the federal Clean Air Act[2] ("CAA"), specifically the 1990 Clean Air Act Amendments. Among other things, this Law requires the development of rules for the issuance of permits to stationary sources and provides new mechanisms to enforce rules and permits. The Hawaii Department of Health ("Department") has promulgated administrative rules, effective November 1993 and amended in 1998, to implement the legislative changes made to the Air Pollution Control Law. These rules set forth general requirements and prohibitions regarding open burning, permits for noncovered and covered sources, fees, the prevention of significant deterioration review, new source standards of performance, and hazardous air pollutant sources.[3]

The United States Environmental Protection Agency ("EPA") and the Department are the two agencies primarily responsible for regulating air pollution from stationary sources in Hawaii. Hawaii's air pollution control program follows the requirements set out in the CAA. The CAA requires the preparation and submission of State Implementation Plans for the attainment of National Ambient Air Quality Standards ("NAAQS") by given target dates. The CAA requires each state to enact regulations sufficient to attain and maintain the federal NAAQS.

---

1 Haw. Rev. Stat. ch. 342B (Michie 1999). All references to the Hawaii Revised Statutes are made to the printed version of the statutes current through the 1999 legislative session, unless otherwise noted. Where appropriate, references to acts passed during the 2000 legislative session have also been added.

2 42 U.S.C. §§ 7401-7671q.

3 See Haw. Admin. Rules tit. 11, ch. 60.1 (Weil's 2000). All references to the Hawaii Administrative Rules are current through the date of publication of this Handbook unless otherwise noted. Chapter 60.1 differs substantially from the old rules, Hawaii Administrative Rules tit. 11, ch. 60, which were repealed concurrent with the adoption of the new rules. Chapter 60.1 was reviewed by an Air Advisory Committee, comprised of representatives of government, business and environmental interests.

Under the Air Pollution Control Law, the Director of the Hawaii Department of Health ("Director") is empowered to prevent, control and abate air pollution, promulgate rules controlling air pollution and appoint hearings officers for contested case hearings.[4] Specifically, the Director sets the state ambient air quality standards, establishes and administers the air permit program, regulates open burning activities and vehicle emissions, and establishes standards of performance for stationary sources, standards of technology for the control of hazardous air pollutants, and rules for the prevention of significant deterioration of air quality.[5] The air pollution control laws are administered by the Clean Air Branch, whose mission is to protect Hawaii's air environment through a strong and effective statewide program, and through the cooperative efforts of governmental bodies, affected facilities, communities, and the general public.[6]

The Department may use revenues generated by the environmental response tax and deposited into the environmental response revolving fund to address concerns relating to air quality.[7]

2.0 RELATIONSHIP TO THE FEDERAL CLEAN AIR ACT

Enacted in 1963, the federal Clean Air Act was substantially amended in 1970, 1977 and 1990. The amendments provide for federal research, interstate compacts and financial support of state control programs. In addition, the amended CAA gives the EPA direct authority to adopt emission standards for several sources including new vehicles,[8] all aircraft[9] and sources of hazardous air pollutants under the National Emission Standards for Hazardous Air Pollutants

---

4 Haw. Rev. Stat. § 342B-3.

5 *Id.* § 342B-12.

6 Hawaii State Department of Health, *Strategic Plan for Hawaii's Environmental Protection Programs* at 30 (January 1999).

7 2000 Haw. Sess. Laws 245 (to be codified at Haw. Rev. Stat. § 128D-2).

8 42 U.S.C. §§ 7404, 7521-7554.

9 *Id.* §§ 7571-7574.

("NESHAPs") regulations.[10] The EPA also is empowered to establish emission standards for new stationary sources which cause or contribute to the endangerment of public health or welfare, under the New Source Performance Standards ("NSPS") regulations.[11] Under the administrative rules, each owner or operator of a stationary source is to comply with all applicable requirements of 40 CFR Part 60, entitled "Standards of Performance for New Stationary Sources."[12]

The EPA and the Department cooperate to enforce and implement air quality standards set forth in the CAA. On the federal level, the CAA requires the EPA to establish National Ambient Air Quality Standards ("NAAQS") for certain pollutants.[13] These NAAQS for individual pollutants apply nationwide. On the state level, the CAA requires each state to establish a State Implementation Plan ("SIP") which imposes emission controls on stationary sources to ensure compliance with the NAAQS.[14] Currently, there are seven NAAQS: sulfur dioxide (SO_2), particulate matter smaller than ten microns in size (PM_{10}), particulate matter, carbon monoxide (CO), ozone (O_3), nitrogen oxides (NO_x), and lead (Pb).[15] Hawaii's Ambient Air Quality Standards for carbon monoxide, nitrogen dioxide and ozone are more stringent than the NAAQS.[16] In accordance with the CAA's requirements, each state lists the attainment status of each of its air quality control regions, or portions thereof, for each of the NAAQS.[17] If an area meets the NAAQS, it receives "attainment" status; if it does not meet the NAAQS, it receives "non-attainment" status for that pollutant.

---

10 *Id.* § 7412.

11 *Id.* § 7411.

12 Haw. Admin. Rules § 11-60.1-161.

13 42 U.S.C. § 7409.

14 *Id.* § 7410.

15 40 C.F.R. Part 50.

16 Hawaii State Department of Health, *Strategic Plan for Hawaii's Environmental Protection Programs* at 27 (January 1999). *Cf.* 40 C.F.R. Part 50 and Haw. Admin. Rules § 11-59-4.

17 42 U.S.C. § 7410.

Those areas falling under attainment status are subject to the requirements for Prevention of Significant Deterioration ("PSD"), which includes the requirement that most new or modified sources use Best Available Control Technology ("BACT").[18] On the other hand, those areas falling under the non-attainment status are required to meet stringent technological control standards of the Lowest Achievable Emission Rate ("LAER"), in addition to meeting the NSPS regulations.[19] All of Hawaii's designated areas achieved the NAAQS for the extended 1987 attainment status deadlines.[20]

Enforcement of NESHAPS may be delegated to the states by the EPA under the CAA.[21] There are currently NESHAPs for asbestos, arsenic, beryllium, mercury, vinyl chloride, benzene, and radionuclides.[22] The CAA requires NESHAPs to be maintained at a level providing "an ample margin of safety to protect the public health" from the hazardous air pollutant."[23] Each owner or operator of a stationary source must comply with all applicable requirements of 40 C.F.R. Part 61, National Emission Standards for Hazardous Air Pollutants.[24] The authority to enforce NESHAPs has not yet been delegated to Hawaii. Hawaii and EPA operate under a memorandum of agreement which provides that the State investigates potential violations of NESHAPs and reports to EPA, which makes decisions regarding enforcement.

Like the NESHAPs, the authority to delegate the enforcement of the NSPS, for new sources,[25] is also given to the EPA under the CAA. New sources are subject to the NSPS if the source falls within the EPA's list of sources causing, or significantly contributing to air pollution

---

18 *Id.* § 7475(a)(4).

19 *Id.* § 7503(a)(2).

20 For a complete list of the designation status of Hawaii's designated areas, see 40 C.F.R. § 81.311.

21 42 U.S.C. § 7412(l).

22 40 C.F.R. §§ 61.20-61.340.

23 42 U.S.C. § 7412(f)(2)(a).

24 Haw. Admin. Rules § 11-60.1-180. The rules identify 40 C.F.R. Part 61, Subparts A, E, J, V, BB, and FF as applicable subparts.

25 42 U.S.C. § 7411(c).

which may reasonably be anticipated to endanger public health or welfare.[26] The NSPS may be designated as either operational standards or numerical emission limitations. Additionally, the Governors may petition the EPA to include any category of major stationary sources which are not subject to NSPS to be included within the EPA's designation.[27]

The standards set forth in the CAA may be enforced by the EPA, the State or a private citizen. Although the EPA delegates enforcement authority to the states, it retains several enforcement devices for violations of NESHAPs, NSPS and designated pollutant standards.[28] The EPA may also enforce the provisions of an approved SIP or any other requirement or prohibition relating to air quality and emission limitations.[29] Additionally, each state has the power to enforce its own SIP. Finally, under the citizen suit provision, any person may sue for a violation of an emission standard or limitation under the CAA or in a SIP provided the EPA or the state has not already commenced an action for the same violation.[30]

3.0 AMBIENT AIR QUALITY STANDARDS AND THE AIR POLLUTION CONTROL LAW

The Ambient Air Quality Standards for the State of Hawaii are found in the Hawaii Revised Statutes[31] and the Hawaii Administrative Rules.[32]

---

26 *Id.* § 7411(b)(1)(A).

27 *Id.* § 7411(g)(1).

28 *Id.* §§ 7411-7413.

29 *Id.* § 7413.

30 *Id.* § 7604.

31 Haw. Rev. Stat. ch. 342B.

32 Haw. Admin. Rules tit. 11, chs. 59 and 60.1. The former Hawaii Administrative Rules tit. 11, ch. 60 was repealed concurrent with the adoption of Chapter 60.1.

3.1 DISTRICT ATTAINMENT PLANS

The Director must establish ambient air quality standards for the State as a whole or for any part thereof.[33] The rules define "ambient air" as "the general outdoor atmosphere to which the public has access."[34] Under the rules, the ambient air quality standards are to protect public health and welfare and prevent the significant deterioration of air quality.[35] There are state ambient air quality standards ("SAAQS") for carbon monoxide (CO), nitrogen dioxide (NO_2), particulate matter (PM), ozone (O_3), sulfur dioxide (SO_2), lead (Pb), and hydrogen sulfide (H_2S).[36] No person may cause, allow or contribute to the violation of any ambient air quality standard.[37] Violators of this prohibition are liable for penalties and remedies as provided for in the Air Pollution Control Law.[38]

3.1.1 AREA CLASSIFICATION

Under the Hawaii Administrative Rules, all geographical areas in the State are designated Class I, Class II or Class III for purposes of air quality control. Class I areas include federal lands specified as Class I by the CAA on August 7, 1977, including international parks, national wilderness areas and national memorial parks which exceed 5,000 acres in size, and national parks which exceed 6,000 acres in size. Class II areas are all those areas not designated as Class I. Most of the State is designated as the less strict Class II area. Class III areas are those areas designated Class III by the State.[39]

---

33 Haw. Rev. Stat. § 342B-12(1).

34 Haw. Admin. Rules § 11-59-2.

35 *Id.* § 11-59-1.

36 *Id.* § 11-59-4.

37 *Id.* § 11-59-5.

38 *Id.* § 11-59-6. *See infra* § 13 of this Chapter.

39 *Id.* § 11-60.1-131.

Redesignation of Class I, II and III areas is subject to federal rules.[40] Under the rules, Haleakala National Park, Volcanoes National Park and the other Class I areas may not be redesignated.[41] Class II areas may be redesignated as a revision to the State Implementation Plan following submission of the request to the EPA, public notice, public hearing, notice to the appropriate federal land manager and consultation with the affected county government.

Each area classification has limits for the amount by which air pollutant concentration may increase over an established baseline. The limits vary by area and type of pollutant. Specific standards and ceilings for particular pollutants are found in the Hawaii Administrative Rules.[42]

3.1.2 NAAQS ATTAINMENT PLANS

The Hawaii SIP provides specific attainment plans for both visible emissions[43] and ambient air quality standards. Ambient air quality standards are established for emissions from fugitive dust, motor vehicles, incineration, fuel combustion and the storage of volatile organic compounds. The Department diligently monitors sources of air pollutants, and its measurements demonstrate that Hawaii's air quality is better than that required by federal and state standards for air pollution control.[44]

Fugitive dust controls prohibit any person from causing or permitting any visible fugitive dust to become without taking reasonable precautions. Fugitive dust is the emission of solid airborne particulate matter from any source other than combustion, and fugitive emissions are emissions which could not reasonably pass through a stack, chimney, vent or other such opening. Precautions must be taken against fugitive dust in demolition, construction, grading or clearing

40 *See* 40 C.F.R. § 52.21(g).

41 Haw. Admin. Rules § 11-60.1-136.

42 *Id.* § 11-59-4.

43 *Id.* § 11-60.1-32. *See infra* § 4.1 of this Chapter.

44 Hawaii State Department of Health, *Strategic Plan for Hawaii's Environmental Protection Programs* at 27 (January 1999).

of land. Other precautions against fugitive dust include the installation and use of hoods, fans and filters as well as covering open-bodied trucks and conducting agricultural operations to minimize fugitive dust. The discharge of visible fugitive dust beyond the lot line of the property from which the dust originates is prohibited unless the person is engaged in agriculture, or can show the use of best practical operation or treatment.[45]

Motor vehicles (and their parts) subject to the rules include gasoline-powered motor vehicles, diesel-powered vehicles, engines and equipment. The rules generally prohibit operation of a gasoline-powered motor vehicle which emits visible smoke. Operation of diesel-powered motor vehicles which emit visible smoke for a period of more than five seconds is also prohibited. Stationary vehicles may not allow their engines to idle unless the engine is being repaired, the engine provides a power source for other equipment such as a hoist or crane, or for more than a three minute period while passengers are loading or unloading. The removal, dismantling, or failure to maintain a motor vehicle's air pollution control equipment is also prohibited.[46] Although motor vehicles are an important air pollutant source, the Department is not considering implementation of a motor vehicle emission program at this time as it believes that technological improvements, strict federal limits on internal combustion engine emissions and turnover in the older vehicle population should stabilize pollution levels well below NAAQS.[47]

Incineration, non-fossil fuel burning boilers and process industries are controlled by limiting the emissions produced. Emissions of particulate matter from incinerators is limited to 0.20 pounds per one hundred pounds (two grams per kilogram) of refuse.[48] Similarly, biomass fuel burning boilers are limited to 0.40 pounds of emissions per one hundred pounds of

45 Haw. Admin. Rules §§ 11-60.1-1 and 11-60.1-33.

46 *Id.* § 11-60.1-34.

47 Hawaii State Department of Health, *Strategic Plan for Hawaii's Environmental Protection Programs* at 28 (January 1999).

48 Haw. Admin. Rules § 11-60.1-35(a).

biomass.[49] The rate of emissions from process industries is governed by an equation based emissions and process weight rate and in any event may not exceed forty pounds per hour.[50]

Sulfur oxides from fuel combustion are controlled by limiting the sulfur level in any fuel burned or sold in the State. The burning of any fuel containing in excess of two percent sulfur by weight is prohibited, except for fuel used in ocean-going vessels.[51] Similarly, no person may burn any fuel containing in excess of 0.50 percent sulfur by weight in any fossil fuel fired power and steam generating facility which generates an output greater than twenty-five megawatts.[52] The use of such fuels, however, may be allowed at the Director's sole discretion, if such use will result in equivalent or lower emission rates of sulfur oxides.

Emissions from the storage of volatile organic compounds, volatile organic compound water separation, pump and compressor requirements and waste gas disposal are controlled by specifying the types of equipment and control devices used in such activities. Strict limits are placed on the storage of volatile organic compounds ("VOCs"). Storage of VOCs is allowed only with vapor loss control devices, such as a floating roof, vapor recovery system or other similar equipment.[53] The rules also set forth similar requirements for VOC water separation, pump and compressor requirements, and waste gas disposal.[54]

4.0 OTHER STATEWIDE AIR POLLUTION PROVISIONS

The Hawaii Air Pollution Control Law gives the Director specific authority to develop standards and regulations to address particular sources of air pollution.[55] Visible emissions and open burning, both agricultural and nonagricultural, are regulated.

---

49 *Id.* § 11-60.1-36.

50 *Id.* § 11-60.1-37.

51 *Id.* § 11-60.1-38.

52 *Id.* § 11-60.1-38(b).

53 *Id.* § 11-60.1-39(a).

54 *Id.* § 11-60.1-40-42.

55 Haw. Rev. Stat. § 342B-12.

4.1 VISIBLE EMISSIONS

There are currently two visible emission restrictions for stationary sources. The first restriction applies to stationary sources which commenced construction or were in operation before March 21, 1972; the second restriction applies to stationary sources whose construction, modification or relocation commenced after March 20, 1972. The first restriction limits emission of visible air pollutants of a density equal to or darker than forty percent opacity while the second restriction allows only twenty percent opacity. Under both restrictions, the visible emissions are limited to a density not darker than sixty percent opacity for more than six minutes in any sixty minute period when igniting or creating a fire, or when breakdown of equipment occurs. Compliance with the restrictions is determined by the methods for evaluating actual opacity readings incorporated into the rules.[56] Emissions of uncombined water, such as water vapor, are exempt and do not constitute a violation of the rules.[57]

4.2 OPEN BURNING

Open burning is generally prohibited. However, agricultural burning is allowed by permit, and certain non-agricultural burning is exempt from regulation under the rules. The general prohibition against open burning does not apply to fires for the cooking of food or for recreational or ceremonial purposes.[58]

4.2.1 AGRICULTURAL BURNING

The rules define "agricultural burning" as the use of open outdoor fires in agricultural operations, forest management or range improvements.[59] A permit is required for agricultural burning.[60] Violations of the terms and conditions of the permit are subject to penalties and

---

56 Haw. Admin. Rules § 11-60.1-32. Opacity is measured pursuant to 40 C.F.R. Part 60, Appendix A, Method 9 and other EPA approved Methods.

57 Haw. Admin. Rules § 11-60.1-32.

58 *Id.* § 11-60.1-52.

59 *Id.* § 11-60.1-51.

60 *Id.* § 11-60.1-53.

remedies provided for in state and federal air pollution control laws, rules, and regulations. The Director may regulate open burning by districts rather than by island. A district is a geographic area, as designated by the Director, to distinguish appropriate air basins for the purpose of smoke management.

The Department conducts a special monitoring project regarding the agricultural practice of burning sugar cane before harvesting. The Department established two particulate stations on Maui to monitor ground-level effects from cane burning, and is also evaluating the effectiveness of burn forecasting which uses meteorological and topographic information to minimize smoke impact to communities and residential areas.[61]

Many small farmers, as well as sugar companies, apply for agricultural burning permits. Applications for agricultural burning permits, made on forms from the Department, must include maps of the burn areas, the direction of prevailing winds and the location of nearby residences, schools, airports and the fields to be burned. Each application, signed by the applicant, constitutes an agreement with the Department that the applicant will comply with the terms and conditions of the permit.[62] In processing agricultural burning permits, the Department evaluates the application based on the location, size and frequency of burn, potential community impacts and verification of agricultural activity. An agricultural burning permittee must maintain a record of the conditions existing at the time of each burn, including the location and type of material burned, and meteorological conditions.[63] The Director must act on a permit application within ninety days of receipt of the completed application. If the Director has not acted within ninety days, the application is deemed to be approved.[64]

The rules describe "no burn" conditions under which agricultural burning will not be permitted. These periods occur under conditions of widespread haze or elevated levels of carbon

---

61 Hawaii State Department of Health, *Strategic Plan for Hawaii's Environmental Protection Programs* at 27 (January 1999).

62 Haw. Admin. Rules . § 11-60.1-54.

63 *Id.* § 11-60.1-56.

64 *Id.* § 11-60.1-57.

monoxide or particulate matter. Notices of "no-burn" periods are provided by radio broadcast through the National Weather Service.[65]

4.2.2 NON-AGRICULTURAL BURNING

The following are non-agricultural exceptions to the prohibition of open burning: fires to abate a fire hazard; fires for prevention or control of disease or pests; fires for training personnel in the methods of fighting fires; fires for the disposal of dangerous materials which have received advance approval by the Director; fires for residential bathing purposes; and fires for recreational, decorative or ceremonial purposes.[66] These types of open burning are generally permitted, however, some require the Director's approval. Fires for burning leaves, grass, weeds, wood, paper and similar materials on one's own premises are allowed under certain conditions on all islands except Oahu.[67]

5.0 PERMITTING OF SOURCES

Under the operating permits program, no person may engage in, cause, allow or maintain any activity which causes air pollution without first securing written approval from the Director.[68] The operating permits program was granted interim approval by the EPA on December 1, 1994.[69] The new operating permits program replaces the old Authority to Construct and Permit to Operate permit process with a single permit process. An application for a covered source or noncovered source permit must be submitted to the Director for approval.[70] The permit may be issued for any term not to exceed five years.[71] The permit may also be used to prove the

---

65 *Id.* § 11-60.1-55.

66 For more exemptions, *see id.* § 11-60.1-52.

67 Haw. Admin. Rules § 11-60.1-52.

68 Haw. Rev. Stat. § 342B-11.

69 59 Fed. Reg. 61,549.

70 Haw. Rev. Stat. § 342B-22(c).

71 *Id.* § 342B-25.

applicant's knowledge that it was not complying with the NAAQS and SAAQS.[72] Violation of any condition of the permit may result in modification, suspension or revocation of the permit as determined by the Director, but only after the permittee is afforded the opportunity for a hearing. The hearing must be held as a contested case hearing in accordance with Hawaii Administrative Procedure Act.[73]

For each application for a permit to build or operate a covered source, the Director must provide for public notice, opportunity for public comment and an opportunity for public hearing.[74] Public notice is usually given by placement of a classified advertisement in Hawaii newspapers of statewide circulation. The public comment period is not less than thirty days.[75] Once the application is complete, fees have been paid and public notice requirements have been fulfilled, the Director must approve or deny the application. In general, the Director must approve an application for a noncovered or covered source permit if the applicant can demonstrate compliance to the satisfaction of the Director with all applicable requirements, including the maintenance of NAAQS, SAAQS and the applicable NSPS, NESHAP and PSD review requirements. Each application is also subject to federal oversight. The Department must take final action on each permit application within eighteen months.[76]

5.1 COVERED SOURCE AND NONCOVERED SOURCE PERMITS

Permits are required for covered sources and noncovered sources. The rules define "covered source" to include any major source, any source subject to standards of performance for stationary sources, any source subject to an emission standard for hazardous air pollutants, and any source subject to the rules for prevention of significant deterioration ("PSD") of air quality.

---

72 *Unitek Environmental Services, Inc. v. Hawaiian Cement*, 1997 U.S. Dist. LEXIS 19261, *10-11.

73 *Id.* § 342B-27. *See infra* ch. 13 of this Handbook.

74 Haw. Rev. Stat. § 342B-24(d). *See also* § 342B-13.

75 *Id.* § 342B-13(a)(4).

76 *Id.* § 342B-24.

A noncovered source is any stationary source constructed, modified or relocated after March 20, 1972, that is not a covered source.[77]

5.1.1 COVERED SOURCE PERMIT

A covered source permit is required prior to burning used oil and prior to the construction, reconstruction, modification, relocation or operation of an emission unit or air pollution control equipment.[78] The rules identify insignificant activities which are exempt from the requirement of obtaining a covered source permit. However, certain insignificant activities must be identified in the covered source permit application. Examples of insignificant activities include storage tanks, certain fuel burning equipment, steam generators, kilns, standby electricity generators, paint spray booths, hand-held equipment, ocean-going vessels, ovens, grills, stoves and air conditioning systems. All sources and source categories subject to the national emission standard for asbestos during demolition and renovation activities,[79] are also exempt from covered source permit requirements.[80] Where the PSD requirements conflict with the requirements regarding covered source permits, the most stringent of the two requirements is to apply.[81]

5.1.2 NONCOVERED SOURCE PERMIT

The administrative rules for noncovered source permits prohibit any activity which causes air pollution or causes or allows the emission of any regulated or hazardous air pollutant unless approval has been secured in writing from the Director.[82] The Director must grant a noncovered source permit before any person may burn used or waste oil or begin construction, reconstruction, modification, relocation or operation of an emission unit or air pollution control equipment. The noncovered source permit remains valid past its expiration date until the

---

77 Haw. Admin. Rules § 11-60.1-1.

78 *Id.* § 11-60.1-82(a).

79 40 C.F.R. § 61.145.

80 Haw. Admin. Rules § 11-60.1-82.

81 *Id.* *See infra* § 7.0 of this Chapter for PSD requirements.

82 *Id.* § 11-60.1-62.

Director has issued or denied a renewal application, provided the application and any requested additional information has been submitted to the Director prior to permit expiration. The rules exempt certain activities from the requirement of obtaining a noncovered source permit.[83] The list of activities from the noncovered source permit requirement follows the list of activities exempt from the covered source permit requirement.[84]

5.2 TRANSITION PERIOD

During the transition period, from November 26, 1993 through November 26, 1996,[85] all owners or operators of an existing covered source submitted an initial covered source permit application.[86] Certain types of covered sources, such as mining, manufacturing and electric services were given four to eight months from the effective date of the rules to submit an application. All others were submitted within ten months of the effective date of the rules.[87]

During the transition period, the effect of a covered source permit application varied. An owner or operator who had applied for, but not received an authority to construct permit pursuant to repealed Chapter 11-60 of the administrative rules, for example, was required to submit a covered source permit application and refrain from constructing or operating the source. However, if the covered source was in existence prior to March 21, 1972, or was exempt pursuant to repealed Chapter 11-60, the owner or operator could continue to operate the source without violation for failure to obtain a covered source permit, provided the owner or operator submitted a timely application under the new rules.

Similarly, where an authority to construct or permit to operate expired prior to the issuance of the covered source permit, the party could continue to construct or operate if they submitted a timely covered source permit application. In effect, the authority to construct or

83 *Id.*

84 *Compare with* Haw. Admin. Rules § 11-60.1-82.

85 *Id.* § 11-60.1-81.

86 *Id.* § 11-60.1-87(f).

87 *Id.*

permit to operate remained valid until the covered source permit was issued or denied.[88] In the event that an authority to construct or permit to operate expired prior to the required submission date for the initial application, the owner or operator was permitted to continue construction or operation provided a timely application was submitted.

Except for applications subject to the PSD requirements, the Director was required to approve, conditionally approve, or deny at least one-third of all complete covered source permit applications submitted within one year of the effective date of the rules, or by November 26, 1994. The Director was required to act on applications for new covered sources or modifications subject to PSD requirements within twelve months of receipt of the application.[89] The covered source application submittal deadline was extended by the Director to twelve months from the effective date of the rules, *i.e.*, to November 26, 1994. Therefore, the deadline for the submittal of all initial covered source applications for existing sources has passed.[90]

Noncovered source permits followed similar guidelines during the transition period. The owner or operator of a noncovered source with an authority to construct permit, issued pursuant to repealed Chapter 60, submitted a noncovered source permit application sixty days prior to expiration of the permit. During this period, the owner or operator could continue construction or operation of the source until the noncovered source permit was issued. The owner or operator of a noncovered source who had not received the permit to operate was also required to apply for a noncovered source permit. Finally, an owner or operator who applied for, but did not receive an authority to construct permit was required to obtain a noncovered source permit prior to construction or modification. If the authority to construct or permit to operate expired before the issuance of the noncovered source permit, the owner or operator could continue to construct or operate only if a timely permit application was submitted.[91]

---

88 *Id.* § 11-60.1-87(d).

89 *Id.* § 11-60.1-88.

90 *Id.* § 11-60.1-87.

91 *Id.* § 11-60.1-66.

5.3 PERMIT APPLICATION

The covered source permit application is submitted on forms furnished by the Department and is reviewed by the Engineering Section of the Clean Air Branch. It must include the name, address, and telephone number of the company, the owner and owner's agent, and the plant site manager or other contact person. The application must provide information regarding the facility including location, typical operating schedules, specifications and drawings, and reasonably anticipated operating scenarios. The application also includes maximum emission rates, all points of emissions, a detailed description of air pollution control equipment and compliance monitoring devices, and a detailed schedule for construction of the source or modification.[92] If emission trading is proposed, the application must include information to define permit terms and conditions. An applicant must also include maximum emissions rates, a detailed description of air pollution control equipment, a description of applicable requirements along with the applicable test methods for determining compliance, and current operational limitations or work practices. The application must also include a description of all emission points in enough detail to establish a basis for fees and applicability of regulatory requirements.[93]

For new and existing covered sources, and significant modifications, the application must include an assessment of the ambient air quality impact of the source. The Director may request a risk assessment and information regarding other available control technologies. Finally, the application must include a compliance plan.[94]

Unless the Director requests additional information or notifies the applicant within sixty days after receiving the application that the application is incomplete, it is deemed complete. The Director must approve, conditionally approve, or deny the covered source permit within eighteen months after receiving the application. If the application contains an early reduction demonstration, the Director must act on the application within nine months. The Director is required to approve, conditionally approve, or deny the application for new covered sources or

92 *Id.* § 11-60.1-83(a).

93 *Id.*

94 *Id.* *See infra* § 5.3.1 of this Chapter.

significant modifications within twelve months after receiving it. The Director is required to provide a statement, which sets forth the legal and factual basis for the draft permit conditions, to the EPA and any other person requesting it.[95]

The owner or operator must submit to both the EPA and the Department a copy of all covered source permit applications. The Department then submits a copy of each proposed covered source permit to the EPA. The Director cannot issue the covered source permit, amendment or renewal if within forty-five days of receiving the proposed permit the EPA objects to its issuance. The Director then has ninety days to amend the proposed covered source permit and resubmit it to the EPA.[96]

Each application for a covered source, temporary covered source and general covered source permit must include a compliance certification. The compliance certification, which is to be submitted to the Director and to the EPA, must include a description of methods used to determine compliance, a schedule for submissions of compliance certifications during the permit, and a statement indicating compliance with enhanced monitoring and certification requirements. After permit issuance, the permittee must submit a compliance certification every six months which identifies the terms or conditions of the permit, the compliance status, the methods used for determining compliance status, and which also indicates whether compliance was continuous or intermittent.[97] Any applicant who fails to submit relevant facts or submits incorrect information has a duty, under the rules, to submit the relevant or correct information.[98]

An application for a noncovered source permit, also submitted on forms provided by the Director, must provide similar information. The Director may likewise request an assessment of the ambient air quality impact of the noncovered source or modification as part of the application.[99]

95 Haw. Admin. Rules § 11-60.1-83.

96 *Id.* § 11-60.1-95.

97 *Id.* § 11-60.1-86.

98 *Id.* § 11-60.1-84.

99 *Id.* § 11-60.1-63(a)(9).

The rules require certification, by a responsible official, of the truth, accuracy, and completeness of every application form, report, compliance plan, or compliance certification submitted to the Department. The certification must state that, based on information and belief formed after reasonable inquiry, the statements are true, accurate and complete.[100]

5.3.1 COMPLIANCE PLAN

Each initial application for a covered source permit, temporary or general covered source permit, or application for renewal or significant modification must include a compliance plan. A compliance plan also must be submitted with every initial application for a noncovered source, temporary noncovered source and general noncovered source permit, or application for a modification to a noncovered source.[101]

The compliance plan must describe the current compliance status of the source and identify those requirements with which the source is in compliance. The compliance plan must also describe applicable requirements with which the source is not in compliance, and provide a detailed schedule explaining how the source will achieve compliance. It must include a schedule of compliance under which the owner or operator will submit progress reports to the Director no less frequently than every six months if the compliance plan is to remedy a violation. The compliance plan must contain specific dates for achieving activities, milestones or compliance, along with an explanation of why scheduled dates were not met and any preventative or corrective measures adopted.[102]

5.4 PERMIT TERM AND CONTENT

The covered source permit may be issued or renewed for a fixed term of five years.[103] A covered source permit is to include, among other items, emission limitations and standards,

---

100 *Id.* § 11-60.1-4.

101 *Id.* § 11-60.1-65.

102 *Id.* §§ 11-60.1-85 and 11-60.1-65.

103 *Id.* § 11-60.1-89.

control technology, monitoring methods and a requirement for the prompt reporting of deviations.[104] The rules allow emissions trading, the terms and conditions of which must also be included in the permit.[105]

The permit may allow the designation of confidential records. The permit also may allow the Director to enter the premises to inspect records and the emission-related activity, including monitoring and air pollution control equipment, and to conduct sampling or monitoring. Terms and conditions included in a covered source permit are enforceable by the EPA and through a citizen suit under the federal CAA unless specifically designated otherwise.[106]

Similarly, a noncovered source permit may be issued or renewed for any term not to exceed five years.[107] The permit may include, among other things: emission limitations; emissions tests, monitoring, and recordkeeping; anticipated operating scenarios; and provisions regarding compliance with the permit terms and conditions. The permit also may contain provisions regarding modifications and reporting of equipment shutdown. The permit must comply with certification requirements.[108]

5.5 TYPES OF PERMITS

In addition to standard covered source permits and noncovered source permits, the rules provide for temporary and general permits as well as administrative permit amendment.[109]

---

104 *Id.* § 11-60.1-90.

105 *Id. See infra* § 12.0 of this Chapter.

106 *Id.* § 11-60.1-93.

107 *Id.* § 11-60.1-67.

108 *Id.* § 11-60.1-68.

109 *Id.* §§ 11-60.1-69, 11-60.1-70, 11-60.1-75, 11-60.1-91, 11-60.1-92, 11-60.1-102.

5.5.1 TEMPORARY PERMIT

An owner or operator of a temporary covered source, to be operated at various locations with the same equipment and similar methods of operation, may apply for a temporary covered source permit. The application and issuance of a temporary covered source permit is subject to the same procedures and requirements as those for covered source permits. The Director is to provide for public notice and comment, as well as a statement setting forth the legal and factual basis for the draft temporary covered source permit conditions. Each application is subject to EPA oversight.[110]

The owner or operator is required to identify any changes in location of the temporary covered source permit, and notify the Director at least thirty days prior to the change in location. In doing so, the owner or operator must submit a location map and the projected dates of operation at the new location, as well as certification that no modification will be made to the equipment. Prior to relocation, the Director must approve, conditionally approve, or deny in writing each location change. With the exception of the initial locations, if a source remains at a location for longer than twelve consecutive months, the Director may request an ambient air quality impact assessment.[111]

Noncovered source owners and operators may apply for a temporary noncovered source permit, subject to the same procedures and requirements for a noncovered source permit. The owner or operator must certify that no modification will be made to the equipment or operational methods. If the noncovered source remains in any one location for longer than twelve consecutive months, the Director may request an ambient air quality impact assessment of the source.[112]

---

110 *Id.* § 11-60.1-91.

111 *Id.*

112 *Id.* § 11-60.1-69.

5.5.2 GENERAL PERMIT

At the Director's discretion, a covered source general permit may be issued for similar covered sources. Nonmajor covered sources qualifying for a general permit must have the same Standard Industrial Classification ("SIC") Code, as well as similar equipment design and air pollution controls. No general permit is available for covered sources requiring case-by-case determinations regarding air pollution control requirements. At present, the Department has only issued a general permit for drycleaners.[113] General permits require public notice, an opportunity for the public to request a hearing, and an opportunity for public comment.

The covered source general permit application must identify and describe all points of emissions, including current operational limitations or work practices.[114] The Director must approve an application for coverage under a general permit within six months after receipt of a complete application.

The Director may approve an application for coverage under a covered source general permit without repeating the public participation procedures. Such approval, however, is not considered final permit action for purposes of administrative and judicial review.[115]

The Department may issue a noncovered source general permit for similar noncovered sources,[116] if they have the same SIC Code, similar equipment design and air pollution controls, and the same applicable requirements. As with covered source general permits, no general permit may be considered for noncovered sources requiring a case-by-case determination for air pollution control requirements.

The Director may request an assessment of the ambient air quality impact of the noncovered source with the general permit application. The Director must approve,

---

113 Interview with Scott Takamoto, Clean Air Branch, Hawaii Department of Health (August 1, 2000).

114 *Id.* § 11-60.1-92.

115 *Id.*

116 *Id.* § 11-60.1-70.

conditionally approve or deny an application for coverage under a noncovered general permit within six months after receiving the completed application.[117]

5.5.3 ADMINISTRATIVE PERMIT AMENDMENT

An administrative permit amendment is a permit amendment which corrects typographical errors, requires more frequent monitoring or reporting, consolidates two or more covered or noncovered source permits into one permit, or allows for a change in ownership or control of the source. Administrative permit amendments are available for covered[118] and noncovered[119] sources. The Director must take final action on a request for an administrative permit amendment within sixty days of receiving the written request, and the Director may amend the permit without providing notice to the public.

5.5.4 APPLICATIONS FOR MODIFICATIONS

A covered source may wish to change operations in response to changing technical, economic or environmental circumstances. Source modifications may require permit modifications. "Modification" is defined by the covered source rules as a physical change or change in the method of operation of a stationary source, excluding routine maintenance, repair, and replacement.[120] The modification may increase emissions of pollutants or result in the emission of air pollutants not previously emitted. Covered source modifications may be either minor or significant.

Applications for minor modification to a covered source are to include a description of all changes, why the modification is determined to be minor, maximum emission rates and certification that the modification is minor along with related information. The minor modification is to be approved only if it will be in compliance with all applicable requirements.

---

117 *Id.*

118 *Id.* § 11-60.1-102.

119 *Id.* § 11-60.1-75.

120 *Id.* § 11-60.1-81.

Each application is subject to EPA oversight.[121] Within fifteen days following the end of the EPA's forty-five day review period, the Director must either amend the permit to reflect the minor modification, deny the minor modification, determine that the requested modification is actually a significant modification, or amend the proposed permit and resubmit the amendment to the EPA for reevaluation.

Applications for significant modifications to a covered source are subject to the same requirements as for an initial covered source permit application.[122] The application is to include a description of the significant modification, including changes to equipment design and source emissions. For significant modifications which increase the emissions of any air pollutant or result in the emission of any air pollutant not previously emitted, the applicant must also submit an ambient air quality impact assessment.[123]

The Director must approve, conditionally approve or deny an application for a significant modification within eighteen months of receiving the complete application. The rules also require the Director to provide reasonable procedures and resources to complete the review of the majority of the applications for significant modification within nine months of receiving a complete application. The Director must provide for public participation regarding significant modifications.[124]

A noncovered source may also be modified for various reasons. The noncovered source rules define "modification" as a physical or operational change in a stationary source which increases the amount of any air pollutants or which results in the emission of any air pollutant not previously emitted; it may also include significant changes in existing monitoring requirements or in reporting or recordkeeping requirements. As with covered sources, routine maintenance, repair, and replacement are not considered modifications.[125]

---

121 *Id.* § 11-60.1-103.

122 *Id.* § 11-60.1-104.

123 *Id.*

124 *Id.*

125 *Id.* § 11-60.1-61.

An application for a modification to a noncovered source must provide information describing modification of the emissions rates, a schedule for construction or modification of the noncovered source and a compliance plan. The application for modification is deemed complete if the Director does not notify the applicant of its incompleteness within sixty days. The Director must approve, conditionally approve or deny an application for modification within six months of receiving the completed application.[126]

5.5.5 PERMIT RENEWAL

Applications for covered source permit renewal are subject to the same requirements as those for an initial permit application. Each application for covered source permit renewal must be submitted to the Director a minimum of twelve months prior to the date of permit expiration. If the application for renewal has not been approved or denied within twelve months, the covered source permit and all its terms and conditions are to remain in effect and not expire until approval or denial provided that the applicant has submitted any additional information requested by the Director.[127]

For covered source general permits, the Director is required to approve or deny the renewed application within six months. If the renewal has not been approved or denied within six months, the covered source general permit remains in effect. The Director is required to provide a statement that sets forth the legal and factual basis for the draft permit renewal conditions to the EPA and any other person requesting it: each application for renewal is subject to EPA oversight.[128]

Noncovered source permit renewals are granted based on similar considerations. The application for a noncovered source permit renewal must comply with the requirements for the initial permit application. Each permit renewal application is to be submitted to the Director at least sixty days prior to the date of permit expiration. The Director must approve, conditionally

---

126 *Id.* § 11-60.1-76.

127 *Id.* § 11-60.1-101.

128 *Id.*

approve or deny the application for renewal within six months of receipt of the complete application. If the application has not been approved or denied within six months, the noncovered source permit is to remain in effect and will not expire until the application for renewal has been approved or denied.[129]

5.6 PERMIT FEES

The collection of fees from covered sources is required by the 1990 Clean Air Act Amendments and its implementing regulations to cover the direct and indirect costs to develop, support and administer the covered source permit program and the Small Business Assistance Program, which is intended to provide small business covered sources with guidance in complying with the new regulations. Owners and operators are to pay application fees and annual fees.[130] If, upon evaluation, the Director finds fee adjustments are required, the Director must afford the opportunity for public comment in accordance with the Hawaii Administrative Procedure Act and the Air Pollution Control Law.[131]

5.6.1 APPLICATION FEES

No covered source permit application is complete until the application fee is paid in full. The administrative rules provide a fee schedule for PSD sources, major covered sources, nonmajor covered sources, temporary covered sources, sources seeking coverage under a general covered source permit, major air toxic sources and nonmajor air toxic sources. If a covered source falls under more than one category listed in the schedule, the owner or operator is to pay the highest application fee applicable to the source. Administrative permit amendment fees are to be assessed only if the change is requested by the owner or operator.[132] Application fees for

---

129 *Id.* § 11-60.1-74.

130 *Id.* § 11-60.1-112.

131 *Id.* § 11-60.1-112(g). *See infra* ch. 13 of this Handbook.

132 *Id.* § 11-60.1-113.

noncovered source permits are applicable to noncovered sources, temporary noncovered sources and air toxic sources and are subject to substantially similar requirements.[133]

No application for an agricultural burning permit will be acted upon or considered unless the application fee is paid in full. The rules provide a fee schedule from $50 to $1,500 based on the number of acres to be burned.[134]

5.6.2 ANNUAL FEES

Annual fees are to be paid in full within sixty days after the end of each calendar year, and within thirty days after the permanent discontinuance of any covered source. Fee worksheets are provided by the Director to aid the owner or operator in calculating annual fees. The Director, upon written request submitted fifteen days prior to the due date, may extend the annual fee submittal deadline if reasonable justification exists. If the Director disapproves an extension for annual fee submittal, the owner or operator is to pay the fees within thirty days of receiving the disapproval notification or the original submittal deadline, whichever is later.[135]

Annual fees are based upon the calculated tons of regulated air pollutants emitted during the prior calendar year. The rules define "regulated air pollutant" as (1) nitrogen oxides or any volatile organic compound; (2) any air pollutant for which a national or state ambient air quality standard has been promulgated; (3) any air pollutant subject to standards adopted pursuant to the Hawaii Air Pollution Control Law,[136] or Section 111 of the CAA; (4) certain air pollutants subject to a standard under Section 112 of the CAA; and (5) any Class I or Class II subject to standards under Title VI of the CAA.[137] For purposes of annual fee calculations, carbon

---

133 *Id.* § 11-60.1-117 and 120.

134 *Id.* § 11-60.1-121.

135 *Id.* § 11-60.1-114.

136 Haw. Rev. Stat. Ch. 342B.

137 Haw. Admin Rules. §§ 11-60.1-1 and 11-60.1-114.

monoxide emissions, fugitive emissions, emissions from insignificant activities, and anything greater than four thousand tons per year of each regulated air pollutant are excluded.[138]

The annual fee assessed for each regulated air pollutant is determined by multiplying the appropriate dollar per ton charge by the calculated emissions in tons per year for each regulated pollutant. Since January 1, 1995 the dollar per ton charge has been adjusted by the percentage increase in the Consumer Price Index. The rules provide guidelines for determining the calculated emissions in tons per year.[139]

The minimum annual fee for each covered source facility or covered source permit held during the prior calendar year is $1,000. A covered source facility may have more than one source under common control of the same person(s) and be located on adjacent or contiguous properties.[140] The annual fee for a noncovered source is $500 for each valid permit.[141] Although fees for regulated air toxic pollutant emissions are deferred until calendar year 2001, the owner must nonetheless report such emissions greater than one ton per year upon submittal of the annual fee.[142] If any part of the annual fee is not paid within thirty days after the due date, a late payment penalty of five percent of the amount due is added to the fee. If any annual fee is not paid in full within thirty days after the due date, the Director may terminate or suspend any or all of the covered source permits.[143] Before doing so the Director must afford an opportunity for a hearing in accordance with the Hawaii Administrative Procedure Act[144] and the Air Pollution Control Law.[145]

---

138 *Id.* §11-60.1-114(e).

139 *Id.* §§ 11-60.1-114 and 115.

140 *Id.* § 11-60.1-114(l).

141 *Id.* § 11-60.1-119.

142 *Id.* § 11-60.1-114(p).

143 *Id.* §§ 11-60.1-114 and 119.

144 Haw. Rev. Stat. ch. 91. *See infra* ch. 13 of this Handbook.

145 Haw. Admin. Rules § 11-60.1-114.

5.7 PUBLIC PARTICIPATION

The Director must provide public notice, including the method by which a public hearing may be requested, and an opportunity for public comment, on all draft covered source permits. Public notice is to be provided for permit renewal, initial issuance or for significant modification of a covered source.[146] The Director must notify the public of the availability of the application and the Department's analysis by publishing notice once in the county affected by the proposed action and by posting notice on the Department's web site.[147] Persons may object to the issuance of any proposed covered source permit by petitioning the EPA pursuant to federal rules.[148] The Director may not issue the permit if the EPA objects to the proposed permit as a result of public petition.[149]

The applicant, and any person who participated in the public comment or hearing process and who objected to the grant or denial of a covered source permit or permit amendment, may petition the Department for a contested case hearing. The petition for a contested case hearing is to be filed within ninety days of the date of approval or disapproval of the proposed draft permit.[150] Any person aggrieved by a final administrative decision and order, including the denial of any contested case hearing, may petition for judicial review pursuant to the Hawaii Administrative Procedure Act.[151]

In considering any application for a noncovered source permit, the Director may provide for public notice and public comment, but is not required to do so.[152] A public hearing may be requested during the public comment period. The request should provide reasons why public comment or hearing is warranted. The Director is to make available for public inspection all

---

146 *Id.* § 11-60.1-99(a).

147 2000 Haw. Sess. Laws 150 (to be codified at Haw. Rev. Stat. 342B-13).

148 *Id.* § 11-60.1-100(a). See 40 C.F.R. § 70.8(d).

149 Haw. Admin. Rules § 11-60.1-100.

150 *Id.*

151 Haw. Rev. Stat. ch. 91. *See infra* ch. 13 of this Handbook.

152 Haw. Admin. Rules § 11-60.1-73.

non-confidential information submitted by the applicant, the Department's analysis and proposed action, and other relevant information.

Interested persons may submit written comments during the public comment period.[153] The notice of public comment period and public hearing must contain information regarding the facility, the applicant and the emissions change involved in any permit amendment, along with the identity of a contact person from whom interested persons may obtain additional information, including copies of the draft permit and application. The Director is to maintain a record of the comments and the issues raised during the public participation process.[154]

5.8 PUBLIC ACCESS TO INFORMATION

All permit applications, supporting information, compliance plans and schedules, reports and results from tests and monitoring, certifications, permits, and public comments and testimonies are considered government records available for public inspection pursuant to the Hawaii Uniform Information Practices Act.[155] Any owner or operator, however, may submit a written request for confidential treatment of specific information, provided the owner or operator documents how each item of confidential information concerns secret processes or methods of manufacture, or is confidential in nature, who has access to the information, what steps have been taken to protect the secrecy of each item, why the applicant believes each item must be accorded confidential treatment and the anticipated prejudice should disclosure be made. The permit contents and emissions data will never be entitled to confidentiality protection. Any person whose claim for confidentiality of records, reports or other information is denied by the Director may obtain administrative and judicial review subject to the Administrative Procedure Act.[156]

---

153 *Id.*

154 *Id.* § 11-60.1-73(b)(6).

155 Haw. Rev. Stat. ch. 92F.

156 Haw. Admin. Rules § 11-60.1-14; Haw. Rev. Stat. ch. 91. *See infra* ch. 13 of this Handbook.

The Department is required to maintain records on all covered and noncovered source permit applications for a minimum of five years.[157] The Director may require an owner or operator to maintain files on information necessary to determine compliance with state and federal air pollution control laws, rules and regulations.[158] This information is to be summarized and reported to the Director at intervals specified in the rules.[159]

5.9 PERMIT ACTION

The Director may terminate, suspend, reopen or amend a permit. The Director may take such action upon finding a material mistake with regard to emissions limitations, noncompliance or violation of a permit condition, or where the permit was obtained by misrepresentation, where action is necessary to ensure compliance with the Clean Air Act or Hawaii Air Pollution Law, where changed conditions requires a reduction or elimination of the discharge, where more frequent monitoring is required, or where such action is in the public interest. The Director may impose more restrictive conditions in a noncovered or covered source permit to further limit the emissions of air pollutants or the operation of the source.[160]

The Director may reopen and amend a covered source permit if additional requirements become applicable to a major covered source and the permit has a term of three or more remaining years. No such permit reopening is required if the effective date of the requirement is later than the date on which the permit is due to expire. A permit may also be reopened if it contains material mistake or if inaccurate statements were made in establishing emissions limitations or other permit conditions. The Director is to provide written notification to the permittee on reopening the permit.[161]

---

157 Haw. Admin. Rules §§ 11-60.1-71(b) and 11-60.1-94(d).

158 Haw. Rev. Stat. § 342B-28.

159 Haw. Admin. Rules § 11-60.1-11.

160 *Id.* § 11-60.1-5.

161 *Id.* § 11-60.1-98.

For covered sources, the permit may be cancelled if construction is not commenced within eighteen months, is discontinued for eighteen months or is not completed within a reasonable time.[162] Permits are not transferable from between persons, locations or pieces of equipment without approval from the Director.[163]

A noncovered source permit may be reopened and amended upon the Director's determination that the permit contains a material mistake or inaccurate statements were made in establishing emissions standards or other terms or conditions of the permit. The permit may be terminated if termination is required to assure compliance with applicable requirements.[164] The Director is required to provide written notification to the permittee on the reopening of the permit at least thirty days prior to the reopening date, unless immediate action is required to prevent an imminent peril to public health and safety or the environment.[165] A noncovered source permit may be cancelled if construction authorized by the permit is not commenced within twelve months after the permit takes effect, is discontinued for twelve months or is not completed within a reasonable amount of time.[166]

5.10 REPORTING REQUIREMENTS

In 1997, the Hawaii Administrative Rules were revised to require every owner or operator of a major source within Campbell Industrial Park or Kahe Valley and every geothermal facility which emits criteria air pollutants in excess of 100 tons per year to submit an annual report to the Department. The facility must describe the type and quantity of criteria pollutants and a description of measures to control criteria pollutants.[167]

---

162 *Id.* § 11-60.1-9.

163 *Id.* § 11-60.1-7.

164 *Id.* § 11-60.1-72.

165 *Id.*

166 *Id.* §11-60.1-9(a).

167 Haw. Rev. Stat. § 342B-18(a).

After submission of pollutant information, the Department then reviews all facility reports and produces its own report summarizing the ambient air quality data for each criteria pollutant, a comparison of the modeling data against state and federal ambient air quality standards, the impacts of the criteria pollutants on human health and the environment, as well as a report on air quality trends over a five-year period.[168]

If the Department determines that any unpermitted releases may have an adverse impact on human health, the Department must notify the neighborhood boards or community associations of the adjacent communities as soon as the circumstances warrant.[169]

The Department also monitors air quality with three monitoring stations adjacent to Campbell Industrial Park. Monitoring data indicate that although air quality is good, air pollution incidents do occur at times as a result of equipment malfunction or breakdown. The Department is also assisting the Campbell Industrial Park Air Quality Task Force, created by the 1997 Legislature, in assessing the air quality of the area and evaluating air planning strategies to accommodate future growth of the industrial park.[170]

6.0 EQUIPMENT SHUTDOWN AND FAILURE

Permanent discontinuance of the operation of any noncovered or covered source must be reported to the Director within thirty days.[171] Shutdown of air pollution control equipment for necessary scheduled maintenance must be reported to the Director at least twenty-four hours prior to the shutdown. This notice must include the location and permit number of the specific equipment, the length of time the equipment will be out of service, the expected length of the shutdown period, air pollutants likely to be emitted, measures taken to minimize the length of the shutdown period and the reasons why it would be impossible or impractical to halt the source

168 *Id.* § 342B-18(b).

169 *Id.* § 342B-18(c).

170 Hawaii State Department of Health, *Strategic Plan for Hawaii's Environmental Protection Programs* at 28 (January 1999).

171 *Id.* § 11-60.1-8.

operation during the maintenance period.[172] Similarly, the rules require immediate notification to the Department of the failure or breakdown of an emission unit or air pollution control equipment, unless such notification is infeasible due to emergency circumstances.[173]

7.0 PREVENTION OF SIGNIFICANT DETERIORATION OF AIR QUALITY

The Prevention of Significant Deterioration ("PSD") requirements are additional requirements for a certain covered source permits.[174] No stationary source or modification to which the PSD requirement applies may begin actual construction without the covered source permit stating that the PSD requirements will be met. PSD requirements apply to all major stationary sources or modifications constructed in an attainment or unclassifiable area under the CAA.[175] The EPA "Prevention of Significant Deterioration Workshop Manual" may be used for general guidelines on PSD Review.[176]

7.1 PSD EXEMPTIONS

The rules provide various exemptions from the PSD review requirements.[177] The PSD review requirements do not apply if the construction began before August 7, 1977.[178] Nonprofit health or nonprofit educational institutions may be exempt from the PSD review requirement at the discretion of the Director. Furthermore, the PSD requirements do not apply to major stationary sources or modifications with respect to a particular pollutant if the owner or operator

---

172 *Id.* § 11-60.1-15.

173 *Id.* § 11-60.1-16(a).

174 *Id.* § 11-60.1-132.

175 *Id.* See CAA, § 107(d)(1)(d)-(e).

176 Interview with Scott Takamoto, Clean Air Branch, Hawaii Department of Health (August 1, 2000).

177 Haw. Admin. Rules § 11-60.1-133.

178 *Id.* § 11-60.1-133(a).

can show that the source or modification is located in an area designated as nonattainment.[179] Nor do these requirements apply to sources or modifications where the allowable emissions[180] or net emissions increase of the pollutant would be temporary and would not impact a Class I area.[181] Certain exemptions also apply to Class II areas.[182] The exemption from any PSD review requirement does not, however, exempt the owner or operator from the covered source permit requirements of the rules.[183]

7.2 AMBIENT AIR INCREMENTS AND CEILINGS

In general, the owner or operator of the proposed source or modification must demonstrate that allowable emissions[184] increases would not cause or contribute to air pollution in violation of any NAAQS, or any applicable maximum allowable increase over the baseline concentration in any area.[185] The rules limit increases in pollutant concentrations over the baseline concentration in Class I, II or III areas. A baseline concentration is determined for each pollutant. The baseline area is the area in which the major stationary source or major modification would have an air quality impact equal to or greater than the annual average of the pollutant for which a baseline date has been established.[186] In any case, no concentration of a pollutant may exceed that permitted by the national primary or secondary ambient air quality standard, or the State ambient air quality standard.[187]

---

179 *Id.* § 11-60.1-133(b). In a nonattainment area, more stringent Lowest Available Emissions Rate ("LAER") technical requirements apply.

180 See definition of "allowable emissions," Haw. Admin. Rules § 11-60.1-1.

181 Haw. Admin. Rules § 11-60.1-133(c).

182 *Id.* § 11-60.1-133(d).

183 *Id.* § 11-60.1-133(l)

184 See definition of "allowable emissions," Haw. Admin. Rules § 11-60.1-1.

185 Haw. Admin. Rules § 11-60.1-141.

186 *Id.* § 11-60.1-134.

187 *Id.* § 11-60.1-135.

7.3 CONTROL TECHNOLOGY REVIEW

A source or modification must meet the applicable emissions limitations and standards pursuant to the state and federal administrative rules.[188] It may do so through a number of different methods. A new major stationary source must apply Best Available Control Technology ("BACT") for each regulated pollutant it would have the potential to emit in significant amounts. A major modification also must use BACT for each pollutant where a net emissions increase will result from the physical change or change in method of operation of the unit.[189]

An owner or operator of a proposed major stationary source or major modification may attempt to comply with PSD requirements by using techniques specifically suited to its unique circumstances. As such, the owner or operator may request the Director to approve a system of innovative control technology.[190] Such technologies may be employed if they will not result in an unreasonable risk to public health, welfare or safety, the owner or operator agrees to continuous emissions reductions and the source or modification will not contribute to a violation of any applicable requirement. The Director must withdraw approval of such a technology if the system fails to achieve the required continuous emissions reduction or contributes to an unreasonable risk to public health, welfare or safety.[191] If a source or modification fails to meet the required level of continuous emission reduction, the Director may allow up to three years to meet the BACT requirement through the use of a demonstrated system of control.

7.4 PSD AIR QUALITY AND ADDITIONAL IMPACT ANALYSIS

The rules require pre-application ambient air quality analysis as part of the PSD review requirements. Any application for a permit pursuant to the PSD review rules must contain an analysis of each pollutant potentially emitted in a significant amount, and for modifications each

---

188 *Id.* § 11-60.1-140.

189 *Id.*

190 *Id.* § 11-60.1-149.

191 *Id.* § 11-60.1-149(c).

pollutant that would cause a significant net emissions increase. In general, continuous air quality monitoring data should be gathered over a period of at least one year.[192]

The owner or operator of a major stationary source or modification is required to conduct ambient monitoring, as the Director determines is necessary, to assess the effect emissions may have on air quality in any area.[193] All estimates of ambient concentrations are to be based on applicable air quality models, databases and other requirements pursuant to the rules.[194]

In addition, the owner or operator must provide an analysis of impacts upon visibility, soils, and vegetation associated with the source or modification as well as general commercial, residential, industrial, and other growth associated with the source or modification along with the projected air quality impact of such growth. The Director may require monitoring of visibility in any Class I area near the proposed source or modification.[195]

The Director is required to provide notice to the federal land manager and the federal official charged with responsibility for the land of any covered source permit application for a source or modification which may affect a Class I area. The rules define "federal land manager" as the Secretary of the Department with authority over such lands.[196] The Director must also provide the federal land manager and federal officials with a copy of his or her preliminary determination.[197]

The Director must consider any analysis performed by the federal land manager which shows that the source or modification may have an adverse impact on visibility in a Class I area. "Adverse impact on visibility" means visibility impairment which interferes with the

---

192 *Id.* § 11-60.1-143.

193 *Id.*

194 *Id.* § 11-60.1-142.

195 *Id.* § 11-60.1-145.

196 *Id.* § 11-60.1-131.

197 *Id.* § 11-60.1-146(a).

management, protection, preservation or enjoyment of a visitor's visual experience of a Class I area.[198] If the Director concurs, the covered source permit will not be issued.[199]

The owner or operator of a source or modification which cannot be approved, based on the federal land manager's conclusion that emissions would have an adverse impact on air quality-related values, may seek a variance from the Governor.[200] Subject to the federal land manager's recommendations, the Governor may grant such a variance. Where the Governor recommends a variance, but the federal land manager does not concur, the recommendations of both are to be transmitted to the President of the United States. The President may approve the Governor's recommendation if the President finds that the variance is in the national interest.[201]

7.5 DISPERSION TECHNIQUES

The rules limit the use of stack height or dispersion techniques to effect the degree of emission limitation required for control of any air pollutant. The rules do not apply to stack heights or dispersion techniques implemented before December 31, 1970.[202] Dispersion techniques include attempts to affect the concentration of a pollutant by using excessively tall stacks, varying the rate of emission or increasing the final exhaust gas plume rise by manipulating the source process parameters. Other techniques approved pursuant to federal rules[203] which would increase sulfur dioxide emissions,[204] such as reheating of gas streams, merging of exhaust gas streams or smoke management in agricultural burning are not considered to be dispersion techniques.

---

198 *Id.* § 11-60.1-131.

199 *Id.* § 11-60.1-146(c).

200 *Id.* § 11-60.1-146(e).

201 *Id.* § 11-60.1-146(f).

202 *Id.* § 11-60.1-139.

203 *See* 40 C.F.R. § 51.100(hh)(2).

204 Haw. Admin. Rules § 11-60.1-131.

8.0 OTHER EMISSION CONTROL REGULATIONS

In addition to the above protections, the Department has adopted rules which enable the Director to take timely action as necessary in an emergency situation. Hazardous air pollutants and emissions from municipal waste incinerators are regulated. Also, the Legislature has enacted an ozone protection law which allows the Department to adopt specific prohibitions against the use of certain products which may be hazardous to the environment.[205]

8.1 EMERGENCY AIR POLLUTION CONTROLS

In an emergency, the Governor or the Director has the power to order any person causing or contributing to the release of an air pollutant discharge to immediately reduce or stop such discharge or emission. As may be necessary, the Governor or Director may take any and all other actions without public hearing, if the situation requires emergency procedures. The trigger for such emergency situations is the Governor or the Director's determination that an "imminent peril to the public health and safety is or will be caused by the release of any air pollutant or any combination of air pollutants which requires immediate action."[206]

The Department also may take steps to prevent air pollution emergency episodes. To this end, the Department has adopted rules designed to prevent the buildup of air contaminants during air pollution episodes. Under these rules, the Director may proclaim an air pollution "alert," "warning" or "emergency" whenever it is determined that the accumulation of air contaminants in any place is attaining or has attained levels which could, if such levels are sustained or exceeded, lead to a threat to public health.[207] The rules specify pollutant levels which determine the degree of crisis.

An "air pollution alert" calls for first stage control action which may require an "air pollution forecast," an internal watch by the Department actuated by a national weather service advisory that an atmospheric stagnation advisory is in effect. The Director must issue health

---

205 Haw. Rev. Stat. ch. 342C.

206 *Id.* § 342B-43.

207 Haw. Admin. Rules § 11-60.1-17.

advisories and may declare the source activities be curtailed. An "air pollution warning" indicates that air quality is continuing to degrade and that additional health advisories and abatement procedures are necessary. Finally, an "air pollution emergency" indicates that the warning level for a pollutant has been exceeded. At this stage, the public is evacuated from the affected area if necessary. After an episode level has been determined, the episode level will remain in effect until the criteria for that level are no longer met. At that time, the next lower episode level will be assumed.

The determination of an air pollution emergency episode is made by the Governor or the Director, who is guided by specific criteria. The criteria for the various stages of an air pollution "warning," "alert" or "emergency" depend on the level of concentration of the following pollutants: sulfur dioxide, particulate matter, sulfur dioxide combined with particulate matter, carbon monoxide, ozone and nitrogen dioxide. The objective of abatement measures during emergency air pollution episodes is the prevention of emergency situations due to the effects of contaminants on the public health.[208]

8.2 HAZARDOUS AIR POLLUTANTS

Any stationary source which emits or has the potential to emit any hazardous air pollutant is subject to the hazardous air pollution rules. The rules define 189 chemicals as "hazardous air pollutants."[209] These rules prohibit the emission of hazardous air pollutants in such quantities that result in or contribute to an ambient air concentration which endangers human health.[210] The Director will not approve a permit for a new major source or modification if the Director has reason to believe emissions may result in an unacceptable ambient air concentration.[211] The rules also guard against an accidental release, or unanticipated emission of a regulated substance or other extremely hazardous substance into the ambient air from a stationary source.[212] Under

208 *Id.*

209 *Id.* § 11-60.1-172.

210 *Id.* § 11-60.1-179(a).

211 *Id.* § 11-60.1-179(b).

212 *Id.* § 11-60.1-171.

the hazardous air pollutant rules, an owner or operator may be required to prepare, submit and implement a risk management plan pursuant to Section 112(r) of the CAA.[213] The rules furthermore prescribe the use of the "maximum available control technology" for control of hazardous air pollutants.

8.2.1 MACT AND EQUIVALENT MACT STANDARDS

The rules define "maximum achievable control technology" ("MACT") to mean the maximum degree of reduction in emissions of hazardous air pollutants on a case-by-case basis, taking into account the costs of emission reduction and any non-air quality health and environmental impacts and energy requirements.[214] No construction, reconstruction or modification of any major source of hazardous air pollutants may be done unless the Director has determined that the MACT emission limitation, or equivalent MACT, will be met. The Director may exempt a modification from the MACT requirements, if the owner or operator can show the increase in emissions from any hazardous air pollutant will be offset by an equal or greater decrease in emissions of another more hazardous air pollutant.[215] Electric utility steam generating units are exempt from the MACT requirements.[216] Upon written request, the Director may issue a covered source permit which grants an extension allowing the owner or operator up to one additional year to comply with any applicable MACT standard pursuant to the CAA,[217] if time is necessary for the installation of controls.[218]

The rules also describe the process to be followed where the MACT limitation has not been promulgated.[219] First, the owner or operator is to submit a complete application for an

---

213 *Id.* § 11-60.1-178.

214 *Id.* § 11-60.1-171.

215 *Id.* § 11-60.1-174(b).

216 *Id.* § 11-60.1-174(d).

217 CAA § 112(g)(2), 42 U.S.C. § 7412(g)(2).

218 Haw. Admin. Rules § 11-60.1-174(f).

219 *Id.* § 11-60.1-175.

initial covered source permit or modification. The Director then will determine on a case-by-case basis an equivalent MACT emission limitation. This equivalent MACT emission limitation becomes an applicable requirement.[220]

In determining the equivalent MACT emission limitation, the Director must consider the cost of achieving such emission reduction, and any other non-air quality health and environmental impacts and energy requirements.[221] The equivalent MACT emission limitation may be achievable by reducing the volume of pollutants through process changes; substitution of materials; system enclosure; and design or operational standards.[222] The maximum degree of reduction in emissions deemed achievable must not be less stringent than the emission control achieved in practice by the best controlled similar source, as determined by the Director.[223] If it is not feasible to prescribe or enforce an emission limitation for the control of hazardous air pollutants, the Director may, in the alternative, consider design, equipment, work practice or operational standards consistent with this section.[224]

9.0 MUNICIPAL WASTE COMBUSTORS

The rules restrict the discharge of metals and metal compounds emitted in the exhaust gases from municipal waste combustors ("MWC").[225] Units combusting medical waste combined with other municipal solid waste are subject to NSPS requirements.[226] Units combusting solely medical waste, however, are not regulated under these rules.[227]

---

220 *Id.*

221 *Id.* § 11-60.1-176.

222 *Id.* § 11-60.1-176(a).

223 *Id.* § 11-60.1-176(b).

224 *Id.* § 11-60.1-176(d).

225 *Id.* § 11-60.1-162(c).

226 *Id.* § 11-60.1-162(b)(4).

227 Such units are subject to regulation under the Infectious Waste Law, Haw. Rev. Stat. § 321-21. *See infra* ch. 5 of this Handbook.

The discharge of dioxin/furan emissions from MWC in levels in excess of those identified in the rule is prohibited.[228] Discharge of sulfur dioxide, hydrogen chloride and carbon monoxide is restricted to the concentration levels listed in Tables in the rules.[229] Finally, the rules provide standards for MWC operating practices.[230] These standards govern operating load levels, operating temperatures, operator's certifications, operating manuals, shift supervisors and the compliance and performance test methods.[231]

10.0 OZONE LAYER PROTECTION

The Ozone Protection Law restricts the sale and use of chlorofluorocarbon chemicals (CFCs), including CFC-11, CFC-12, CFC-13, CFC-14, CFC-113, CFC-114, CFC-115, CFC-116, CFC-500, CFC-502 and CFC-503.[232] Effective January 1, 1991, no person in the State of Hawaii may sell or offer for sale any CFC refrigerant used in air conditioners or mobile air conditioners in containers which are smaller than fifteen pounds net.[233] The purchase, distribution, manufacture, import or sale of any halon fire extinguisher is also prohibited, as is the repair of portable fire extinguishing systems without using a reclamation system to properly recapture and dispose of unspent halons. The Ozone Protection Law further prohibits any person from willfully causing or allowing CFCs to be released into the air from any source or process regulated by that chapter. Refrigerators and freezers are exempt from this Law.

Violation of these provisions may result in a fine not to exceed $1,000 for each separate offense. Each unit of CFC refrigerant sold or offered for sale, and each willful release of CFCs into the air and each purchase, sale, or servicing of a halogen-containing fire extinguisher

---

228 Haw. Admin. Rules § 11-60.1-162(d), Table 2.

229 *Id.* § 11-60.1-162(e)-(f).

230 *Id.* § 11-60.1-162(g).

231 *Id.* § 11-60.1-162(g)-(h).

232 Haw. Rev. Stat. ch. 342C.

233 *Id.* § 342C-2.

constitutes a separate offense.[234] Any action to impose or collect the fine is considered a civil action.

11.0 VARIANCES FROM AIR POLLUTION STANDARDS

Variances which authorize the emission of pollutants in amounts greater than the applicable standard may be requested from the Department. Applications for a variance may be made on forms furnished by the Department and are required to be accompanied by a complete and detailed description of present conditions and how the present conditions do not conform to applicable standards.[235] The application for a variance should include a calculation and description of the change in emissions and expected ambient air quality concentrations.[236]

11.1 TYPES OF VARIANCES

Variances are granted for emission or discharge of specific pollutants. Therefore, each application is reviewed in light of the descriptions, statements, plans, histories and other supporting information submitted with the variance application.[237] In reviewing a variance application, the Department considers the public interest in continuation of the function or operation involved in the discharge, the potential substantial endangerment of human health or safety, and whether the hardship caused to the applicant is without equal or greater benefits to the public.[238] No variance may be granted which will prevent or interfere with the maintenance or attainment of NAAQS.[239] In addition, no variance prevents or limits the application of any emergency provisions and procedures under the law.[240]

---

234 *Id.* § 342C-5.

235 *Id.* § 342B-14(a).

236 Haw. Admin. Rules § 11-60.1-18.

237 Haw. Rev. Stat. § 342B-14(b).

238 *Id.* § 342B-14(c).

239 Haw. Admin. Rules § 11-60.1-18(a).

240 Haw. Rev. Stat. § 342B-14(g).

11.2 VARIANCE CONDITIONS

If the variance is granted on the ground that there is no practicable means known or available for the adequate prevention, control or abatement of the air pollution involved, it will be granted for a limited period of time and continue until the necessary means for prevention, control, or abatement becomes practicable. The variance is subject to the substitute or alternate measures that the Department may prescribe.[241] The term of each variance may not exceed five years and is subject to renewal. All variances granted by the Department require the grantee to perform air or discharge sampling and report the results of such sampling to the Department.

11.3 VARIANCE PROCEDURE

The variance application procedure allows the Director to afford a hearing to the applicant to present arguments in favor of the variance.[242] Further, each application for the issuance, renewal or modification of a variance is subject to public participation requirements including public notice and written comments by interested persons.[243]

12.0 EMISSIONS TRADING

The Director may allow emissions trading within a permitted facility without requiring a permit amendment.[244] The emissions trading must not constitute a modification of the source or exceed the allowable emissions,[245] and the owner or operator must provide seven-day minimum advance written notification of the proposed emissions trading.[246] The advance notification is to

---

241 *Id.* § 342B-14(d).

242 *Id.* § 342B-14(f).

243 *Id.* § 342B-14(h).

244 Haw. Admin. Rules § 11-60.1-96(a).

245 *Id.* See definition of "allowable emissions," Haw. Admin. Rules § 11-60.1-1.

246 Haw. Admin. Rules § 11-60.1-96(a).

include the date on which the change will occur, a description of the change, the permit requirements and how the source will comply with the permit terms and conditions.

13.0 ENFORCEMENT MECHANISM FOR AIR POLLUTION CONTROL

Enforcement of rules, permits and variances is carried out by the Director. Upon determining that there has been a violation of a rule, permit or variance, the Director may issue a written notice requiring the violator to correct the violation within a specified, reasonable time and to give periodic progress reports.[247] The notice may include an order imposing penalties on the alleged violator and directing the alleged violator to appear before the Director for a hearing. For continuing violations, the Director may, by written notice, demand a schedule of compliance from the violator, and may issue cease and desist orders and impose further administrative penalties.[248]

13.1 ADMINISTRATIVE PENALTIES

The Director may impose an administrative penalty for violation of the Air Pollution Control Law, the rules or a permit. Administrative penalties may be imposed in the same amounts as provided in civil penalties, discussed in Section 13.2, below. The factors considered in imposing an administrative penalty include the nature and history of the violation, any prior violations, the opportunity, difficulty and history of corrective action, good faith efforts to comply and such other matters as justice may require. The violator has the burden of proof to show he or she is unable to pay the penalty due to economic and financial conditions.[249]

13.2 CIVIL PENALTIES

Violations may be penalized by civil enforcement options available to state and local authorities. Violations of air pollution rules, permits, or variances, other than those for vehicular smoke emissions and open burning control, are subject to the imposition of civil fines not to

---

247 Haw. Rev. Stat. § 342B-42(a).

248 *Id.* § 342B-42(b).

249 *Id.* § 342B-48.

exceed $25,000 for each separate offense.[250] Fines are deposited into the environmental response revolving fund established by the Environmental Response Law.[251] The Director may institute a civil action in any court of competent jurisdiction for injunctive relief to prevent any violation of the air pollution rules without the necessity of prior revocation of the permit or variance.[252] State of mind of the alleged violator or violators is not an element of proof for civil violations.[253]

Any person denying, obstructing or hampering the entrance and inspection by any duly authorized officer or employee of the Department, of any building, place or vehicle that the officer or employee is authorized to enter and inspect, may be fined not more than $25,000 for each violation.[254]

The penalty for violation of the vehicular smoke emission rules adopted by the Department may result in fines of not less than $25 nor more than $2,500 for each separate offense.[255] Penalties for the violation of open burning control rules may result in fines not to exceed $10,000 for each separate offense.[256] Each day of either type of violation constitutes a separate offense.

The Department's Clean Air Branch has established a civil penalty policy ("Penalty Policy") which is used as guidance for branch personnel in assessing penalties under various air pollution control statutes and regulations.[257] The Penalty Policy uses deterrence as an

---

250 *Id.* § 342B-47(c).

251 *Id.* § 128D-2.

252 *Id.* § 342B-44.

253 *Id.* § 342B-47(e).

254 *Id.* § 342B-47(d).

255 *Id.* § 342B-47(a).

256 *Id.* § 342B-47(b).

257 Hawaii State Department of Health, Environmental Management Division, Clean Air Branch, *Guidelines for the Exercise of Prosecutorial Discretion Under the State of Hawaii Air Pollution Control Act, Chapter 342B, H.R.S.* (Draft 8/00).

important goal and seeks to remove any significant benefits resulting from non-compliance and include an additional amount to reflect the seriousness of the violation. The preliminary deterrence amount is calculated by adding the economic benefit component and the gravity component.[258] In cases with multiple violations, each violation is treated separately and the penalty for each violation is added to arrive at the total assessed penalty.[259] Although the Department recognizes the advantage of a cash penalty as a deterrent, the Department will consider allowing the violator to undertake a mitigation project if the project would protect the environment or public health better than a deposit of the penalty into the environmental response revolving fund.[260]

The Penalty Policy calculates the violator's economic benefit of non-compliance by examining the economic benefits derived from delayed compliance costs and from permanently avoided costs. The economic benefit calculations runs from the start of non-compliance up to the point when the facility will be in compliance.[261] Although the Clean Air Branch generally will not settle a case for less than the economic benefit amount, it may consider settling for less if the benefit amount is less than $5,000, if there are compelling public concerns, or where the Department's realistic changes of recovering the full penalty by going to court is not good.[262]

The gravity component of any penalty reflects the seriousness of the violation and ensures that the violator is worse off than if the law was obeyed. The gravity component is therefore calculated to take into account the actual or possible harm to health or the environment, including pollutant amounts, pollutant toxicity, the sensitivity of the environment and the duration of the violation. The gravity component will also look at the importance of the regulatory scheme and the size of the violator. The gravity component of a penalty is adjusted to

---

258 *Id.* at 13.

259 *Id.* at 22-23.

260 *Id.* at 29.

261 *Id.* at 13-14.

262 *Id.* at 21-22.

promote equitable treatment of the regulated community, to account for the unique factors in each case, and to maintain consistency in treating similar violations in the same manner. The gravity component may be adjusted upwards based on the violator's degree of willfulness or negligence, the history of noncompliance, or the environmental damage resulting from the violation. The gravity component will only be adjusted downwards based on the violator's ability to pay and degree of cooperation to remedy the violation, prompt reporting of noncompliance, prompt correction of environmental problems and cooperation during the pre-filing investigation period.[263]

The Department will seek penalties for violations of continuous emissions monitoring systems ("CEMS") reporting requirements and for violations of emission limits identified via the CEMS monitoring reports. Due to technological advances in CEMS methodology and instrumentation, CEMS units have evolved from being compliance monitoring tools to being established as enforceable indirect and direct compliance determinations. Facilities' quarterly excess emissions and monitoring systems performance reports ("EERs") are reviewed by the Clean Air Branch to determine the percentage of excess emissions to demonstrate sources' abilities to maintain compliance with emission limits. The percentage downtime of CEMS units is examined in relation to sources' abilities to achieve and maintain continuous CEMS operation. The Clean Air Branch will issue informal notices if the percentage of excess emissions or downtime is between five and ten percent per quarter. Formal notices of violation will be issued if similar violations are found for two consecutive quarters, for two occurrences in a rolling twelve month period, or if the percentage of excess emissions or downtime exceeds ten percent.[264]

The Clean Air Branch will provide incentives to companies for due diligence, disclosure and the prompt correction of violations that are discovered during the performance of environmental audits. The Department will consider providing incentives under the following conditions:

---

263 *Id.* at 15-20.

264 *Id.* at 28.

1. Violations were found and reported by the company through voluntary audits and/or due diligence;

2. Violations were identified voluntarily and not by required monitoring, sampling or auditing procedures;

3. "Voluntary disclosure" involves reporting the violation prior to commencement of any regulatory agency inspection, investigation, information request or imminent discovery of the violation due to citizen's suits, third party complaints, "Whistle blowers" and other factors;

4. Violations were promptly corrected and any environmental harm resulting from the violation was promptly remedied;

5. The company has taken appropriate measures to prevent recurrence of the violation;

6. The violation is not a repeated violation, meaning that the same or a closely related violation has not occurred at the same facility for three years, and the violation is not part of a recurring pattern of violations at the facility for five years;

7. The violation did not present an imminent and substantial endangerment to human health or the environment or result in serious actual harm;

8. The violation does not involve noncompliance with any specific terms and conditions of any judicial or administrative order;

9. The company has cooperated in providing all necessary information to determine the applicability of the violations to the Department's guidance.

When examining the applicability of incentives for environmental audits, the Clean Air Branch will follow the Department's general audit guidance and the related EPA final policy statement.[265] In the event that all of the EPA's final policy conditions are met, the Department would not seek gravity-based penalties and would generally not recommend criminal prosecution against the company if the violation results from the unauthorized criminal conduct of an

---

265 *See* Memorandum to Environmental Health Administration Program Managers from Bruce S. Anderson, Ph.D., Deputy Director for Environmental Health dated January 15, 1998; and the EPA's *Final Policy Statement, Incentives for Self-Policing: Discovery, Disclosure, Correction and Prevention of Violations*, 60 Fed. Reg. 66,706 – 66,712 (December 22, 1995). Note that although the EPA has replaced its 1995 audit policy with a new policy effective May 11, 2000, see 65 Fed. Reg. 19,618 – 19,627 (April 11, 2000), the Clean Air Branch's Penalty Policy has not adopted this new guidance.

employee. The Department, however, retains its discretion to recover economic benefit gained as a result of noncompliance. Corporations remain criminally liable for violations resulting from conscious disregard of their legal duties, and individuals remain liable for criminal wrongdoing.

The Department will also consider up to a seventy-five percent reduction of gravity-based penalties for a company which voluntarily discovers violations by means other than environmental audits and/or due diligence, but promptly discloses and corrects those violations and meets all other conditions of the audit guidance.

13.3 CRIMINAL PENALTIES

The Air Pollution Control Law provides criminal penalties for violations of the Law or the release of hazardous materials into the air. A person who knowingly violates any statutory air standard, any permit condition or any order, rule, or any fee or filing requirement is subject to a fine of up to $25,000 per day of violation, or imprisonment of up to five years, or both, for each violation.[266] A person who knowingly fails to make any report or makes any false statement in any report as required by the statute, or renders any required monitoring device inaccurate, is subject to a fine of up to $25,000 per day of violation or imprisonment of up to two years, or both, for each violation.[267]

A person convicted of negligently releasing into the air any hazardous air pollutant or extremely hazardous substance, placing another person in imminent danger of death or serious bodily injury, is subject to a fine of not more than $25,000 or imprisonment for not more than one year, or both.[268] Subsequent convictions for an offense under the same subsection are subject to a doubling of the maximum fine and imprisonment.

---

266 Haw. Rev. Stat. § 342B-49(a).

267 *Id.* § 342B-49(b).

268 *Id.* § 342B-49(c).

Furthermore, a person who knowingly releases a hazardous air pollutant or extremely hazardous substance into the air, knowing that such action places another person in imminent danger of death or serious bodily injury, is subject to a fine of not more than $25,000 or imprisonment of not more than fifteen years, or both.[269] Subsequent convictions for an offense under the same subsection are subject to a doubling of the maximum fine and imprisonment. An organization violating this subsection is subject to a fine of not more than $1,000,000.

13.4 PROCEDURE AND DEFENSES

The Director may receive or initiate complaints, hold hearings and institute legal proceedings in the name of the State for the prevention, control or abatement of air pollution.[270] The Attorney General of the State of Hawaii represents the Director and the Department in legal proceedings. The Director is authorized to appoint a master to conduct investigations and hearings.

Any action brought for noncompliance with the terms of an air pollution control permit may be defended against by the affirmative defense that an emergency occurred. The administrative rules define "emergency" as any situation, including acts of God, arising from sudden and reasonably unforeseeable events beyond the control of the owner or operator of the source. An emergency does not, however, include noncompliance caused by improper design, lack of preventative maintenance, improper operation or operator error.[271] The emergency must be documented in operating logs or other relevant evidence. The source must have properly operated during the period of emergency, and the owner or operator must have taken reasonable steps to minimize levels of emissions during the emergency period. The owner or operator must submit notice of the emergency to the Director within two working days. The notice must contain a description of the emergency, steps taken to mitigate omissions, and corrective actions

---

269 *Id.* § 342B-49(d).

270 *Id.* § 342B-15.

271 Haw. Admin. Rules § 11-60.1-81.

taken. The owner or operator has the burden of proof in establishing the existence of the emergency.[272]

In 1992, the Legislature provided for citizen suits for violations of the statute. Since June 30, 1995, any person may bring a civil action against any alleged violator of the Air Pollution Control Law for violations of the Air Pollution Control Law including emission limits, violation of any order issued by the Director.[273] Citizen suits may also be filed against any person who proposes to construct a new or modify a major emitting facility without a required permit or who is alleged to be in violation of a permit condition. In addition, a citizen suit may be used to enforce specific limitation and emission standards of the Hawaii SIP, including fugitive dust emission limits.[274] Violations of agricultural burning permits, however, became subject to citizen suits after April 1, 1996. Any penalties paid as a result of a successful citizen suit are deposited into the clean air special fund established by the Air Pollution Control Law.[275] These amounts are to remain available to finance air compliance and enforcement activities.[276] Any person also may bring a civil action against the Director for an alleged failure to perform any nondiscretionary duty under the statute.

The citizen bringing suit must give sixty days notice to the alleged violator, the Department, and the Director before commencing any action.[277] No action may be commenced if the Director or the Department has commenced and is diligently prosecuting a civil action to enforce the subject violation. The citizen, however, may intervene in such an action. Likewise, the Director, if not a party, may intervene as a matter of right at any time in a citizen suit.

---

272 *Id.* § 11-60.1-97.

273 Haw. Rev. Stat. § 342B-56(a).

274 *Unitek Environmental Services, Inc. v. Hawaiian Cement*, 1997 U.S. Dist. LEXIS 19261, *17-20.

275 *Id.* § 342B-56(h) and 342B-32.

276 *Id.* § 342B-56(h).

277 *Id.* § 342B-56(c).

When issuing a final order in a citizen suit, the court may award costs of litigation, including reasonable attorney and expert witness fees to any party. If a temporary restraining order or preliminary injunction is sought, the court may require the filing of a bond or equivalent security in accordance with the Hawaii Rules of Civil Procedure.

The applicant for a permit or any person who participated in the public comment process may obtain judicial review of any decision as to permit issuance or denial.[278] Appeals of any decision of the Director regarding the penalties imposed for violation of a rule or permit may be made with the Circuit Court.[279] The procedures for an appeal are provided for in the Hawaii Administrative Procedure Act.[280]

In 1992, the Hawaii Supreme Court found the Department had inappropriately issued a permit to a geothermal energy project. The permit included permissible levels of hydrogen sulfide (H_2S) emissions from the project.[281] The Court found the permit improper because the Department had not promulgated any rules specifically for ambient air quality standards for H_2S. The Court remanded the case for an issuance of an injunction against the further construction or operation of the project under the permit and issued an order requiring the Department to promulgate rules governing H_2S emissions. The Hawaii Administrative Rules have been amended in compliance with the order.[282]

13.5 MISCELLANEOUS ENFORCEMENT PROVISIONS

All state and county health authorities and police officers are authorized to enforce air pollution control laws, administrative rules, orders and permits.[283] Additionally, any county may adopt ordinances and rules governing any matter relating to air pollution control not already

---

278 *Id.* § 342B-30.

279 *Id.* § 342B-46.

280 *Id.* ch. 91. *See infra* ch. 13 of this Handbook.

281 *Aluli v. Lewin*, 73 Haw. 56, 828 P.2d 802 (1992).

282 Haw. Admin. Rules § 11-59-4(g).

283 Haw. Rev. Stat. § 342B-51.

governed by a rule of the Department. For example, the County of Maui has enacted an ordinance declaring the emission of smoke, soot, poisonous gases, dirt, dust or debris from any building, smokestack, incinerator or smoldering open fires to be an unlawful public nuisance punishable of a fine not to exceed $100.[284] Any county rules regarding air pollution become null and void upon adoption of a rule regarding that same matter by the Department.

In 1997, the Hawaii Air Pollution Control Law was revised to allow the issuance of summons or citation for any person who violates the vehicular smoke emission rules or open burning control rules. Such violations are enforced by police officers. The summons or citation will warn the person to appear and answer the charge against them within seven days of issuance. If any person fails to comply with a summons or citation, the issuer must cause a complaint to be issued against the person and secure the issuance of a warrant for the person's arrest. Failure to comply with a summons or citation is a misdemeanor.

14.0 ASBESTOS AND LEAD

The 1991 Legislature established statutory authority to implement an integrated asbestos program in Hawaii by creating the Asbestos Law, which regulates asbestos emissions and abatement, and provides enforcement powers and a penalty schedule.[285] In 1998, the Legislature revised the Asbestos Law to include regulation of lead.

The Asbestos and Lead Law is administered by the Department's Noise, Radiation and Indoor Air Quality Branch.

---

284 Maui, Haw., Maui County Code ch 20.04 (February 2000).

285 *Id.* ch. 342P. At the present time, the Department conducts investigations under the federal asbestos NESHAPs program and reports to the EPA. The EPA handles all enforcement decisions and actions in the State through federal EPA administrative actions or civil actions commenced in the United States District Court.

14.1 ASBESTOS AND LEAD EMISSION CONTROL

Asbestos and lead emissions are controlled by the prohibition of activities which cause them.[286] The Asbestos and Lead Law does not define pollution, but defines "emission" to mean the act of releasing or discharging asbestos or lead into the ambient air from any source. "Asbestos" is defined as "asbestiform varieties of spacing serpentine (chrysotile), riebeckite (crocidolite), cummingtonite-grunerite (amosite), anthophyllite, actinolite, and tremolite.[287] The Asbestos and Lead Law also regulates the abatement of asbestos and lead paint, and defines "abatement" as any measures designed to permanently eliminate asbestos or lead-based paint hazards, including removal, enclosure, encapsulation or disposal.[288]

The Director is authorized to promulgate rules controlling and prohibiting asbestos pollution, lead-based paint hazards and regulating asbestos and lead abatement.[289] The Director may establish emissions standards and lead hazard exposure, which may include an indoor nonoccupational exposure standard, for the State.[290] The Director may also establish a model accreditation program for provider certification requirements, establish work practice standards and notification requirements for demolition and renovations of facilities containing asbestos and for lead-based abatement activities. In the regulation of asbestos or lead abatement activity, the Director may require the owner or operator of the activity to install and use monitoring equipment, sample emissions, monitor hazards, and establish certain records.[291]

Contractors that engage in the application, enclosure, removal, encapsulation, renovation, repair or demolition of friable asbestos or asbestos containing material which may become friable during the activity are required to be licensed as specialty asbestos contractors.[292] The

---

286 *Id.* § 342P-40.

287 *Id.* § 342P-1.

288 *Id.*

289 *Id.* § 342P-3.

290 *Id.* § 342P-41. As of the printing of this Handbook, the State asbestos rules had not been adopted.

291 Haw. Rev. Stat. § 342P-42.

292 *Id.* § 444-7.5.

licensing requirements, procedures and standards of conduct are established by the contractors license board. Persons who conduct asbestos-related activities without a license in violation of this statute are subject to a fine of $5,000 for each violation, each day.[293] A list of licensed asbestos contractors is provided by the Clean Air Branch of the Department.

The Director is authorized to handle complaints on asbestos pollution or lead hazard violations, hold hearings and institute legal action on behalf of the State in connection with asbestos pollution or lead hazards.[294] In the event that an asbestos emission or the presence of lead hazards poses or will pose an imminent peril to public health and safety, the Governor or the Director may order the person causing the emission or creating the hazard to cease the emission or the creation of the hazard and to take abatement measures as the Governor or the Director deems necessary.[295] In the event the Director uses this emergency power, he or she must set a hearing within twenty-four hours.

14.2 VARIANCES FROM ASBESTOS OR LEAD-BASED PAINT HAZARDS STANDARDS

The Department may issue variances authorizing deviation from established asbestos or lead-based paint hazards standards. Variances may only be granted if the applicant can demonstrate that the deviation is in the public interest, that the variance will not substantially endanger human health or safety, and that compliance with established standards would produce a serious hardship without equal or greater benefits to the public. All variance applications are subject to public approval.[296]

Any variance issued by the Director may not exceed six months and must require sampling of air or dust and reporting of the results to the Department. If the variance is granted

---

293 *Id.* § 444-7.5(f).

294 *Id.* § 342P-43.

295 *Id.* § 342P-6.

296 Haw. Rev. Stat. § 342P-5.5.

on the basis that there is no practical means for the adequate prevention, control, or abatement of the asbestos or lead, the variance will only last until the means becomes practicable.[297]

Variances may be renewed for a six month period only if the renewal application has met all the conditions imposed by the initial variance. Renewal applications must be made sixty days before the variance expires.[298]

The Director may allow a hearing in connection with the issuance, renewal or modification of a variance.[299] The hearing will be conducted in accordance with the Hawaii Administrative Procedure act.[300]

14.3 ENFORCEMENT OF THE ASBESTOS AND LEAD LAW

The Director or an authorized representative may enter any building to determine whether asbestos or lead is present and to determine compliance with the Asbestos and Lead Law.[301] Entry must be in accordance with any other laws. The Director may take samples and have them tested. All Department, county health officials and police officers are authorized to enforce the Asbestos and Lead Law.[302]

To prevent violation of the Asbestos and Lead Law, the Director may seek injunctive relief through a civil action.[303] The Hawaii Rules of Civil Procedure apply to all requests for injunctions.

---

297 *Id.*

298 *Id.*

299 *Id.* § 342P-5.5(f).

300 *Id.* Ch. 91. See infra ch. 13 of this Handbook.

301 *Id.* § 342P-4.

302 *Id.* § 342P-31.

303 *Id.* § 342P-26.

Upon violation of the Asbestos and Lead Law, the Director is required to serve written notice to the alleged violator which may contain educational information necessary in performing abatement activities and may also contain an order to correct the violation.[304] The notice may require the alleged violator to attend a hearing or it may impose penalties. If a person continues to violate the Asbestos and Lead Law, another notice may be served on the alleged violator which requires the preparation of a written schedule which specifies corrective measures.[305] This written schedule must be submitted within thirty days. The Director may accept the submitted schedule or may issue a cease and desist order against the alleged violator. The cease and desist order remains in effect until the Director accepts the written schedule. The Director may impose penalties in the notice for continued violations.

Any order issued by the Director becomes final in twenty days, unless the person named in the notice requests a hearing.[306] If a hearing is requested, any penalty imposed by the notice becomes payable only after the hearing and upon the issuance of a final order.

All hearings are conducted as contested cases in accordance with the Hawaii Administrative Procedure Act.[307] Orders which are issued after the hearing may impose or rescind the penalty, and may establish a timetable to correct the violation.[308] Any penalty imposed by the final order which is not paid within thirty days after it becomes due may be recovered through a civil action.[309] The Director's decision in the hearing may be appealed to the Circuit Court.

---

304 *Id.* § 342P-5(a).

305 *Id.* § 342P-5(b).

306 *Id.* § 342P-5(d).

307 *Id.* ch. 91. *See infra* ch. 13 of this Handbook.

308 Haw. Rev. Stat. § 342P-5(e).

309 *Id.* § 342P-5(f).

14.4 PENALTIES UNDER THE ASBESTOS AND LEAD LAW

The Asbestos and Lead Law provides administrative and civil penalties for violations of the law or rules.[310] Criminal fines and imprisonment may be sought for negligent and knowing violations, and knowing endangerment.[311]

Civil penalties of not more than $10,000 for each separate offense may be imposed for violation of the Asbestos and Lead Law.[312] Each day of each violation is considered a separate offense. A civil penalty of $5,000 maximum may be imposed on a person who obstructs or hampers entry and inspection by an authorized representative of the Department.[313] These penalties may also be imposed administratively.[314] Factors considered in the imposition of an administrative penalty include the nature and history of present and past violations, and the opportunity, difficulty and history of corrective action. Financial ability to pay the penalty is presumed: the violator has the burden of proving otherwise.

Criminal penalties may be imposed for negligent and knowing violations, and for knowing endangerment. A person who negligently violates the Asbestos and Lead Law is subject to a fine of $2,500 to $25,000 per day for each violation or imprisonment for one year, or both.[315] Subsequent convictions carry a fine of $50,000 maximum per day of violation or imprisonment up to two years, or both.

Knowing violations of the Asbestos and Lead Law carry even harsher consequences. The first conviction for a knowing violation carries a prison term up to three years or a fine ranging

---

310 *Id.* §§ 342P-20, -21.

311 *Id.* §§ 342P-22, -23, -24.

312 *Id.* § 342P-20(a).

313 *Id.* § 342P-20(b).

314 *Id.* § 342P-21.

315 *Id.* § 342P-22.

from $5,000 to $50,000 per day, per violation or both.[316] Subsequent convictions carry a fine up to $100,000 per day of each violation or imprisonment for a maximum of six years or both.

Knowing endangerment is defined as a knowing violation of the Asbestos and Lead Law with knowledge at the time that the violation places another person in imminent danger of death or serious bodily injury.[317] The penalties for a conviction of an individual for knowing endangerment is a fine of $250,000 or imprisonment for fifteen years or both. Conviction of an organization for knowing endangerment carries a maximum penalty of $1,000,000.

---

316 *Id.* § 342P-23.

317 *Id.* § 342P-24.

CHAPTER 3

WATER POLLUTION CONTROL

1.0 INTRODUCTION

The Water Pollution Law[1] provides a comprehensive regulatory program for discharges of pollutants to the waters of Hawaii. The Water Pollution Law establishes a permitting program, provides for water quality testing by the Hawaii Department of Health, provides enforcement mechanisms to the Department of Health and to the Attorney General, and establishes penalties for violations of the Water Pollution Law, its rules and permits. In addition to the Water Pollution Law, this Chapter discusses the Nonpoint Source Pollution Management and Control Law.[2]

2.0 RELATIONSHIP TO THE FEDERAL CLEAN WATER ACT

The Hawaii Water Pollution Law establishes the National Pollutant Discharge Elimination System ("NPDES") permit program required under the Clean Water Act.[3] Permits issued under the NPDES program are issued by the Hawaii Department of Health ("Department") and are subject to review by the Environmental Protection Agency ("EPA"). The federal government retains the right to enforce provisions of the Clean Water Act in civil and criminal proceedings. Finally, the State is required to establish and enforce water quality standards under the Clean Water Act.

---

1 Haw. Rev. Stat. ch. 342D (Michie 1999). All references to the Hawaii Revised Statutes are made to the printed version of the statutes current through the 1999 legislative session, unless otherwise noted. Where appropriate, references to acts passed during the 2000 legislative session have also been added.

2 Haw. Rev. Stat. ch. 342E.

3 33 U.S.C. § 1251 *et seq.*

3.0 STATE POLICIES AND PROGRAMS

The Department administers the NPDES permit program, which establishes certain levels of performance that the permit holder must maintain with respect to discharges of pollutants to the state waters. The program is a self reporting program, as it requires the permit holder to report failures to meet those permit limits to the Department. The Water Pollution Law and its rules[4] establish objectives to achieve a level of water quality which provides for the protection and propagation of fish, shellfish and wildlife. Accordingly, the State designates uses for each body of water and adopts water quality criteria to protect those uses. The permit and sampling program carried out by the Department and the diligent enforcement of the Water Pollution Law, its rules and permits are designed to achieve these objectives. The 1995 and 1999 amendments to the Water Pollution Law expanded the Director's regulatory powers over domestic sewage, sewage sludge and recycled water.[5] The Director now is authorized to regulate management practices for domestic sewage, sewage sludge and recycled water regardless of whether such practices cause water pollution.[6]

The state's policy is to promote water pollution prevention by financing eligible county and state projects. This financing occurs through a revolving fund loan program and a leveraging program that uses revenue bonds and revolving fund loan programs.[7] In 1997, the Legislature created the water pollution control revolving fund which is administered by the Director. The fund provides financial assistance to counties or state agencies for the planning, design and construction of Publicly Owned Wastewater Treatment Works, and for the

4 Haw. Admin. Rules, tit. 11, chs. 54 and 55 (Weil's 2000). All references to the Hawaii Administrative Rules are current through the date of publication of this Handbook, unless otherwise noted.

5 Act approved June 14, 1995, ch. 180, §§ 5-15, 1995 Haw. Sess. Laws 320 (codified throughout Haw. Rev. Stat. ch. 342D and other locations).

6 Haw. Rev. Stat. § 342D-4.

7 *Id.* § 342D-81.

implementation of conservation and management plans.[8] Projects receiving financing must conform with the state water quality management plan and must receive the Director's certification that they are entitled to priority on the basis of financial and water pollution control needs. Wastewater treatment works construction projects must ensure proper and efficient operation and maintenance after construction, and must also ensure that a fee structure will be instituted so that new developments will pay their appropriate share of costs of the wastewater treatment works.[9]

The Department may use revenues generated by the environmental response tax and deposited into the environmental response revolving fund to address concerns relating to clean water and polluted runoff.[10]

3.1 MAINTAINING THE HIGH QUALITY OF STATE WATERS

The Department has established a general policy of water quality antidegradation.[11] This policy requires that waters whose quality is higher than the water quality standard not be lowered in quality, unless the change is justifiable for important social or economic developments. In addition, any decrease in water quality may not injure or interfere with uses that were already assigned to those waters.

The water quality antidegradation policy is supplemented by the Department's policy of water pollution control.[12] This policy supports the conservation of Hawaii waters and the protection and improvement in the quality of water for drinking, marine and aquatic life, oceanographic research, preservation of wilderness and coral reefs, and other legitimate uses of water. The water pollution control policy also provides for effective wastewater treatment and water pollution control. Finally, the water pollution control policy mandates the "highest and

---

8 *Id.* § 342D-83.

9 *Id.* § 342D-97.

10 2000 Haw. Sess. Laws 245 (to be codified at Haw. Rev. Stat. § 128D-2).

11 Haw. Admin. Rules § 11-54-01.1.

12 *Id.* § 11-55-02.

best degree of waste treatment practicable under existing technology" in project designs for all new or increased sources of water pollution.[13]

In the year 2000, the Legislature created a Watershed Protection Board under the Department of Land and Natural Resources. Recognizing that Hawaii's forested watersheds are vital recharge areas for Hawaii's underground aquifers and a dependable source of clean water for streams, the Legislature created the Watershed Protection Board to develop a watershed protection master plan to provide for the protection, preservation, and enhancement of important watershed areas. The master plan must include an identification of potential watershed management areas, the development of criteria for eligible watershed management projects, and a designation and implementation plan for projects, including an assessment of required funding and potential funding sources. The Watershed Protection Board is required to submit its master plan to the Legislature no later than June 30, 2001.[14]

3.2 WATER QUALITY MONITORING PROGRAM

The Clean Water Branch of the Department implements and maintains the statewide clean water program for recreational and ecosystem protection through services including engineering analysis and permitting, water quality monitoring and investigation, water quality violation enforcement, and polluted runoff or nonpoint source pollution control monitoring.[15] As part of its duties, the Monitoring Section of the Clean Water Branch identifies sources of water pollution through area surveillance, routing inspections and complaint investigations. The Monitoring Section also evaluates the impact of water pollutants on public health; determines compliance with rules via source testing, water sampling and special studies; and submits data that appear to indicate non-compliance to the Enforcement Section.[16]

---

13 *Id.* § 11-55-02(b).

14 2000 Haw. Sess. Laws 152.

15 Hawaii State Department of Health, *Strategic Plan for Hawaii's Environmental Protection Programs* at 90 (January 1999).

16 *Id.* at 91.

The Department of Health's goals are to ensure that Hawaii's coastal waters are safe and healthy for people plants and animals, and also to protect and restore the quality of Hawaii's streams, wetlands, estuaries and other inland waters for fish and wildlife, recreation, aesthetic enjoyment and other appropriate uses. The Department of Health has achieved success in working toward these goals. Beach closures due to sewer and chemical spills in calendar year 1998 were down to thirteen days, a fifty-four percent reduction from calendar year 1997. Recently, the Department of Health has also developed a new water quality monitoring protocol to better assess and protect the state's inland (and coastal) waters.[17]

The statewide monitoring strategy is being completely revised, and major components of the new monitoring program will be: (1) routine monitoring of public beaches, followed by management action when bacteria levels are significantly above water quality standards; (2) collection of surface water chemistry data to determine if long-term trends in water quality are present; and (3) assessment of the condition of the State's streams and watersheds. Monitoring data will be summarized and will be placed on the Clean Water Branch web site on a quarterly basis. Monitoring data is used to prepare reports required by the EPA, including the Clean Water Act Section 303(d) list of water quality-limited segments and the 305(b) report on the state of the State's waters. These reports are prepared in the spring of even-numbered years and are made available to the public.[18]

3.3 CLASSIFICATION OF STATE WATERS AND WATER USES

The Water Quality Standards program must be consistent with the goal of attaining "swimmable and fishable" waters as mandated by the federal Clean Water Act. Through the program, the Department designates uses for each body of water in the State and adopts water quality criteria to protect those designated uses. The Water Quality Standards are found in the Hawaii Administrative Rules, Title 11, Chapter 54. The standards were revised in October 1992,

17 The Environmental Council and the Office of Environmental Quality Control, *Environmental Report Card, 1999,* at 46.

18 Hawaii State Department of Health, *Strategic Plan for Hawaii's Environmental Protection Programs* at 93 (January 1999).

and EPA granted its approval of the revised standards in November 1992.[19] The 1992 revisions added criteria for pollutants in fresh and coastal waters, standards for acute and chronic exposure, and fish consumption standards.

The Clean Water Act requires that state water quality standards be reviewed, updated and amended on a three year cycle. Although overdue, the first triennial revision was moved through the public hearing process and was adopted in April 2000. The April 2000 revisions have been forwarded to EPA for approval and the Department anticipates that they will be duly approved. In addition, the Department has already begun working on the next triennial revision to its water quality standards.[20]

The State water quality standards are applicable to all state surface waters, including fresh, brackish and saline waters.[21] Groundwater, ditches, flumes, ponds and reservoirs required as part of a pollution control system are excluded from the water quality classification program.[22] State waters are classified either as inland waters or marine waters. Inland waters may be fresh, brackish or saline and may be classified further as: flowing waters such as streams (perennial and intermittent), flowing springs and seeps and ditches and flumes that discharge into any other State waters; standing waters such as natural freshwater lakes and reservoirs; and wetlands including elevated wetlands such as bogs, marshes and swamps as well as low wetlands.[23] Marine waters are classified as embayments, open coastal or oceanic waters. Marine waters are further classified according to the following bottom subtypes: soft bottom communities, reef flats, artificial basins, marine pools and protected coasts, lava rock shorelines, and sand beaches.

---

19 *See* 60 Fed. Reg. 51,793, 51,797 (Oct. 3, 1995).

20 Telephone interview with June Harrington, State of Hawaii, Department of Health, Environmental Planning Office (July 26, 2000)

21 Haw. Rev. Stat. § 342D-1; Haw. Admin. Rules § 11-54-01.

22 Haw. Admin. Rules § 11-54-01.

23 *Id.* § 11-54-02.

The designation of uses permitted in inland waters is divided into two classes: Class 1 and Class 2 waters.[24] Class 1 waters are further divided into Class 1.a. and 1.b. designations. Class 1 waters are to be protected in their natural state as much as possible with an absolute minimum of pollution from human caused sources. Waste discharges into these waters and any activities which result in increased levels of point or nonpoint source contamination are prohibited. Class 1.a. waters are protected for scientific and educational purposes. Other non-degrading uses which are compatible with the protection of the ecosystems in this class may be permitted such as compatible recreation and aesthetic enjoyment. Class 1.b. waters are so designated to protect their use for domestic water supplies, food processing, support and propagation of aquatic life, compatible recreation and aesthetic enjoyment. Public access to waters in this class may be restricted to protect water quality.

In Class 2 waters, a much broader range of uses is allowed. NPDES discharges and storm water discharges which satisfy the basic water quality criteria are permitted in Class 2 waters. These waters also can act as receiving waters for discharges which have received the best degree of treatment or control compatible with the criteria established for this class. No new treated sewage or industrial discharges are permitted within Class 2 estuaries, except that certain discharges are acceptable within the Pearl Harbor estuary on Oahu.[25]

Marine waters are classified as either Class AA or Class A.[26] Class AA waters are intended to remain in their natural state with a minimum of pollution from human caused sources. Zones of mixing are not permitted in defined reef areas where the water is less than ten fathoms or in waters less than 1,000 feet offshore if there is no defined reef area and if the depth is greater than ten fathoms. Uses which are protected in Class AA waters are the conservation of coral reefs and wilderness, support and propagation of marine life, oceanographic research, aesthetic enjoyment and compatible recreation. Other compatible uses which conform to Class AA criteria may be permitted.[27]

---

24 *Id.* § 11-54-03(b).

25 *Id.* § 11-54-03(b)(4).

26 *Id.* § 11-54-03(c).

27 *Id.* § 11-54-03(c)(1).

Class A waters are intended for recreational purposes and any other uses which are compatible with recreation and the protection and proliferation of fish, shellfish and wildlife. Class A waters may act as receiving waters for NPDES and storm water discharges, and discharges which have received the best degree of treatment or have controls compatible with criteria for this class. New sewage discharges will not be permitted in embayments. Industrial discharges and certain other discharges are permitted in embayments at the following locations: Honolulu Harbor, Barbers Point Harbor, Keehi Lagoon Marina Area, Ala Wai Boat Harbor and Kahalui Harbor.[28] Finally, storm water discharges which meet the basic water quality criteria and NPDES discharges approved by a general permit are permitted in Class A waters.

Marine bottom ecosystems are divided into Classes 1 and 2. Class 1 marine bottom ecosystems are intended to remain in their natural pristine state with a minimum of pollution from human induced sources. Passive human uses are allowed for marine bottom ecosystems in this class so long as they do not interfere with or alter the marine bottom in its natural state. Class 2 marine bottom ecosystems may be used for the propagation of fish, shellfish, and wildlife and for recreational purposes. Actions which modify, alter or consume the marine bottom may be allowed with the approval of the Director of Health ("Director"). Navigational structures, structural shore protection and wastewater effluent outflow structures also may be permitted by the Director.[29]

The Environmental Planning Office ("EPO") is responsible for describing baseline conditions in surface waters and for developing reliable, risk-based water quality standards and improving methods of water quality monitoring. The EPO will also prepare and revise a State Water Quality Management Plan in conjunction with the State Commission on Water Resources Management, and will revise the Clean Water Act list of impaired waters. As required by the EPA, the EPO also develops reliable biological and land use assessments for use in preparing Total Maximum Daily Load estimates on a watershed basis.[30]

---

28 *Id.* § 11-54-03(c)(2).

29 *Id.* § 11-54-03(d).

30 Hawaii State Department of Health, *Strategic Plan for Hawaii's Environmental Protection Programs* at 24 (January 1999).

4.0 REGULATION OF WASTE DISCHARGES TO WATER

Waste discharges are regulated by the Hawaii NPDES permit program which was authorized by the EPA on November 28, 1974.[31] The general policy of the water pollution control program provides that no waste is to be discharged into any waters of Hawaii without first being given the degree of treatment necessary to protect the legitimate beneficial uses of such waters.[32] To this end, pursuant to the Clean Water Act, an NPDES permit must be issued by the Department before discharging any pollutant into state waters or substantially altering the quality or quantity of any discharge. In addition to the NPDES permit requirements, any person who discharges any water pollutant or effluent into a publicly owned treatment work or sewage system may be required to apply for a pretreatment permit issued by the Department or by the appropriate county government. Discharges to publicly owned treatment works or sewage systems must comply with the pretreatment standards established by the Department or the county government.[33] The State of Hawaii pretreatment program was authorized by the EPA on August 12, 1983.[34] Finally, certain discharges of storm water are regulated by the NPDES permit program and by Hawaii's general permit system, which was adopted by rule on October 29, 1992 and amended in 1997.[35]

4.1 NPDES PROGRAM

In November of 1974, EPA delegated the administration of the NPDES program in Hawaii to the Department.[36] The Clean Water Branch administers the NPDES permit program. All discharges of water pollutants to state waters must be in compliance with the Water Pollution

---

31 *See* 56 Fed. Reg. 55,502 (Oct. 28, 1991).

32 Haw. Admin. Rules § 11-55-02 (a)(3).

33 Haw. Rev. Stat. § 342D-50(c).

34 *See* 56 Fed. Reg. 55,502 (Oct. 28, 1991).

35 Haw. Admin. Rules §§ 11-55-34 to -34.12.

36 Hawaii State Department of Health, *Strategic Plan for Hawaii's Environmental Protection Programs* at 90 (January 1999).

Law, its rules and the NPDES permit or variance provisions issued by the Director.[37] The NPDES permit program serves two objectives: the regulation of water pollutants which are discharged to state waters and the requirement of monitoring and reporting by the permittee to the State. Applications for NPDES permits and variances are made to the Director by the owner or operator of the facility. The application for an NPDES permit will be granted if the Director determines that the application is in the public interest. Each application for an NPDES permit is subject to public notice and comment, and may be subject to a public hearing. Variances to NPDES permit requirements may be granted by the Director after the fulfillment of procedural requirements, including public notice.[38]

4.1.1 PERMIT APPLICATION

Each application for an NPDES permit must be made on the application forms furnished by the Department.[39] The application package must include siting information, a plan description, specifications, drawings and other detailed information regarding the treatment works or waste outlet. With the exception of county, state and federal agency applicants, each NPDES permit application requires a filing fee of $1,000.00. This fee is nonrefundable.[40]

The NPDES permit application form must be signed by a responsible corporate officer such as a president, secretary, treasurer or vice-president or any other person who performs similar policy or decision-making functions. Corporate applications may also be signed by managers of large corporations who have the authority to sign such documents. In the case of a partnership, the application must be signed by a general partner, and in case of a sole proprietorship, by the sole proprietor. For public facilities, including municipal, state or other

---

37 Haw. Rev. Stat. § 342D-50.

38 *Id.* §§ 342D-6 to -7.

39 Applications for the NPDES Individual Permit and the NPDES General Permit Coverage are available from the Department's website at http://www.hawaii.gov/health/eh/cwb/forms/index.html (visited August 12, 2000).

40 Haw. Admin. Rules § 11-55-04.

public facilities, a principal executive officer, a ranking elected official or some other authorized employee is required to sign the NPDES permit application.[41]

4.1.2 PERMIT PROCEDURE

After the NPDES permit application is received by the Department, the Director is required to promptly transmit a copy of it to the Regional Administrator of the EPA. The Department also is required to submit the NPDES permit application to the National Data Bank. The Regional Administrator of the EPA is given the opportunity to object, in writing, to any deficiencies in the NPDES permit application.[42]

After the NPDES permit application is considered by the Director and the Department, the Director is required to prepare a tentative determination with respect to the application prior to public notice. The tentative determination must indicate an intent to issue or deny the NPDES permit. If the determination is to issue the permit, the tentative determination must include the proposed effluent limitations for the appropriate pollutants and a proposed schedule of compliance with dates, if one is required. The tentative determination to issue the permit must also contain monitoring requirements along with a brief description of any special conditions which will have a significant impact upon the discharge for which the NPDES permit application is submitted.[43]

The Director is required to notify the public of every complete NPDES permit application. The permit applicant is responsible for payment of all public notice costs associated with processing of the application. This public notice must be circulated in and around the geographical area of the proposed discharge. The notice must be posted near the entrance to the applicant's premises, in the local post office or in other public places near the applicant's premises. The notice must be published in a local newspaper or in a daily newspaper of general circulation. The public notice also must be mailed to any person or group who has requested

---

41 *Id.* § 11-55-07.

42 *Id.* § 11-55-06.

43 Haw. Admin. Rules § 11-55-08.

notice, including those persons on the mailing list to receive copies of notices for all NPDES permit applications within the State.

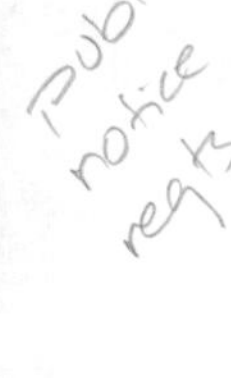

The public notice must include pertinent information regarding the applicant, the applicant's activities or operations which involve the NPDES permit application, the name of the waterway to which each discharge is proposed, the tentative determination made by the Director, a brief description of the procedures for the formulation of the final determination and the contact person at the Department from whom further information can be obtained.[44] For proposed permits for a major facility or activity, Class I sludge management facilities, proposed variances or sewage land applications, and for every draft permit which is the subject of widespread public interest or raises major issues, the Director must prepare a fact sheet for the proposed discharge and send it to the applicant and any person who requests it. The fact sheet must include a sketch or detailed description of the discharge location and a description of the type of facility, along with a quantitative description of the discharge including rate, temperature, and amount of pollutants. The fact sheet will also include the Director's tentative determination, a brief identification of state water classification and water quality standards and a more detailed description of the procedures for the formulation of final determinations.[45]

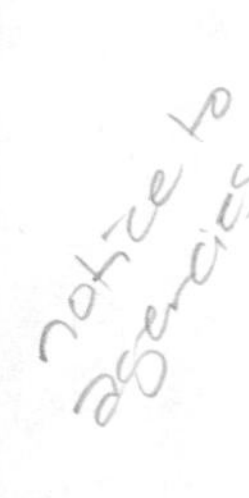

The Director is required to give notice to other governmental agencies of each NPDES permit application. Each government agency is then given the opportunity to comment on the proposed NPDES discharge. Notice to the Army Corps of Engineers must be given simultaneously with the public notice for all discharges into navigable waters. Any written agreement reached between the Director and the District Engineer for the Corps of Engineers must be forwarded to the Regional Administrator for the EPA. This written agreement must also be made available to the public.[46]

---

44 *Id.* § 11-55-09(c).

45 *Id.* § 11-55-10.

46 *Id.* § 11-55-11.

The public notice given for a NPDES permit application must include public access to information. All NPDES forms, including the draft permit, must be made available to the public for reviewing and copying during office hours. Certain confidential information, such as trade secrets, may be withheld from the public by the Director, with concurrence of the Regional Administrator of the EPA. The Director must provide a facility for public inspection of the information and the means for copying the forms.[47]

Following publication of the public notice for the NPDES permit application, the Director must allow at least thirty days for interested persons to submit their comments on the Director's tentative determination with respect to the application. Written comments which are received during the thirty day period must be retained by the Director and considered in the formulation of the final determination.[48]

Any interested person or group of persons, the Regional Administrator, any interested agency or the applicant may request a public hearing with respect to the NPDES permit application. This request for a public hearing must be filed within the thirty day comment period indicating the reason why a hearing is warranted and the interest of the person requesting the hearing. The Director must consider the request and must hold a hearing if there is significant public interest in holding a hearing. The Director is to be guided by federal regulations in determining whether a public hearing would be in the public interest.[49] The public hearing must be held in the geographical area of the proposed discharge or in another appropriate area.[50] The substantive content of the notice of a public hearing is similar to that contained in the notice of the NPDES permit application. The notice for a public hearing must be published in a newspaper of general circulation, sent to all persons and governmental agencies which received a copy of the notice or fact sheet for the NPDES permit application and any person who has made

---

47 *Id.* § 11-55-12.

48 *Id.* § 11-55-09.

49 Haw. Rev. Stat. § 342D-6(f).

50 Haw. Admin. Rules § 11-55-13.

a prior request. The notice of public hearing must be given at least thirty days in advance of the hearing.[51]

After the public notice and comment requirements are fulfilled and the Director has held a public hearing, if one is required, the Director may issue or deny the NPDES permit. A NPDES permit may be issued for any period not exceeding five years. All renewals for permits also shall not exceed five years. Issuance of a permit does not convey any property rights or exclusive privileges.[52]

The 1995 Legislature added a provision to the Water Pollution Control Law which prioritized the processing of certain permit applications.[53] Pursuant to this new provision, permit applications for the repair, reuse, restoration or reconstruction of Hawaiian fishponds[54] are to be processed by the Department before all other permit applications.[55] The Director is required to render a decision on the completeness of an application within thirty days of receipt and a decision on a complete permit application for any fishpond within 150 days.[56]

4.1.3 PERMIT STANDARDS

The Director may issue or renew a NPDES permit subject to certain conditions and standards. For existing publicly owned treatment works, either secondary treatment or the best practicable waste treatment technology is required. For other existing treatment works or waste outlets, the best practicable control technology or the best available technology economically

---

51 *Id.* § 11-55-14.

52 *Id.* § 11-55-15(a), (g).

53 Act approved June 14, 1995, ch. 177, 1995 Haw. Sess. Laws 29 (partially codified at Haw. Rev. Stat. § 342D-6.5).

54 "Hawaiian fishponds" are defined in Haw. Rev. Stat. § 183B-1.

55 Act 177 also exempted the restoration, reconstruction, use or repair of Hawaiian fishponds from the Environmental Impact Statement Law, Haw. Rev. Stat. ch. 343. In addition, the Act expedites processing of land use applications for Hawaiian fishponds in the Conservation district. *See* 1995 Haw. Sess. Laws 177.

56 Haw. Rev. Stat. § 342D-6.5 and Haw. Admin. Rules § 11-54-09.1.01(c).

achievable or the best pollutant control technology for point sources other than publicly owned treatment works is required. For new treatment works or waste outlets, compliance with the applicable standards of performance is required, as well as operation consistent with applicable rules of the Department. All new or existing treatment works or waste outlets must not endanger the maintenance or attainment of applicable water quality standards. The facility also must comply with effluent limitations, water quality standards, and monitoring and record keeping requirements. The NPDES applicant may be required to provide facilities for the monitoring of the authorized waste discharge into state waters and the effects of such wastes on the receiving waters.[57] The permit may also require compliance with effluent standards and limitations, water quality standards, as well as conditions imposed by the Director, the Corps of Engineers, or other government agencies.

The Director may issue an NPDES permit to an existing facility which does not or cannot comply with the requirements for an NPDES permit. These facilities are subject to a schedule of compliance with specific deadlines for bringing the facility into compliance.[58]

For facilities which cannot conditionally or otherwise meet the requirements of the NPDES permit as described above, the NPDES permit must be denied. Also, the Director may not issue a NPDES permit for, or grant a modification or variance for the discharge of radiological, biological warfare agents or high level radioactive waste into navigable water. The Director may not grant a NPDES permit for discharges which the Secretary of the Army has determined would substantially impair anchorage and navigation, discharges to which the Regional Administrator has objected in writing, or discharges which conflict with federal law.[59]

4.1.4 WASTE DISCHARGE REPORTS AND REQUIREMENTS

Each discharge subject to an NPDES permit is subject to monitoring and reporting requirements. Minor discharges, those which have total daily volume less than 50,000 gallons, are subject to monitoring and reporting requirements as established by the Director. Any

57 Haw. Admin. Rules § 11-55-15(c).

58 *Id.* § 11-55-15(d).

59 *Id.* § 11-55-15(e)-(f).

discharges classified as "major," which contains toxic pollutants subject to effluent standards established by the Regional Administrator, or other discharges which the Regional Administrator requests, in writing, be monitored are subject to monitoring and reporting requirements for specific parameters and pollutants as determined by the Director and by the EPA.[60] Monitored items include flow, pollutants which are the subject of reduction or elimination under the terms and conditions or the NPDES permit, pollutants which could have a significant impact on the quality of state waters, and pollutants which the EPA has designated as subject to monitoring. Effluent flows or pollutants must be monitored at intervals sufficiently frequent to yield data which reasonably characterizes the nature of the discharge. Variable effluent flows and pollutant levels must be monitored more frequently than relatively constant flows and levels. The monitoring and reporting results must be submitted to the Department on the NPDES Discharge Monitoring Report ("DMR"). The DMRs contain the quantity or loading units, the quality or concentration of various physical, biological and pollutant parameters and the permit limitations. The completed DMRs must be submitted to the Department at a frequency indicated in the particular NPDES permit, at least once per year.[61] The permittee must maintain monitoring records and results for a minimum of three years.[62] Testing and sampling must be performed by someone knowledgeable in the field of water pollution control, using a methodology approved by the Director or published by the EPA. The Director may also conduct tests of waste discharges from any source.[63]

4.1.5 SCHEDULE OF COMPLIANCE

The Director may issue an NPDES permit for a discharge which is not in compliance with applicable effluent limitations, water quality standards or other legally applicable requirements. In such cases, the NPDES permit must require the permittee to take specific steps to achieve compliance. The timing of the schedule of compliance is based on the most stringent

---

60 *Id.* § 11-55-28.

61 *Id.* § 11-55-30.

62 *Id.* § 11-55-29(3).

63 *Id.* § 11-55-31.

effluent standards and limitations or, in the absence of any legally applicable schedule of compliance, in the shortest reasonable period of time consistent with the guidelines and requirements of the Clean Water Act.[64] Where the schedule of compliance specifies compliance more than one year after the issuance of the NPDES permit, the schedule of compliance must include interim requirements and the corresponding dates of their achievements. The schedule of compliance must require the completion of interim requirements at a maximum of one year between interim dates. If the project cannot be divided into stages of one year or less, the schedule of compliance must specify interim dates for the submission of progress reports by the permittee. Each NPDES permit which contains a schedule of compliance must also include interim dates, reporting dates and the final date for compliance.[65]

The compliance schedule will require progress reports within fourteen days following the interim dates and the final date of compliance. Each report must provide the Director with written notice of compliance or noncompliance with the requirements specified in the NPDES permit. Reports are submitted by the Director to the EPA Regional Administrator on a quarterly basis and are made available to the public for inspection. The Department is required to compile a list of facilities which have not complied with the interim or final requirements of the compliance schedule in the NPDES permits. Noncompliance with interim or final requirements in an NPDES permit may be considered a violation of the permit and may subject the violator to enforcement action by the Director.[66]

4.2 WATER QUALITY CERTIFICATION

Water quality certification from the State is required for all federal licenses or permits which may result in a discharge to navigable waters.[67] The Clean Water Branch issues Clean Water Act Section 401 Water Quality Certifications for federal permits for construction in near-

64 *Id.* § 11-55-21.

65 *Id.*

66 *Id.* § 11-55-22. *See infra* § 7.0 of this Chapter.

67 33 U.S.C. § 1341(a)(1). *See also* 33 C.F.R. § 325.2(b)(1).

shore and inland waters.[68] In Hawaii, the Director is authorized to issue the certification that the proposed discharge complies with state water quality standards as required by the Clean Water Act.[69] For example, a permit to discharge dredge and fill material into wetlands under the Clean Water Act, Section 404 or a permit to conduct ocean dumping of dredged and non-dredged material with a Section 102 or Section 103 Permit under the Marine Protection, Research and Sanctuaries Act requires a Section 401 Water Quality Certification ("Certification") from the Director.

As with NPDES permit application processing, Certification applications for activities involving Hawaiian fishponds are prioritized for expedited handling. Applications for the repair, reuse, restoration or reconstruction of Hawaiian fishponds are to be processed before any other applications. The Director must determine whether an application is complete within thirty days of receipt. The Director must make a decision on any complete application for Certification involving a Hawaiian fishpond within 150 days of receipt of the application.[70]

The Department of Health has developed Section 401 Water Quality Certification Application Guidelines ("Guidelines").[71] The Department provides an application package which includes the application form, accompanying instructions and a checklist for the Certification application. The application for a Section 401 Water Quality Certification is also available from the Department's website.[72] The Guidelines explain how to complete the application package, and also include monitoring guidelines and flow charts explaining Section 401 Water Quality Certification processing.

---

68 Hawaii State Department of Health, *Strategic Plan for Hawaii's Environmental Protection Programs* at 91 (January 1999).

69 Haw. Rev. Stat. § 342D-53.

70 *Id.* § 342D-6.5.

71 Department of Health, Clean Water Branch, Guidelines for the Section 401 Water Certification Application (rev. 06/26/00). The guidelines are available from the Department's website at http://www.hawaii.gov/health/eh/cwb/forms/index.html (visited August 12, 2000).

72 http://www.hawaii.gov/health/en/cwb/forms/index.html (visited August 12, 2000).

A Water Quality Certification application must include the scope of work or a description of the overall project, a description of equipment or facilities to control discharges and a description of the methods used to monitor the quality and characteristics of discharges along with a map showing the locations of the monitoring points.[73] A Best Management Practices Plan must accompany the application. The plan should address the methods to be used to prevent or reduce the pollution of the waters of the United States and must contain proposed mitigative measures and monitoring. The Rules were recently amended in April 2000 to include more detailed application requirements including supporting documentation such as maps and plans, copies of associated federal permits or licenses and Environmental Assessments or Environmental Impact Statements, as applicable. A nonrefundable filing fee of $1,000 is required with the submission of the application to the Department.

If the application is deficient or incomplete, the Director will notify the applicant in writing and must include a description of the additional information necessary to complete the water quality certification application or to correct the deficiency. If the applicant fails to provide the requested information, application processing will be terminated and the application may be denied. Once an application is complete, the applicant will be notified in writing. The Director must then act on the application within one year of determining that the application was complete. During this one year period, the applicant must notify the Department in writing of any changes which may affect the application or the certification process.[74]

The Clean Water Branch follows its general monitoring guideline for the development of an applicable monitoring and assessment plan. The guideline is available from the Department's website.[75]

---

73 Haw. Admin. Rules § 11-54-09.1.02.

74 Haw. Admin. Rules § 11-54-09.1.02.

75 State of Hawaii Department of Health, Clean Water Branch, *General Monitoring Guideline for Section 401 Water Quality Certification Projects* (rev. 04/07/00). The guideline is available from the Department's website at http://www.hawaii.gov/health/eh/cwb/forms/index.html (August 12, 2000).

After the Fact water quality certification applications may be submitted if a project or activity requiring a federal permit or license involves or may involve the discharge of pollutants and is initiated or completed without a water quality certification. The Director may only accept and process these applications for the purpose of deeming federally licensed or permitted activities to be properly permitted or licensed forward of the date the water quality certification was issued. After the Fact applications may only be approved if the activity is not the subject of an ongoing enforcement action, adverse impacts upon water quality have been mitigated to the maximum extent feasible, and the activity will not contribute to any lack of attainment of state water quality standards.[76]

Once an application has been submitted, the Director may provide the opportunity for public comment or hearings. The Director will publish a notice and inform the applicant. All publication and mailing costs are borne by the applicant, and failure to pay such costs may result in a delay in the certification process.[77]

The person who has been issued a Certification or waiver is required to give the Director an opportunity to conduct an inspection of the project prior to commencement to ensure compliance with the applicable water quality standards.[78] If the Director determines that operation of the proposed facility or activity will violate applicable water quality standards, the Director will notify the owner and the licensing or permitting agency.[79] Following such notification, the licensing or permitting agency may suspend a license or permit, following a public hearing. The owner is then afforded the opportunity to submit evidence that the facility or activity has been modified so as not to violate applicable water quality standards. If the Director determines that the applicable water quality standards have not been and will not be violated, the Director must notify the licensing or permitting agency.[80]

---

76 Haw. Admin. Rules §11-54-09.1.02.

77 *Id.* § 11-54-09.1.03.

78 *Id.* § 11-54-09.1.06.

79 *Id.* § 11-54-09.1.07.

80 *Id.* § 11-54-09.1.08.

Licensees or permittees must comply with any new water quality standards adopted by the Department. In any case where a certification or waiver was issued without applicable water quality standards, where water quality standards are established for the receiving waters before the activity is completed, or where the Director determines that new water standards are being violated, the licensee or permittee along with the licensing or permitting agency is notified of the violation. The licensee or permittee then has 180 days to cease the violation. If the violation does not cease, the Director will notify the licensing or permitting authority of the failure to comply with the standards. At the Director's discretion, the Director may revoke the certificate or waiver or recommend suspension of the applicable license or permit pursuant to Section 401 of the Clean Water Act. After suspension of a license of permit, if the Director forms the opinion that applicable water quality standards will not be violated because the licensee a permittee took appropriate action, the Director must notify the licensing or permitting agency of this opinion.[81] In addition, the Department may take enforcement action.[82]

4.2.1 WAIVERS

The requirements for a Section 401 Water Quality Certification shall be automatically waived if the Director fails to act on the request for certification in one year.[83] Certification requirements may also be waived for minor noncontroversial activities subject to a nationwide permit for the discharge of dredge and fill materials.[84] If the discharge resulting from an activity receives a determination that it is covered under a nationwide permit authorization, the Director will determine on a case by case basis which of these dredge and fill activities are minor and noncontroversial, and may waive certification requirements within one year of receipt of a completed application for certification.[85]

---

81 *Id.* § 11-54-09.1.05.

82 *See infra* § 7.0 of this Chapter.

83 Haw. Admin. Rules § 11-54-09.1.04.

84 33 C.F.R. § 330.4(c).

85 Haw. Admin. Rules § 11-54-09.1.04.

4.3 WATER QUALITY CRITERIA

Water quality criteria for specific parameters have been established for all waters of the State. Uses and specific criteria have been established for inland waters, marine waters, various marine bottom types and recreational areas. In addition, the rules designate certain areas which are to be protected and are subject to special conditions.

4.3.1 USES AND SPECIFIC CRITERIA

The basic water criteria are applicable to all waters and require that all waters be free of substances which are attributable to controllable sources of pollutants such as industrial and domestic sources. These controllable sources of pollutants are further defined to include floating materials, sludge or bottom deposits, deleterious substances which are toxic or harmful to animal, plant, human or aquatic life, and soil particles resulting from erosion caused by construction, agriculture, industry and development.

All state waters are subject to monitoring for discharges containing harmful or toxic substances, including field monitoring. For control of soil particles resulting from erosion, a management plan in accordance with soil conservation practices is required. Numerical standards for almost one hundred pollutants have been adopted by rule to serve as the water quality standards. These numerical standards have been established for acute and chronic levels of pollutants in fresh and salt water. The water quality standards also include numerical standards for fish consumption.[86]

Inland waters are classified into the following categories for application of use and specific criteria: flowing waters, standing waters, elevated wetlands, low wetlands, and brackish or saline waters such as anchialine pools, saline lakes, coastal wetlands and estuaries.[87] Inland water areas which have been designated as "Class 1" or "Class 2" protected areas include established preserves and sanctuaries, state and national parks, state and federal wildlife and fish refuges, critical habitat for endangered species and protective subzones designated by the state

86 *Id.* § 11-54-04.

87 *Id.* § 11-54-05.1.

board of land and natural resources, along with all waters in the Wai-Manu National Estuarine Research Reserve. For all Class 1 and 2 flowing waters in which water quality exceeds state standards, the quality must not be lowered unless the change is justifiable as a result of important economic or social development and will not interfere with or injure any assigned uses of those waters.[88]

Springs and seeps, ditches and flumes that discharge into any state waters, natural lakes, reservoirs, anchialine pools, low and coastal wetlands are subject to the basic criteria. In addition, the "no discharge" policy is applicable to anchialine pools and natural lakes. Specific criteria for streams, elevated wetlands and estuaries are provided for several biological, physical and chemical parameters.[89]

The marine waters category includes embayments, open coastal waters and oceanic waters. The most stringent specific criteria are designated for oceanic waters which are not influenced by fresh water discharge to the volume and extent that embayments are influenced by fresh water discharge.[90] Marine bottom types have been classified into sand beaches, lava rock shoreline and solution benches, marine pools and protected coves, reef flats, reef communities and soft bottom communities. The specific criteria applicable to these bottom types designate the following parameters: grain size distribution of sediment, oxidation reduction potential and episodic deposits of flood-borne soil sediment. Artificial basins such as shallow boat harbors and deep draft commercial harbors are classified with specific criteria.[91]

In April 2000, the Department adopted area-specific criteria for the Kona (west) coast of the Island of Hawaii.[92] The nutrient criteria of the open coastal waters of the Kona coast were revised to take into account the unique physiographic conditions of that coastline. Kona coastal waters naturally receive high nutrient groundwater from seeps and springs along the coast. The

---

88 *Id.* § 11-54-05.1.

89 *Id.* § 11-54-05.2.

90 *Id.* § 11-54-06.

91 *Id.* § 11-54-07.

92 *Id.* § 11-54-07.

new criteria take the mixing of natural groundwater into account and are designed to detect any human-caused increase in nutrients. The rules proscribe a unique sampling process that specifies the frequency and location of water quality sampling. These sample results are analyzed using a statistical procedure that takes saltwater/groundwater mixing into account.[93]

In addition to the specific criteria designated for the various types of waters and bottoms, additional bacterial criteria have been established for recreational areas. For inland recreational waters, fecal coliform content criteria are applicable; for marine recreational waters within 1,000 feet of the shoreline, enterococci content criteria are used. For both inland and marine recreational waters, there is to be no raw or inadequately treated sewage or other pollutants of public health significance, as determined by the Director.[94] The marine recreational water standard authorizes the Director to post warnings of a risk to human health from exposure to waterborne microorganisms in waters adjacent to coastlines receiving storm drain or stream discharges, or where water exchange is limited through breakwaters and where the bacterial standard is chronically exceeded.[95]

4.3.2 ZONES OF MIXING

The zone of mixing is the limited area around outfalls and other facilities where the discharge does not comply with existing water quality standards. The zone of mixing allows for the initial dilution of waste discharges.[96] The rules recognize that zones of mixing are necessary and regulate them to achieve the highest attainable level of water quality. A zone of mixing permit may be required in addition to an NPDES discharge permit under the program. Applications to establish a zone of mixing should be submitted concurrently with the NPDES

---

93 Executive Summary, Amendments to Hawaii Administrative Rules, Title II, Chapter 54, Water Quality Standards at pp. 1-2.

94 *Id.* § 11-54-08.

95 *Id.* § 11-54-08(b)(2).

96 *Id.* § 11-54-09(a).

permit application. Applications are reviewed in light of the supporting information and the effect and probable effect of the discharge upon water quality standards.[97]

Public notice must be given for all applications for zones of mixing. The public notice must be given in the county where the source is located. The Director may hold a public hearing or may provide a public notice and comment period concurrently with an NPDES permit application for the same discharge. The zone of mixing may be established by the Director only if the discharge has received the best degree of treatment control, if the discharge will not violate basic standards applicable to all waters and if the discharge will not unreasonably interfere with use of the water. In addition, the Director must determine that the operation involved with the discharge and zone of mixing is in the public interest and that the discharge occurring does not substantially endanger human health or safety.[98]

A zone of mixing may be established or renewed for a maximum time period of five years. The Director may attach conditions to the zone of mixing, including sampling of the effluent and the receiving waters, monitoring of the bottom biological communities and research on methods of treatment. Renewals for zones of mixing may be granted for a maximum of five years, provided that the renewal does not provide for a larger discharge and provided that the applicant has satisfied the conditions required in the previous zone of mixing. Applications for renewal of a zone of mixing must be made at least 180 days prior to the expiration of the zone of mixing.[99] After the zone of mixing expires, no rights become vested in the designee or permittee.[100]

The Director's establishment of a zone of mixing requires the concurrence of the EPA. The Director may revoke, suspend or modify any zone of mixing if the Director determines that

---

97 *Id.* § 11-54-09(c).

98 *Id.* § 11-54-09(c)(4)-(5).

99 *Id.* § 11-54-09(c)(6)-(7).

100 *Id.* § 11-54-09(c)(12).

the Water Pollution Law has been violated and after notice and opportunity for a contested case hearing pursuant to the Hawaii Administrative Procedure Act.[101]

4.4 WETLAND MANAGEMENT

The Hawaii Wetland Management Policy ("Wetland Policy") was adopted in April 1999. The Wetland Policy was prepared by the Hawaii Wetland Management Policy Workgroup working closely with federal, state, county, developers, planning professionals and conservation groups. With the exception of existing legal obligations, the policy is intended for use on a voluntary basis.[102]

Although wetlands account for approximately 110,000 acres of Hawaii's landscape, an estimated one-third of the coastal wetlands have been lost to development in the last two centuries. The Wetland Policy's vision is therefore to integrate Hawaii's wetlands into the watershed, or ahupua'a, extending from the uplands to the coastal waters. The Wetland Policy also seeks to preserve, conserve, restore and create wetlands in order to maintain habitat, support species biodiversity, nurture fisheries, control floods, improve water quality, sustain cultural resources and provide scenic vistas.[103]

The goals of the Wetland Policy are to promote better understanding of the functions and values of wetlands, to promote the preservation, conservation, resaturation and creation of wetlands and to improve public participation in the wetland management process.[104]

The Wetland Policy encourages public participation to the maximum extent practical in wetland management. Regional and statewide planning is encouraged to integrate wetland conservation, and private landowners are encouraged to become involved in wetland resources

---

101 *Id.* § 11-54-9(c)(9)-(10). *See infra* ch. 13 of this Handbook.

102 Hawaii Wetland Management Policy Workgroup, Hawaii Wetland Management Policy at ii (April 1999).

103 *Id.* at ES-i.

104 *Id.* at 3.

management. The Wetland Policy also seeks to foster a training program to encourage wetland managers, technical staff, developers, private landowners and others to implement wetland management measures.[105]

In order to encourage more efficient processing of wetland-related permits or approvals, the Wetland Policy promotes better understanding of the roles and responsibilities of agencies with wetland permits or approval programs. To this end, the Wetland Policy encourages cooperation between applicants, government agencies, the general public, and groups with conservation interests throughout project planning and implementation.[106]

The Wetland Policy only considers wetland mitigation after the avoidance and minimization of wetland loss. To this end, the Wetland Policy encourages wetland preservation and conservation. Compensatory mitigation compensates only for unavoidable adverse impacts that remain after all appropriate and practicable avoidance and minimization have been accomplished. The Wetland Policy also prefers on-site and in-kind compensatory measures to off-site and out-of-kind measures.[107]

The Wetland Policy takes a watershed management approach which seeks to develop procedures for evaluating the functions and values of Hawaii's wetlands, and to establish a geographic information system-based database in Hawaii, including a wetland inventory, for compiling and storing information.[108]

To minimize cultural impacts, the Wetland Policy encourages consultation with Hawaiians and other cultural practitioners on the cultural significance for wetlands of interest. The Wetland Policy also encourages the establishment of a kupuna and traditional knowledge database for use by Hawaiians and other interested parties. Hawaiians and other cultural

---

105 *Id.* at 110-11.

106 *Id.* at 13, 19.

107 *Id.* at 19.

108 *Id.* at 21-22.

practitioners are engaged to preserve, restore and reclaim cultural values in a manner consistent with conservation principles and encourage the sustainable sue of wetland resources.[109]

The Wetland Policy attempts to prevent or minimize disputes by education, clarifying existing rules and guidelines, proactive planning, and using an effective public participation process. Along those lines, the Wetland Policy encourages the use of alternative dispute resolution methods such as mediation and arbitration to resolve conflicts.[110]

4.5 NONPOINT SOURCE POLLUTION MANAGEMENT

The Director has broad authority under the Water Pollution Law to prevent, control and abate water pollution in Hawaii and to adopt necessary rules.[111] This authority encompasses regulation of nonpoint source pollution as well as the point source pollution under the NPDES program. Polluted runoff from agriculture, urban development, forestry, recreational boating and marinas, and wetlands activities are the leading cause of water pollution in waters across the country and in Hawaii.[112] For this reason, the 1993 Legislature passed a bill, which added a new statute specifically providing for the management and control of nonpoint source pollution.[113] The Nonpoint Source Pollution Law authorizes the Director to adopt rules to regulate nonpoint source pollution as required by the Clean Water Act.[114] Hawaii is currently seeking to obtain approval of its Coastal Nonpoint Pollution Control Program and Management Plan which was prepared by the Hawaii Coastal Zone Management Program in collaboration with the Department and the Department of Business, Economic Development and Tourism.[115]

---

109 *Id.* at 23.

110 *Id.* at 25.

111 Haw. Rev. Stat. § 342D-4 to -5.

112 http://www.epa.gov/region09/water/nonpoint/hi/index.html (visited July 27, 2000).

113 Act approved July 1, 1993, ch. 345, 1993 Haw. Sess. Laws 817 (codified at Haw. Rev. Stat. ch. 342E).

114 Clean Water Act § 319, 33 U.S.C. § 1329.

115 Hawaii State Department of Health, *Strategic Plan for Hawaii's Environmental Protection Programs* at 90 (January 1999).

Hawaii's Coastal Nonpoint Pollution Control Program (CNPCP) was submitted to EPA and the National Oceanic and Atmospheric Administration (NOAA) for approval in 1996.[116] EPA and NOAA announced their conditional approval of Hawaii's CNPCP on July 9, 1998.[117]

Nonpoint source pollution means water pollution that does not originate from a point source. A point source is a discrete, confined or discernible conveyance such as a pipe, container, ditch, channel or conduit. Discharges which are return flows from agriculture irrigation and agricultural storm water discharges are specifically excluded from the definition of point source.[118] For the nonpoint source pollution program, "state waters" is defined to include coastal waters, rivers, streams, wetlands and all other waters of the State. However, reservoirs, ponds, canals, drainage ditches and wetlands which are part of an irrigation system or water pollution control system do not fall within the definition of "state waters."[119]

Pursuant to the Nonpoint Source Pollution Law, the Director is authorized to adopt rules to implement the law, comply with federal requirements and work cooperatively with other federal, state and local agencies to achieve the purposes of the law and the Clean Water Act. The Director may facilitate implementation of best management practices programs, convene statewide and regional forums and provide funding for the program and related projects.[120] As of the printing of this Handbook, rules to implement the Nonpoint Source Pollution Law had not been adopted.[121]

The Nonpoint Source Program is managed by the Environmental Planning Office ("EPO"). The EPO has been instrumental in providing public education to raise awareness of nonpoint source pollution and its effects.[122] An ongoing public education and participation

---

116 http://www.epa.gov/region09/water/nonpoint/hi/index.html (visited July 27, 2000).

117 63 Fed. Reg. 37094-37095 (July 9, 1998).

118 Haw. Rev. Stat. § 342E-1.

119 *Id.*

120 *Id.* § 342E-3(a).

121 Interview with Dennis Lau, State of Hawaii, Department of Health, Clean Water Branch (July 26, 2000).

122 *See e.g.*, State of Hawai:, Department of Health, Nonpoint Source Pollution (pamphlet, undated).

project regarding nonpoint source pollution is the stenciling of drains that flow to the storm water collection system with the following statement: "Don't dump here, goes to ocean."

The Office of State Planning facilitated the development of a draft management plan for a statewide program to control polluted runoff.[123] The Coastal Nonpoint Pollution Control Program Management Plan was developed with community input, and public hearings were held in early 1995.[124] The Management Plan incorporates management measures based on EPA guidance.[125] The management measures are separated into six categories: agriculture, forestry, urban, marinas and recreational boating, wetlands and riparian areas, and hydromodification.[126] The final Plan will provide a statewide program for control of polluted runoff to be implemented by several existing state agencies.

To enforce the Nonpoint Source Pollution Law, the Director is authorized to enter and inspect any area suspected of nonpoint source pollution, inspect records and test any waters, aquatic and other life forms.[127] Violation of any rule adopted under the Law may be punished by a civil fine of $10,000 for each offense, and each day of violation. The denial or obstruction of any inspection by a Department employee or authorized officer is subject to a civil fine of $5,000 per day. Fines collected are deposited in the Environmental Response Fund.[128]

---

123 The Management Plan is based upon federal guidance from EPA and the National Oceanic and Atmospheric Agency. 58 Fed. Reg. 5182 (Jan. 19, 1993).

124 State of Hawaii, Office of Environmental Quality Control, The Environmental Notice, at 21 (Jan. 23, 1996).

125 State of Hawaii, Office of State Planning, Coastal Nonpoint Pollution Control Program Management Plan (Executive Summary draft, Dec. 1995).

126 "Hydromodification" means alteration of the hydrogeologic characteristics of coastal and noncoastal waters. *Id.* at 13.

127 Haw. Rev. Stat. § 342E-3(b).

128 *Id.* § 342E-4.

4.6 STORM WATER REGULATIONS

Pursuant to the federal Clean Water Act regulations,[129] general permits for the federal storm water and effluent limitation guidelines were developed by the Department[130] and approved by the EPA in September 1991.[131] Control of storm water discharges is a high priority for the EPA and the State.[132] The Department adopted the general permit program rules which establish general permits for discharges associated with the following industrial activities: storm water associated with certain industrial activities, construction activities involving five acres or more,[133] leaking underground storage tank remediation sites, once-through non-contact cooling water of one million gallons per day, non-polluted discharges of hydrotesting waters, dewatering from construction sites and the discharge of treated process wastewater effluent from petroleum bulk stations and terminals or associated with well drilling activities.[134]

Of the total NPDES Permits granted by the Clean Water Branch, 82% are general permits and only 18% are individual permits.[135] Of the total general permits, 163 were for industrial storm water, 170 were for construction storm water, 48 were for construction dewatering, 27 were for hydrotesting and 3 were for non-contact cooling water.[136]

---

129 40 C.F.R. § 122.26(b)(14).

130 Haw. Admin. Rules §§ 11-55-34 to -34.12.

131 56 Fed. Reg. 55,502 (Oct. 28, 1991).

132 Hawaii State Department of Health, *Strategic Plan for Hawaii's Environmental Protection Programs* at 94 (January 1999).

133 The United States District Court for the District of Hawaii has ruled that the calculation of disturbed land area should exclude acreage which falls within other exceptions to NPDES permitting requirements, such as the exclusion for agricultural or slivicultural activities. *Na Mamo O'aha 'Ino v. Galiher*, 28 F. Supp. 2d 1258, 1262 (1998).

134 Haw. Admin. Rules § 11-55-34.02(b).

135 Hawaii State Department of Health, *Strategic Plan for Hawaii's Environmental Protection Programs* at 44 (January 1999)

136 *Id* at 44.

General permits are valid for a maximum term of five years.[137] Discharges covered by the general permit program are subject to a number of standard conditions and must comply with the water quality standards. In October 1997, the Department adopted Standard General Permit Conditions which apply to each general permit.[138] In addition, each general permit is subject to additional conditions.[139]

The Department's Standard General Permit Conditions ("Conditions") require compliance with basic water quality criteria. The Conditions specify sampling requirements, including sampling points, flow measurements, calibration of monitoring equipment, and formulae for calculating daily, weekly, monthly, and maximum daily discharge as well as concentration measurements. After expiration of the notice of general permit coverage, the permitee must reapply. The Conditions also require that the permittee take all reasonable steps to minimize or prevent any discharge in violation of the general permit or applicable law. Although most of the Conditions require compliance with federal regulations, the Conditions sometimes differ from federal regulations, as with the requirements for monitoring and recordkeeping.

Permittees are also required to report any "upset," defined as an exceptional incident in which there is unintentional and temporary noncompliance with technology based permit effluent limitations because of factors beyond the reasonable control of the permitee. If the permittee meets the conditions necessary for the demonstration of upset, an upset constitutes an

---

137 *Id.* § 11-55-34.03.

138 *Id.* § 11-55-34-04(b) and Department of Health Standard General Permit Conditions, attached as Appendix A.

139 *Id.* tit. 11, ch. 55, apps. B-I. *See Id.* § 11-55-34.04. Appendix B covers the NPDES General Permit Authorizing Discharges of Stormwater Associated With Industrial Activities; Appendix C covers the NPDES General Permit Authorizing Discharges of Stormwater Associated With Construction Activity; Appendix D addresses the NPDES General Permit Authorizing Discharges of Treated Effluent from Leaking Underground Storage Tank Remedial Activities; Appendix E addresses the NPDES General Permit Authorizing Discharges of Once Through Cooling Water Less Than One (1) Million Gallons Per Day; Appendix F covers the NPDES General Permit Authorizing Discharges of Hydrotesting Waters; Appendix G addresses the NPDES General Permit Authorizing Discharges Associated With Construction Activity Dewatering; Appendix H covers the NPDES General Permit Authorizing Discharges of Treated Effluent From Petroleum Bulk Stations and Terminals; and Appendix I covers the NPDES General Permit Authorizing Discharges of Treated Effluent from Well Drilling Activities.

affirmative defense to an action brought for noncompliance with the technology based permit effluent limitations. The permittee, however, bears the burden of proving in any enforcement action that an upset has occurred.

The Director may require any person who is covered by a general permit to apply for and obtain an individual permit. An individual permit may be required of persons whose discharge is not in compliance with the general permit, if a change has occurred in the availability of demonstrated technology or practices for the control of pollutants, if effluent limitation guidelines are promulgated for point sources covered by the general permit, if a water quality management plan containing requirements applicable to point sources is approved, if circumstances have changed so that the permittee is no longer appropriately controlled under the general permit, if applicable standards for sewage sludge use or disposal have been promulgated, or if the discharger is a significant contributor of pollutants to state waters.[140] When the individual permit is issued to the source, the general permit coverage is automatically terminated. Conversely, a party that holds an individual permit but qualifies for coverage under the general permit system may request revocation of the individual permit. Upon revocation of the individual permit, the general permit is applicable.[141]

Persons seeking coverage under a general permit must submit a Notice of Intent ("NOI") to the Department. Each NOI must be accompanied by all pertinent information, including engineering reports, a schedule of progress, plans, specifications, maps, records and a nonrefundable filing fee of $500. The NOI must be submitted thirty days prior to the start of activities causing the discharge.[142] If the Director notifies the owner or operator that the application is incomplete, the thirty day period starts over again upon receipt of the revised notice of intent.

The Director is required to notify the person submitting the NOI in writing whether the proposed discharge is covered by a general permit (Notice of General Permit Coverage or

---

140 *Id.* § 11-55-34.05.

141 *Id.* § 11-55-34.06.

142 *Id.* § 11-55-34.08.

"NGPC") or whether an individual permit application is required. The Director may add additional conditions to the NGPC and may limit the NGPC for a term less than five years. The NGPC holder must submit an NOI for renewal of the NGPC before expiration of its term or before five years, whichever is less. The Director may extend the NGPC administratively.[143]

Any interested person may petition the Director under the Administrative Procedure Act[144] for a declaratory ruling on the applicability of a general permit or the requirement for an individual permit. During the proceedings on the petition, the Director's decision regarding the applicability or nonapplicability of a general permit remains effective.[145]

An NGPC may be revoked, modified, reissued or terminated after notice and opportunity for a contested case hearing.[146] Violations of terms of the general permit are subject to enforcement and penalties.[147]

The EPA promulgated its NPDES Storm Water Phase II Final Rule ("Phase II Final Rule") in December 1999.[148] The Phase II Final Rule contains a conditional exclusion applicable to all categories of industrial activity, with the exception of construction activity, with no exposure of industrial materials and activities to storm water. A condition of "no exposure" exists at an industrial facility when all industrial materials and activities are protected by a storm resistant shelter to prevent exposure to rain, snow, snowmelt and/or runoff. The rule does not alter the types of industrial facilities regulated under the industrial permitting program. The Clean Water Branch is in the process of adopting the related Federal Regulations.[149] In the

143 *Id.* § 11-55-34.09.

144 *See infra* ch. 13 of this Handbook.

145 Haw. Admin. Rules § 11-55-34.10.

146 *See infra* ch. 13 of this Handbook. *See also* Haw. Admin. R. § 11-55-34.11.

147 Haw. Rev. Stat. §§ 11-55-34.12, -35. *See infra* § 7.0 of this Chapter.

148 64 Fed. Reg. 68,722-68,851 (Dec. 8, 1999).

149 http://www.hawaii.gov/health/eh/cwb (visited July 26, 2000).

interim, the Clean Water Branch has developed an application for "No Exposure" certification for facilities qualifying for the no exposure exclusion.[150]

The general permit program adopted by the Department may be revised under the decision in *Natural Resources Defense Council v. EPA.*[151] In the *NRDC* case, the Court of Appeals for the Ninth Circuit invalidated the exemptions from the nonpoint management program which had been established by the EPA for eighteen light industries and for construction activity involving less than five acres.

4.7 REGULATION OF RECYCLED WATER AND SEWAGE SLUDGE

In 1995, the Legislature expanded the authority of the Director to regulate reclaimed water and sewage sludge. Notably, the amendments authorized the Director to regulate management practices for sewage sludge irrespective of whether the management practices cause water pollution.[152] In 1999, the Hawaii Water Pollution Law was again revised and the "reclaimed water" was redefined as "recycled water."

The Director is authorized to issue permits for management practices for sewage, sewage sludge and recycled water.[153] Sewage sludge means any liquid, semi-solid or solid residue removed during the treatment of domestic sewage or municipal wastewater. Sewage sludge specifically includes sewage sludge products, portable toilet pumping, certain marine sanitation device pumpings, scum, septage and solids removed during primary, secondary or advanced wastewater treatment.[154] Specifically, sewage sludge does not include ash generated from

---

150 State of Hawaii Department of Health, Clean Water Branch, "No Exposure" Certification for Conditional "No Exposure" Exclusion from NPDES Storm Water Associated with Industrial Activity Permitting (Rev. 04/28/00). This form is available from the Department's website at http://www.hawaii.gov/health/eh/cwb/forms/.index.html (visited August 12, 2000).

151 966 F.2d 1292 (9th Cir. 1992).

152 Haw. Rev. Stat. §§ 342D-4 and 342-6(c).

153 *Id.* § 342D-6(c).

154 *Id.* § 342D-1.

sewage sludge incineration, grit or screenings. “Recycled water” and “reclaimed water” broadly include treated wastewater that by design is intended or used for beneficial purpose.[155]

The Director is authorized to enter and inspect actual or suspected management practices for domestic sewage, sewage sludge and recycled water operations[156] and issue emergency orders to reduce, change or stop the domestic sewage, sewage sludge, or recycled water management practice, regardless of whether the practice causes water pollution.[157] Finally, the Director may impose recordkeeping and monitoring requirements on any person who owns or operates any effluent source, works, system or plant or any effluent discharger.[158]

The Director may make grants to any county or state agency for the construction of treatment plants and other wastewater reclamation and management projects which use unconventional means to prevent discharge. Any projects which apply for funding must have the Director’s certification that they are entitled to priority over other eligible projects on the basis of financial as well as other water pollution control needs.[159]

4.8 REGULATION OF GRAY WATER

"Gray water" is defined to include all water from residential domestic plumbing systems, except toilets. "Gray water," in order to qualify for the recycling program, may not contain any household hazardous waste. As of April 1993, each County may be authorized by the Department to implement a gray water recycling program. Under the program, the use of the recycled gray water is limited to irrigation of gardens and lawns.

Each County gray water recycling plan must be approved by the Department prior to its implementation. Each County plan must include procedures for the proposed plan and address

---

155 *Id.*

156 *Id.* § 342D-8.

157 *Id.* § 342D-10.

158 *Id.* § 342D-55.

159 *Id.* § 342D-54.

the environmental impacts, cost and appropriateness of the program for the geographic area. Finally, authorization for the County gray water recycling plans may be revoked by the Department at any time.[160]

4.9 VARIANCES

Variances may be issued by the Director to discharge wastes in excess of applicable standards or to act in a manner which is not in compliance with the administrative rules.[161] Applications for a variance must include a detailed description of present conditions and how present conditions do not conform to the applicable standards. Applications for variances will be reviewed in light of the effect or probable effect on the water quality standards as supported by the information submitted with the application.[162]

4.9.1 CONDITIONS

Variances authorizing the discharge of pollutants in excess of the water quality standards may be granted if three conditions are met: continuation of the activity involving the subject discharge is in the public interest; the discharge does not substantially endanger human health or safety; and compliance with the applicable rules or standards from which the variance is sought would produce serious hardship without equal or greater benefits to the public.[163]

Any variance issued by the Director will be subject to sampling and reporting requirements. Variances which are granted on the grounds that there are no practicable means for the control of the water pollution will be granted only until such means of control become available. The Department may prescribe alternative methods for control of the water pollution. Every variance will require the permittee to sample the discharge or effluent and report the results to the Department. The Director may grant a variance for a maximum of five years.[164]

---

160 *Id.* § 342D-70.

161 *Id.* § 342D-1.

162 *Id.* § 342D-7(a)-(b).

163 *Id.* § 342D-7(c).

164 *Id.* § 342B-7(d).

4.9.2 PROCEDURES

All applications for variances are subject to public participation. Public notice of every completed application for a variance must inform all potentially interested parties. Public notice must be circulated in the geographical area of the proposed discharge. Notice also must be mailed upon request to any person or group and must be mailed to all persons on the mailing list for variance applications.[165]

The public notice must contain descriptive information about the applicant, a description of the activity causing the discharge and the location of the discharge. The notice must contain the procedures for formulation of the final determination and the location and contact at the Department where more information can be obtained.[166]

The Director must provide a comment period of at least thirty days during which time interested persons may submit written comments to the Department. After reviewing the written comments, the Director may hold a public hearing if he or she determines that a hearing is warranted. The hearing must be held in the geographical area of the proposed discharge or some other appropriate area.[167]

A variance or renewal of a variance may be granted for a maximum period of five years. Renewal variances may not provide for a greater discharge than the preceding variance. An application for renewal of a variance must be submitted at least 180 days prior to the expiration of the variance. The Director is required to act on an application for issuance, renewal or modification of a variance within 180 days of receipt[168] and may hold a hearing in connection with the renewal application[169] pursuant to the Hawaii Administrative Procedure Act.[170]

---

165 *Id.* § 342D-7(i)(1).

166 *Id.* § 342D-7(i)(3).

167 *Id.* § 342D-7(i)(2), (4).

168 *Id.* § 342D-7(e).

169 *Id.* § 342D-7(f).

170 Haw. Rev. Stat. ch. 91. *See infra* ch. 13 of this Handbook.

5.0 REGULATION OF DISCHARGES TO PUBLICLY OWNED TREATMENT WORKS

The pretreatment program establishes general standards and numerical limitations for certain substances entering the public sewer system. In Hawaii, the publicly owned treatment works are owned and operated by the respective county governments. Discharges to publicly owned treatment works ("POTW") are regulated by pretreatment programs. County programs which are implemented for the design, construction and operation of sewage treatment plants must be approved by the Director.[171] The Clean Water Branch oversees the City and County of Honolulu in administering the POTW Pre-Treatment Program.[172] The wastewater infrastructure in some counties has become inadequate due to rapid development. In order to prevent overloading the existing infrastructure, some counties have imposed limitations on the use of county wastewater systems. On Oahu, the county imposed a moratorium on sewer connections in 1994 to prevent spillage and discharges of untreated sewage in the Windward and West Oahu areas until additional treatment facilities were available.[173]

Each county that establishes a pretreatment program must adopt standards at least as stringent as those established by the EPA.[174] The users of POTWs who discharge any effluent or pollutant into the sewers are subject to inspection and reporting requirements. The Director is authorized to inspect records and monitoring equipment required by the pretreatment program and may take samples of any pollutant or effluent. In addition, the Director may require the discharger to make and submit records, install and use specific methods and monitoring equipment, and sample the effluent and state waters.[175]

---

171 Haw. Rev. Stat. § 342D-19 and Haw. Admin. Rules § 11-55-24.

172 Hawaii State Department of Health, *Strategic Plan for Hawaii's Environmental Protection Programs* at 91 (January 1999).

173 State of Hawaii, Office of Environmental Quality Control, *1994 Annual Report of the Environmental Council*, at 16 (1995).

174 33 U.S.C. § 1317(b)-(c).

175 Haw. Admin. Rules § 11-55-24.

On Oahu, the City and County of Honolulu is responsible for the operation of the sewage treatment plants and the establishment of pretreatment standards.[176] Specific pretreatment and permitting requirements apply to discharges of industrial wastewater into the public sewer system.[177]

The ordinances of the City and County of Honolulu ("C&C") establish an industrial user permitting program and prescribe requirements and prohibitions applicable to the C&C wastewater collection and treatment system. Inflow is not permitted into the sewer system, and discharges of subsurface drainage, roof runoff, ground, surface or storm water runoff into public sewers are prohibited.[178] The C&C has issued guidance documents for discharges into sanitary sewers and storm drains.[179]

The City and County of Honolulu has established restrictions on temperature, pH, oil and grease, metals and pollutants in accordance with EPA requirements pursuant to the Clean Water Act.[180] For example, the following substances may not be discharged into the public sewer system: petroleum, wastes, pollutants having a pH lower than 5.5 or higher than 11.0, wastes exceeding the National Categorical Pretreatment Standards,[181] any substance causing the POTW to violate its NPDES permit, and wastes containing certain substances in excess of numerical limitation. Maximum limitations are prescribed for arsenic, cadmium, total chromium, copper, total cyanide, lead, mercury, nickel, selenium, silver, zinc, oil and grease, and phenolic compounds.[182] In addition to these specific pollutant limitations, the disposal of wastewater

---

176 Honolulu, Haw., Rev. Ordinances of Honolulu, ch. 14 (rev. April 5, 2000).

177 *Id.* ch. 14, art. 5.

178 *Id.* § 14-1.9(a).

179 *See, e.g.*, City and County of Honolulu, Dept. of Public Works, Criteria for Handling Drainage Discharge from Buildings and Appurtenant Structures (Memorandum, June 14, 1995).

180 Honolulu, Haw., Rev. Ordinances of Honolulu § 14-1.9. *See also* 40 C.F.R. § 403.5.

181 40 C.F.R. ch. I, subch. N, pts. 405-471.

182 Honolulu, Haw., Rev. Ordinances of Honolulu § 14-1.9(g). Wastewater discharge from cooling water systems can contain high concentrations of metals corroded from copper and other metal piping. The City and County of Honolulu, Department of Environmental Services has therefore published Best Management Practices (BMPs) for Cooling Water Systems (November 1997).

containing concentrations exceeding EPA national categorical pretreatment standards; radioactive materials; toxic pollutants such as herbicides or insecticides at elevated concentrations; and wastes capable of causing obstruction or damage to the sewer system are prohibited.[183] The installation of grease and oil interceptors is required for certain industries. Any business that discharges fats, oils and grease must connect all kitchen fixtures to a grease interceptor. Kitchens fixtures include sinks, floor drains and dishwashers, among others. Grease interceptors must be properly maintained and are subject to inspection by city inspectors. To assist with compliance, several guidance documents are available.[184]

Industrial users who discharge above a certain concentration of suspended solids or biological oxygen demand are required to pay a surcharge.[185] Dilution of industrial wastewater as a substitute for treatment is prohibited. Finally, any waste which would be considered hazardous waste if disposed of differently, is expressly prohibited from the sewer system.[186]

The discharge of industrial wastewaters into public sewers requires an industrial wastewater discharge permit from the City and County of Honolulu, Director of the Department of Wastewater Management ("WW Director"). Applications for Industrial Wastewater Discharge Permits along with application instructions are available from the City and County of Honolulu, Department of Environmental Services webpage.[187] Permits may be issued for a maximum period of five years and are only transferable to a new owner or operator with written approval from the WW Director. The permits must contain effluent limitations and may require

---

183 Honolulu, Haw., Rev. Ordinances of Honolulu § 14-1.9(g).

184 City and County of Honolulu, Department of Wastewater Management, *Environmental Information Bulletin for Restaurants and Food Processing Industry*; City and County of Honolulu, Department of Environmental Services, *Best Management Practices (BMPs) for: The Food Processing Industry* (Dec. 1998); City and County of Honolulu, Department of Environmental Services, *Policy for Grease Interceptor Self-Cleaners* (March 1998); City and County of Honolulu, Department of Environmental Services, *Policy For: Grease Interceptor Program Compliance* (June 1999); City and County of Honolulu, Department of Environmental Services, *Grease Inteceptor Sizing Criteria; Grease Interceptor Sizing Criteria Guidelines* (May 1999). These guidance documents are available from the Department of Environmental Services website, http://www.co.honolulu.hi.us/env/rc/index.html (visited July 27, 2000).

185 Honolulu, Haw., Rev Ordinances of Honolulu § 14-1.9(h).

186 *Id.* § 14-1.9(m)and (n).

187 http://www.co.honolulu.hi.us/env/rc/index.html (visited July 27, 2000).

pretreatment of the industrial wastewater prior to discharge to the public sewer. The permits may impose monitoring, sampling and analysis reporting, recordkeeping and notification requirements. Finally, the permits may require a compliance schedule.[188] The WW Director is authorized to change permit conditions as required by federal or state law or by ordinance. The WW Director may modify, suspend or revoke any industrial wastewater discharge permit.[189]

6.0 WASTE DISCHARGES

The Director or Governor, after determining that a discharge of waste is or will cause an imminent peril to the public health or safety, may order the person causing or contributing to the discharge to immediately cease or reduce the discharge. If these emergency powers are used to order a person to cease or reduce a discharge, the Director must allow an opportunity for a hearing within twenty-four hours.[190] The Director may take any other actions as necessary, including testing of the water and aquatic life.[191]

Discharges of water pollutants into state waters are prohibited. Any person who causes or allows an unpermitted discharge of a water pollutant into state waters is liable under the Water Pollution Control Law. Violation of the Law, rules, permits and variances issued under the Law is prohibited. Unpermitted discharges to publicly owned treatment works or sewage systems are prohibited, as is establishing or altering any drainage, sewage outfall area or water supply without approval from the Director.[192] Violation of these prohibitions is subject to administrative, civil and criminal penalties.

---

188 Honolulu, Haw., Rev. Ordinances of Honolulu § 14-5.1. *See also.* §§ 14-5.10, -5.11.

189 *Id.* §§ 14-5.4, -5.5, -5.7.

190 Haw. Rev. Stat. § 342D-10.

191 *Id.* § 342D-52.

192 *Id.* § 342D-50.

6.1 REPORTING OF DISCHARGES

The Water Pollution Law imposes an affirmative duty to report discharges which are not in compliance with the Law, rules, a permit or variance. The person who has caused the unlawful discharge is required to report the incident to the Director within twenty-four hours of the discharge, unless a valid NPDES permit specifies another reporting time for the specific discharge.[193] Additional reporting requirements may apply under other Hawaii statutes, such as the Environmental Response Law.[194]

7.0 ENFORCEMENT OF DISCHARGE LIMITATIONS

The Director is authorized to enforce the Water Pollution Law, the rules, permits and variances. Enforcement activities are aided by the Director's investigatory powers, as well as the record keeping and monitoring requirements imposed by the conditions in NPDES permits and zones of mixing. The State may take enforcement action by imposing an administrative penalty, by bringing a civil action for a penalty in state court and by instituting a criminal prosecution to seek imprisonment and fines. Finally, the Director may seek injunctive and other relief and may take emergency actions to prevent a violation of the Water Pollution Law, rules and permits.

The Department, county health authorities and county police officers are authorized to enforce the Water Pollution Law, rules and orders of the Department.[195] Generally, enforcement actions are deferred to the Department and the Attorney General's office.

7.1 INVESTIGATORY POWERS AND CONFIDENTIAL INFORMATION

The Director is authorized to enter and inspect any facility or place which is subject to a permit or pretreatment requirement under the Water Pollution Law. The Director may investigate any facility or place which is an actual or suspected source of water pollution to ascertain compliance with the Law. The Director may also inspect actual or suspected domestic

193 *Id.* § 342D-51.

194 *See infra* ch. 9 of this Handbook for reporting requirements.

195 Haw. Rev. Stat. § 342D-17.

sewage, sewage sludge and recycled water operations, whether or not their management practices cause water pollution. In addition to conducting an inspection, the Director may take samples of the effluent or water pollutants and make other reasonable tests.[196] Confidential information secured as a result of an inspection may not be disclosed unless the information relates directly to water pollution.[197] Information concerning secret processes or methods of manufacture will be protected from release to the public. However, all other reports submitted to the Department on discharges of waste, such as DMRs, will be made available to the public. Improper disclosure of confidential information by an agent of the Department, except as required by court order or at an administrative hearing, is subject to a maximum fine of $1,000.[198]

7.2 ADMINISTRATIVE AND CIVIL PENALTIES

Civil and administrative penalties may be imposed for violation of the Water Pollution Law, the rules, a permit or variance. A civil penalty up to $25,000 may be imposed for each day of each violation.[199] Violation of each parameter or limitation of a permit may be considered a separate violation. For example, violation of every parameter of a permit which specifies five parameters will subject the violator to a $125,000 penalty per day of violation. However, a single operational upset which leads to simultaneous violations of more than one water pollutant parameter is treated as a single violation.[200] Civil penalties consider the seriousness of the violation, the economic benefit resulting from the violation, the history of violations, good-faith efforts to comply with applicable requirements, the economic impact of the penalty on the violator. If the violator claims that their economic and financial conditions are insufficient to pay a penalty, the violator bears the burden of proof on this issue.[201]

---

196 *Id.* § 342D-8(a)-(b).

197 *Id.* § 342D-8(c).

198 *Id.* § 342D-14.

199 *Id.* § 342D-30.

200 *Id.* § 342D-36.

201 *Id.* § 22342D-30.

Denial, hampering or obstruction of the entrance and inspection of a facility or place by the Department is subject to a maximum penalty of $10,000 per day of violation.[202] All fines and penalties collected under the Water Pollution Law are deposited into the environmental response revolving fund,[203] which was established under the Environmental Response Law. Civil actions to impose these penalties may be brought by the Attorney General in state courts.

These civil penalties also may be imposed by the Director through an administrative proceeding.[204] The Director may take a number of administrative actions in response to a violation of the Water Pollution Law, rules, a permit or variance. The Director may give written notice of the violation and impose a compliance order for corrective action, may order a hearing on the alleged violations and may impose civil penalties.[205] Notice must be given by certified mail or personal service. If the person continues the violation after having been served the notice of violation, the Director is required to order the violator to submit within thirty days a written schedule which will bring that person into compliance. The Director must modify or approve the submitted schedule within thirty days, or the schedule will be deemed accepted. If the alleged violator does not submit a written schedule to the Director within thirty days, the Director is required to issue a cease and desist order which remains effective until the Director accepts a written schedule from the alleged violator. In addition to the compliance schedule requirement, the Director may impose civil penalties up to $25,000 per day per violation.[206] Violation of an accepted schedule or of an order issued by the Department is also subject to these civil penalties.[207]

Any order issued or penalty imposed by the Department is subject to administrative review. An order or penalty will become final unless the person named in the notice of order or

---

202 *Id.* § 342D-30.

203 *Id.* § 342D-39. *See infra* ch. 8 of this Handbook.

204 *Id.* §§ 342D-30, -31.

205 *Id.* § 342D-9(a).

206 *Id.* § 342D-9(b).

207 *Id.* § 342D-9(c).

notice of penalty requests a hearing within twenty days of service. An administrative hearing will be set by the Director and the hearing will be conducted as a contested case[208] in accordance with the Hawaii Administrative Procedure Act.[209] In an administrative hearing, the following factors must be considered by the Director: nature, circumstances, extent, gravity, and history of the violation and prior violations, the economic benefit to the violator, history, opportunity and difficulty of corrective action good-faith efforts to comply, and degree of culpability. The burden to show inability to pay the proposed penalty is on the violator.[210] After the hearing, the Director may affirm or modify the order or penalty contained in the notice. The Director may rescind the order or penalty upon finding that no violation has occurred or is occurring. Penalties which are affirmed and not paid within thirty days after they become due are subject to collection through a civil action.[211]

The Department has adopted an administrative and civil penalty policy ("Policy") for the clean water and wastewater programs.[212] The Policy is intended to guide the settlement of clean water and wastewater enforcement cases. It states the following goals: deter violations, remove the economic benefit of violations, provide fair treatment of the regulated community, account for litigation considerations and the violator's socio-economic condition and give the violator an opportunity to perform environmentally beneficial projects in lieu of a monetary fine.[213]

The Policy, by its own terms, serves only as guidance for the Department and is not to be deemed to grant rights to any party. The Policy is applicable to enforcement under the Hawaii

---

208 *Id.* § 342D-9(d)-(e).

209 Haw. Rev. Stat. ch. 91. *See infra* ch. 13 of this Handbook.

210 Haw. Rev. Stat. § 342D-31.

211 *Id.* § 342D-9(e)-(f).

212 State of Hawaii, Department of Health, *Administrative and Civil Penalty Policy, Clean Water and Wastewater Programs* (Jan. 19, 1994, revised March 15, 1999).

213 *Id.* at 1.

Water Pollution Control Law and the Hawaii Administrative Rules, chapters 54, 55 and 62. Particularly, the Policy applies to the following violations:[214]

1. Discharges without an NPDES permit;
2. Reporting and monitoring violations;
3. Discharges in violation of pretreatment requirements;
4. Sludge disposal or use violations; and
5. Discharges in violation of NPDES permits.
6. Hawaii Wastewater Systems Rules

The minimum penalty calculation for settlement purposes is based upon three components: economic benefit, gravity and adjustment factors. The economic benefit component is the amount of money that the violator has saved by being in noncompliance. This figure may reflect a temporary deferral cost or a permanent avoidance cost. The gravity component reflects the seriousness of the violation and the offense to the regulatory program. This figure incorporates the pollutant concentration of the exceedance, the number of violations, the duration of the violation, and the health and environmental risk presented by the discharge.[215]

The final component of the penalty calculation is the adjustment factors. There are three adjustment factors which may raise or lower the calculated penalty: environmental history of the violator, conduct of the violator with respect to alleged violation, and consequences of the alleged violation. Two adjustment factors may reduce the penalty calculation: litigation considerations regarding the strength or weakness of the case, and the defendant's inability to pay the calculated penalty. Other unique factors may be considered in adjustments to the penalty, such as the equitable consideration given to a defendant who reasonably, conclusively and detrimentally relied on a state or federal agency's representations or actions.[216]

---

214 *Id.* at 2.

215 *Id.* at 2-5. Numerical penalty adjustments for gravity components are provided as an attachment. *Id.*

216 *Id.* at 5-7. Numerical penalty adjustments are provided in the attachment. *Id.*

The Policy permits the Department to evaluate and accept an environmentally beneficial project in lieu of or credited against a cash penalty. Considerations include the value of the project, the environmental benefit of the project and that the project is not otherwise required by law or planned by the defendant. Generally, the following types of projects are eligible for credit: pollution reduction, pollution prevention, sewering of facilities that are on cesspools, sludge and effluent reuses, and completion of studies on the environmental impacts of a regulated activity.[217] Supplemental environmental projects have been accepted in civil enforcement cases involving the City and County of Honolulu and private parties.[218]

7.3 CRIMINAL PENALTIES

The Water Pollution Law provides criminal penalties for negligent and knowing violations of the Law, rules, permits and pretreatment requirements. Negligent violations are subject to fines of $2,500 to a maximum of $25,000 per day of violation or imprisonment for one year, or both, upon conviction. Subsequent convictions for negligent violations are subject to fines up to $50,000 per day of violation or by imprisonment for two years, or both.[219]

Knowing violations of the Water Pollution Law, rules, permits or pretreatment requirements are subject to harsher penalties. Persons who are convicted of knowing violations are subject to imprisonment for a maximum of three years or a fine of $5,000 to $50,000 per day of violation or both upon conviction. Subsequent convictions are subject to fines up to a maximum of $100,000 per day of violation or imprisonment for a maximum of six years or both.[220]

Criminal penalties may be imposed for knowingly making a false statement or representation in any report or other document filed or maintained under the Water Pollution

---

217 *Id.* at 7-8.

218 *See, e.g., U.S. v. City and County of Honolulu*, Consent Decree as Modified by Stipulation, at 31, Civ. No. 94-00765 DAE (D. Haw. filed May 15, 1995) (Cash penalty of $1.2 million imposed in addition to supplemental environmental project).

219 Haw. Rev. Stat. § 342D-32.

220 *Id.* § 342D-33.

Law. Persons who knowingly falsify, render inaccurate or tamper with a sampling method, analytical method or monitoring device required by the Water Pollution Law are subject to criminal penalties. These acts are punishable by imprisonment for up to two years or by imposition of a fine to a maximum of $10,000, or both, upon conviction. Subsequent convictions are subject to double penalties: a maximum $20,000 fine per day of violation or imprisonment for up to four years or both.[221]

The crime of knowing endangerment is subject to the harshest criminal penalties under the Water Pollution Law. "Knowing endangerment" is defined as a knowing violation of the Water Pollution Law, rules or a permit, with knowledge at that time that the violation places another person in imminent danger of death or serious bodily injury.[222] Knowledge, for the purpose of determining whether the individual defendant knew that his or her conduct placed another person in imminent danger of death or serious bodily injury, is further defined as actual awareness or actual belief, or circumstantial evidence of possession of actual knowledge, such that the defendant took affirmative steps to shield him or herself from relevant information.[223] Knowing endangerment is punishable by a fine up to $250,000 or imprisonment for up to fifteen years or both upon conviction of a defendant who is an individual. The maximum penalties for subsequent convictions of an individual for knowing endangerment are doubled. Where the defendant convicted is an organization, which includes all established legal entities except governments, the crime of knowing endangerment is punishable by a fine up to $1,000,000.[224]

In 1991, the United States prosecuted two individuals accused of improperly bypassing partially treated sludge through an outfall off a popular Oahu beach.[225] In *United States v. Weitzenhoff*,[226] two managers of the Hawaii Kai Wastewater Treatment Plant were convicted of

221 *Id.* § 342D-35.

222 *Id.* § 342D-34(a).

223 *Id.* § 342D-34(c).

224 *Id.* § 342D-34(a)-(b).

225 For a narrative of the *United States v. Weitzenhoff* trial, *See* Environment Hawai'i (Nov. 1991).

226 U.S.D.C. Cr. No. 90-01568-DAE (D. Haw.).

six counts each of violating the Clean Water Act, including conspiracy to violate the Clean Water Act, knowing discharge of pollutants, knowing falsification of the Discharge Monitoring Reports and knowing tampering with the monitoring device.[227] This criminal case is notable for the District Court's ruling on the *mens rea* requirement. In ruling on the *mens rea* issue before trial started, the court held that the government was required to prove that defendants knowingly discharged pollutants from a point source into a navigable waterway in violation of the permit. The court further held that the government did not have to prove that defendants knew that the discharges violated the NPDES permit or the permit conditions. As licensed plant operators, the defendants were presumed to have understood the permit provisions under which they acted and operated the plant.[228] The convictions for "knowingly" violating the permit conditions required only the showing that defendants knowingly engaged in conduct that resulted in permit violation were affirmed on appeal.[229]

In 1999, the Environmental Crimes Task Force, which is co-chaired by the Assistant U.S Attorney, the State Attorney General's Office and the resident EPA Criminal Investigation Special Agent, assisted with a Clean Water Act prosecution. Affordable Grease Trap Services, the operator of a grease trap cleanout truck, was convicted after dumping waste into a streambed.[230]

7.4 RECORD KEEPING AND MONITORING REQUIREMENTS

The Director is authorized to require the owner or operator of an effluent source, works, system, or plant or any discharger of effluent along with any persons engaged in management

---

227 *United States v. Weitzenhoff*, U.S.D.C. Cr. No. 90-01568-DAE, Verdict (D. Haw. Oct. 2, 1991), *aff'd*, 1 F.3d 1523 (9th Cir. 1993), *aff'd and amended on denial of reh'g and reh'g en banc*, 35 F.3d 1275 (9th Cir. 1275 (9th Cir. 1994), *cert. denied sub nom*, Mariani v. U.S., 115 S.Ct. 939 (1995).

228 *United States v. Weitzenhoff*, *supra*, Order granting Plaintiff's Motion in Limine (D. Haw. Sept. 13, 1991).

229 *U.S. v. Weitzenhoff*, 35 F.3d 1275, 1285 (9th Cir. 1994).

230 Hawaii Department of Health, *Report to the Twentieth Legislature, State of Hawaii, in Compliance with Hawaii Revised Statutes 128D and 128E on the Activities of the Department of Health Environmental Health Administration Office of Hazard Evaluation and Emergency Response and Use of the Environmental Response Revolving Fund* at 23 (2000).

practices with regard to domestic sewage, sewage sludge, and recycled water to make reports, establish and maintain records, and to sample effluent, state waters and sewage sludge. The Director may require the use of certain sampling and analytical methods and monitoring equipment. The Director may require permit applicants and facility owners to submit plans and reports relating to existing situations and proposed additions, modifications and alterations. The plans and reports are completed at the applicant's or owner's expense on forms provided by the Director or by a competent person acceptable to the Director.[231]

A permit applicant or owner may be required to submit several types of reports and plans to the Department. A permittee subject to a compliance order must submit quarterly reports of progress as required by compliance schedule.[232] Permittees of publicly owned treatment works are required to submit periodic reports of progress towards compliance with the pretreatment requirements.[233] Periodic reporting of monitoring results is required in all NPDES permits.[234]

Monitoring is required of all major NPDES discharges and NPDES discharges which contain a toxic pollutant for which a standard has been established. The Director may require any other NPDES discharge to be subject to monitoring requirements.[235] The NPDES permit conditions will contain the monitoring and reporting requirements, including the timing, location and analysis parameters designated for monitoring. These monitoring records must be maintained by the permittee for a minimum of three years, including the original charts generated from continuous monitoring.[236] Sampling and analysis pursuant to the permit monitoring requirements must be conducted according to test procedures approved by the Director or according to EPA methodology. The sampling and testing facilities must be made available to the Director upon request.[237]

---

231 Haw. Rev. Stat. § 342D-55.

232 Haw. Admin. Rules §§ 11-55-21 to -22.

233 *Id.* § 11-55-23(a).

234 *Id.* § 11-55-30.

235 *Id.* § 11-55-28(a)-(b).

236 *Id.* § 11-55-29.

237 *Id.* § 11-55-31.

7.5 CITIZEN SUITS

The Water Pollution Law does not contain a citizen suit provision. However, that absence has not delayed citizen enforcement of the Clean Water Law, rules and permits as several citizen suits have been initiated in Hawaii under the federal Clean Water Act citizen suit provision.[238] Environmental groups have taken the enforcement of federal clean water laws into their own hands by filing complaints against the City and County of Honolulu and BYU-Hawaii in Laie.[239] While the majority of these citizen suits target violations at the publicly owned sewage treatment plants, suits have been brought against private and military sewage treatment plant owners.[240]

The City and County of Honolulu has been targeted for several citizen's suits involving violations at the two largest sewage treatment plants in the State: Sand Island and Honouliuli. In *Sierra Club v. City & County of Honolulu*[241] the City was sued for violations of NPDES permit limitations and for operation of the Sand Island Wastewater Treatment Plant without a valid permit for over five years. After summary judgment was granted to plaintiffs on liability for violation of the secondary treatment requirements, settlement negotiations were accelerated.[242] The settlement ultimately reached in this case included thirteen million dollars to be spent on a number of projects: a study of the impact of the discharge in Mamala Bay, reinstallation of treatment equipment previously dismantled by the City & County of Honolulu at the Sand Island Plant and a study of high BOD (biological oxygen demand) industrial discharges to the Sand Island Plant. In addition, both parties agreed to withdraw their objections to the

---

238 33 U.S.C. § 1365.

239 Hawaii State Department of Health, *Strategic Plan for Hawaii's Environmental Protection Programs* at 93 (January 1999).

240 For a discussion of citizen suits, civil and criminal actions involving Hawaii sewage treatment plants, *See* Environment Hawai'i (Oct. & Nov. 1991).

241 Civ. No. 90-00219-ACK (D. Haw. filed Mar. 28, 1990). Order approving consent decree (D. Haw. filed Nov. 10, 1991).

242 *Sierra Club*, *supra*, Civ. No. 90-00219-ACK, Order partially granting and partially denying parties' motions for summary judgment (D. Haw. filed Dec. 31, 1990).

§ 301(h) waiver which was issued by the EPA in January 1990 and which permitted the Sand Island Plant to operate at less than secondary treatment levels. The Mamala Bay Commission Report was finalized and made available to the public in late 1995 and early 1996.

The City and County of Honolulu was also sued in *Hawaii's Thousand Friends v. City & County of Honolulu*[243] for violations at the State's second largest plant, the Honouliuli Wastewater Treatment Plant. This case involves alleged numerous improper bypasses, failure to report bypasses and failure to meet secondary wastewater treatment levels since July 1, 1988. Plaintiffs prevailed in 1993 for civil penalties and an additional allocation of funds by the City and County to the Mamala Bay Study Commission.[244]

7.6 ENFORCEMENT OF INDUSTRIAL WASTEWATER DISCHARGE PERMITS

Industrial wastewater users who discharge or cause a discharge in violation of the law and who damage the sewer system are liable to the City and County of Honolulu Wastewater Department.[245] Any industrial user that violates the ordinances, rules or permit is subject to administrative, civil and criminal enforcement. The WW Director may issue an order seeking injunctive relief or penalties for violations. Judicial enforcement of an order also may be sought. The ordinance specifies the types of orders that may be issued by the WW Director: consent orders, show cause orders, compliance orders, cease and desist orders, cleanup and abatement orders, termination of discharge orders and orders imposing administrative fines.[246] The terms of a permit or the WW Director's order may be appealed to the WW Director. If the appeal is not acted upon within thirty days, the petition shall be deemed to have been denied.[247]

---

243 Civ. No. 91-00739-ACK (D. Haw. filed Dec. 24, 1991). This case was consolidated with Civ. No. 90-00218-HMF (D. Haw. filed Mar. 27, 1990) which involves the same parties and different violations at the Honouliuli Treatment Plant.

244 *Hawaii's Thousand Friends*, *supra*, Civ. Nos. 90-00218 and 91-00739, Judgment on behalf of plaintiffs (D.Haw. May 24, 1993).

245 *Id.* § 14-5.13.

246 *Id.* §§ 14-5.15, -5.16, -5.17.

247 *Id.* § 14-5.18.

Administrative and civil penalties up to $1,000 per violation, per day, may be imposed by the WW Director. Where violation of a monthly or long-term discharge limit has occurred, penalties will accrue for each day during the period of violation.[248]

Criminal penalties and fines may be sought for certain types of violations. Willful, intentional, reckless or negligent violation of the ordinance, permit, order or a pretreatment requirement is subject to a minimum fine of $1,000 or by imprisonment for a maximum of ninety days. Each day of violation may be considered a separate offense, after due notice to the alleged violator. Knowingly making a false statement or misrepresentation in any submission to the WW Director is subject to a criminal fine up to $25,000 or imprisonment for six months, or both. Knowingly tampering with or rendering inaccurate any sampling or analysis method or any monitoring device required by ordinance or by law is subject to criminal prosecution. A fine up to $25,000 or imprisonment up to six months, or both, may be imposed upon conviction.[249]

7.6 MISCELLANEOUS ENFORCEMENT PROVISIONS

The State may seek an injunction to prevent violations of the Water Pollution Law, rules, permits or variance.[250] The Director may also institute a civil action to collect administrative penalties or obtain other relief. These types of civil actions do not require the Director to revoke a permit or variance before seeking an injunction or other relief. The Hawaii Rules of Civil Procedure apply to the State's action.[251]

If a discharge of waste requires immediate action and if the discharge causes or will cause imminent peril to the public health and safety, the Director or Governor may take emergency action. The Director or Governor may order the person causing or contributing to the

---

248 *Id.* § 14-5.19(a).

249 *Id.* § 14-5.19(b).

250 In 1994, the United States and the State of Hawaii filed suit against the City and County of Honolulu to force compliance with the pretreatment requirements and establish a collection system compliance program. The terms of the settlement are set forth in the consent decree. *United States of America v. City and County of Honolulu*, Consent Decree as Modified by Stipulation, Civ. No. 94-00765 DAE (D. Haw. filed May 15, 1995).

251 Haw. Rev. Stat. § 342D-11.

discharge to reduce or stop the discharge and is then required to hold a hearing on the matter within twenty-four hours.[252]

In addition to the enforcement mechanisms provided in the Water Pollution Law, certain discharges may be subject to enforcement and response actions under the Environmental Response Law.[253]

---

252 *Id.* § 342D-10.

253 *Id.* ch. 128D. *See infra* ch. 8 of this Handbook.

CHAPTER 4

SAFE DRINKING WATER

1.0 INTRODUCTION

Chapter 340E of the Hawaii Revised Statutes provides standards and procedures designed to maintain an adequate supply of safe drinking water for the State. To this end, the Hawaii Administrative Rules establish state standards for drinking water contaminant levels, treatment, testing and reporting requirements for public water systems, procedures for the provision of drinking water in emergency situations and public notification in the event of drinking water contamination. Underground injection activities which are likely to cause drinking water contamination also are regulated. The Hawaii Wellhead Protection Program establishes a groundwater protection program. Finally, the Hawaii Safe Drinking Water Law[1] creates a system of penalties and remedies applicable in the event of violation of the Law or its rules.

All rules promulgated under the Law are implemented and enforced by the Director of the State Department of Health ("Director"). The Department of Health ("Department"), Safe Drinking Water Branch ("Branch") conducts the drinking water monitoring program for chemical, microbiological, radiological and turbidity parameters.

The Department may use revenues generated by the environmental response tax and deposited into the environmental response revolving fund to address concerns related to drinking water.[2]

---

1 Haw. Rev. Stat. ch. 340E (Michie 1999). All references to the Hawaii Revised Statutes are made to the printed version of the statutes current through the 1999 legislative session, unless otherwise noted. Where appropriate, references to acts passed during the 2000 legislative session have also been added.

2 2000 Haw. Sess. Laws 245 (to be codified at Haw. Rev. Stat. § 128D-2).

2.0 RELATIONSHIP TO FEDERAL SAFE DRINKING WATER ACT

The federal Safe Drinking Water Act ("SDWA")[3] provides for the promulgation of National Primary Drinking Water Regulations, which set federal standards for maximum contaminant levels ("MCLs") in public supplies of drinking water. The Hawaii Safe Drinking Water Law provides for the promulgation of the State Primary Drinking Water Regulations ("State Regulations"). The standards set by the State Regulations may not be any less stringent than the federal standards in effect at the time.[4] Specific contaminant level ceilings and contaminant level monitoring requirements regarding organic and inorganic chemicals, radionuclides, microbiological contaminants and turbidity are established in the State Regulations.[5]

The Branch has been delegated primary enforcement authority from Environmental Protection Agency ("EPA") to administer the SDWA. The EPA has approved the Hawaii State Water System Supervisor Program and program revisions.[6] The Branch is required to comply with new federal regulations to retain primary authority to administer the SDWA program. Recent State program revisions through rules have adopted federal requirements pertaining to fluoride, filtration and disinfection of surface water systems and ground water systems influenced by surface water, and new organic and inorganic compounds. The federal Underground Injection Control program is administered by EPA.[7] However, the Department has adopted rules regulating certain classes of injection wells in the State.[8]

Hawaii's public water systems provide piped water for human consumption such as drinking and washing. They include both municipal and private facilities for the collection,

---

3 42 U.S.C. § 300f *et seq.*

4 Haw. Rev. Stat. § 340E-2.

5 Haw. Admin. Rules tit. 11, ch. 20 (2000 Weil's). All references to the Hawaii Administrative Rules are current through the date of the publication of this Handbook, unless otherwise noted.

6 *See* 60 Fed. Reg. 7962 (Feb. 10, 1995), 58 Fed. Reg. 45,491 (Aug. 30, 1993) and 58 Fed. Reg. 17,892 (April 6, 1993).

7 40 C.F.R. § 147.601.

8 49 Fed. Reg. 45,292, 45,298. *See* Haw. Admin. Rules, tit. 11, ch. 23.

treatment, storage and distribution of water. In 1998, 99.8% of Hawaii's population, or 1,331,353 individuals, were served drinking water in compliance with 1994 MCLs.[9]

The maintenance of safe drinking water supplies is especially important in Hawaii which only has 126 ground water systems, the fewest number of ground water systems of any state in the country.[10] The federal SDWA permits the EPA to designate certain aquifers as the sole or principal source of drinking water for population districts.[11] Pursuant to this authority, the EPA has made two final aquifer determinations for the State of Hawaii: the Southern Oahu Basal Aquifer in the Pearl Harbor Area of Oahu[12] and the Molokai Aquifer in Maui County.[13] As a result of these determinations, projects which are federally assisted and which are constructed in the areas designated by the determinations are subject to EPA review. The purpose of the EPA review is to ensure that the projects do not contaminate the sole source or principal source aquifer through a recharge zone which would create a significant hazard to public health.

2.1 SOURCE WATER ASSESSMENT PROGRAM

The 1996 reauthorization of the SDWA included an amendment requiring states to develop a program to assess sources of drinking water and encouraging states to establish protection programs.[14] The assessment requires delineation of the area around a drinking water source which may convey contaminants which could reach the drinking water supply. The assessment also requires an inventory of activities that might lead to the release of microbiological or chemical contaminants within the delineated area. The Department submitted

---

9 State of Hawaii, The Environmental Council, *The 1999 Environmental Council Annual Report* at 27 (1999).

10 65 Fed. Reg. at 30,199 (May 10, 2000).

11 SDWA, § 1424(e), 42 U.S.C. § 300h-3(e).

12 52 Fed. Reg. 45,496 (Nov. 30, 1987).

13 59 Fed. Reg. 26,063 (May 4, 1994).

14 SDWA § 1453, 42 U.S.C. § 300j-13.

a program plan in February 1999[15] and has received EPA approval. Hawaii's Source Water Assessment Program ("SWAP") is scheduled for completion in December 2001.[16]

The goals of the Hawaii SWAP include the development of guiding principles for the assessments of sources of drinking water supply to benefit public water systems, the assessment of potential impacts to drinking water quality, the encouragement of proactive community based strategies to protect drinking water sources, and to develop linkages to other water resource protection and planning efforts and to upcoming water quality regulations. The SWAP also seeks to raise awareness of drinking water issues and to prioritize cleanup and pollution prevention efforts for al sources of drinking water.[17]

Once complete, the results of the Hawaii SWAP will be used to updated the Hawaii Water Quality Plan administered by the Commission on Water Resource Management.[18]

3.0 STATE PRIMARY DRINKING WATER REGULATIONS

The State Primary Drinking Water Regulations are set forth in the rules relating to potable water systems.[19] The State Regulations were revised in January 1993 to incorporate federal requirements for total coliform and the surface water treatment rule. In December 1994, the State Regulations were again revised to adopt the EPA's lead and copper rule.[20] The State

---

15 A final draft of the SWAP is available on the internet at http://www.aloha.net/~will/hiswap.html (visited August 13, 2000).

16 State of Hawaii, Department of Land and Natural Resources, Commission on Water Resource Management, *Statewide Framework for Updating the Hawaii Water Plan* at p. 3-7 (February 2000).

17 *Id.* at 3-8.

18 *Id.* For further discussion regarding the Hawaii Water Quality plan, *see infra* ch. 14 of this Handbook.

19 Haw. Admin. Rules, tit. 11, ch. 20.

20 40 C.F.R. § 141.88.

Regulations establish specific numerical MCLs for approximately fifty inorganic and organic chemicals,[21] turbidity,[22] microbiological contaminants,[23] and radionuclides.[24] In addition, special monitoring for unregulated contaminants is required.[25]

The State Regulations establish sampling and analytical requirements. The minimum monitoring frequency for microbiological contaminants is based upon the population served by the water system, ranging from a minimum of one sample per month up to 480 samples per month. The time intervals for the taking of samples, procedures for taking routine and repeat samples, and the performance of sanitary surveys are set out in the Regulations.[26] Specific sampling and analytical requirements have been established for turbidity, inorganic and organic chemicals, and radionuclides.[27] Samples taken for analysis of microbiological, chemical and radionuclide contaminants must be analyzed by a laboratory approved by the Director.[28]

The water supplier is required to notify Director of any required test result within the first ten days following the month in which the test result is received or within ten days following the required monitoring period, whichever is shorter. In the event of a failure to comply with any primary drinking water regulations, including a failure to comply with monitoring requirements, the Director must be notified within forty-eight hours.[29]

The SDWA Amendments of 1996 required each state to develop and implement capacity development plans for public water systems which would enable systems to consistently provide

---

21 Haw. Admin. Rules §§ 11-20-3 to -4.

22 *Id.* § 11-20-5.

23 *Id.* § 11-20-6.

24 *Id.* § 11-20-7.

25 *Id.* §§ 11-20-36 to -37.

26 *Id.* § 11-20-9.

27 *Id.* §§ 11-20-10 to -14.

28 *Id.* § 11-20-15.

29 *Id.* § 11-20-17.

safe drinking water.[30] In 1997 the Legislature gave the Director the authority to adopt rules to ensure that public water systems demonstrate technical, managerial and financial capacity.[31] The Branch has now adopted a New Public Water Systems Plan to evaluate new water systems beginning operation after October 1, 1999 and an Existing Public Water Systems Plan to implement capacity development strategies for existing water systems most in need of improvement.

3.1 FILTRATION AND DISINFECTION REQUIREMENTS

The federal filtration and disinfection requirements, also called the Surface Water Treatment Rule ("SWTR") went into effect on January 2, 1993. This rule applies to public water systems that are supplied by either a surface water source or by a groundwater source that is under the direct influence of surface water. The SWTR establishes treatment requirements for microbiological contaminants and turbidity in lieu of MCLs.

Public water systems which are subject to the SWTR rule are required to install and operate water treatment processes which achieve virtually complete removal or inactivation of *Giardia lamblia* cysts, heterotrophic plate count bacteria, Legionella, turbidity and viruses. The SWTR provides specific disinfection and filtration requirements and technologies.[32] The SWTR also establishes requirements for analytical methods and monitoring, reporting and recordkeeping.[33]

The State Regulations reference and adopt the national primary drinking water regulations for lead and copper. By incorporating the national standards for lead and copper, they are made a part of the State Regulations.[34] Copper and lead are two metals which have

---

30 Hawaii Safe Drinking Water Branch, The Water Spot at 1, vol. 3, iss. 2 (April/May 1999).

31 Haw. Rev. Stat. § 340E-2.5.

32 *Id.* § 11-20-46. *See also* State of Hawaii, Department of Health, Safe Drinking Water Branch, Surface Water Treatment Rule Administrative Manual (July 1, 1994).

33 Haw. Admin. Rules § 11-20-46.

34 *Id.* § 11-20-48.

frequently been used in the assembly and installation of water systems, including distribution systems in public buildings and private homes. Both metals have the potential to leach into the water supply in the distribution system.

The Legislature revised the Hawaii Safe Drinking Water Law in 1997 to require the Department to establish a program to conduct annual testing of water catchment systems for lead and copper. Under this program, residents who rely on water catchment systems may have their water tested once a year at an analytical laboratory designated by the Department. Residents will pay $25 for the tests, and the remaining costs will be paid by the Department. The Department is required to recommend practical and affordable methods to improve water quality, based on the specific design and conditions of the water catchment system.[35]

3.2 VARIANCES AND EXEMPTIONS

The Director is authorized to grant a variance from any MCL requirement upon finding that the characteristics of the raw water source, which are reasonably available to the water system, cannot meet the MCL requirement, despite the application of best technology. The Director also must find that the variance will not result in an unreasonable risk to the health of the water supply consumers. The Director may grant a variance from a specified treatment technique if the applicant demonstrates that the technique is not necessary to protect the health of the system's consumers due to the nature of the raw water source. However, variances from the total coliform MCL and the filtration and disinfection criteria may not be granted.[36]

A public water system may apply for an exemption from an MCL or treatment technique requirement under limited circumstances. First, the system must be unable to comply with the requirement due to compelling factors, including economic factors. Second, the system must have been in operation on the effective date of the MCL or treatment technique requirement. Lastly, the Director must find that the granting of the exemption will not result in an

---

35 Haw. Rev. Stat. § 340E-4.8.

36 Haw. Admin. Rules § 11-20-20(c) and (d). For procedure on applying for a variance, *see id.* §§ 11-20-21 to -22, and -26 to -28.

unreasonable risk to health. As with variances, exemptions cannot be granted for the total coliform MCL. In addition, exemptions will not be granted for disinfection requirements where the public water system is a surface water system or groundwater system under the direct influence of surface water.[37]

4.0 NOTIFICATION REQUIREMENTS

The operators of a public water system are required to notify the public and the Department whenever the system exceeds any MCL or fails to comply with a required treatment technique, testing or monitoring requirement established by the State Regulations. Operators are also required to submit consumer confidence reports.[38] A "public water system" is a system which provides piped water for human consumption and has at least fifteen service connections or regularly serves at least twenty-five individuals.[39] Public notification also is required when the water is for any reason deemed exempt from compliance with the MCLs or has not met any schedule prescribed by a variance or exemption.[40]

4.1 NOTIFICATION PROCEDURE

In the event of a violation of a MCL, a failure to perform required monitoring, or if the public water system is subject to a variance or exemption, notification to the users and Department is required. The operator of the public water system involved is required to promptly notify the Department, advising it as to the violation, variance or exemption and as to the extent of the risk to human health. If the violation involves an exceedance of the MCL, failure to comply with a treatment technique or testing procedure, or if a variance or exemption is applicable, the water system must publish notification in a local newspaper of general circulation within fourteen days of the violation. A notice must also accompany the water bills or be

---

37 *Id.* §§ 11-20-22. For procedure on requesting an exemption, *see id.* §§ 11-20-24 to -28.

38 40 C.F.R. § 141.151 *et seq.*

39 Haw. Rev. Stat. § 340E-1(3).

40 *Id.* § 340E-6(a). *See also id.* §§ 340E-22 and -24.

provided by direct mail.[41] In the event of a violation of an MCL of contaminants that may pose an acute risk to human health, the local radio and television media must be notified within seventy-two hours of the violation.[42] Notice of any violation determined by the Director to pose a serious adverse health effect as a result of short term exposure must be given as soon as possible, and no later than twenty-four hours after the violation.[43]

In the event of potential lead contamination, the water system operators must identify and provide notice to all persons who may be affected. The notice must include a clear explanation of the following items: the potential source(s) of lead in the drinking water; the potential adverse health effects; the reasonably available methods of mitigating known or potential lead contamination in drinking water; any steps the system is taking to mitigate lead contamination in drinking water; and the necessity for seeking alternative water supplies, if any.[44]

4.2 CONSUMER CONFIDENCE REPORTS

In August 1998 the EPA promulgated rules requiring that community water systems prepare and produce to their customers annual consumer confidence reports on the quality of the water delivered by the systems. The community reporting requirements were mandated by the 1996 amendments to the SDWA and were adopted by Hawaii in September 1999.

Consumer confidence reports must disclose the detection of any regulated contaminants, along with the MCL goal for those contaminants, the MCL, and the level of the contaminant in the water system. For any exceedence of an MCL, the report must contain a brief statement in plain language regarding the health concerns that resulted in regulation of the contaminant. The reports must also include the telephone number for the Safe Drinking Water Hotline,[45] which will

41 *Id.* § 340E-6; Haw. Admin. Rules § 11-20-18.

42 Haw. Admin. Rules § 11-20-18(a)(1)(C).

43 Haw. Rev. Stat § 340E-6(b).

44 *Id.* § 340E-4.7.

45 The telephone number for the Safe Drinking Water Hotline is 1-800-426-4791.

provide more information about contaminants and potential health effects. The information contained in consumer confidence reports is intended to raise consumers' awareness of where their water comes from, help them understand the process by which safe drinking water is delivered to their homes, and educate them about the importance of preventative measures, such as source water protection, that ensure a safe drinking water supply.[46]

5.0 STATE INTERIM ACTION LEVELS

If the Department discovers a potentially hazardous contaminant in a public water system for which no federal maximum contaminant level has been set by the EPA, the Department may set a state interim action level for that contaminant. Where appropriate, the Department may utilize federal drinking water guidelines in setting the interim action level. Levels of contamination above this level will be considered unacceptably dangerous to public health.[47]

Upon setting an interim action level, the Department must inform the public of its establishment and must issue such guidance as may be necessary to protect the health of persons who are or who may be users of the contaminated water.[48] The Department may, after reviewing all pertinent scientific information, establish an official state standard which supersedes an interim action level.[49] To date, the Department has not set any state interim action levels or state standards for contaminants without an applicable MCL.

6.0 EMERGENCY PLAN FOR SAFE DRINKING WATER

The State Emergency Plan for Safe Drinking Water ("Emergency Plan") prescribes procedures to be utilized by the Department and other state and county agencies to provide safe

---

46 63 Fed. Reg. 44,512-44,536 (August 19, 1998).

47 *Id.* § 340E-22.

48 *Id.* § 340E-22(d). *See also id.* § 340E-24.

49 *Id.* § 340E-23.

drinking water during emergency situations.[50] The Emergency Plan applies to two types of emergency situations, which are categorized as types "A" and "B." Type "A" emergencies are major state or county catastrophes, such as nuclear disasters, tsunamis, earthquakes, volcanic eruptions, floods, hurricanes and tornadoes.[51] Type "B" emergencies are limited situations affecting only water systems. Type B emergencies include drought, major contamination of a basic water source, and major destruction or impairment of a water system's physical facilities which substantially interferes with the quantity and quality of water delivered to the public.[52] In either type of emergency, the Department and the other state and county agencies are responsible for ensuring an adequate supply of water to deprived areas, sampling and analysis to determine the levels of contamination, notifying the public and prescribing appropriate procedures to minimize health risks.[53]

7.0 CROSS-CONNECTION AND BACKFLOW CONTROL

The Hawaii Safe Drinking Water Law provides for the regulation of cross-connection and backflow prevention control.[54] The purpose of this program is to protect public water systems from the possibility of contamination by pollutants which could backflow or backsiphon into the system, and to promote the elimination or control of existing cross-connections through periodic inspection and testing.[55]

Backflow preventors are required to be installed between public water systems and any secondary water system.[56] Secondary water systems may include potable and non-potable water

---

50 Haw. Admin. Rules tit. 11, ch. 19.

51 *Id.* §§ 11-19-1 and -22.

52 *Id.* § 11-19-2.

53 For Department of Health responsibilities, *see id.* §§ 11-19-4, -6, -8 and -9. For responsibilities of other State and county agencies, *see id.* §§ 11-19-5 to -7.

54 Haw. Rev. Stat. § 340E-2(d). *See* Haw. Admin. Rules, tit. 11, ch. 21.

55 Haw. Admin. Rules § 11-21-1.

56 *Id.* § 11-21-6.

systems, plumbing fixtures and industrial piping systems. The backflow prevention device must satisfy nationwide specifications and standards.[57] The rules also contain guidelines for installation of backflow prevention devices for irrigation systems[58] and maintenance requirements which include periodic inspection and testing of the backflow preventors by a certified tester.[59]

Knowing violation of the backflow control rules is subject to a civil penalty of $500 and criminal prosecution for a misdemeanor. Failure to correct the violation may result in termination of water service to the affected building or facility.[60]

8.0 UNDERGROUND INJECTION CONTROL PROGRAM

The Safe Drinking Water Law establishes an Underground Injection Control ("UIC") Program designed to protect the State's underground sources of drinking water from pollution by subsurface disposal of fluids.[61] The function of the UIC Program is to protect the quality of Hawaii's underground sources of drinking water from chemical, physical, radioactive and biological contamination that could originate from injection well activity.[62] The rules set certain minimum standards regarding the location, design, construction, operation and monitoring of injection wells.[63] All persons are required to obtain a permit from the Department before constructing, operating, modifying or abandoning an injection well.[64] Specific rules also pertain

57 *Id.* § 11-21-4.

58 *Id.* § 11-21-7.

59 *Id.* § 11-21-8.

60 *Id.* § 11-21-9.

61 Haw. Admin. Rules tit. 11, ch. 23.

62 Hawaii State Department of Health, *Strategic Plan for Hawaii's Environmental Protection Programs* at 77 (January 1999).

63 *Id.* § 11-23-01. For siting and pre-construction requirements, *see id.* § 11-23-09. For well location requirements, *see id.* § 11-23-10. For operational requirements, *see id.* § 11-23-11. For well operation monitoring requirements, *see id.* § 11-23-18.

64 *Id.* § 11-23-12. For plugging and abandonment requirements, *see id.* § 11-23-19.

to the acquisition of injection well permits.[65] Through enforcement of the UIC program, the Department may revoke the permit of any party failing to meet state underground injection well standards. The Department also may seek civil and criminal fines from such parties.[66]

8.1 UNDERGROUND INJECTION CONTROL STANDARDS

The underground injection control program establishes standards which govern the location, construction and operation of injection wells so that the injected fluids do not migrate or pollute an underground source of drinking water. The UIC rules regulate all wells through which the subsurface disposal of fluids occurs or is intended to occur by means of injection. Individual waste water systems which serve a single family residential household and certain non-residential waste disposal systems which receive only sanitary wastes are exempted from the UIC standards.[67] The residential or non-residential waste disposal system must generate less than 1,000 gallons of waste per day in order to qualify for the exemption. Wells used for ground stabilization and test borings used for hydrologic or geotechnical investigations are also exempt, so long as the wells are plugged thereafter with an impermeable material.[68]

Underground sources of drinking water ("USDW") are defined as aquifers or portions of aquifers which supply a public or private drinking water system, or contain a sufficient quantity of groundwater to supply a public water system. All aquifers are considered to be USDW unless they are expressly exempted. Aquifers may be exempted from USDW status if they meet two criteria. First, the aquifer must not currently serve as a source of drinking water. Second, the aquifer cannot now and will not in the future serve as a source of drinking water due to one of three factors: recovery of water for drinking water is impractical; the water is so contaminated that it would be impractical to render the water fit for drinking; or the total dissolved solids

---

65 *Id.* §§ 11-23-12, -17.

66 *Id.* §§ 11-23-20 to -22.

67 *Id.* § 11-23-02.

68 *Id.*

concentration in the groundwater is above a certain level.[69] In terms of location, exempted aquifers under the State's rules are separated from USDW by the application of the UIC line. The UIC line is a line that circles or partitions portions of each island's inland areas and separates the USDW which are located mauka (mountainside) of the line from the exempted aquifers, which are located makai (oceanside) of the line. Unless an aquifer is expressly exempted as described on a UIC map, it is considered an USDW.[70]

The construction and operation of injection wells is limited in the State of Hawaii. Injection wells are categorized by the type of fluids which are injected into the well, and are designated into classes I through V. Wells in classes I through IV are completely prohibited. Class I wells involve disposal of hazardous, industrial or municipal waste. Class II wells involve fluids injected for use in oil or natural gas production or storage. Class III wells include wells used for extraction of minerals such as metals, sulfur, uranium, salts or potash. Class IV wells involve disposal from hazardous or radioactive waste management facilities.[71]

Only Class V wells may be installed and operated in the State. Class V wells are divided into several subclasses.[72] Subclass A includes injection wells which inject sewage or certain industrial fluids into USDWs. Subclass AB includes injection wells which inject sewage or certain industrial fluids only into exempted aquifers. After 1984, subclass A and AB wells may be constructed and operated only in an exempted aquifer.[73]

Subclasses B, C and D of Class V wells include all injection wells which inject non-polluting fluids into any geohydrologic formation, and may be permitted in both USDWs and

---

69 *Id.* § 11-23-04.

70 *Id.* §§ 11-23-04 to -05. The UIC maps are available for viewing and reproduction from the Department of Health, Safe Drinking Water Branch and are also available from the Branch's website at http://www.state.hi.us/doh/eh/sdwb/uicmaps.html (visited August 12, 2000).

71 *Id.* § 11-23-06(a).

72 *Id.* § 11-23-07(a).

73 *Id.* § 11-23-07(b).

exempted aquifers.[74] Subclass B wells include: air conditioning return flow wells; cooling water return flow wells; recharge wells used to replenish or store water in an aquifer; certain salt water intrusion barrier wells; wells used in aquaculture; and injection wells used in an experimental technology. Subclass C injection wells consist of storm runoff water drainage wells. Subclass D injection wells consist of wells for overflows or relief flows from potable water systems. Subclass E injection wells consist of wells associated with geothermal energy, brine, condensate and entrained gas injection. Subclass E injection wells may be constructed at various depths, provided the injection meets certain characteristics of the receiving formation water.[75]

8.2 INJECTION WELL PERMITS

A UIC permit is required prior to the construction of any injection well. Any new injection well must be sited at least one-quarter mile from any part of a drinking water source. Where the drinking water source draws water from an artesian aquifer located below an exempted caprock aquifer, the new injection wells must be located at least one-quarter mile from the drinking water source[76] and outside of a one-half mile wide area extending from the drinking water source, upgradient to the UIC line.

Subclasses B, C and E injection wells which are proposed to be mauka (mountainside) of the UIC line are required to be located a minimum of one-quarter mile from any drinking water source. In addition, an applicant for a Subclass B, C or E well permit can be required to submit water quality data representative of local conditions to the Department as part of the application. The water quality parameters which must be identified include and are not limited to the following: chloride concentration, total dissolved solids and coliform counts. The construction design of the injection well must prevent vertical migration of the fluids which would result in undesirable mixing of fluids from the aquifers.[77] Additional conditions are applicable for

---

74 *Id.* § 11-23-06.

75 *Id.* § 11-23-06(b)(6).

76 *Id.* § 11-23-09.

77 *Id*

construction of an injection well to be located in a caprock formation which overlies a volcanic underground source of drinking water.[78]

Operation, modification or abandonment of an injection well also requires a UIC permit or approval from the Department. Permit applications which involve injection wells on leasehold property must include written proof of consent from the landowner. An applicant may apply for a system permit instead of an individual permit if all the wells are to be owned by the same person, operated by the same person, similar in design, serve the same purpose and inject into the same aquifer or injection zone at the same property. Each application must be accompanied by a filing fee of $100 and specified data regarding the facility, proposed injection well, operating and testing plans.[79] In addition, the applicant must pay for all fees assessed for public notice where public notice is required.[80]

The Director must give public notice for all underground injection well applications for wells proposing to inject into an USDW. One purpose of the public notice is to inform the public of the impact of injecting and to minimize waste generation.[81] A minimum thirty day comment period must be provided by the Director, which may be extended at the Director's discretion. Any interested person may request a public hearing with respect to a UIC application which has received public notice. The Director may hold a public hearing if significant public interest is expressed. The public hearing must be held in the geographical area of the proposed injection well or another appropriate area.[82]

The operator of an injection well is required to keep records of the operation of the well, including the type and quantity of the injected fluids, and the method and rate of injection for each well. Any change in ownership of the well must be reported to the Director in writing

78 *Id.* § 11-23-10. Areas in the State which are known to have extensive caprock formation are listed in this rule.

79 *Id.* § 11-23-13(a).

80 *Id.* § 11-23-12.

81 State of Hawaii, Office of Environmental Quality Control, *1994 Annual Report of the Environmental Council*, at 19 (1995).

82 Haw. Admin. Rules § 11-23-14 to -15.

within one month.[83] Transfer of a UIC permit to a new owner must be approved by the Director.[84]

A permit application must be submitted for plugging and abandonment of an injection well. The Department may require that an abandoned well be plugged such that the detrimental movement of fluids between formations will not occur. The plugging should be completed by grouting by the tremie method in accordance with Department standards.[85] The Department also may order an injection well to be plugged if it is determined to be a threat to the groundwater resource or if the underground injection well no longer serves its intended purpose.[86]

8.3 UIC PROGRAM ENFORCEMENT AND PENALTIES

The Director may revoke, suspend or revise any UIC permit after the Director determines that there has been a violation of any term or condition of the permit, the permit was obtained by misrepresentation or the UIC permit was altered. A UIC permit also may be revoked or revised if there is a change in conditions which requires reduction or elimination of the permitted injection or if there has been a failure to comply with the Safe Drinking Water Law or the rules. The permittee must be given notice and an opportunity for a contested case hearing in accordance with the Hawaii Administrative Procedure Act.[87]

9.0 CERTIFICATION OF DRINKING WATER TREATMENT PLANT OPERATORS

Chapter 340F of the Hawaii Revised Statutes establishes the mandatory certification of operating personnel in water treatment plants ("Certification Law"). The Certification Law

83 *Id.* § 11-23-18.

84 *Id.* § 11-23-16(e).

85 *Id.* § 11-23-19. *See* City and County of Honolulu, Hawaii, Honolulu Board of Water Supply, Water Systems Standards (Mar. 1977).

86 Haw. Admin. Rules § 11-23-19.

87 *Id.* § 11-23-20. *See infra* ch. 13 of this Handbook.

requires that all water treatment plants be operated by a certified operator. Individuals who are not certified may not perform the duties of a water treatment plant operator.[88] The Certification law is administered by the Branch's Water Treatment Plant Operator Certification Program, whose function is to assure that drinking water treatment plants are staffed by qualified operators. The Certification Program receives applications and conducts operator certification training and testing.[89]

The Certification Law sets forth requirements for the minimum qualification of various levels of treatment plant operators and requires that all water treatment plants be operated under the direct supervision of an appropriately certified operator.[90] The Certification Law establishes a Board of Certification to carry out the functions of the law, including the classification of treatment plants and the establishment of criteria for issuance of operator certification, classes of certification and criteria for reciprocal recognition of other state certified personnel.[91] Rules have been adopted pursuant to the Certification Law to govern operation of the Board, application for certification, testing requirements, fees for certification, procedures for revocation, suspension and refusal to renew certification, continuing education credit requirements, education and work experience, issuance and renewal of certification.[92] The Rules provide that the classification of treatment plants is to be based upon the complexity of treatment processes utilized.[93]

The Certification Law imposes civil and criminal penalties for violation of the Law, rules or certificate. Injunctive relief may be granted to prevent further violations and civil penalties up to $25,000 may be imposed for each day of violation. Knowing misrepresentations made in any

---

88 Haw. Rev. Stat. § 340F-8.

89 Hawaii State Department of Health, *Strategic Plan for Hawaii's Environmental Protection Programs* at 78 (January 1999).

90 *Id.* § 340F-6.

91 *Id.* §§ 340F-4, -11, -12.

92 Haw. Admin. Rules tit. 11, ch. 25.

93 *Id.* § 11-25-11.

application, report, record or statement are subject to criminal prosecution for a misdemeanor.[94]

The Safe Drinking Water Branch anticipates that certification requirements for drinking water treatment plant operators will be expanded to include distribution system operators as well. As of the date of publication of this Handbook, the Safe Drinking Water Branch is hopeful that the public comment period for these amended rules will be completed in the latter half of the year 2000.[95]

10.0 WELLHEAD PROTECTION PROGRAM

The Hawaii Wellhead Protection Program was developed by the Department and approved by the EPA in May 1995.[96] The Wellhead Protection Program is administered by the Department's Safe Drinking Water Branch. The Wellhead Protection Program was developed by the Groundwater Protection Program in the Environmental Planning Office and was transferred to the Safe Drinking Water Branch in 1997.[97] The Program is a comprehensive, preventive, voluntary and community-based program intended to protect potable ground water in the State. The Program identifies the roles and responsibilities of the Department and county agencies and groups, delineates wellhead protection areas, identifies and inventories potential contamination sources within each protection area, and assists in the development of management strategies and contingency plans. The Program also establishes procedures for siting new drinking water wells, public participation and education, and management of information.

The Program anticipates the development of County Wellhead Protection Plans and the formation of working and advisory groups to assist the counties in the planning and implementation of the County Plans.

---

94 Haw. Rev. Stat. §§ 340F-9 to -10.

95 Interview with Stewart Yamada, State of Hawaii Department of Health, Safe Drinking Water Branch, July 31, 2000.

96 State of Hawaii, Department of Health, Hawaii Wellhead Protection Program Plan (May 1995). *See* Act approved May 27, 1986, ch. 220, 1986 Session Laws 385 (Act establishing Groundwater Protection Program).

97 Hawaii State Department of Health, *Strategic Plan for Hawaii's Environmental Protection Programs* at 75 (January 1999).

11.0 DRINKING WATER TREATMENT REVOLVING LOAN FUND

In 1997, the Legislature established the Drinking Water Treatment Revolving Loan Fund ("Fund").[98] The Fund is administered by the Branch's State Revolving Fund Program to assure low cost loans for qualifying public water systems and the Branch reports to EPA on the use of the funds.[99] Consistent with the State's policy of protecting and improving drinking water quality by financing eligible projects, the Director may approve grants, loans, and other financial assistance. The Fund may only be used for loans and financial assistance for facilitating compliance with national primary drinking water regulations or otherwise significantly furthering the health protection objectives of the SDWA. The Director must submit an annual report to the Legislature addressing the operations of the Fund, including information regarding each grant, loan, or other financial assistance made during the year.[100]

12.0 ENFORCEMENT MECHANISMS

Violators of the Safe Drinking Water Law and its rules face administrative, civil and criminal penalties.[101] Although the Branch realizes that formal enforcement actions are not the most expedient or desirable means of achieving compliance, the compliance section reviews public water system performance and achieves system compliance through technical assistance, formal enforcement and other means.[102] Violation of the UIC rules is subject to a civil penalty of $25,000 maximum per day of violation. Any party who violates the contaminant notification requirements is subject to penalties of not more than $25,000 for each violation.[103] Parties who violate any other provision of the Safe Drinking Water Law are also subject to civil penalties of

98 Haw. Rev. Stat. § 340E-35.

99 Hawaii State Department of Health, *Strategic Plan for Hawaii's Environmental Protection Programs* at 78 (January 1999).

100 Haw. Rev. Stat. § 340E-32, -33 and -36.

101 Haw. Rev. Stat. §§ 340E-7.

102 Hawaii State Department of Health, *Strategic Plan for Hawaii's Environmental Protection Programs* at 75, 77 (January 1999).

103 Haw. Rev. Stat. § 340E-8(e).

not more than $25,000 for each violation.[104] Willful violators of underground injection well rules are subject to criminal fines not more than $25,000 for each violation and may be imprisoned for not more than three years.[105] In addition, a party may be enjoined from engaging in any activity which violates the Law.[106]

Civil penalties may be imposed through administrative or judicial proceedings. The Director may issue a notice of violation, which becomes final in twenty days unless the alleged violator requests a hearing from the Director in writing. The hearing is conducted as a contested case hearing pursuant to the Hawaii Administrative Procedure Act.[107] If the Director orders immediate action to protect public health from an imminent and substantial harm, the Director must provide an opportunity for a hearing within twenty-four hours.[108] The Director may file a civil action to enforce an order, seek injunctive relief or any other appropriate remedy.[109]

Parties who tamper, attempt to tamper, or threaten to tamper with a public water system are subject to criminal penalties of imprisonment of not more than five years and fines in an amount not exceeding $500,000 upon conviction. If the party is an individual, the fine shall not exceed $250,000.[110] In addition, such parties are subject to civil penalties of not more than $50,000.[111] For purposes of enforcement, the term "tamper" is defined as the introduction of a contaminant into a public water system with the intention of harming persons, or to otherwise interfere with the operation of a public water system with the intention of harming persons.[112]

---

104 *Id.* § 340E-8(a).

105 *Id.* § 340E-8(b).

106 *Id.* § 340E-8(c).

107 Haw. Rev. Stat. ch. 91. *See infra* ch. 13 of this Handbook.

108 Haw. Rev. Stat. §§ 340E-4 and -8(d).

109 *Id.* § 340E-8(d)(2).

110 *Id.* § 340E-4.5(a).

111 *Id.* § 340E-4.5(b).

112 *Id.* § 340E-4.5(c).

The Director or an authorized representative may enter any facility of a supplier of water to determine compliance with the Safe Water Drinking Law and its rules. The inspection may extend to inspection of equipment, operation or sampling methods, taking samples of the public water system, inspection and copying of records.[113]

113 *Id.* § 340E-4.6; Haw. Admin. Rules § 11-20-33.

CHAPTER 5

SOLID WASTE MANAGEMENT

1.0 INTRODUCTION

Chapter 342H of the Hawaii Revised Statutes, the Solid Waste Management Law ("Solid Waste Law"), contains provisions for solid waste management and control of solid waste pollution.[1] The rules establish standards for solid waste management facilities and the permit program.[2]

The 1991 Legislature enacted a bill which promoted integrated solid waste management on both the state and county levels.[3] Chapter 342G, the Integrated Solid Waste Management Law, requires the establishment of integrated solid waste management plans with source reduction as the priority practice, promotes the use of recycled materials and mandates public education. This Law also established the Office of Solid Waste Management ("OSWM"), which has program responsibilities in three primary areas: municipal solid waste, special waste and alternative waste management. Specific program tasks include permitting, inspections, complaint response and enforcement. The OSWM also provides technical assistance and training, regulatory and policy development, and responds to requests for public records and information.[4] The Law also establishes the position of "recycling coordinator" within the OSWM.[5]

---

1 Haw. Rev. Stat. ch. 342H. All references to the Hawaii Revised Statutes are made to the printed version of the statutes current through the 1999 legislative session, unless otherwise noted. Where appropriate, references to acts passed during the 2000 legislative session have also been added.

2 Haw. Admin. Rules tit. 11, ch. 58.1 (Weil's 2000). All references to the Hawaii Administrative Rules are current through the date of the publication of this Handbook, unless otherwise noted.

3 Haw. Rev. Stat. ch. 342G.

4 State of Hawaii, Department of Health, *Strategic Plan for the Solid and Hazardous Waste Branch* at 11 (Draft Dec. 1995).

5 Haw. Rev. Stat. § 342-12.5.

The Department may use revenues generated by the environmental response tax and deposited in the environmental response revolving fund to address concerns related to solid waste.[6]

This chapter also addresses separate statutes which govern the recycling of lead acid batteries and used motor vehicle tires, the management and disposal of infectious waste and the recycling, transportation and disposal of used oil.

2.0 RELATIONSHIP TO FEDERAL LAW

The State is responsible for regulation of nonhazardous waste under Subchapter 4 of the Solid Waste Disposal Act.[7] The Hawaii Department of Health ("Department") is responsible for implementation and enforcement of solid waste laws and rules. The Environmental Protection Agency ("EPA") is authorized to promulgate rules which establish minimum criteria for control and monitoring requirements for solid waste disposal facilities.[8]

The Department is responsible for ensuring compliance with EPA's minimum requirements for municipal solid waste landfill units, which became effective on October 9, 1993. Within the Department, the OSWM is assigned this task. The Solid Waste Disposal Act requires states to develop permit programs for municipal solid waste landfills[9] which comply with the federal criteria.[10] The Department adopted rules to comply with EPA requirements in December 1993.[11] The rules were accepted by EPA as meeting the minimum federal requirements in June 1994.[12] EPA's determination of adequacy for the Hawaii program means

---

6 2000 Haw. Sess. Laws 245 (to be codified at Haw. Rev. Stat. § 128D-2).

7 42 U.S.C. § 6941 *et seq.*

8 Hazardous and Solid Waste Amendments of 1984, § 4010, 98 Stat. 3221. The implementing regulations are found in 40 C.F.R. Parts 260 - 281.

9 42 U.S.C. § 6945(c)(1)(B).

10 40 C.F.R. Part 258.

11 Haw. Admin. Rules, tit. 11, ch. 58.1.

12 Environmental Protection Agency, Notice of final determination of full program adequacy for Hawaii's application. 59 Fed. Reg. 28,523 (June 2, 1994).

that any covered facility owner or operator complying with the provisions of the Hawaii program is considered to be in compliance with the federal requirements.[13] The rules establish the minimum standards for design, construction, installation, operation and maintenance of solid waste disposal, recycling, reclamation and transfer systems.[14] The rules also apply to medical waste treatment, foreign waste treatment, used oil transport and recycling, hazardous waste, infectious waste and radioactive waste.[15]

3.0 DEFINITION OF SOLID WASTE

The statutory definition of solid waste includes any waste, without regard to its physical state. Solid waste is defined as:

> garbage, refuse, and other discarded materials, including solid, liquid, semisolid, or contained gaseous materials resulting from industrial, commercial, mining and agricultural operations, sludge from waste treatment plants and water supply treatment plants, and residues from air pollution control facilities and community activities, but does not include solid or dissolved materials in domestic sewage or other substances in water sources such as silt, dissolved or suspended solids in industrial waste water effluents, dissolved materials in irrigation return flows, or other common water pollutants, or source, special nuclear or by-product material. . .[16]

3.1 GENERAL RESPONSIBILITIES

The rules impose general responsibilities for the management of solid waste. Responsibility for the sanitary, aesthetic and nonhazardous storage of solid waste is placed upon the owner, operator or manager of the facility where the solid waste is accumulated. Generally, all persons who own, operate or manage a business, property, industry or establishment are required to remove accumulated solid waste to an approved solid waste disposal facility before

---

13 59 Fed. Reg. 28,523, -28,524.

14 Haw. Admin. Rules § 11-58.1-01.

15 Haw. Admin. Rules § 11-58.1-02.

16 Haw. Rev. Stat. § 342H-1 and Haw. Admin Rules § 11-58.1-03.

the solid waste creates a health or safety hazard, or nuisance condition.[17] Land owners and occupants are responsible for the disposal of animal carcasses found on their property. The carcass must be immediately disposed of, either by on-site burial or some other method approved by the Director.[18]

Owners and operators of solid waste disposal facilities are required to develop and implement a plan at the facility to detect and prevent the disposal of hazardous waste[19] and polychlorinated biphenyls ("PCBs"). Pesticide containers must be prepared for disposal pursuant to Department of Agriculture rules. Soil which is determined to be hazardous must be treated and disposed of as hazardous waste.[20] Infectious waste which has been treated and rendered non-infectious may be incinerated or disposed of at municipal solid waste landfills. Infectious waste which is generated within a household may be disposed of as residential solid waste.[21] The disposal of radioactive wastes is subject to state regulation,[22] as well as regulation by the U.S. Nuclear Regulatory Commission.[23]

In addition to the general responsibilities, additional responsibilities are imposed on owners and operators of solid waste disposal facilities for special wastes, such as scrap cars, white goods, tires and green waste. All solid waste facilities must develop a plan to separate or ban green waste. The plan must require diversion of seventy-five percent of commercially generated green waste and fifty percent of residentially generated green waste. If the Director determines, from data submitted by the facility on its annual report, that these diversion rates are

---

17 Haw. Admin. Rules § 11-58.1-61(b). For exemptions, *see* § 11-58.1-04(b).

18 *Id.* § 11-58.1-61(c).

19 *See infra* ch. 6 of this Handbook.

20 Haw. Admin. Rules § 11-58.1-62.

21 *Id.* § 11-58.1-63.

22 *See infra* ch. 11 of this Handbook.

23 Haw. Admin. Rules § 11-58.1-64. For a discussion of Hawaii's radiation control rules, *see infra* ch. 11 of this Handbook.

not achieved, then the acceptance of all commercial and residential green waste may be banned.[24] In addition to the restrictions placed on the acceptance of green waste, solid waste disposal facilities may not accept scrap cars, white goods such as electrical or mechanical appliances or whole motor vehicle tires.[25] All solid waste disposal facilities must develop and implement a plan to enforce this ban.[26]

4.0 PERMITS

Written approval from the Director of the Department of Health ("Director") is required to operate a solid waste management system.[27] A permit is required to establish, operate or modify any solid waste management facility, part, addition or extension.[28] The following activities and facilities are exempted from the permitting requirement: composting of vegetative solid waste by single family or duplex residential property; agricultural solid waste disposal facilities for waste from product processing; private landfills for up to 150 tons per year of rock, soil, concrete or other nondecomposable, uncontaminated inert materials generated on-site; incinerator facilities with a total rated capacity of less than one ton per hour; and other minor sources as determined by the Director.[29] Permitting requirements apply to all persons, including state and county government. Solid waste disposal other than at a permitted solid waste disposal system, in amount greater than one cubic yard requires prior written approval of the Director.[30] The operation of an open dump is flatly prohibited.[31]

---

24 *Id.* § 11-58.1-65(a)-(b).

25 These items may be accepted at transfer facilities. *See id.* § 11-58.1-31.

26 *Id.* § 11-58.1-65(c).

27 Haw. Rev. Stat. § 342H-30.

28 Haw. Admin. Rules § 11-58.1-04(a).

29 *Id.* § 11-58.1-04(b).

30 Haw. Rev. Stat. § 342H-30(c).

31 *Id.*

4.1 REQUIREMENTS

Applications for permits are made to the Department and must contain detailed plans and specifications for the facility, certification of compliance with local ordinances and zoning requirements and a detailed operations report. In addition, the operation of a disposal facility must be recorded with the Bureau of Conveyances. The operations report must include the proposed method of operation, population and area to be served, the characteristics, quantity and source of the material to be processed, the proposed ultimate use of the land, the method of processed residue disposal, and emergency procedures and equipment to be used.[32] In addition, a closure and land use plan which includes identification of contaminant compounds and a plan to address the contaminants must be submitted as part of the application. A detailed assessment and final closure plan must be submitted 180 days before closure.[33]

Applications must be accompanied by the appropriate filing fee. The fees range from $50 for composting, salvage, recycling and materials recovery facilities to $1,000 for incinerators and landfills handling over twenty tons per day. Facilities which qualify for "permit by rule" are assessed a $25 filing fee.[34]

4.2 PERMIT PROCEDURE

The signing applicant must be a person who will assume responsibility for the construction, modification or operation of the facility in accordance with the State laws and rules. When the applicant is a partnership or group other than a corporation, one member of the group must submit the application. If the applicant is a county or a corporation, one individual, such as an officer of the corporation or general manager of the facility, or an authorized representative of the county shall make the application and assume this responsibility.[35]

---

32 Haw. Admin. Rules § 11-58.1-04(c)(1).

33 State of Hawaii, Department of Health, Permit Application for Solid Waste Disposal Facilities, Attachment P-4 (Rev. Nov. 1997). The OSWM anticipates that the application form will be revised shortly after publication of this Handbook. Interview with Lene Ichinotsubo, Solid and Hazardous Waste Branch, Department of Health (August 3, 2000).

34 Haw. Admin. Rules § 11-58.1-04(h).

35 *Id.* § 11-58.1-04(c)(2).

The Department has 180 days to notify the applicant in writing of its approval or disapproval of the permit application. Except for those permits which are part of a federally approved or delegated program, the failure of the Director to act upon an application shall be deemed a grant of the application.[36] Permits for municipal solid waste landfill units are part of the federally approved program and therefore are not subject to the 180 day automatic permit approval.

No application may be denied without the opportunity for an administrative hearing in accordance with the Hawaii Administrative Procedure Act.[37] The rules direct the Director to approve the application for the permit if the application and the supporting information show that the issuance of the permit is in the public interest, and that the solid waste disposal facility is designed, built and equipped in accordance with the best practicable technology so that the facility can operate in compliance with applicable rules.[38]

The factors which the Director must consider in determining the public interest include the environmental impact of the proposed action, any adverse environmental effects which cannot be avoided should the action be implemented, the alternatives to the proposed action, the relationship between local short-term uses of the environment, and the maintenance and enhancement of long-term productivity. The Director must consider any irreversible and irretrievable commitments of resources which would be involved in the proposed action. The Director may prescribe by rule any other factors to be considered. The Solid Waste Law requires that "any determination of public interest must promote the optimum balance between economic development and environmental quality," but does not indicate what that optimum balance shall be.[39]

---

36 Haw. Rev. Stat. § 342H-4(d) and Haw. Admin Rules § 11-58.1-04(c)(3). The applicant must act consistently with the plans and specifications submitted in the application. *Id.*

37 Haw. Admin. Rules § 11-58.1-04(c)(4). *See* Haw. Rev. Stat. ch. 91. *See also infra* ch. 13 of this Handbook.

38 Haw. Admin. Rules § 11-58.1-04(c)(4).

39 Haw. Rev. Stat. § 342H-4(c).

The issuance of a permit is conditioned upon compliance with established requirements.[40] Conditions of the permit may include a requirement that the applicant provide necessary facilities for sampling and testing to determine the degree of pollution from the solid waste facility. Commencement of the work by the applicant is deemed to be an acceptance of all the permit conditions.[41]

The maximum duration of a permit is five years, with additional renewal periods of up to five years each.[42] Permits are not transferable without the written approval of the Director.[43] The permit holder is required to notify the Director within ninety days of permanent termination of a solid waste facility operations.[44]

The Director may modify, suspend or revoke a permit, if after an administrative hearing, the Director determines that any condition of the permit was violated, the permit was obtained by misrepresentation or failure to disclose fully all relevant facts, or that such action is in the public interest. Additionally, the Director is authorized to modify, suspend or revoke a permit if there is a change in any condition that requires either a temporary or permanent reduction or elimination of the permitted disposal.[45]

4.3 VARIANCES

A variance is a written authorization from the Director for disposal of solid waste not in conformance with the applicable standards and rules.[46] An application for a variance is made by providing the Department with a detailed description of the present conditions of the solid waste

---

40 Haw. Admin. Rules § 11-58.1-04(c)(6).

41 *Id.*

42 Haw. Rev. Stat. § 342H-4; Haw. Admin. Rules § 11-58.1-04(e)(1).

43 Haw. Admin. Rules § 11-58.1-04(e)(2).

44 *Id.* § 11-58.1-04(e)(3).

45 Haw. Rev. Stat. § 342H-4(c).

46 *Id.* § 342H-1.

disposal facility, how the conditions do not conform to the applicable standards and any supporting information which may be relevant or which the Director may require.[47] Variances may not be granted for municipal solid waste landfill units unless variances are specifically allowed in the rules adopted by the Director.[48]

Any successful application for a variance must show that the continuation of the function or operation involved in the solid waste disposal which requires the variance is in the public interest, that the disposal occurring or proposed to occur does not substantially endanger human health or safety, and that compliance with the applicable standards or rules from which variance is sought would produce serious hardship without equal or greater benefits to the public.[49]

If the variance is granted on the ground that there is no practicable means known or available for the adequate prevention, control or abatement of the solid waste pollution involved, the variance will be granted only until such means become practicable.[50] Variances which are granted on this "no practicable means" basis are subject to prescription by the Department of any substitute or alternate methods of treatment. Every variance is subject to such conditions as the Director may prescribe and variance renewals will be allowed only after a thorough review of the practicable technology.[51]

The Director may hold an administrative hearing in relation to an application for the issuance, renewal or modification of a variance, but is not required to do so.[52] However, every application for a variance is subject to public notice and comment requirements.[53] These requirements include provisions for public notice within the geographical area of the facility and

---

47 *Id.* § 342H-5(a)-(b).

48 *Id.* § 342H-5(i).

49 *Id.* § 342H-5(c).

50 *Id.* § 342H-5(d)(1).

51 *Id.* § 342H-5(d)(3).

52 *Id.* § 342H-5(f).

53 *Id.* § 342H-5(h).

to other interested persons. At least thirty days must be allowed for the receipt of written comments from the public.

5.0 STANDARDS FOR SOLID WASTE DISPOSAL FACILITIES

The Solid Waste Law prohibits the operation of an open dump or solid waste disposal system without written approval from the Director. In addition, the dumping or discharge of solid waste, or arranging directly or indirectly for the disposal of solid waste in an amount greater than one cubic yard is prohibited, without prior written approval from the Director.[54] Counties are permitted to adopt rules regarding the control and management of solid waste, so long as the matter is not governed by either state law or Department rules.[55]

New solid waste facilities are required to provide for the detection of groundwater contamination and for corrective action. Existing dumps are permitted to upgrade to satisfy these requirements. The application of EPA's minimum criteria determines whether a facility is considered an "open dump." An "open dump" is defined as a disposal site that is not operating in conformance with applicable standards, rules, permits or the Solid Waste Law.[56] The 1992 revisions to the Solid Waste Law require all entities, including the county, state and federal governments, to obtain a permit from the Director prior to construction, operation, modification or closure of a municipal solid waste landfill ("MSWL") unit.[57]

5.1 STANDARDS FOR MUNICIPAL SOLID WASTE LANDFILLS

Municipal solid waste landfills ("MSWLs") accept waste from residential and commercial sources, and are generally owned by the counties.[58] The minimum state criteria for

---

54 *Id.* § 342H-30.

55 *Id.* § 342H-19.

56 *Id.* § 342H-1.

57 *Id.* § 342H-52.

58 On Oahu, Waimanalo Landfill is the only solid waste landfill in operation. Interview with Lene Ichinotsubo, Solid and Hazardous Waste Branch, Department of Health (August 3, 2000).

MSWLs were adopted in December 1993.[59] The criteria are applicable to owners and operators of new and existing MSWLs as well as lateral expansions of existing MSWLs. Those MSWL units which did not receive waste after October 9, 1991 are exempted. MSWL units that received waste after October 9, 1991, but stopped receiving waste before October 9, 1993 are exempt from the criteria except for the installation of a final cover as specified in the rules.[60] In order to maintain this conditional exemption, the MSWL must install the final cover within six months from the date of the last receipt of waste.[61]

Open dumps are prohibited.[62] All MSWLs are required to obtain a permit issued by the Department.[63] Public notice is given for all applications regarding MSWL construction, operation, modification or renewal.[64] The public notice must be circulated within the subject geographical area by publication and mailing. A public comment period of at least thirty days must be given. A public hearing may be held if the Director determines that a public hearing is warranted, based upon the comments received.[65]

5.1.1 MUNICIPAL SOLID WASTE LANDFILL CRITERIA

The MSWL criteria apply several design, operation and closure requirements to new and existing MSWLs, including MSWLs that are used to dispose of sewage sludge. First, the criteria require that owners and operators of new, expanded and existing MSWLs perform a site analysis.[66] The site analysis must include criteria such as bird hazard to aircraft, floodplains,

---

59 Haw. Admin. Rules tit. 11, ch. 58.1.

60 Haw. Rev. Stat. 342H-53 and Haw. Admin. Rules § 11-58.1-11. For final cover requirements, *see id.* § 11-58.1-17(a)(1).

61 Haw. Rev. Stat. § 342H-53 and Haw. Admin. Rules § 11-58.1-11.

62 Haw. Admin. Rules § 11-58.1-11(h)-(i).

63 *Id.* § 11-58.1-12.

64 *See id.* § 11-58.1-12(b)(5) for content requirements of the public notice.

65 *Id.* § 11-58.1-12(b)(6).

66 *Id.* § 11-58.1-13.

wetlands, marine sanctuary requirements, fault areas, seismic impact zones, unstable areas and tsunami zones. Second, the MSWL criteria establish design requirements such as exceedence of aquifer contaminant levels and composite liners.[67] Third, the operating requirements for MSWLs should include criteria such as procedures to exclude the receipt of hazardous waste, and should cover material requirements, disease vector control, explosive gases control, air criteria, access requirements, runoff control systems and surface water requirements.[68]

Generally, liquid waste in bulk form and noncontainerized liquid waste may not be disposed of in MSWLs. However, there are two exceptions to this prohibition. Household waste other than septic waste, and leachate or gas condensate water derived from the leachate collection system may be placed in the MSWL. Containerized liquid waste is permitted in MSWL only if the liquid waste is household waste, the container is a small size normally found in household waste or the container is designed to hold liquids for a use other than storage. Oil filters which are crushed or drained for at least twenty-four hours and are not a regulated hazardous waste may be disposed of in a MSWL.[69]

Records of all required plans, inspections, results and procedures must be kept near the facility or in another location approved by the Director. The Director is authorized to impose any other requirements necessary to protect public health, safety and welfare.[70]

Groundwater protection provisions apply to all MSWLs, unless the owner or operator can certify, through a qualified groundwater scientist and site specific field measurements and transport predictions, that there is no potential for the migration of hazardous constituents from the MSWL to the uppermost aquifer. MSWLs must conduct groundwater monitoring throughout the active life and post-closure care period for the MSWL by using a goundwater monitoring system sufficient to yield samples from the uppermost aquifer. The rules specify sampling and

---

67 *Id.* § 11-58.1-14.

68 *Id.* § 11-58.1-15.

69 *Id.* § 11-58.1-15(i).

70 *Id.* § 11-58.1-15(j)-(k).

analysis criteria and also require a detection monitoring system for certain constituents such as heavy metals.[71]

When MSWL's detect a statistically significant increase in groundwater contaminants, an assessment monitoring program is triggered. The MSWL must perform an assessment of corrective measures, and select a remedy which is protective of human health and the environment, which will attain groundwater protection standards and reduce or eliminate the source of releases. The MSWL must then implement the selected remedy.[72]

5.1.2 CLOSURE AND POST-CLOSURE CARE OF MSWLs

The closure criteria for MSWLs require the installation of a final cover which is designed to minimize erosion and infiltration. A written closure plan must be prepared by the owner or operator of each MSWL which describes the steps that need to be taken to close the MSWL at any time during its active life. The closure plan for each MSWL is due on the initial date waste is received. Generally, closure activities must be started within thirty days after final receipt of wastes. Closure must be completed within 180 days unless an extension is granted by the Director.

Post-closure care must be conducted for thirty years, unless the time period is decreased by the Director. Post-closure care includes, at a minimum, maintenance and repair of the final cover, maintenance and operation of the leachate collection system, groundwater monitoring, and maintenance and operation of the gas monitoring system.[73]

5.1.3 FINANCIAL ASSURANCE REQUIREMENTS FOR MSWLs

The financial assurance requirements are applicable to all owners and operators of MSWLs, except owners and operators who are state or federal government entities. Financial

---

71 *Id.* § 11-58.1-16.

72 *Id.* § 11-58.1-16(e)-(g).

73 *Id.* § 11-58.1-17. Following completion of closure activities, the owner or operator must record a notation on the deed to the facility property indicating its use as a landfill facility and that its use is restricted.

assurance requirements became effective in April 1994 and apply closure, post-closure care and corrective action. The financial assurance must be continuous and adequate to cover the cost of hiring a third party to close the largest area of the MSWL unit. All estimates for financial assurance must be adjusted upward to reflect the maximum costs of closure, post-closure care or corrective action. The owner or operator must also annually adjust the closure cost estimate for inflation. Owners and operators must choose one or a combination of the following allowable financial assurance mechanisms: trust fund, surety bond, letter of credit, insurance, other state approved mechanism or assumption of responsibility.[74]

5.2 CONSTRUCTION AND DEMOLITION WASTE LANDFILLS

Construction and demolition waste is defined as solid waste resulting from the repair, construction, razing or demolition of roads, buildings and other structures.[75] Construction and demolition waste includes debris which is generated from land clearing activities in preparation for construction. The rules provide the following examples of construction and demolition waste: plaster, roofing, hollow tile, concrete, glass, wood, dirt, rock, stumps and boulders. In addition, the following wastes are specifically exempted from classification as construction and demolition waste: cleanup materials contaminated with hazardous substances, friable asbestos, waste solvents or similar materials, paints, adhesives and sealers.[76] A construction and demolition landfill which is used only by the site owner or person in control of the site and accepts less than 150 tons per year of concrete, rock, soil and other inert or non-decomposable materials generated on-site is exempt from permitting requirements.[77]

---

74 *Id.* § 11-58.1-18.

75 *Id.* § 11-58.1-03, definition of "construction and demolition waste."

76 *Id.* § 11-58.1-19(a).

77 *Id.* §11-58.1-04(b)(3).

A permit is required for all construction and demolition waste landfills, unless exempted.[78] An operations plan and engineering report must be included with the permit application. The plan must include methods to control drainage, nuisance conditions, disease vectors and an emergency fire plan. The report must provide for controlled access to the landfill, a leachate management plan, and information regarding user population, site description, land utilization and the characteristics and volume of the construction and demolition solid waste.[79] Three minimum design requirements must be incorporated into landfill design. First, construction and demolition waste landfills must not be located near fault areas prone to flooding, wetlands, close to potable water supplies, near fault areas or other unstable locations. Second, a minimum of three groundwater monitoring wells must be installed to provide for adequate groundwater quality and flow analysis. Third, a minimum underlying soil liner, two feet thick, with specific permeability characteristics, must be installed.[80]

The operation of construction and demolition landfills are subject to several requirements. The following wastes may not be accepted at the landfill: hazardous waste, liquids, pesticide containers (unless they qualify as household waste),[81] electrical transformers which contain PCBs or any other type of oil, and electrical transformers from a non-demolition project site. Friable asbestos containing materials may be accepted at the landfill as long as the asbestos waste conforms to federal requirements.[82] In addition, petroleum contaminated soil which complies with the facility permit special conditions may be disposed of in the landfill.[83]

---

78 On the Island of Oahu, the sole commercial construction and demolition landfill is located at Nanakuli, on the Waianae Coast of Oahu. Interview with Lene Ichinotsubo, Solid and Hazardous Waste Branch, Department of Health (August 3, 2000).

79 Haw. Admin. Rules § 11-58.19(b).

80 *Id.* § 11-58.1-19(c). Alternative liner and groundwater monitoring systems may be required and approved by the Director.

81 *See infra* ch. 6 of this Handbook.

82 *See* 40 C.F.R. Part 61.

83 Haw. Admin. Rules § 11-58.1-19(d)(2), (6), (7).

The operating requirements include an interim minimum earthen cover of six inches and a final minimum earthen cover of two feet. Daily operating records must be kept by the facility owner or operator which include waste volume and description data. Records must also be kept of major deviations from the operation plan such as fires or explosions at the facility. Finally, a notation on the deed or some other real property instrument normally reviewed during a title search must be made to notify potential purchasers of the landfill use and restrictions on future land use of the property.[84]

Generally, a groundwater protection and monitoring plan is required for construction and demolition waste landfills, unless exempted by the Director. The groundwater monitoring plan must include the location and description of each well constructed, boring logs and a monitoring wellhead protection plan. Baseline groundwater data must be obtained before starting operations. A series of heavy metal analyses, as well as cyanide, total petroleum hydrocarbons, total organic carbon and chemical oxygen demand analyses must be completed. Sampling plans must be submitted to the Director and corrective actions must be taken if the testing results are deficient.[85] Closure, post-closure and financial assurance requirements which have been established for MSWLs are applicable to construction and demolition landfills.[86] An annual report must be submitted to the Department by July 30 of each year. The annual report must detail the origin and transporter of all waste received at the facility, as well as the weight or volume of the waste received.[87]

6.0 STANDARDS FOR RECYCLING FACILITIES

The construction and operation of recycling and material recovery facilities are regulated under the Solid Waste Law. Recycling facilities are facilities at which the following activities take place: on-site separation of recyclables from nonrecyclables; processing of source separated

84 *Id.* § 11-58.1-19(d)(3)-(5).

85 *Id.* § 11-58.1-19(e).

86 *Id.* § 11-58.1-19(f)-(g).

87 *Id.* § 11-58.1-19(h).

materials such as metal sludges, motor oil and batteries; and collection, purchase, brokering, bailing, compacting or shredding of recyclable materials. Certain facilities are exempt from regulation under this section. Composting facilities that treat or separate ash, sludge or green waste are exempt.[88] Recycling drop-off centers, facilities which buy back refillable containers and facilities which process regulated or hazardous waste only and do not produce a solid waste or recycled material are exempt from this section. In addition, the repair and re-sale of clean, source separated furniture and clothing, and manufacturing processes using clean, source separated plastic, glass or paper products as feedstock for production of an end-product for resale are exempt.[89]

A permit is required to construct and operate a facility engaged in the treatment, storage, collection or recovery of recyclable material. The application must include a site analysis and design specifications which address equipment, drainage, nuisance, health and safety control. An operations plan must be submitted which discusses residue disposal, the recoverable materials collected, the means used to weigh or measure all materials accepted by the facility, recyclables recovered, bypass waste and residue disposal. A closure plan must be prepared for the facility by the owner or operator.[90] Finally, each recycling facility must submit an annual report to the Director by July 30 of each year which summarizes the volume of recoverable material that was accepted, processed, transported and disposed.[91]

7.0 STANDARDS FOR SOLID WASTE INCINERATION

Facilities which reduce the volume of solid waste through use of an enclosed combustion device are subject to regulation under the Solid Waste Law.[92] Solid waste incinerators which

---

88 *See infra* § 10.0 of this Chapter.

89 Haw. Admin. Rules § 11-58.1-32(a).

90 *Id.* § 11-58.1-32(b).

91 *Id.* § 11-58.1-32(c).

92 *Id.* § 11-58.1-20.

dispose of infectious waste also must comply with the Infectious Waste Law requirements.[93] Solid waste incinerators may be subject to the Air Pollution Control Law requirements.[94] Incinerators which have a total rated capacity of less than one ton per hour are exempt from solid waste permit requirements.[95] All municipal solid waste incinerators are required to obtain a permit from the Director. The permit application must include a site plan and analysis which addresses public access, surrounding land uses, a description of area and the location of any equipment. The Director may require a description of mitigative measures.[96]

The design requirements for an incinerator are similar to the requirements for a MSWL. An engineering report must address the overall process, include a process flow diagram, describe anticipated performance and design criteria. The following issues must also be addressed in the permit application: equipment, drainage, nuisance, health and safety control, ash residue system, operation plan, compliance with state air pollution regulations and provisions for periodic cleaning to maintain the plant in a sanitary and clean condition.[97]

The operating requirements applicable to incinerators are similar to the MSWL and construction waste landfill requirements. Incinerators may not accept hazardous waste, liquids or pesticide containers unless they qualify as household waste,[98] electrical transformers containing PCBs or any other oil, or transformers generated from a non-demolition project.[99] The facility must be operated in accordance with the operations plan which has been approved by the Director. The ash residue must be treated as special waste and must be disposed of in an ash monofill landfill which accepts only ash residue from incinerators. Daily operating records must be maintained at the facility, which should include information regarding the solid waste

---

93 *See infra* § 15 of this Chapter.

94 *See supra* ch. 2 of this Handbook.

95 Haw. Admin. Rules §§ 11-58.1-04(b)(4), -20(b).

96 *Id.* § 11-58.1-20(c).

97 *Id.* § 11-58.1-20(d).

98 *See infra* ch. 6 of this Handbook.

99 Haw. Admin. Rules § 11-58.1-20(e)(6).

accepted at the facility and the ash residue generated by the facility. An annual report must be submitted to the Director by July 30 of each year which addresses the facility's operations for the previous fiscal year.[100]

Specific sampling and analysis requirements have been established for incinerators. The ash residue must be tested within one month of beginning operation and twice per year thereafter, or as otherwise determined by the Director. Representative samples of the solid waste and ash residue must be tested for heavy metals and other parameters determined by the Director. Organic matter content in the ash residue must be limited to a maximum of ten percent. All analyses must be completed in accordance with EPA methods.[101]

8.0 STANDARDS FOR TRANSFER STATIONS

All owners and operators of solid waste transfer stations must obtain a permit to construct and operate. The permit application must include a site analysis and satisfy design requirements for drainage, machinery and equipment, facility signage and nuisance, health and safety controls. The application must include an operation and a closure plan. Transfer stations may accept only household and commercial waste.[102] Industrial, hazardous, infectious, construction or demolition waste may not be accepted at transfer stations. Solid waste collected at a transfer facility must be treated, recycled, collected or disposed of at a permitted solid waste disposal facility. The operations plan must provide a plan for transfer of the accepted waste to a solid waste disposal facility.[103]

Operating records must be kept at the transfer facility, including a daily log of the solid waste received and transported, as well as the identification of the disposal site. An annual report listing the volume or weight of waste received, origin and transporter of the solid waste

---

100 *Id.* § 11-58.1-20(e).

101 *Id.* § 11-58.1-20(f).

102 Commercial waste is waste generated by nonmanufacturing entities. *Id.* § 11-58.1-03.

103 *Id.* § 11-58.1-31(b).

and the ultimate disposal site must be filed with the Director by July 30 of each year. Owners of more than one transfer station may submit a combined annual report.[104]

9.0 STANDARDS FOR SOLID WASTE SALVAGE FACILITIES

The construction and operation of salvage or materials recovery facilities is regulated under the Solid Waste Law. Salvage facilities include junkyards, processors of white goods (large electrical and mechanical appliances), scrap metal and automobile dismantlers. Small facilities which store fewer than twenty-five units of white goods or cars are exempt.[105]

As with other solid waste facilities, a permit is required for construction and operation of a salvage or materials recovery facility. The permit application must include the standard application components: site analysis, design requirements for equipment, drainage, nuisance, health and safety control, operation plan and closure plan.[106] Annual reporting to the Director is required by July 30 of each year. The report must summarize the volume of incoming material, the salvageable materials recovered and how it was disposed.[107]

10.0 STANDARDS FOR RECLAMATION FACILITIES

Composting facilities are regulated as solid waste reclamation facilities. The construction and operation of composting facilities for solid wastes, including sewage sludge and green waste (yard waste) requires a permit from the Director. Small composting facilities which process less than three thousand tons of green waste per year are exempt from the individual permit requirements and instead are permitted by rule.[108]

---

104 *Id.* § 11-58.1-31(c).

105 *Id.* § 11-58.1-33(a).

106 *Id.* § 11-58.1-34(b).

107 *Id.* § 11-58.1-34(c).

108 *Id.* § 11-58.1-41(a).

Permit applications must include several standard minimum components. Site analysis, design requirements, operation and closure plans must be part of the permit application. The design requirements must include engineering plans, manufacturer performance data for the equipment, temperature monitoring plan, nuisance, health and safety controls. The facility must be located to minimize leachate release, and a leachate collection and treatment system is required. For sewage sludge composting facilities, the maximum contaminant levels must meet federal requirements.[109]

The operation plan should include a description and process flow diagram for the facility. A description of the source, quantity and quality of the solid waste, bulking materials and analysis of sewage sludge (if applicable) must be included in operation plan. The operation plan must require that the compost product be free of offensive odors, be chemically and biologically stable, free of injurious components or pathogens and able to sustain plant growth. Solid waste that may be pathogenic is permitted to be composted, provided that a method specified by the rules is utilized. The operation plan must describe the ultimate use for the compost, disposal for compost that cannot be used and the method of removal of compost from the site. Finally, a closure plan must be submitted with each permit application.[110]

Each composting facility is required to submit an annual report to the Director by July 30 of each year. The annual report must include a summary of monitoring activities, type and quantity of solid waste received, and amount of compost produced and removed from the facility.[111]

11.0 STANDARDS FOR REMEDIATION FACILITIES

The requirements under this section are applicable to the construction and operation of off-site remediation facilities. Facilities which are developed for one-time operation are exempt from these rules. Remediation facilities may use biological, chemical or physical conversion

109 *See* 40 C.F.R. Part 503.

110 Haw. Admin. Rules § 11-58.1-41(b).

111 *Id.* § 11-58.1-41(c).

processes to treat wastes. As a basic requirement, each facility must be in the best interest of the public and must utilize best practicable technology.[112]

Each permit application for a remediation facility must include a site analysis and design requirements. Design requirements which are specific to remediation facilities include protection of groundwater resources and prevention of soil contamination. Remediation facilities must be located in an impermeable area so as to prevent contamination. A liner of sufficient thickness may be used to satisfy this requirement. A leachate and runoff collection system must be installed at the remediation facility. As with other solid waste processing facilities, an operation plan and closure plan is required.[113] An annual report must be submitted to the Director by July 30 of each year which summarizes the amount of incoming material and the amount of material treated from the remediation process.[114]

12.0 SPECIAL WASTE MANAGEMENT

The solid waste regulations identify and separate certain solid waste to be handled and disposed of as "special wastes." Special wastes include any solid wastes which require proper processing or disposal because of their source or physical, chemical or biological characteristics.[115] The following special wastes have specific management and disposal requirements: asbestos, incinerator ash, medical waste, lead acid batteries, used motor vehicle tires, foreign waste, municipal waste, and petroleum contaminated soil.

Owners and operators of landfills that accept special wastes are required to obtain a permit from the Director. The permit application must include the standard solid waste permit application components: site analysis, design requirements and operation plan. The annual reporting requirement also applies to special waste landfills.[116]

---

112 *Id.* § 11-58.1-42(a).

113 *Id.* § 11-58.1-42(b).

114 Haw. Admin. Rules § 11-58.1-42(c).

115 *Id.* § 11-58.1-03.

116 *Id.* § 11-58.1-51.

12.1 PETROLEUM CONTAMINATED SOIL

Petroleum contaminated soil ("PCS") is frequently generated in the course of response actions to leaking underground storage tanks, above ground tanks and surface spillage of petroleum products. In the State of Hawaii, petroleum contaminated soil is the most common non-hazardous contaminated media that presents environmental risk and requires special handling. "Petroleum contaminated soil" is defined to mean soil that has been contaminated by a release of petroleum to a degree that exceeds certain levels determined to be acceptable to the Director.[117] The transportation of PCS requires a permit from the Department, unless the transporter provides written notification to the Department at least forty-eight hours before any proposed transportation of PCS.[118] The remediation of PCS may be accomplished at permitted solid waste remediation facilities.[119] Several commercial PCS remediation facilities have begun operation on the Island of Oahu since 1992, employing a variety of technologies, including bioremediation and thermal remediation.

12.2 FOREIGN SOLID WASTE

Foreign solid waste means garbage generated by carriers which have left foreign ports and whose first port of entry into the United States is the State of Hawaii.[120] The treatment and disposal of foreign solid waste must comply with the United States Department of Agriculture regulations regarding garbage.[121] For treatment and disposal of foreign wastes, sterilization and incineration are the methods approved by the rules.[122] Treatment facilities which treat foreign

---

117 Haw. Rev. Stat. § 342H-1.

118 *Id.* § 342H-4.5.

119 *See supra* § 11.0 of this Chapter.

120 Haw. Admin. Rules §§ 11-58.1-03 and 11-58.1-53. Although the term "port" is not defined in the Solid Waste Law or rules, other Hawaii statutes use "port" with reference to both aircraft and vessels. *See, e.g.*, Haw. Rev. Stat. § 142-8.

121 7 C.F.R. § 330.400.

122 Haw. Admin. Rules § 11-58.1-53(a).

solid waste are required to comply with the requirements applicable to solid waste incinerators, refuse-derived fuel processing facilities,[123] and medical waste treatment and disposal facilities.[124]

13.0 INTEGRATED SOLID WASTE MANAGEMENT PLAN

In 1991, the Legislature enacted the Hawaii Integrated Solid Waste Management Act ("Integrated Management Act" or "Act") which requires that a comprehensive integrated solid waste management plan ("Plan") be developed by each county and by the State.[125] The most recent revision of Hawaii's Integrated Solid Waste management Plan was finalized in July 2000.[126]

The Integrated Management Act promotes source reduction, recycling and bioconversion of municipal solid waste as preferable methods for solid waste management as compared to the options of incineration and landfilling. The purposes of the Plan are several: minimization of the amount of waste generated; prevention of unnecessary generation of waste; proper municipal solid waste practices; public agency purchases of recycled goods; development of public and private recycling and bioconversion activities; promotion of markets for recovered materials; and public education on citizen participation in the recycling of consumer goods and in waste reduction programs. The Plan must contain a component which addresses the collection, recycling and disposal of household hazardous waste.

The Integrated Management Act establishes solid waste management priorities. Source reduction is accorded the highest priority, followed by recycling and bioconversion. Incineration and landfilling are designated as the least preferable alternatives for solid waste management. The Plan's goals were to reduce the solid waste stream prior to disposal by 25% by January 1,

---

123 *Id.* § 11-58.1-20. *See supra* § 7.0 of this Chapter.

124 *Id.* §§ 11-58.1-52, -53(b). *See infra* § 15.0 of this Chapter.

125 Haw. Rev. Stat. ch. 342G.

126 Hawaii Department of Health, OSWM, *Hawaii 2000 Plan for Integrated Solid Waste Management* (July 2000).

1995 and by 50% by January 1, 2000.[127] These reductions were to be implemented through the waste management priorities. An additional goal of the Plan was to reduce the amount of office paper generated by state and county agencies by 25% by January 1, 1995.[128] To this end, the Integrated Management Act promotes more efficient use of office paper by mandating double-sided copying as the standard operating practice for all agencies and offices. Recycling of office paper and other materials was to be commenced by the Department by January 1, 1992, and by all other agencies by June 30, 1993.[129]

The Integrated Management Act established the Office of Solid Waste Management ("OSWM") within the Department.[130] Both the Department and the OSWM are responsible for administration of the Integrated Management Act, including compliance with the federal Resource Conservation and Recovery Act.[131] The Department is responsible for rule making and enforcement duties, whereas the OSWM is responsible for establishing and administering goals and guidelines under the Act, public promotion of the Plan, studying the impact of disposal fees and acting as a liaison between the federal, state and county agencies.[132] The OSWM is required to prepare a detailed annual report describing its activities.[133] Each county was required to submit their plan to the OSWM by January 1, 1993. The county plans must be adopted by the

---

127 The State did not meet the reduction goals for 1995, or the year 2000. In 1998/99 the State's overall recycling rate was 24%, which did not increase from a year earlier. The County of Maui had the highest waste diversion rate in the State: 29.8%. The OSWM still believes that the fifty percent diversion rate is achievable, but will require a far greater commitment of resources for both collection and processing capabilities. The OSWM has therefore suggested that the goal be revised to fifty percent diversion by the year 2005. *See* State of Hawaii, Department of Health, *Report of the Twentieth Legislature, State of Hawaii, Pursuant to Section 342g-15 Hawaii Revised Statutes Relating to Integrated Solid Waste Management* at 3-5 (2000). More recently, OSWM recommended that the fifty percent waste diversion goal be extended to 2010. *See* Hawaii Department of Health, OSWM, *Hawaii 2000 Plan for Integrated Solid Waste Management* at 4-2 (July 2000).

128 Haw. Rev. Stat. § 342G-3.

129 *Id.* §§ 342G-44, -45.

130 Haw. Rev. Stat. § 342G-12.

131 42 U.S.C. § 6901 *et seq.*

132 Haw. Rev. Stat. § 342G-14.

133 *Id.* § 342G-15. *See, e.g.*, State of Hawaii, Department of Health, *Report to the Twentieth Legislature Pursuant to Section 342G-15 Hawaii Revised Statutes Relating to Integrated Solid Waste Management* (2000).

governing entity of each county and approved by the OSWM.[134] The first revised county plan was required to be submitted to the OSWM by July 1, 1995 and subsequent revised plans are due every five years thereafter.[135]

The Integrated Management Act makes it the policy of all state and county public agencies to give purchase preference to products made from recycled materials. The OSWM and the State Procurement Office are responsible for providing technical assistance and information to the county and state purchasing agencies to promote procurement of goods with recycled content.[136] The OSWM, in conjunction with the Department of Business Economic Development and Tourism (DBEDT), is responsible for identifying and developing markets for recycled materials, including coordination with other state agencies.[137]

In 1994, the Legislature created the Clean Hawaii Center. The center's purpose is to work in partnership with business and government to develop and expand commercial markets for recyclable materials, recycled content products, and to facilitate recycling environmental and technology development.[138] The Clean Hawaii Fund was subsequently created by the Legislature in 1999. The Clean Hawaii Fund is administered and used to market and promote the development of local processing and manufacturing industries for collected recycled materials.[139]

DBEDT's Clean Hawaii Center publishes many informative materials regarding recycling in Hawaii. The *Hawaii Recycling Industry Guide* is a listing of businesses, government agencies and non-profit organizations directly involved in addressing Hawaii's

---

134 Haw. Rev. Stat. §§ 342G-21, -22, -23.

135 *Id.* §342G-24.

136 *Id.* § 342G-42.

137 *Id.* § 342G-48. For example, the Hawaii Housing Finance Development Corporation requires preferential use of recycled content building materials by their permittees. State of Hawaii, Office of Environmental Quality Control, 1994 Annual Report of the Environmental Council at 9 (1995).

138 1994 Haw. Sess. Laws 202.

139 1999 Haw. Sess. Laws 112 (codified at Haw. Rev. Stat. Ch. 201).

unique solid waste challenges.[140] The *Recycling/Remanufacturing in Hawaii Industry Report* describes the current state of affairs among Hawaii's recycling in relation to past practices and national circumstances.[141] The *Y2K Directory of Environmental Businesses* in Hawaii lists major recycling businesses in Hawaii.[142] *A Contractor's Waste Management Guide* provides practical methods contractors can use to practice responsible construction waste management in Hawaii.[143] DBEDT also publishes factsheets regarding: construction, demolition and waste management facilities; glass recycling in Hawaii; greenwaste recycling in Hawaii; paper recycling in Hawaii; and plastic recycling. All of these publications are available through Clean Hawaii Center's website.[144]

Each county solid waste management plan must contain certain program elements. A waste stream assessment must be completed, measures for achieving source reduction, recycling and bioconversion must be assessed, and the energy-balance must be increased. In addition, each county plan is required to address special waste handling and disposal practices. The plan must include current and proposed programs for reuse, handling and long-term disposal of the following special wastes: asbestos, agricultural wastes, derelict vehicles, lead acid batteries, medical wastes, municipal waste combustion ash, petroleum contaminated soil, sewage sludge, tires, used oil and white goods.[145] The plan must also address landfill and incineration options, marketing and procurement of materials derived from solid waste, and program funding.

The Integrated Management Act also requires the county plans to develop a household hazardous waste collection program. The disposal of the collected household hazardous waste is

---

140 State of Hawaii, Department of Business, Economic Development & Tourism, Energy, Resources & Technology Division, *Hawaii Recycling Industry Guide* (May 1999).

141 Hawaii Small Business Development Center Network, *Recycling/Remanufacturing in Hawaii – An Industry Report* (1999).

142 State of Hawaii, Department of Business, Economic Development & Tourism, Energy, Resources & Technology Division, *Y2K Directory of Environmental Businesses in Hawaii* (April 2000).

143 State of Hawaii, Department of Business, Economic Development & Tourism, *A Contractor's Waste Management Guide*.

144 http://www.state.hi.us/dbedt/ert/chc/ (visited August 12, 2000).

145 Haw. Rev. Stat. § 342G-26.

to be conducted by the Department and coordinated with the counties.[146] Household hazardous waste means those wastes which result from products purchased by the general public for household use, but may pose a substantial known or potential hazard to human health or the environment when these products are improperly treated, disposed of or otherwise managed.[147]

Since 1994, the Department has imposed a solid waste management surcharge for solid waste disposed within the State at permitted and unpermitted solid waste disposal facilities. In 1997, the surcharge was adjusted to thirty-five cents per ton.[148] The surcharge is payable to the owner or operator of the solid waste disposal facility.[149] The total solid waste management surcharge collected for fiscal year 1998-99 was $509, 481.[150] Each county may, but is not required to assess residential real property owners an annual solid waste collection surcharge.[151]

The surcharges paid to the solid waste disposal facilities are submitted to the Department on a quarterly basis. The surcharges are deposited into the Environmental Management Special Fund.[152] The Special Fund is used to fund operating costs of the integrated solid waste management program, development of waste reduction and diversion activities, fund statewide education, demonstration and market development programs, and provide for annual training of municipal solid waste operators.[153]

---

146 *Id.* § 342G-26(f).

147 *Id.* § 342G-1.

148 However, the surcharge may not exceed $1.50 per ton. *Id.* § 342G-62(c).

149 Haw. Rev. Stat. § 342G-62.

150 Interview of Lene Ichinotsubo, Solid and Hazardous Waste Branch, Department of Health (August 3, 2000).

151 Haw. Rev. Stat. § 342G-61.

152 *Id.* § 342G-62.

153 *Id.* §§ 342G-63, -64.

14.0 RECYCLING

The Director is required to encourage the recycling of solid wastes, including animal and non-hazardous industrial wastes, for agricultural purposes. The use of treated sludge effluent for fertilizer and other agricultural purposes is also encouraged.[154] To promote recycling, pilot household waste recycling programs have been established in the Counties of Maui, Hawaii, Kauai and the City and County of Honolulu. Recycling of lead acid batteries, used motor vehicle tires and used oil also are regulated by the Solid Waste Law. A glass container recovery program was enacted in 1994.[155]

The State has a budgetary incentive to pursue recycling efforts. The disposal of the State's almost two million tons of rubbish each year costs the public and private sectors more than $250,000,000 annually. Recovered materials such as waste paper, waste glass, plastic, aluminum cans, and tree and grass trimmings can have value reaching an average of $45 per ton, with certain waster paper reaching as high as $200 per ton and aluminum valued at $700 per ton. The legislature therefore believes that the value of recycling is a "critical goal" for the State's economy.[156]

14.1 GLASS CONTAINER RECOVERY

The glass container recovery program was enacted by the 1994 Legislature as an initiative to protect Hawaii's energy resources and physical environment.[157] The program imposes an "advance disposal fee" on glass container importers for glass containers. For the initial period of September 1994 to September 1996, the fee is set at one and one-half cents per glass container.[158] The Legislature is now authorized to set the fee at a rate to fund the county

---

154 *Id.* § 342H-36.

155 *Id.* ch. 342G, part VII, §§ 81 to 89.

156 1996 Haw. Sess. Laws 83.

157 Act approved June 21, 1994, ch. 201, § 1, 1994 Haw. Sess. Laws 483.

158 Haw. Rev. Stat. § 342G-82(a). Plates, bowls, drinking glasses, cups, ashtrays and similar tempered glassware are exempt from the fee. *Id.*

glass recovery programs. In the fiscal year 1998/99, the total revenue from the advance disposal fee was $2, 208,468.[159] Glass recycling in Honolulu is estimated to be forty-three percent.[160]

Glass container importers are required to register with the Department and maintain manufacture, import and export records for glass containers.[161] The revenues collected from the advance disposal fee program are deposited into a special account, to be used for funding county glass recovery programs. Distribution of the revenues is based upon the county's *de facto* population. The program imposes one limitation on the distribution of funds: no more than ten percent of the yearly revenues may be used for educational and administrative purposes by the Department.[162] Payment of the advance disposal fee is made quarterly to the Department and is based upon manufacture, import, sale and distribution and export documentation provided by the glass importers. Importers of fewer than 5,000 glass containers within a year are exempt, as are glass containers designed to hold two and one-half fluid ounces of product or less for human consumption. Glass container importers who import between 5,000 and 100,000 glass containers within a year are permitted to pay their fee annually, rather than quarterly.[163]

The counties must establish glass recovery programs in order to receive funding from the Department. Each county program must include two components. First, the program must contain a "buy back" or other incentive to encourage participation by private and public collectors. Second, the county program must include a research and demonstration project utilizing glassphalt for a portion of a two lane asphalt roadway.[164]

In addition, the county glass recovery programs may fund the collection and processing of glass containers, subsidize transportation of processed containers, develop a collection facility,

---

159 *Report to the Twentieth Legislature,* note 133, at 12.

160 *Id.* at 10.

161 *Id.* § 342G-83.

162 *Id.* § 342G-84.

163 *Id.* § 342G-85.

164 Haw. Rev. Stat. § 342G-86(a).

conduct and provide grants for research and development programs, and provide public education and awareness programs.[165]

Violation of the glass recovery program law is subject to a $10,000 fine for each offense, per day.[166] The Department is charged with enforcement of the glass recovery program.[167]

14.2 RECYCLING OF HOUSEHOLD WASTE

In response to public interest, curbside community recycling programs for aluminum cans, glass, plastics and newspaper were established in Kailua, Kaneohe and Lanikai in 1991.[168] This one year pilot program was planned to expand to the entire island of Oahu. Recycling bags or bins were provided to the community by the City and County of Honolulu at no cost, and the recyclable items were picked up curbside on a weekly basis.[169] Although the curbside recycling program was discontinued, other recycling programs have been developed on Oahu and the Neighbor Islands.

In an effort to prevent theft of recyclable materials, the ownership of recyclable materials was clarified by a bill enacted by the 1992 Legislature. Pursuant to the bill, recyclable materials which have been segregated and placed at designated collection sites for recycling may not be removed by any unauthorized person.[170]

All the counties have established landfill diversion and recycling programs that target residents and businesses alike. The counties generally provide guidance and drop-off sites to

---

165 *Id.* § 342G-86(b).

166 *Id.* § 342G-88.

167 *Id.* § 342G-89.

168 For a narrative describing the development of recycling programs on Oahu, *see* Environment Hawai'i (July 1992).

169 Telephone interview with the City and County of Honolulu's Recycling Office (July 30, 1991). The curbside recycling pilot program expired and was not reinstituted due to funding shortages. *Id.*

170 Haw. Rev. Stat. § 342H-21.

encourage the recycling of many types of solid waste. For example, the County of Maui has established drop boxes for cardboard, newspaper, glass, some plastic, aluminum and metal cans. The County of Maui also has a curbside recycling program for source-separated recyclables accepted at drop boxes, provides for collection of up to two gallons of used oil collection at more than nine locations and conducts a composting program.[171] The County of Hawaii generally conducts household hazardous waste collection programs twice a year, has recycling centers where paper, glass and other recyclables are collected and has an ongoing green waste management program with collection centers in Waimea, Hilo and Kona.[172]

The City and County of Honolulu funds the "Recycle Hawaii" program. Through the program, community recycling bins at approximately 77 locations accept aluminum cans, cardboard, glass bottles and jars, newspaper, colored office paper, white office paper, plastic beverage bottles and telephone books. Large appliances are delivered to a metal recycler, as are all junk autos, car batteries and tires. Curbside greenwaste pickups are also available in many Oahu communities.[173] The City and County of Honolulu buys only recycled-content paper and uses the Honolulu Zoo as a showcase for recycled products from plastic benches remanufactured from milk jugs to glassphalt-paved walkways.[174] In 1999, Oahu recycled 36% of its total waste including 38,900 tons of corrugated cardboard and 11,000 tons of newspaper.[175]

As another encouragement and aid to recycling, all plastic bottles or containers that are intended for single use are required to be labeled as to the type of resin used to produce that container.[176] The labeling requirement became effective on January 1, 1992, after which date the

---

171 County of Maui, Department of Public Works, Recycle Maui County website http://www.maui.net/~recyclemaui/ (visited August 2, 2000). The County of Maui Recycling Section can be reached at (808)270-7874.

172 Interview with Jim Ushijima, Hawaii County Solid Waste Office (August 2, 2000).

173 http://www.opala.org/recycwhat.html (visited August 2, 2000).

174 http://www.opala.org/recyccity.html (visited August 2, 2000).

175 http://www.opala.org/facts2.html (visited August 2, 2000).

176 Haw. Rev. Stat. § 342H-42. The labeling must include the triangular "recycle" symbol, certain letters and a code number which identified the type of resin used to manufacture the plastic object.

manufacture, distribution, sale or exposure for sale of unlabelled plastic bottles or containers was prohibited. In addition, nondegradable plastic connecting devices, such as those used for beverages, may not be sold in the State.[177]

14.3 RECYCLING OF SPECIAL WASTES

The Special Wastes Recycling Law ("Special Wastes Law") regulates the collection, recycling and disposal of lead acid batteries and used motor vehicle tires.[178] The Special Wastes Law prohibits the disposal of used lead acid batteries and whole motor vehicle tires into municipal solid waste.[179] The Special Wastes Law also establishes affirmative recycling programs which require retailers to assist consumers in disposal of these items.

14.3.1 LEAD ACID BATTERIES

The State promotes the recycling of lead acid batteries by requiring retailers and wholesalers who sell batteries to accept used batteries from their customers. Retailers and wholesalers must accept at least the number of batteries purchased from them, and they are required to post written notice of the recycling program at their facilities.[180] Furthermore, the price of a new lead acid battery must include disposal of the old battery, and this must be stated in any advertising pertaining to the price of new lead acid batteries.[181] The Department is responsible for printing and distributing the notices to the battery retailers.[182]

Persons who accept lead acid batteries for recycling must transport the batteries to a transfer station or permitted lead smelter with the liquid intact or have the liquid electrolyte

177 *Id.* § 339-22.

178 Haw. Rev. Stat. ch. 342I

179 *Id.* §§ 342I-1, -22.

180 *Id.* §§ 342I-2, -4.

181 *Id.*

182 *Id.* § 342I-3.

neutralized prior to transporting the batteries to a lead smelter.[183] Facilities which accept five or more batteries per day are required to maintain certain records to track the batteries. The facility accepting the batteries must keep the following information for at least three years: the name, address and telephone number of the person submitting the batteries; the date of receipt of the batteries; and records which indicate the date of shipment and the ultimate destination of the batteries.[184]

Disposal of a used lead acid battery into municipal solid waste or by any other means, except by delivery to a battery wholesaler or retailer, permitted recycling facility or permitted secondary lead smelter, is prohibited.[185] In addition, the disposal of battery electrolyte into the ground, groundwater, surface or marine water, sewer or drainage system is prohibited.[186]

14.3.2 USED MOTOR VEHICLE TIRES

In 1993, the Legislature added provisions to the Special Wastes Law governing the recovery and handling of used motor vehicle tires, which became effective in July 1994.[187] The tire recovery program has been very successful. In 1994 alone, following the disposal ban effective in July 1994, over 900,000 automobile tire equivalents were recycled.[188] In fiscal year 1998/99, 7,053.60 tons of tires were collected.[189] Under the Special Wastes Law, motor vehicle tire retailers are required to accept used tires from their customers. Retailers are required to accept at least the number of tires that are purchased from them without any additional charge.

---

183 *Id.* § 342I-2.5.

184 *Id.* § 342I-6.

185 *Id.* § 342I-1.

186 *Id.* §342I-1.5.

187 Motor vehicle tires includes any tire designed for or used on a motorized vehicle such as an automobile, bus, truck or heavy equipment. Haw. Rev. Stat. § 342I-21.

188 State of Hawaii, Department of Health, Report to the Eighteenth Legislature on Integrated Solid Waste Management, at 15 (1994).

189 Interview with Lene Ichinotsubo, Solid and Hazardous Waste Branch, Department of Health (August 3, 2000)

Like the lead acid battery provisions, retailers are required to post written notice of the tire recycling and disposal program.[190]

Motor vehicle tire wholesalers also are required to accept used tires at least equal to the number of new tires purchased. The wholesaler accepting tires must remove the used tires from the retailer collection point within ninety days.[191]

The disposal of whole motor vehicle tires into municipal solid waste is prohibited. All persons must dispose of motor vehicle tires by delivery to a tire retailer or wholesaler, or to an authorized tire recycler.[192] A variance to the tire disposal requirements may be made in writing to the Director by a permitted disposal facility.[193]

Effective July 1, 2000, all facilities that accept used tires are expected to maintain a record documenting the person from whom used tires were received, the date of receipt and quantity of tires, a record of shipment indicating the ultimate destination of the used tires, identification of the transporter, as well as the date and quantity of shipment. Records must be kept for a minimum of three years, and a summary of the records must be submitted to the Department each July. Municipal solid waste disposal facilities are exempt from these recordkeeping requirements, if they received used tires incidental to the disposal of municipal solid waste.[194]

All tire importers must register with the Department by September 1, 2000, and after that time, any person who desires to conduct a tire import business must register with the Department

---

190 Haw. Rev. Stat. § 342I-23.

191 *Id.* § 342I-25.

192 *Id.* § 342I-22(a)-(b).

193 *Id.* § 342I-22(e).

194 2000 Haw. Sess. Laws 173 (to be codified at Haw. Rev. Stat. § 342I-A).

one month prior to the commencement of business. Importers must also maintain records reflecting importation of tires.[195]

Between September 30, 2000 and January 1, 2006, the State has imposed a $1 per tire surcharge on all tires imported into Hawaii, including those tires imported on motor vehicles. The surcharge must be paid by the person who imports the tires. Car rental companies are entitled to subtract the number of tires on exported vehicles when calculating the motor vehicle surcharge.[196] Importers of less than fifty tires per year are exempt from the surcharge. Payment of the surcharge is generally due to the Department on a quarterly basis, but importers of between fifty and two hundred tires are permitted to provide a summary report and surcharge payment on an annual basis.[197]

Money collected from the surcharge will be deposited into a special account in the environmental management special fund and may be used by the Department to support permitting, monitoring, and enforcement activities regarding used tire management, collection, recycling and disposal facilities. The fund may also be used to develop opportunities for the reuse of motor vehicle tires, to support programs to prevent illegal dumping and to clean up improper tire disposal sites.[198] If the Department undertakes any tire cleanups or associated environmental assessments, all associated costs, plus interest, are recoverable from the liable persons.[199]

195 *Id.*

196 2000 Haw. Sess. Laws 173 (to be codified at Haw. Rev. Stat. § 342I-B).

197 2000 Haw. Sess. Laws 173 (to be codified at Haw. Rev. Stat. §342I-C).

198 2000 Haw. Sess. Laws 173 (to be codified at Haw. Rev. Stat. §342I-D).

199 2000 Haw. Sess. Laws 173 (to be codified at Haw. Rev. Stat. §342I-E).

14.3.3 ENFORCEMENT OF SPECIAL WASTE PROVISIONS

The Department is authorized to enter, inspect, copy records and take samples at any facility.[200] Warnings and citations may be issued to tire retailers and wholesalers who fail to comply with the motor vehicle tire recovery provisions.[201] Persons who violate the Special Wastes Recycling Law are subject to civil and criminal penalties. Retailers who fail to post the required notice regarding lead acid batteries are subject to a $2,000 fine per offense, after first being issued a warning by the Director. Persons who fail to post required notices regarding collection of used tires for recycling are subject to a $1,000 penalty for each separate offense.[202] Other violations of the Special Wastes Law subject a person to a $10,000 fine per offense or per battery, per tire, or per violation of the used tire recordkeeping requirements. A person who knowingly or willfully violates the chapter is also subject to prosecution for a misdemeanor.[203] Violators of the motor vehicle tire provisions are also subject to penalties under the Solid Waste Law.[204]

15.0 INFECTIOUS WASTE MANAGEMENT

Although the total quantity of infectious waste generated in the State comprises less than one-tenth of one percent of the entire solid waste stream,[205] issues relating to the handling and disposal of infectious waste generated by health care facilities have received substantial community and media attention in the last few years. The potential health risks posed by the improper management and disposal of infectious waste have generated considerable public involvement in proceedings which involve the siting, construction and operation of infectious waste treatment and disposal facilities.

---

200 *Id.* §§ 342I-7, -24, 342I-E.

201 *Id.* § 342I-24.

202 Id. § 342I-I

203 *Id.* §§ 342I-8, -22(c)-(d), 342I-I.

204 *See supra* § 16.0 of this Chapter.

205 Interview with Lene Ichinotsubo, Solid and Hazardous Waste Branch, Department of Health (August 3, 2000).

Following the 1989 Legislative Session, a statute regulating the management and disposal of infectious wastes was signed into law ("Infectious Waste Law").[206] The Department promulgated rules in 1990 to implement and enforce the Infectious Waste Law. The rules establish minimum requirements for the management, treatment, transport, storage and disposal of infectious waste and treated infectious waste.[207] The Solid Waste rules impose permit requirements upon infectious waste treatment and disposal facilities.[208]

Those subject to the Infectious Waste Law and rules include persons who generate infectious wastes; persons who by contract, agreement or otherwise arrange to treat, store, transport or dispose of infectious waste; and persons who accept or have accepted any treated or untreated infectious waste for treatment, storage, transport, or disposal. Virtually every hospital, medical school, medical research facility, clinic, physician and dentist is subject to the Infectious Waste Law and rules. Infectious wastes which are generated within households are exempt from the Infectious Waste Law and may be disposed of as residential solid waste.[209]

The rules establish six categories of infectious wastes: infectious isolation wastes; cultures and stocks of infectious agents; blood, blood products and body fluids; pathological waste; contaminated sharps (such as needles); and contaminated animal carcasses, body parts and bedding.[210] Infectious waste must be segregated from all other waste at the point of generation. Treatment methods are specified for each category of infectious waste. Methods of approved treatment for infectious waste include autoclaving, incineration, sterilization and chemical disinfection, followed by wastewater disposal.[211]

---

206 Haw. Rev. Stat. § 321-21 (1993).

207 Haw. Admin. Rules tit. 11, ch. 104.

208 *Id.* § 11-58.1-52.

209 *Id.* § 11-58.1-63.

210 *Id.* § 11-104-4.

211 *Id.* § 11-104-5.

15.1 TRANSPORTATION AND DISPOSAL OF INFECTIOUS WASTE

Transportation of infectious waste within a facility and transportation of infectious waste for treatment away from the generating facility are subject to certain requirements. Both classes of transportation require complete containment of the waste in nonsoluable plastic bags, either red in color or clearly labeled with the Universal Biological Hazard symbol ("the Symbol"); rigid puncture resistant and leak proof containers, either red in color or clearly marked with the Symbol for contaminated sharps; or sturdy leak proof containers clearly marked with the Symbol. All bags and other containers of infectious wastes must be tightly closed before transport and placed into a rigid or semirigid tightly closed, leak proof containment system, which is clearly marked with the Symbol. Reusable carts, bins or other containment systems used to transport infectious wastes within a facility must be cleaned after each use and disinfected daily when in use.

In addition, infectious waste being transported for treatment away from the generating facility must be fully enclosed in a rigid, leak proof container or vehicle compartment which will prevent scattering, spillage or leakage of the waste during transport. The transport vehicle must be labeled with a clearly visible Symbol. Disposable containers which have been in contact with infectious waste must be incinerated or sterilized prior to disposal. Reusable containers must be cleaned after each use and disinfected daily when in use.

Untreated infectious waste must be segregated from noninfectious waste. Untreated infectious waste that is transported for treatment away from the generating facility may not be transported with noninfectious waste unless all waste in the load is managed as infectious waste.[212]

Infectious waste which is being stored awaiting treatment must be stored in a disposable or reusable sturdy leak proof container with tight fitting lids or a leak proof fully enclosed room, which is clearly labeled with the Symbol. The containers must be fully enclosed and the locations must be secured to prevent access by animals and unauthorized persons. Infectious waste which has been treated and is awaiting transport for disposal must be stored in fully

---

212 *Id.* §§ 11-104-5 to -6.

enclosed and secured areas or containment systems which are accessible only to authorized persons.[213]

Infectious waste and treated infectious waste may be disposed of in approved waste water disposal systems. Infectious waste may also be incinerated, and the resulting incinerator ash may be disposed of only in state permitted landfills or authorized disposal sites.[214] Treated infectious waste which has been rendered non-infectious may also be incinerated or disposed of in a municipal solid waste landfill.[215]

15.2 INFECTIOUS WASTE MANAGEMENT PLAN AND ENFORCEMENT

Each infectious waste generator and transporter of untreated infectious waste must develop a written infectious waste management plan ("Plan") which contains policies and procedures for the safe and effective management of infectious waste. The Plan must be kept in the administrative offices of the generator or transporter. The Plan must provide for emergency situations and must include procedures for the following circumstances: spills of liquid infectious waste, rupture of plastic bags or other loss of containment, and equipment failure.[216]

Violation of the Infectious Waste Law or rules carries administrative penalties of $1,000 maximum per offense, per day. Persons who have received a notice of violation are entitled to a contested case hearing pursuant to the Hawaii Administrative Procedure Act.[217]

---

213 *Id.* § 11-104-8.

214 *Id.* § 11-104-9.

215 *Id.* § 11-58.1-63.

216 *Id.* § 11-104-10.

217 Haw. Rev. Stat. ch. 91. *See infra* ch. 13 of this Handbook.

15.3 INFECTIOUS WASTE TREATMENT AND DISPOSAL FACILITIES

The Solid Waste rules regulate infectious waste treatment and disposal facilities.[218] Under these rules infectious waste is regulated from the point that it is received from a health care facility which generated the waste, for the purpose of transporting the waste off-site for treatment, storage or disposal.[219]

All facilities which transfer, treat, store or dispose of infectious wastes are required to obtain a permit from the Director. In the State, several hospitals and private medical facilities operate autoclaves and incinerators for the treatment and disposal of their own infectious waste. Autoclave facilities in lower Kalihi and Sand Island have been permitted to treat infectious waste from other sources, and one facility has recently received a permit to treat waste using microwave technology.[220] Infectious waste transfer and storage facilities are prohibited from accepting treated or destroyed medical waste, solid waste or low level radioactive waste, unless authorized by the Director. The rules give one exemption to the permitting requirement: health care facilities which treat and dispose of infectious waste generated on-site with treatment and disposal units located on-site are not required to obtain a permit. Permit applications must include a site analysis, security analysis, fire plan, drainage plan and operation plan.[221] An annual report which details the amount of incoming material must be filed with the Director by July 30 of each year by every facility.[222]

---

218 Haw. Admin. Rules § 11-58.1-52.

219 *Id.* § 11-58.1-52(a).

220 Interview with Lene Ichinotsubo, Solid and Hazardous Waste Branch, Department of Health (August 3, 2000).

221 Haw. Admin. Rules § 11-58.1-52(b).

222 *Id.* § 11-58.1-52(c).

16.0 ENFORCEMENT AND PENALTIES

The Department, county health officials and county police departments are authorized to enforce the Solid Waste Law, rules, and permits of the Department.[223] The Department may authorize county agencies to investigate alleged violations involving unauthorized dumping of solid waste in any place other than a permitted solid waste disposal system.[224] The Solid Waste Law provides for the imposition of civil and administrative penalties for violations.

If the Director determines that any person is violating the Solid Waste Law, rules, permit or variance for solid waste disposal, the Director may issue an order which requires compliance and assesses an administrative penalty for the violation. In the alternative, the Director may commence a civil action in circuit court for relief, including an injunction. The order also may suspend, modify or revoke a permit issued under the law.[225]

Orders issued by the Director become final in twenty days unless a hearing is requested by the person named in the order. Penalties imposed by an order become due and payable in twenty days after the notice of penalty is served unless the named person request a hearing. All hearings are conducted as contested case hearings pursuant to the Hawaii Administrative Procedure Act.[226]

16.1 INSPECTIONS

The Director may enter and inspect any facility, building or place to investigate an actual or suspected source of solid waste pollution and to ascertain compliance or noncompliance with the Solid Waste Law, rules, permit or variance. The Director may make reasonable tests in connection with the inspection.[227]

---

223 Haw. Rev. Stat. § 342H-17.

224 *Id.* § 342H-2.5.

225 *Id.* § 342H-7(a) - (b).

226 *Id.* § 342H-7(c) - (f). *See infra* ch. 13 of this Handbook.

227 *Id.* § 342H-6.

Any confidential information secured by Department in an inspection is protected from disclosure. Disclosure of that information is prohibited except as it relates directly to solid waste pollution, and then only in connection with the Department employee's official duties within the scope of employment. Improper disclosure of confidential information by an employee or agent of the Department is subject to a civil penalty.[228]

16.2 PENALTIES

Penalties imposed for violations of the Solid Waste Law, the Integrated Solid Waste Management Law, rules, permits or variances shall be not more than $10,000 for each separate offense, with each day of each violation constituting a separate offense.[229] Penalties may be imposed by administrative order or by civil action.[230] Any person who denies, obstructs, or hampers any authorized entrance and inspection by any duly authorized officer or employee of the Department shall be fined not more than $500, and this penalty may be imposed by a civil action. All penalties collected under the Solid Waste Law are deposited into the environmental response revolving fund. If the state and county jointly collect a penalty, the payment is split between the county department which initiated the investigation and the environmental response revolving fund.[231]

If the Director imposes penalties through an administrative action, the following factors must be considered: the nature and history of the violation and of any prior violations, the economic benefit, if any, resulting from the violation, the opportunity, difficulty and history of corrective action, the violator's good faith efforts to comply and any other matters that justice may require. The burden of proving that the violator's financial condition does not allow payment of the penalty is on the violator.[232]

---

228 *Id.* § 342H-14.

229 *Id.* § 342H-9(a), § 342G-71.

230 *Id.* § 342H-10.

231 *Id.* § 342H-10.5. *See id.* § 128D-2.

232 *Id.* § 342H-10.

16.3 MISCELLANEOUS ENFORCEMENT PROVISIONS

The Director may institute an action for injunctive and other relief to prevent any violation of the Solid Waste Law, rules, or any permit or variance relating to solid waste disposal. It is not necessary to revoke a permit or variance before such an injunction is sought or obtained.[233]

233 *Id.* § 342H-11.

CHAPTER 6

HAZARDOUS WASTE MANAGEMENT

1.0 INTRODUCTION

The regulation and management of hazardous waste is a priority for both federal and state government. The federal government has implemented a comprehensive national program that encourages waste reduction and advanced treatment and disposal of hazardous wastes. Under the federal Resource Conservation and Recovery Act ("RCRA"), hazardous wastes are to be treated, stored and disposed of so as to minimize the present and future threat to human health and the environment.[1] Hawaii and other states have sought to implement this mandate through laws and regulations.

The 1991 Hawaii State Legislature amended the Hawaii Hazardous Waste Law[2] to make it substantially similar to RCRA in an effort to gain authorization from the federal Environmental Protection Agency ("EPA") to administer the State hazardous waste program in lieu of the federal program.[3] In 1996, the Hawaii Hazardous Waste Law was revised to include regulation of used oil and used oil fuel.[4] Pursuant to the amended Hazardous Waste Law, the Director of Health ("Director") of the Department of Health ("Department") has promulgated comprehensive rules to govern the management of hazardous waste and to prohibit hazardous waste pollution.[5] These rules took effect June 18, 1994. On March 13, 2000 the Department promulgated rules regarding used oil management.[6]

---

1 42 U.S.C. § 6901 *et seq.*

2 Haw. Rev. Stat. ch. 342J (Michie 1999). All references to the Hawaii Revised Statutes are made to the printed version of the statutes current through the 1999 legislative session, unless otherwise noted. Where appropriate, references to acts passed during the 2000 legislative session have also been added.

3 Senate Conf. Comm. Rep. No. 109, reprinted in 18th Haw. Leg., Reg. Sess., 1991 Sen. J. 788.

4 1996 Haw. Sess. Laws 82 (codified at Haw. Rev. Stat. 342J).

5 Haw. Rev. Stat. § 342J-4. The administrative rules adopted by the Department are found at Hawaii Administrative Rules, tit. 11, chs. 260 - 280. The chapter numbers are analogous to the 40 C.F.R. Part numbers.

6 Haw. Admin. Rules tit. 11, ch. 279 (Weil's 2000). All references to the Hawaii Administrative Rules are current through the date of publication of this Handbook, unless otherwise noted

These rules took effect June 18, 1994. On March 13, 2000 the Department promulgated rules regarding used oil management.[6]

The Department is committed to achieving state authorization and on May 5, 1999 submitted to EPA its authorization package for full delegation of the hazardous waste program to the State.[7] The EPA has made a tentative decision that the state's hazardous waste management program satisfies all of the requirements necessary for final authorization under Subtitle C of the Resource Conservation and Recovery Act ("RCRA").[8] The effect of a final decision to grant authorization to Hawaii is that persons that are subject to RCRA will have to comply with the authorized state requirements instead of equivalent federal requirements. Additionally such persons will also have to comply with any federally issued requirements such as the Hazardous and Solid Waste Amendments regulations issued by EPA for which the state has not received authorization, and RCRA requirements that are not delegable.[9] After close of the public comment period on August 4, 2000, the EPA will make a final decision regarding delegation.[10]

The Department may use revenues generated by the environmental response tax and deposited into the environmental response revolving fund to address concerns related to hazardous waste.[11]

2.0 RELATIONSHIP TO FEDERAL RCRA

The Hazardous Waste Law and rules follow RCRA in attempting to provide "cradle to grave" control of hazardous waste generation, transportation, treatment, storage and disposal. RCRA authorizes states to adopt and enforce state hazardous waste programs if the state program

---

6 Haw. Admin. Rules tit. 11, ch. 279 (Weil's 2000). All references to the Hawaii Administrative Rules are current through the date of publication of this Handbook, unless otherwise noted

7 Hawaii State Department of Health, *Strategic Plan for Hawaii's Environmental Protection Programs*, at 47 (January 1999).

8 65 Fed. Reg. 38802 (June 22, 2000).

9 *See e.g.*, 40 CFR 268.5, 268.6, 268.42(b) and 268.44.

10 *Id. See also* Office of Environmental Quality Control, The Environmental Notice at 20 (July 8, 2000).

11 2000 Haw. Sess. Laws 245 (to be codified at Haw. Rev. Stat. 128D-2).

is substantially equivalent to the federal program.[12] After a state program has been adopted by the state and authorized by the EPA, the EPA retains authority to conduct site inspections and to enforce RCRA.

At the time of publication of this Handbook, the State of Hawaii does not have a state program fully and finally approved by the EPA, and the Hazardous Waste Law and rules operate under a system of dual regulation. As such, the federal program under RCRA is enforced by the EPA in Hawaii. However, to coordinate state and federal hazardous waste management responsibilities, the Department, through a Memorandum of Understanding ("MOU"), has been delegated certain duties under RCRA.[13] Pursuant to the MOU and Letters of Authority,[14] the Department is authorized to conduct compliance inspections, review records and assist the EPA with enforcement and permitting. Pursuant to the Certification of Authority issued by the EPA to the Department, the Deputy Director for Environmental Health is authorized to request information under RCRA.[15] The Letters and Certification of Authority are valid until the Hawaii hazardous waste program is approved by the EPA.

3.0 REGULATED WASTES

Criteria for identifying characteristics of hazardous waste and for listing hazardous waste are based on RCRA, the federal regulations implementing RCRA,[16] the Hazardous Waste Law, and Chapter 261 of the Hawaii Administrative Rules ("rules"). The rules define both solid and hazardous wastes, and set forth exclusions. Both the Hazardous Waste Law and RCRA define hazardous waste in a substantially similar manner. In adopting rules to implement the Hazardous Waste Law, the Director is authorized to establish a list of hazardous wastes and a set of

---

12 42 U.S.C. § 6926. *See generally* 40 C.F.R. Part 271.

13 The Memorandum of Understanding Between the United States Environmental Protection Agency, Region 9 and the State of Hawaii, Department of Health (Sept. 28, 1988).

14 Letters of Authority issued by Jeffrey Zelikson, EPA for Department of Health Hazardous Waste Inspectors (no expiration date).

15 Certification of Authority from Jeffrey Zelikson to Bruce Anderson (no expiration date). The authority to request information is based on RCRA § 3007(a).

16 40 C.F.R. Part 261.

characteristics to identify hazardous wastes.[17] Generally, a waste is designated as a hazardous waste if it exhibits certain characteristics, or if it has been listed as a hazardous waste under state or federal regulations. The characteristics include reactivity, ignitability, corrosivity and toxicity. If the waste in question demonstrates chemical reactivity, ignites under certain conditions, causes corrosion under certain conditions, or is toxic, then that waste may be designated as a hazardous waste.

The Hazardous Waste Law defines hazardous waste to include all solid wastes or combinations of solid wastes which may (1) cause or significantly contribute to an increase in mortality or an increase in a serious irreversible or incapacitating reversible illness; or (2) pose a substantial existing or potential hazard to human health or the environment when improperly treated, stored, transported, disposed of or otherwise managed.[18] Solid waste is defined broadly under the Hawaii law to include the following: garbage; refuse; other discarded materials, including solid, liquid, semisolid, or contained gaseous materials resulting from industrial, commercial, mining and agricultural operations; sludge from waste treatment plants and water supply treatment plants; and residues from air pollution control facilities and community activities.[19]

Certain wastes are excluded from the definition of hazardous waste, and hence from regulation under state or federal hazardous waste law. In general, wastes produced at a particular facility which are excluded by the EPA are not necessarily excluded under state law: for the exclusion to apply, it must be adopted by the State through rulemaking procedures. Solid or dissolved material in domestic sewage, irrigation return flows, or industrial discharges which are subject to permits under the Water Pollution Law,[20] however, are excluded from the statutory definition of solid waste.[21] Drilling fluids, produced waters and other wastes associated with exploration, development, or production of crude oil, natural gas or geothermal energy are

---

17 Haw. Rev. Stat. § 342J-31(3).

18 *Id.* § 342J-2.

19 *Id.*

20 Haw. Rev. Stat. ch. 342D. *See supra* ch. 3 of this Handbook.

21 *Id.* § 342J-2. *See supra* ch. 5 of this Handbook.

regulated as hazardous waste under state rules,[22] although RCRA exempts them from regulation.[23]

Household waste is defined under the Hazardous Waste Law to include any material derived from households, including garbage, trash, and sanitary wastes in septic tanks from residences, campgrounds, and hotels.[24] "Household waste" also includes waste from hotels, motels and day-use recreation areas.[25] Waste generated by hotels is therefore exempt under both state and federal law.[26]

4.0 REGULATION OF GENERATORS, TRANSPORTERS, AND HAZARDOUS WASTE FACILITIES

The Director has established standards applicable to generators,[27] transporters,[28] treatment, storage or disposal facilities,[29] persons who deal with hazardous waste fuel,[30] and hazardous waste brokers.[31] These include standards regarding operating practices, recordkeeping requirements, corrective action plans and other related requirements.

4.1 GENERATORS

As generators are in the position to begin the "cradle-to-grave" monitoring of hazardous waste, the requirements governing generators are of particular importance. Under federal and

22 Haw. Admin. Rules § 11-261-4(b)(5).

23 40 C.F.R. 261.4(b)(5).

24 Haw. Rev. Stat. § 342J-2.

25 *See* Haw. Admin. Rules § 11-261-4(b)(1).

26 Compare RCRA exemption of wastes generated by hotels as household waste at 40 C.F.R. 261.4(b)(1).

27 Haw. Rev. Stat. § 342J-32.

28 *Id.* § 342J-33.

29 *Id.* § 342J-34. Hazardous waste transporters must also comply with Haw. Rev. Stat. ch. 286, Part XII, which regulates the transportation of hazardous materials, hazardous waste and etiologic agents.

30 Haw. Rev. Stat. § 342J-34.5.

31 *Id.* § 342J-34.6

state law,[32] the EPA and the Department are directed to adopt standards for generators to require hazardous waste identification, recordkeeping, labeling, use of appropriate containers, furnishing of information on hazardous waste to others, use of a manifest system, waste minimization certification and preparation of biennial reports.

Small quantity generators are regulated under the Hazardous Waste Law. Small quantity generators are those who produce less than 1,000 kilograms of hazardous waste per month.[33] The types of businesses or operations typically considered small quantity generators include businesses or operations involved in vehicle maintenance, metal manufacturing, equipment repair, photography, laundries and dry cleaners, wood preserving, textile manufacturing, construction, pesticides and application services, laboratories, chemical manufacturing, motor freight terminals, leather and leather products, formulators, cleaning and cosmetics, the paper industry, furniture and wood manufacturing and refinishing, and educational and vocational shops.

Wastes generated by small quantity generators of less than 100 kilograms of non-acute hazardous waste or less than one kilogram of acute hazardous waste per month, as defined in the rules,[34] are not subject to land disposal regulations. Waste pesticides that a farmer disposes of properly also are not subject to these regulations.[35] The rules explicitly prohibit dilution as a substitute for treatment of certain hazardous waste.[36] Combustion is also prohibited, unless the waste can be demonstrated to comply with specific criteria.[37]

---

32 42 U.S.C. § 6922; Haw. Rev. Stat. § 342J-3.

33 Haw. Admin. Rules § 11-260-10.

34 *Id.* § 11-261-5.

35 *Id.* §§ 262-10(f), 11-262-70.

36 *Id.* § 11-268-3. Dilution is permissible only for hazardous waste in specified treatment systems operated under the Federal Clean Water Act. Id. § 11-268-3(b).

37 *Id.* § 11-268-3(c)

4.1.1 MANIFEST SYSTEM

A hazardous waste manifest is the document reviewed by the federal and state government to monitor and ensure proper disposal of hazardous waste. Generators must prepare a manifest on specified EPA forms describing the type of hazardous waste that has been generated.[38] Generators are to use the manifest forms provided by the State to which a shipment of hazardous waste is sent, or if no such form is provided, to use the manifest form of their own state.[39] The manifest must consist of at least the number of copies which will provide the initial transporter, each subsequent transporter, and the owner or operator of the disposal facility with one copy each for their records and another copy to be returned to the generator.[40]

The manifest travels with the hazardous waste. The generator must sign the manifest certification, obtain the signature of the initial transporter and date of acceptance, then retain one copy, and give the remaining copies of the manifest to the transporter.[41] Special rules apply to shipments of hazardous waste within the United States solely by water, for shipments by rail within Hawaii which originate at the site of generation, and for shipments of hazardous waste to a designated facility in an authorized state which has not yet obtained authorization by EPA to regulate that particular waste as hazardous.[42] If the transporter is unable to deliver the hazardous waste to the designated facility or the alternate facility, the generator must designate another facility or instruct the transporter to return the waste.[43] The generator must keep a copy of each manifest, including the signed copy from the designated facility which receives the waste, for three years.[44]

A generator who does not receive the final copy of the hazardous waste manifest must take steps to determine the status of the hazardous waste. For example, a generator who

---

38 *Id.* ch. 262, subchapter B.

39 *Id.* § 11-262-21.

40 *Id.* § 11-262-22.

41 *Id.* § 11-262-23(a) and (b).

42 *Id.* § 11-262-23(c), (d) and (e).

43 *Id.* § 11-262-20.

44 *Id.* §§ 11-262-20(e)(2) and 11-262-40(a).

produces more than 1,000 kilograms of hazardous waste in one calendar month should receive a copy of the manifest, signed by the owner or operator of the facility, within thirty-five days from the date the waste was accepted by the transporter. If no manifest is received, the generator must contact the transporter and the owner or operator to determine the status of the hazardous waste. In addition, if no copy of the manifest is received, an Exception Report must be submitted to the Director. The Exception Report is to include a legible copy of the manifest and a cover letter signed by the generator explaining efforts undertaken to locate the hazardous waste.[45]

4.1.2 OTHER REQUIREMENTS

The rules also prescribe certain pre-transport requirements regarding packaging, labeling, marking and placarding. The hazardous waste must be packaged in accordance with applicable U.S. Department of Transportation ("DOT") regulations.[46] Each container must be labeled, marked and placarded in accordance with DOT regulations.[47]

With certain exceptions, a generator may accumulate hazardous waste on-site for ninety days or less without a permit or without having interim status, provided the waste is placed in specified containers and the generator complies with other requirements as set forth in the rules.[48] A generator who accumulates hazardous waste for more than ninety days, however, becomes an operator of a storage facility subject to the requirements governing operators, unless the generator has been granted a time extension. Such extensions may be granted if the hazardous wastes remain on-site due to unforeseen, temporary, or uncontrollable circumstances. An extension of up to thirty days may be granted at the discretion of the Director on a case-by-case basis.[49]

A generator who generates greater than 100 kilograms but less than 1,000 kilograms of hazardous waste in one calendar month may accumulate hazardous waste on-site for 180 days or

---

45 *Id.* § 11-262-42.

46 *Id.* § 11-262-30.

47 *Id.* §§ 11-262-31, 11-262-32 and 11-262-33.

48 *Id.* § 11-262-34.

49 *Id.*

less without a permit. The generator may do so provided the quantity of waste accumulated on-site never exceeds 6,000 kilograms, and the generator complies with the requirements set forth in the rules.[50] This storage period may be extended to 270 days if the generator must ship wastes more than 200 miles or more for off-site treatment, storage or disposal.

Under Hawaii law, small quantity and large quantity generators are required to submit biennial reports to the Director. RCRA requires only large quantity generators--those who generate more than 1,000 kilograms of hazardous waste per month--to submit biennial reports. Any generator who ships hazardous waste off-site to a temporary storage and disposal facility must prepare and submit a biennial report to the Director by March 1 of each even-numbered year. The report must not only identify the generator, the type of hazardous waste, the transporters and the facilities to which the hazardous waste was shipped, but also must describe efforts undertaken during the year to reduce the volume and toxicity of waste generated, and describe the changes in volume and toxicity of waste actually achieved in comparison to previous years.[51] Likewise, any generator, whether small quantity or large quantity, who treats, stores or disposes of hazardous waste on-site must submit a biennial report covering those wastes.[52]

International exports of hazardous waste are permitted only upon notification to all parties, the receiving country's consent to accept the hazardous waste, EPA acknowledgement of that country's consent and conformance of the shipment to the terms of the consent.[53] Exception Reports are to be submitted where a copy of the manifest is not received by the generator in a timely manner, or the waste is returned to the United States.[54] Finally, exporters must also file annual reports with the EPA.[55]

---

50 *Id.* § 11-262-34(d).

51 *Id.* § 11-262-41.

52 *Id.*

53 *Id.* § 11-262-52.

54 *Id.* § 11-262-55.

55 *Id.* § 11-262-56.

Imports of hazardous waste from a foreign country which stay in Hawaii for more than ten days must be accompanied by a manifest identifying the foreign generator, the importer's name and the EPA identification number. Within thirty days of the arrival of the hazardous waste, the importer must inform the Director of the exact date of arrival of the waste and its current disposition.[56] Imports of hazardous waste from other states must follow similar requirements.[57] Under Hawaii law, persons who import hazardous waste from a foreign country are required to submit specific information in writing to the Director within thirty days,[58] and persons who import hazardous waste from any other state must also submit specific information in writing to the Director within thirty days.[59] RCRA has no similar requirements.

Farmers who dispose of hazardous waste in the form of pesticides need not comply with the standards set forth in Chapter 262, or other hazardous waste regulations, provided specific conditions are met. The waste from pesticides must be from the farmer's own use, the farmer must triple rinse each empty pesticide container and pesticide residues must be disposed of on the farmer's own farm in a manner consistent with the disposal instructions on the pesticide label.[60]

4.2 TRANSPORTERS

Federal and state law[61] establish similar requirements for haulers of hazardous waste. These include requirements for recordkeeping, labeling, compliance with the manifest system, and limiting transportation to the facility listed on the manifest. Regulations governing transporters are found in 40 C.F.R. Part 263, and Chapter 263 of the Hawaii Administrative Rules. In general, if transportation of hazardous waste into, within, or out of a state requires a manifest under Chapter 262 of the state rules, the transporter must comply with the requirements

---

56 *Id.* § 11-262-60.

57 *Id.* § 11-262-61.

58 *Id.* § 11-262-60(d).

59 *Id.* § 11-262-61.

60 *Id.* § 11-262-70.

61 42 U.S.C. § 6923; Haw. Rev. Stat. § 342J-33.

set forth in Chapter 263.[62] On-site transportation of hazardous waste, by generators or owners or operators of permitted hazardous waste management facilities, is not regulated under Chapter 263. Transporters must receive an EPA identification number from the EPA or the Director.[63] Special rules apply for bulk shipments of hazardous wastes shipped by water.[64]

A transporter may not accept hazardous waste from a generator unless it is accompanied by a manifest signed in accordance with the applicable rules.[65] Before transporting the hazardous waste, the transporter must sign and date the manifest acknowledging acceptance of the hazardous waste from the generator, and return the signed copy to the generator before leaving the property.[66] After ensuring that the manifest accompanies the hazardous waste to the point of delivery, the transporter must note the date of delivery and obtain the signature of the owner or operator of the facility to which the hazardous waste is delivered, retain one copy of the manifest and give the remaining copies to the accepting transporter or designated facility.

The transporter must deliver the entire quantity of hazardous waste which the transporter has accepted. If the hazardous waste cannot be delivered in accordance with the rules, the transporter must contact the generator for further directions and revise the manifest according to the generator's instructions.[67]

The transporter must keep a copy of the manifest signed by the generator, the initial transporter, and the next designated transporter, or the owner or operator of the designated facility, for a period of three years from the date the initial transporter accepted the shipment.[68] Similarly, a transporter who transports hazardous waste outside of the United States must keep a copy of the manifest, indicating that the hazardous waste left the United States, for a period of

---

62 Haw. Admin. Rules § 11-263-10.

63 *Id.* § 11-263-11.

64 *Id.* § 11-263-20(e).

65 *Id.* § 11-263-20.

66 *Id.*

67 *Id.* § 11-263-21.

68 *Id.* § 11-263-22.

three years after acceptance by the initial transporter.[69] These three year record retention periods are extended automatically during the course of any unresolved enforcement action regarding the regulated activity, or as requested by the Director.[70]

Transporters are responsible for taking immediate action to protect human health and the environment and cleaning up any hazardous waste discharge that occurs during transportation.[71] This action may include notifying local authorities and sealing off the discharge area. In an emergency situation, notice must be given to the Department[72] and the National Response Center.[73] Written notice must be provided to the DOT. Under such circumstances government officials may, if necessary to protect human health or the environment, authorize the transportation of hazardous waste without a manifest by transporters who do not have an EPA identification number.

4.3 TREATMENT, STORAGE AND DISPOSAL FACILITIES

The Hawaii Administrative Rules provide comprehensive standards for owners and operators of hazardous waste treatment, storage, and disposal ("TSD") facilities. The rules include regulations regarding general facility standards, standards for preparedness and prevention of hazardous waste spills, contingency plans and emergency procedures, manifest systems, recordkeeping, and reporting. The rules also discuss releases from solid waste management units, closure and post-closure activities, and financial requirements for TSD facilities. Furthermore, the rules prescribe requirements for various aspects of the TSD facility operations, including containers, tank systems, surface impoundments, waste piles, land treatment, landfills, incinerators, drip pads, and miscellaneous units. Finally, the rules provide air emission standards for process vents and equipment leaks.

---

69 *Id.* § 11-263-22.

70 *Id.*

71 *Id.* §§ 11-263-30, 11-263-31.

72 Notice should be provided to the Hazard Evaluation and Emergency Response office during business hours at (808) 586-4249 and after hours should be provided to the State Hospital at (808) 247-2191.

73 Telephone: (800) 424-8802 or (202) 426-2675.

The standards, found in Chapter 264 of the Hawaii Administrative Rules, apply to owners and operators of all TSD facilities within the State of Hawaii.[74] The TSD requirements also apply to disposal of hazardous waste in the ocean pursuant to a federally-issued permit, through underground injection, or via publicly owned treatment works. At the time of the publication of this Handbook, there are no TSD facilities currently open in Hawaii to receive wastes from off-site sources.

The TSD requirements do not apply to waste management facilities if the hazardous waste treated by the facility is not regulated under Chapter 264, nor do they apply to facilities managing recyclable materials. Furthermore, the rules do not apply to generators accumulating waste on-site in compliance with the rules, to farmers who dispose of waste pesticides from the farmers' own use, to the owner or operator of a totally enclosed treatment facility, to the owner or operator of an elementary neutralization unit or waste water treatment unit, or to a transporter temporarily storing manifested shipments of hazardous waste at a transfer facility for ten days or less.[75]

Under former state rules, resource recovery facilities that managed municipal solid waste were subject to regulation if they received and burned wastes from hotels. RCRA exempts these activities from regulation. Under the 1995 amendments to the Hazardous Waste Law, which exempted hotel waste from regulation as hazardous waste, this rule became null and void.[76] State rules furthermore require resource recovery facilities to establish contractual requirements or other notification or inspection procedures to assure that no hazardous wastes are received at or burned in the facility.[77]

4.3.1 MANIFESTS AND RECORDKEEPING

Like generators and transporters, all TSD facilities must participate in the hazardous waste manifest system. Upon receiving hazardous waste accompanied by a manifest, the owner

74 Haw. Admin. Rules § 11-264-1.

75 *Id.*

76 Haw. Rev. Stat. § 342J-2.

77 Haw. Admin. Rules § 11-261-4(b)(1). Compare to 40 C.F.R. 261.4(b)(1).

or operator of a TSD facility must sign and date each copy of the manifest and note any discrepancies between the quantity or type of hazardous waste designated on the manifest or shipping paper and the quantity or type actually received by the facility.[78] If a TSD facility discovers a significant discrepancy, it must attempt to resolve the discrepancy with the waste generator or transporter. If the significant discrepancy is not resolved within fifteen days, the TSD facility must provide written notice to the Director of the discrepancy and efforts to resolve it, along with a copy of the manifest.[79] The owner or operator must then give the transporter one copy of the manifest, send a copy to the generator, and retain one copy for at least three years from the date of delivery.[80]

It is possible for a TSD facility to accept hazardous waste from an off-site source without an accompanying manifest or shipping paper. In this situation the owner or operator must prepare and submit an unmanifested waste report, on EPA Form 8700-13B, which is to include the EPA identification number for the facility, the date the facility received the waste, the EPA identification number of the transporter, a description and the quantity of each unmanifested hazardous waste, and a brief explanation of why the waste was unmanifested, if known.[81]

Upon receipt of waste from an off-site source, a TSD facility must inform the generator in writing that the facility has the appropriate permits and will accept the waste. The TSD facility must keep these records for three years.[82]

Owners and operators of TSD facilities must comply with recordkeeping requirements. Under these requirements, TSD facilities must keep written operating records which include detailed descriptions of the quantity of each hazardous waste received and the method and date of treatment, storage or disposal. These records must also include the location of each hazardous waste, the results of waste analyses, reports of incidents, inspections, monitoring and corrective

---

78 Haw. Admin. Rules § 11-264-71(a).

79 *Id.* § 11-264-72.

80 *Id.* § 11-264-71.

81 *Id.* § 11-264-76.

82 *Id.* § 11-264-12(b).

action.[83] Owners and operators also must prepare and submit a biennial report to the Director by March 1st of each even numbered year.[84]

4.3.2 SAFETY MEASURES AND RELEASE RESPONSE

All TSD facilities must be designed, constructed and maintained so as to minimize the possibility of fire, explosion, or other unplanned release of hazardous waste.[85] Toward this end facilities must be equipped with regularly maintained alarm systems, communications systems, fire control equipment, spill control equipment, decontamination equipment and water deliverable through a hose or sprinkler system.[86] Personnel involved in operating the facility must have immediate access to an internal alarm or emergency communication device.[87] The owner or operator of the TSD facility must maintain aisle space to allow the unobstructed movement of personnel.[88] Furthermore, the owner or operator of the facility must arrange to familiarize in advance police, fire and other emergency response teams with the layout of the facility, the hazardous waste handled at the facility and the nature of the operations.[89]

Every facility owner or operator must apply to the State for an EPA identification number.[90] Before the owner or operator treats, stores, or disposes of any hazardous wastes, a detailed chemical and physical analysis of a sample of the waste must be obtained.[91] Certain hazardous wastes pose specific risks which must be guarded against. For example, ignitable or reactive hazardous waste must be separated and protected from sources of ignition or reaction

---

83 *Id.* § 11-264-73.

84 *Id.* § 11-264-75.

85 *Id.* § 11-264-31.

86 *Id.* §§ 11-264-32, 11-264-33.

87 *Id.* § 11-264-34.

88 *Id.* § 11-264-35.

89 *Id.* § 11-264-37.

90 *Id.* § 11-264-11.

91 *Id.* § 11-264-13.

such as open flames, smoking, welding and hot surfaces or radiant heat.[92] Next, the owner or operator must develop and follow a written waste analysis plan which describes the procedures to be carried out to comply with the applicable regulations.[93]

The rules prescribe standards for the location of the TSD facility. Care must be taken when locating any facility near faults, floodplains, salt dome formations or underground mines and caves.[94] The owner or operator must prevent the unknowing entry, and minimize the possibility for unauthorized entry, of persons or livestock onto the active portion of the facility.[95] This may be accomplished by a twenty-four hour surveillance system, an artificial or natural barrier which completely surrounds the active portion of the facility, or other means to control entry at all times. Signs must also be posted warning unauthorized persons to keep out.[96] Furthermore, the owner or operator has a duty to inspect the facility for malfunctions, deterioration, operator errors and discharges which may be causing or may lead to hazardous waste releases or a threat to human health.[97] The owner or operator must also provide classroom instruction or on-the-job training for personnel.[98]

All TSD facilities must have a contingency plan designed to minimize hazards to human health or the environment from fires, explosions, or any unplanned sudden or non-sudden release of hazardous waste or hazardous waste constituents to air, soil or surface water.[99] The contingency plan must: (1) describe in detail the actions facility personnel will undertake in response to such an emergency; (2) describe agreements with police and fire departments, hospitals and emergency response teams; (3) list names, addresses and phone numbers of qualified emergency coordinators; (4) list all emergency equipment at the facility; and (5)

---

92 *Id.* § 11-264-17.

93 *Id.* § 11-264-13.

94 *Id.* § 11-264-18.

95 *Id.* § 11-264-14.

96 *Id.*

97 *Id.* § 11-264-15.

98 *Id.* § 11-264-16.

99 *Id.* § 11-264-51.

include an evacuation plan for facility personnel.[100] Copies of the contingency plan and all revisions to the plan, must be maintained at the facility, and submitted to county police departments, fire departments, hospitals, state and county emergency response teams.[101]

At all times there must be at least one employee of the TSD facility, designated as an emergency coordinator, available to respond to any emergency. The emergency coordinator must be familiar with all aspects of the facility contingency plan, its operations and must have the authority to commit resources necessary to carry out the plan.[102]

In the event of a hazardous waste release a TSD facility may be required to take response actions, including corrective measures which are necessary to protect human health or the environment. The Director may require corrective action beyond the facility boundaries, if necessary to protect human health or the environment. Owners and operators must use their best efforts to obtain permission to complete corrective action beyond the facility boundaries.[103] To initiate response actions to a hazardous waste release, the Director may issue an order requiring the corrective action or file a civil action in state court for injunctive relief. The Director may also impose and collect civil penalties. Failure to comply with an order from the Director is considered a violation of the Hazardous Waste Law.[104]

In addition to completing corrective action, a person who receives an order may be required to submit a proposal to the Director within thirty days describing how the required monitoring, testing and analysis will be accomplished. The Director may prescribe the technical aspects of the corrective action if the Director determines that the owner or operator is unable to complete the action in a satisfactory manner. The cost of the prescribed corrective action remains the responsibility of the operator or owner of the facility. Public notice must be given for proposed Department decisions on a final remedy.[105]

---

100 *Id.* § 11-264-52.

101 *Id.* § 11-264-53.

102 *Id.* § 11-264-55.

103 Haw. Rev. Stat. § 342J-36(a)(2).

104 *Id.* § 342J-36(b).

105 *Id.* § 342J-36.

4.3.3 OTHER REQUIREMENTS

TSD facility owners and operators must conduct monitoring and response programs to assure compliance with applicable regulations.[106] The owner or operator must institute a detection monitoring program. A compliance monitoring program must be instituted when hazardous waste constituents are detected at a compliance point specified in the facility's permit. Compliance points are identified and described in the rules.[107] A corrective action program must be instituted when groundwater protection standards are exceeded.[108] Each permit issued to a TSD facility will specify the specific elements of the monitoring and response program and a groundwater protection standard which is designed to ensure that hazardous constituents do not exceed concentration limits.[109] General groundwater monitoring requirements and the parameters for detection monitoring, compliance monitoring and corrective action programs are also prescribed by the rules.

The closure of a TSD facility triggers specific requirements. TSD facilities must be closed pursuant to a written closure plan approved by the Director in a manner that minimizes the need for further maintenance and controls, minimizes or eliminates the post-closure escape of hazardous waste, leachate, contaminated runoff or other hazardous waste pollution.[110] The owner or operator has ninety days after receiving the final volume of hazardous wastes to treat, remove from the unit or facility, or dispose of on-site, all hazardous wastes in accordance with an approved closure plan.[111] The owner or operator must prepare a post-closure plan, which identifies the activities that will be carried on after closure of each disposal unit.[112] The owner or operator of the facility must have a cost estimate for closure, including a detailed written estimate of the cost of closing the facility in accordance with a applicable closure

---

106 Haw. Admin. Rules § 11-264-91.

107 *Id.* § 11-264-95.

108 *Id.* § 11-264-91.

109 *Id.* §§ 11-264-92 to -94.

110 *Id.* §§ 11-264-111, 11-264-112.

111 *Id.* § 11-264-113.

112 *Id.* § 11-264-118.

requirements.[113] Owners and operators must establish financial assurance for closure of the facility by setting up a closure trust fund or some other means of demonstrating financial ability to satisfy the requirements of the rules regarding closure of TSD facilities.[114]

Owners and operators must also demonstrate financial responsibility for bodily injury and property damage to third parties caused by sudden accidental occurrences. Liability coverage must be provided for sudden accidental occurrences in the amount of at least $1 million per occurrence with an annual aggregate of at least $2 million, exclusive of legal defense costs. Coverage for nonsudden accidental occurrences must also be maintained by owners and operators of surface impoundments, landfills, or land treatment facilities. The liability coverage for nonsudden accidental occurrences must be at least $3 million per occurrence, with an annual aggregate of at least $6 million, exclusive of legal defense costs. An owner or operator may seek exemptions from these financial responsibility requirements.[115]

The rules also prescribe a host of comprehensive technical requirements regarding various types of TSD facilities, including containers, tank systems, surface impoundments, waste piles, land treatment facilities, landfills and incinerators.[116] Such requirements are also provided for: corrective action for solid waste management units; drip pads; miscellaneous units; air emission standards for processed vents and equipment leaks; air emission standards for tanks, surface impoundments and containers; containment buildings; and hazardous waste munitions and explosives storage.[117]

An owner or operator of a facility that has arranged to receive hazardous waste from a foreign source must notify the Director and the EPA in writing at least four weeks before the waste arrives at the facility.[118] Before transferring ownership or operation of the facility, the

113 *Id.* § 11-264-142.

114 *Id.* § 11-264-143.

115 *Id.* § 11-264-147.

116 *Id.* § 11-264, subchapters I-O.

117 *Id.* § 11-264, subchapters S, W, X, and AA-DD.

118 *Id.* § 11-264-12(a).

owner or operator must notify the new owner or operator in writing of the requirements of Chapters 264 and 270 of the rules.[119]

4.3.4 LAND DISPOSAL RESTRICTIONS

The rules provide detailed and comprehensive regulations regarding disposal of hazardous waste on land. In general, the purpose of the land disposal regulations is to identify hazardous waste that cannot safely be disposed of on land and to define limited circumstances under which an otherwise prohibited waste may continue to be disposed of on land.[120] The rules apply to generators, transporters and TSD facilities. These regulations are found in Chapter 268 of the rules. Chapter 268 adopts the federal requirements at 40 C.F.R. Part 268 governing land disposal restrictions, with one exception: the Hawaii regulations have no provisions to allow for exemptions to or extensions to the effective date of any land disposal restriction, whereas federal law allows such applications for such exemptions or extensions to be made to the EPA.[121] The rules prohibit land disposal of certain specific types of hazardous wastes and also set forth treatment standards.

4.3.5 RECYCLING AND RECLAMATION

The rules provide comprehensive regulations for the management of specific hazardous wastes and specific types of hazardous waste management facilities.[122] Chapter 266, which contains these regulations, adopts the federal requirements at 40 C.F.R. Part 266 governing standards for the management of specific hazardous wastes and specific types of hazardous waste management facilities. These include standards for recyclable materials used in a way that constitutes hazardous waste disposal, use of recyclable materials for precious metal recovery and the reclamation of spent lead-acid batteries. Hazardous waste burning boilers and industrial furnaces are also regulated.

---

119 *Id.* § 11-264-12(c).

120 *Id.* § 11-268-1.

121 40 C.F.R. §§ 268.5, 268.6.

122 Haw. Admin. Rules ch. 266.

The provisions regarding recyclable materials used in the manner constituting disposal provide that products produced for public use that are disposed of, and contain recyclable materials, are not subject to regulation, provided certain requirements are met. Under these regulations the use of waste oil which is contaminated with dioxin or any other hazardous waste for dust suppression or road treatment is prohibited.[123]

Persons who reclaim spent lead-acid batteries that are recyclable are subject to certain notification requirements under the rules. Those who generate, transport, or collect spent batteries, or store them but do not reclaim them are not subject to regulation under these rules or the Hazardous Waste Law.[124] Used oil burned for energy recovery that is also a hazardous waste solely because it exhibits hazardous waste characteristics is not subject to regulation under Chapter 266 but is subject to the used oil regulations in Chapter 279.[125]

5.0 HAZARDOUS WASTE BROKERS

In addition to regulating generators, transporters, and TSD facilities, the Hazardous Waste Law also regulates hazardous waste brokers, who are defined by the following three characteristics. First, hazardous waste brokers are persons who act as an intermediary between generators, transporters, other brokers, or facilities which treat, store, or dispose of hazardous waste.[126] Second, brokers are persons who mix hazardous wastes of different descriptions by placing them in a single container, who package or repackage hazardous waste, who label, mark, or manifest hazardous waste, or who perform waste characterization. Third, brokers are persons who arrange for storage, treatment, transportation, disposal or recycling of hazardous waste for a fee based upon the completion of the transaction.[127]

---

123 *Id.* § 11-266-23. The used oil regulations also flatly prohibit the use of any used oil, whether contaminated or not, as a dust suppressant. *See* Haw. Admin. R. § 11-279-12(b) and 40 C.F.R. § 11-279-12(b).

124 *Id.* § 11-266-80.

125 *Id.* § 11-266-100.

126 Haw. Rev. Stat. § 342J-2.

127 *Id.*

Hazardous waste brokers handling any substance listed or identified by its characteristics as a hazardous waste under state or federal rules must apply to the Department for an identification number. Brokers must also file with the Department a notification stating the location and general description of the hazardous waste handling activity of the broker.[128] The broker must provide basic information to the Department regarding the broker's business, including the name, location, and mailing address of business, and the names of the facility owner, land owner and facility operator. A notarized written statement acknowledging the hazardous waste handling activity of the broker must also be submitted.[129]

6.0 TECHNICAL ASSISTANCE AND PUBLIC EDUCATION PROGRAMS

Pursuant to the Hazardous Waste Law, the Department is required to establish a technical assistance program for generators of hazardous waste.[130] The program is intended to assist in the identification of hazardous wastes and in compliance with the hazardous waste management program, particularly for small quantity generators and small businesses. The technical assistance program is required, at a minimum, to establish outreach programs, disseminate relevant information, assist with improvement of hazardous waste management and identify alternate technical solutions to reduce the generation of hazardous waste.

The Department is required to implement a public education program to increase public awareness of the hazardous waste management program.[131] The program's objectives include the dissemination of information so that the public, households, businesses and other institutions can improve their management of hazardous wastes. The Department assists the community by conducting a statewide household hazardous waste collection project[132] and a hazardous waste collection project in public schools.[133]

---

128 *Id.* § 342J-34.6.

129 *Id.*

130 *Id.* § 342J-41.

131 *Id.* § 342J-42.

132 The 1992 Legislature appropriated $350,000 to conduct a statewide hazardous waste collection project. Act approved June 19, 1992, ch. 277, § 3, 1992 Haw. Sess. Laws 723.

133 The 1992 Legislature appropriated $50,000 for the removal of hazardous wastes from public schools in the State. Act approved June 10, 1992, ch. 161, § 2, 1992 Haw. Sess. Laws 300.

7.0 PERMITS

All hazardous waste management facilities must have a permit to treat, store or dispose of hazardous waste. In addition, no person may construct, own or operate a hazardous waste management facility without obtaining a permit.[134] When a facility is owned by one person but operated by another, the duty to obtain the permit falls upon the operator. The owner, however must sign the permit application.[135] The rules governing permits for the hazardous waste program are found in Chapter 270 of the Hawaii Administrative Rules. Chapter 270 adopts the federal requirements at 40 C.F.R. Part 270 governing its state administered hazardous waste permit program, with one exception: State hazardous waste management permits are issued for a maximum fixed term of five years;[136] whereas federal law permits may be issued for a maximum term of ten years.[137]

Hazardous waste management facilities may obtain interim status under RCRA § 3005[138] or under the Hazardous Waste Law. Facility owners and operators with interim status are treated as having been issued a permit until the Department makes a final determination on the permit application.[139] The regulations governing TSD facilities granted interim status are set forth in Chapter 265 of the Hawaii Administrative Rules. Chapter 265 adopts the federal requirements at 40 C.F.R. Part 265 governing interim status standards for owners and operators of TSD facilities.[140] Interim status may be terminated automatically in the event that a schedule of compliance is not met. Hazardous waste management facilities in compliance with federal permitting standards will be authorized to operate under the Hazardous Waste Law when Hawaii becomes an authorized State and enforcement authority is transferred from the EPA.[141]

---

134 Haw. Rev. Stat. § 342J-30.

135 Haw. Admin. Rules § 11-270-10.

136 *Id.* § 11-270-50(a).

137 40 C.F.R. 270.50(a).

138 42 U.S.C. § 6925.

139 Haw. Admin. Rules § 11-270-1.

140 *Id.* ch. 265.

141 Haw. Rev. Stat. § 342J-30.

Temporary emergency permits for treatment, storage and disposal may be issued by the Director upon finding an imminent and substantial endangerment to human health or the environment.[142] Such permits may be written or oral, and are intended to allow nonpermitted facilities or individuals to process or handle hazardous waste under emergency circumstances. Emergency permits are only valid for ninety days, and will clearly specify the type of hazardous waste which may be received by the facility, along with the manner and location of treatment, storage or disposal.

To encourage the development of innovative treatment methods, the Director may issue research, development and demonstration permits for hazardous waste treatment facilities which propose to use experimental technologies or processes for which there are no permit standards promulgated.[143]

All permits issued by the Director will require corrective action for releases of hazardous waste.[144] The permits will require assurance of financial responsibility for corrective action and may contain a schedule of compliance when the corrective action cannot be completed prior to the issuance of the permit. If a permittee's action violates Hawaii's Hazardous Waste Law, a permit will not preclude the Director from taking enforcement action.[145]

Permit applications must be submitted to the Director.[146] As noted, permits may be issued for a maximum of five years, provided that the facility and the applicant have complied with the provisions of the Hazardous Waste Law. At a minimum, permits will be reviewed five years after the date of issuance, and modified, if necessary, to comply with any amended provisions of the chapter. At the Director's discretion, the permit may be reviewed and modified at any time during its term. Conditions necessary to protect human health or the

142 Haw. Admin. Rules § 11-270-61.

143 *Id.* § 11-270-65.

144 Haw. Rev. Stat. § 342J-36(e).

145 *Id.* §342J-36(f).

146 *Id.* § 342J-5.

environment shall be imposed in every permit.[147] Permits are not transferable except after notice to the Director, who may require modification or revocation and reissuance.[148]

The Director may modify a permit, after the permittee is given an opportunity for a hearing, when the permittee has violated a term or condition of the permit, the permit was obtained through misrepresentation, there is a change in circumstance, or the modification is in the public interest.[149] Public notice must be given for a proposed permit issuance, reissuance, modification, denial or suspension. A public hearing may be held, but is not required, prior to the Director's issuance of a final decision on the permit. If the permit expires prior to reissuance, the permittee will not be considered in violation so long as the permittee complies with the terms and conditions of the previous permit. The Director may charge a fee for the issuance of a permit, which is credited to the general fund and is used to enforce and implement the terms and conditions of the permit.[150] As of the date of publication of this Handbook, the Department of Health does not charge a fee for a hazardous waste permit.

The Director must give public notice regarding denial of a permit application, preparation of a draft permit, or scheduling of a hearing. No public notice is required for the denial of a request for permit modification, revocation, reissuance, or termination. Public notice of the preparation of a draft permit must allow at least forty-five days for public comment and notice of public hearing must be given at least thirty days before the hearing. Notice will be given by mailing a copy of the notice to the parties involved and various state and federal agencies. For major permits, notice may be given through publication in a major local newspaper of general circulation. Public notices for hearings must be given at least thirty days before the hearing and include reference to the date of previous public notices relating to the permit and a brief description of the nature and purpose of the hearing, including the applicable rules and procedures.[151]

---

147 *Id.*

148 Haw. Admin. Rules § 11-270-30.

149 Haw. Rev. Stat. § 342J-5(c).

150 *Id.* § 342J-13.

151 Haw. Admin. Rules § 11-271-10.

The public hearing may be requested during the public comment period, at which time any interested person may also submit written comments. The request for public hearing must be in writing and must state the nature of the issues proposed to be raised in the hearing.[152] Alternatively, members of the public may submit comments on the draft permit. The rules require that all comments not only be answered, but also considered in making the final decision.

All hazardous waste management permits require that certain conditions be met. These conditions include the duty to comply with all terms of the permit, the duty to take reasonable steps to minimize releases to the environment in the event of noncompliance, and proper operation and maintenance of the facility.[153] A permittee has a duty to take samples or perform monitoring as required by its permit. Detailed monitoring records must be kept for the active life of the facility. Disposal facilities must keep records during the post-closure care period as well. Monitoring must be reported as required by the permit. Permittees must allow the Director, or an authorized representative, to enter the premises, inspect and copy records, and sample or monitor facility activities.

A permittee must notify the Director of any planned physical alterations to the facility. Hazardous waste may not be stored in the newly-modified portion of the facility until written notification has been given to the Director by the permittee and a professional engineer stating that the modifications are in compliance with the permit, and either the Director has inspected the facility or waived the right to do so.[154]

If a permitee discovers a significant discrepancy in a manifest and cannot reconcile the discrepancy in fifteen days, a written letter report must be submitted to the Director. The receipt of unmanifested waste must also be reported to the Director within fifteen days. Permittees must also submit biennial reports in odd numbered calendar years and have a duty to supplement or correct all information provided to the Director in a permit application or report.[155]

---

152 *Id.* § 11-271-11.

153 *Id.* § 11-270-30.

154 *Id.* § 11-270-30(l).

155 *Id.*

A permit holder has a duty to report to the Department any noncompliance which may endanger health or the environment within twenty-four hours from the time the permittee becomes aware of such circumstances. This reporting must describe any release of any hazardous waste that may endanger public drinking water supplies, or any fire or explosion which may threaten the environment or human health outside the facility along with other information regarding the occurrence, as required by rule. Within five days of the event, a written description of the noncompliance and its cause must be provided to the Department. The written submission must include the exact dates and times of the noncompliance. If the noncompliance has not been corrected, the submission must include the anticipated time it is expected to continue, and steps taken or planned to reduce, eliminate and prevent reoccurrence of the noncompliance. The Director may waive the five day notice requirement in favor of a written report within fifteen days.[156]

8.0 GUARANTORS

The 1991 amendments to the Hazardous Waste Law added a provision relating to guarantors, which are defined as any person, other than the owner or operator, who provides evidence of financial responsibility for an owner or operator under the Hazardous Waste Law.[157] This provision allows claims to be asserted directly against guarantors of owners and operators where the owner or operator is in bankruptcy or reorganization pursuant to the Federal Bankruptcy Code.[158] Claims also may be asserted against guarantors if jurisdiction in state court cannot be obtained over a solvent owner or operator with reasonable diligence. The claims asserted against the guarantor must arise from conduct for which the evidence of financial responsibility is required. Procedurally and substantively, the guarantor may assert all defenses and rights which would have been available to the owner or operator.

The total liability of a guarantor is limited to the aggregate amount provided to the owner or operator as evidence of financial responsibility. However, any contractual or common law liability of the guarantor to the owner or operator is not changed by the guarantor provision. In

156 *Id.*

157 Haw. Rev. Stat. § 342J-10.6(c).

158 *Id.* § 342J-10.6(a).

terms of liability to the State for response costs, the liability of a guarantor does not diminish the liability of a responsible party under the state Environmental Response Law.[159]

9.0 ENFORCEMENT

The Department, county health authorities and police department officers are authorized to enforce the Hazardous Waste Law, the rules and any orders issued by the Department.[160] The Department generally serves as the lead agency for enforcement actions. Although citizen suits were previously allowed to enforce the Hazardous Waste Law, this provision was repealed in 1996.

Upon determining that a person has violated or is violating the Hazardous Waste Law, rules or permits, the Director may require compliance immediately or within a specified time period, issue an order assessing a administrative penalty for any past or current violation, or commence a civil action for an injunction or other appropriate relief. Factors to be considered in imposing an administrative penalty include the nature and history of the violation and any prior violations; the economic benefit, if any, resulting from the violation; the nature of the corrective action; and any other matters that justice may require. The violator carries the burden of proving its economic and financial conditions make it unable to pay any proposed penalty. The Director's order may modify, revoke or suspend a permit issued under the Hazardous Waste Law or under RCRA. Corrective action may be taken for continuing releases at permitted facilities[161] and for releases beyond the facility's boundary.[162]

An order issued by the Director will become final in twenty days after the notice of order is served, unless the person who was served requests a hearing before the Director in writing. An administrative penalty imposed by an order will become final in twenty days after the notice of penalty is served, unless the person served requests a hearing before the Director in writing. If

---

159 *Id.* § 342J-10.6(b). The Environmental Response Law is set forth in Haw. Rev. Stat. ch. 128D. *See infra* ch. 8 of this Handbook.

160 *Id.* § 342J-18.

161 42 U.S.C. § 6924(u).

162 *Id.* § 6924(v).

a hearing is requested, any penalty will become due and payable only after the final order is issued.[163]

All hearings are conducted as contested cases under the Hawaii Administrative Procedure Act.[164] If the Director determines that a violation has occurred and imposes an administrative penalty, that penalty becomes due and payable upon the Director's issuance of a final decision. If the penalty is not paid within thirty days, the Director may file a civil action to recover the fine. To facilitate the hearing process, the Director is empowered to subpoena the attendance of witnesses and the production of evidence.[165] Any person who has an interest which may be adversely affected by the hazardous waste activity may intervene in any civil action to enforce the provisions of the Hazardous Waste Law.[166]

9.1 INSPECTIONS

The Director or a representative may inspect any facility where hazardous wastes are generated, stored, treated, or disposed of, or from which hazardous wastes are transported. Upon the request of the Director, information and records relating to hazardous waste must be furnished by a representative of the facility for review and copying. The Director may inspect and obtain samples of hazardous waste and may obtain all other information, including financial information, to determine compliance with the Hazardous Waste Law.[167]

9.2 CIVIL PENALTIES

Any person who violates the Hazardous Waste Law, its rules, or a permit is subject to a maximum $25,000 penalty for each offense. Any person who denies access or obstructs entrance and inspection, or fails to provide information as requested by an authorized representative of the Director is subject to a maximum $10,000 penalty for each offense. In calculating the number of

---

163 Haw. Rev. Stat. § 342J-7.

164 Haw. Rev. Stat. ch. 91. *See infra* ch. 13 of this Handbook.

165 Haw. Rev. Stat. § 342J-7.

166 *Id.* § 342J-16.

167 *Id.* § 342J-6.

violations for which a penalty may be imposed, each day of violation is considered a separate offense.[168] Any action taken in court to impose or collect the penalty is considered a civil, not criminal, action. This approach parallels the EPA method for the calculation of multi-day civil penalties. All collected penalties and fines are deposited into the environmental response revolving fund.[169]

The Department has adopted an administrative and civil penalty policy ("Policy") for its hazardous waste program.[170] The Policy is intended to provide a logical system for quantifying the gravity of violations of the hazardous waste laws consistent with EPA's penalty policy and to reflect existing State administrative policies. The policy is based on the federal "RCRA Civil Penalty Policy" dated October 1990, with modifications to adapt it to the state's context and to address the Small Quantity Generators who comprise the major percentage of Hawaii's regulated hazardous waste handlers. The Policy is intended only for the guidance of the Department's personnel, and cannot be relied upon to create substantive or procedural rights. The Department has also reserved the right to act at variance with or to change the Policy at any time.

The Policy calculates a penalty figure by computing the economic benefit to the violator and adding a gravity component and a multi-day component.[171] Where a violator has violated several hazardous waste laws, a separate penalty will be calculated for each violation resulting from an independent act, or failure to act, by the violator. For example, failure to implement a groundwater monitoring program, and failure to have a written closure plan, are violations which result from different sets of circumstances and which pose separate risks.

The "economic benefit" is the amount of money that the violator has saved through noncompliance, either by delaying the expenditures necessary to achieve compliance or by permanently avoiding costs associated with compliance.

---

168 *Id.* § 342J-9.

169 *Id.* § 342J-10.5.

170 State of Hawaii, Department of Health, Administrative and Civil Penalty Policy, Hazardous Waste Program (January 2000).

171 *Id.* at 2.

The "gravity" component of a penalty reflects the seriousness of the violation and adds an additional amount to the economic benefit to ensure that the violator is worse off than if the law had been obeyed. The seriousness of the violation is based on its potential for harm and the extent of deviation from a statutory or regulatory requirement. The Policy establishes a matrix for computing the gravity component of a penalty. The axes of the matrix are defined by the potential for harm and the extent of deviation from requirements. For penalties for which the maximum amount is $25,000, the gravity component may range from $100 to $25,000, depending upon which cell of the matrix the violator is categorized. For penalties for which the maximum amount is $10,000, the gravity component may range from $40 to $10,000.[172]

Multi-day penalties are assessed when there are repeated acts, or acts that present considerable risk or harm, such as where someone improperly disposes of large quantities of hazardous waste on more than one occasion, or when someone illegally imports hazardous wastes on separate occasions. Each day of violation is significant and warrants a separate penalty. The gravity-based designations are used to determine the proper cell from the multi-day matrix. Multi-day penalties are then calculated based on the number of days of violation. The policy presumes the assessment of multi-day penalties, when deemed appropriate, for 2 to 180 days. Multi-day penalties beyond the 180th day are discretionary. Under the multi-day matrix, multi-day penalties may range from $20 per day to $2,000 per day. Nothing in the Policy, however, precludes the Department from assessing penalties of up to $25,000, or $10,000 (depending on the violation), for each day of any violation.[173]

The Policy allows adjustment factors which can increase, reduce or have no effect on the penalty amount. Adjustment factors include the degree of willfulness/negligence, history of noncompliance, and other unique factors.[174]

---

172 *Id.* at 3-4.

173 *Id.* at 6-8.

174 *Id.* at 9-11.

The Policy also allows the Department to consider supplemental environmental projects as part of the settlement of a penalty claim. Projects will only be considered if the activity is initiated in addition to all statutory and regulatory compliance obligations, if the penalty deduction reflects the actual cost of undertaking the activity, if the activity demonstrates a good faith commitment to statutory and regulatory compliance and environmental improvement, if the mitigative effect of the project does not detract significantly from the general deterrent effect of the settlement as a whole, if the project is judicially-enforceable and requires little oversight by the Department, and if the activity provides a discernable response to the perceptible risk or harm caused by the violations that are the focus of the Department's enforcement action.[175]

The Policy allows the Department to consider the violator's ability to pay when a violator has met its burden of proving that it cannot afford the penalty prescribed by the policy. The Department may also consider ability to pay once the violator has proven that payment of all or a portion of the penalty will preclude the violator from achieving compliance or from carrying out remedial measures which the Department deems to be more important than the deterrent effect of the penalty.[176]

9.3 CRIMINAL PENALTIES

Any person who knowingly transports hazardous waste to a non-permitted facility is subject to criminal penalties.[177] An Environmental Crimes Task Force has been recently formed to assist in the prevention of illegal disposal activities involving hazardous substances. Criminal penalties may be imposed on any person who knowingly treats, stores or disposes of hazardous waste without first having a permit or on any person who knowingly makes a false statement on an application, report, manifest or any other document which is used to determine compliance with the Hazardous Waste Law. Criminal penalties may also be imposed for the transportation, storage, disposal or handling of used oil or used fuel oil in violation of the rules. The criminal penalties which may be imposed are fines up to $25,000 per day of violation or imprisonment for

---

175 *Id.* at 11-13.

176 *Id.* at 14.

177 Id. § 342J-9(c).

up to one year or both. Subsequent convictions for violations are subject to fines of up to $50,000 per day or imprisonment for up to two years or both.

Emergency orders may be issued by the Director or the Governor, without opportunity for an immediate hearing. The order must set a hearing to be held within twenty-four hours.[178]

9.4 RECORD KEEPING REQUIREMENTS AND ADMINISTRATIVE PROCEDURES

The Director may impose general recordkeeping requirements by rule and may require additional recordkeeping requirements as a condition of a permit. All reports and records which are submitted to the Department are open to the public pursuant to the Hawaii Uniform Information Practices Act, which governs the disclosure of public records.[179] Information such as manufacturing methods and secret processes may be classified as confidential. However, records which must be disclosed to the public under RCRA or the federal Freedom of Information Act cannot be kept confidential by the Department.[180]

Specific guidelines govern requests for information from the Department, as well as for establishing the confidentiality of business information.[181] The Department will disclose records in a manner that is consistent with the rights of individuals to privacy, the rights of business information to confidential treatment, and the need for the Department to safeguard internal policy deliberations from undue disruption.[182] In general, all records maintained by the hazardous waste program will be made available to the public unless they are exempt under the federal Freedom of Information Act.[183] The request must be made in writing and must describe the record sought in a manner that permits their identification and location by the Department.[184]

178 *Id.* § 342J-8.

179 Haw. Rev. Stat. ch. 92F.

180 *Id.* § 342J-14.

181 Haw. Admin. Rules ch. 280.

182 *Id.* § 11-280-101.

183 *Id.* § 11-280-101.

184 *Id.* § 11-280-108.

Chapter 271 of the state rules generally adopts federal rules governing informational public hearings, contested case hearings and declaratory rulings.[185] Chapter 271 also provides specific rules for governing contested case hearings. These rules supersede the procedures established by the Hawaii Administrative Procedure Act.[186] Chapter 280, Public Information, expands and defines procedures established under the Hawaii Uniform Information Practices Act.[187] These procedures apply to requests made with respect to Hawaii hazardous waste program only. Determinations regarding release of requested records must be made by the Department within twenty working days of the date the records were received. Chapter 280 also provides procedures governing claims that records submitted to the hazardous waste program are confidential.

The rules governing informational public hearings describe procedures for issuing, modifying, revoking and reissuing, or terminating hazardous waste permits.[188] The rules governing contested case hearings describe the powers and duties of the hearing officer, including methods to disqualify the officer.[189] The rules also provide for filing, service, and the form of the pleadings and other documents, such as the complaint.[190] Parties may appear in person or by counsel or other representative.[191] Persons who are not yet parties to a proceeding may file a motion for leave to intervene.[192]

9.5 OTHER ENFORCEMENT PROVISIONS

The Director is authorized to institute a civil action for injunctive or other relief to address any release of hazardous waste. Injunctive relief also may be sought to prevent any

---

185 40 C.F.R. Parts 24, 25.

186 Haw. Rev. Stat. ch. 91. *See infra* ch. 13 of this Handbook.

187 *Id.* ch. 92F.

188 Haw. Admin. Rules § 11-271-1.

189 *Id.* § 11-271-104.

190 *Id.* § 11-271-105.

191 *Id.* § 11-271-110.

192 *Id.* § 11-271-111.

violation of the Hazardous Waste Law, rules or a permit.[193] The Director is also authorized to institute a civil action to impose and collect civil penalties and obtain other relief.

In the event of an emergency in which the handling, treatment, disposal or transportation of hazardous wastes may present an imminent and substantial endangerment to the health or the environment, the Governor or the Director, without notice and hearing, may issue an order directing such actions as necessary to abate such danger or threat. The Governor or Director also may file a civil action to secure relief and to abate the danger or threat of a hazardous waste release.[194]

10. MANAGEMENT OF USED OIL

The rules pertaining to the management of used oil became effective March 13, 1999.[195] These rules largely duplicate the federal used oil regulations[196] which have been effective since 1992. The Hawaii rules identify which materials are subject to regulation as used oil. The Hawaii rules classify persons or facilities which handle oil as generators, collection centers, transporters, transfer facilities, processors, re-refiners, used oil burners, or marketers.[197]

"Used oil" means any oil that has been refined from crude oil, or any synthetic oil that has been used and as a result of such use is contaminated by physical or chemical impurities.[198] Mixtures of used oil and hazardous waste may be subject to regulation under the hazardous

---

193 Haw. Rev. Stat. § 342J-11.

194 *Id.* § 342J-8.

195 Haw. Admin. R. § 11-279-1 *et seq.* The former Hawaii solid waste rules regarding the recycling, transportation and disposal of used oil are still published at Haw. Admin. Rules § 11-58.1-54, as of the date of publication of this handbook. Those rules remained in effect until the adoption of the new rules pursuant to the Hazardous Waste Law on March 13, 1999. *See* 1996 Haw. Sess. Laws, Act 82, § 7. The former Hawaii statutes regarding the recycling, transportation and disposal of used oil, Chapter 342N, were repealed by the Legislature in 1996, but remain applicable to rights and duties that matured, penalties that were incurred, and proceedings that were begun, before June 6, 1996. *Id.*

196 40 C.F.R. 279.1 *et seq.*

197 Haw. Admin. R. § 11-279.1 *et seq.*

198 *Id.* at § 11-279-1.

waste rules.[199] There is a rebuttable presumption that used oil containing more than 1,000 ppm total halogens is presumed to be hazardous waste. If used oil is properly drained or removed from materials such that no visible signs of free-flowing oil remain in or on the material, the removed oil is subject to regulation and the material from which the used oil was drained is not subject to regulation as used oil unless burned for energy recovery, but may be subject to regulation as hazardous waste.[200] Generally, mixtures of used oil and fuels are subject to the used oil rules, except that mixtures of used oil and diesel fuel mixed on site by the generator for use in the generator's own vehicles are not subject to regulation.[201]

Used oil which is identified as a hazardous waste may only be disposed of in accordance with the hazardous waste rules. Nonhazardous used oil which cannot be recycled must be disposed of in accordance with the rules regarding solid waste.[202]

Materials reclaimed from used oil that are burned for energy are subject to the rules, but reclaimed materials that are used beneficially (such as for lubrication), are not. Materials reclaimed from used oil that are disposed of are not used oil, but instead are solid wastes subject to the hazardous waste rules. The used oil rules exempt from regulation wastewater contaminated with *de minimis* amounts of used oil, so long as the discharge is regulated by the Clean Water Act. Under specific circumstances, used oil introduced into crude oil pipelines or a petroleum refining facility is also exempt from regulation.[203]

Used oil may not be used as a dust suppressant, nor may it generally be managed in surface impoundments.[204] If used oil does not exceed specification levels for arsenic, cadmium, chromium, lead, flash point, total halogens and PCBs it may be burned for energy recovery

---

199 *Id.* at § 11-279-10.

200 *Id.*

201 *Id.*

202 *Id.* § 11-279-81.

203 *Id.* § 11-279-10.

204 *Id.* §§ 11-279-12, 11-279-82.

without being subject to regulation so long as the requirements for analyses and recordkeeping requirements are met, the EPA is notified and an EPA identification number is obtained.[205]

A permit must be obtained from the department before any person owns, operates, adds, extends or modifies a used oil transportation, marketing or recycling facility.[206] In addition to furnishing information on the application form, recycling facilities must also include an operations manual. Along with their application, transporters must provide a site plan, operations narrative, prevention plan for fires, spills, releases and stormwater runoff, and emergency response plan. Transporters and marketers are also required to apply for a permit to market used oil.[207] The public hearing requirements of the Hawaii Hazardous Waste Law do not apply to used oil permits, but the Director may require a public hearing for permit issuance, denial, revocation, or modification if the Director determines that a hearing is in the public interest.[208] Permits are valid for up to five years and may not be transferred or modified without the approval from the director. Permittees must notify the director within ninety days of termination of the operation of a used oil facility.[209]

Any person who violates the used oil rules is subject to any of the penalties applicable to hazardous waste violations.

10.1 USED OIL GENERATORS

A used oil generator is any person, by site, whose act or process produces used oil or whose act first causes the used oil to become subject to regulation. "Generators" do not include household do-it yourselfers, farmers who generate less than 25 gallons of used oil per month from vehicles or machinery used on the farm, and mixtures or oil and diesel fuel mixed by the generator for use in the generator's own vehicles. Vessels at sea or port are exempt from the used oil regulations, but once the used oil is brought ashore, the owner or operator of the vessel,

205 *Id.* § 11-279-11.

206 *Id.* § 11-279-90.

207 *Id.* § 11-279-92.

208 2000 Haw. Sess. Laws 3 (to be codified at Haw. Rev. Stat. 342J-5 and 342J-54).

209 *Id.* § 11-279-93.

along with the persons removing or accepting the used oil from the vessel are considered co-generators and are subject to regulation.[210]

Depending on a generator's activities, a generator may also be subject to regulation as a transporter, processor, burner and marketer. Generators are subject to the rules regarding the proper disposal of used oil.[211]

Generators may only store used oil in tanks, containers or units which are subject to regulation under the hazardous waste rules. The containers must be in good condition and not leaking. Containers, aboveground storage tanks, and fill pipes used to transfer oil into underground storage tanks must be labeled or marked clearly with the words "used oil."[212] Used oil generators are also subject to the federal Spill Prevention, Control and Countermeasures Regulations[213] and any state and federal underground storage tank rules.[214]

Upon detection of a release, a generator must stop the release, contain the used oil, clean up and manage properly the used oil and other materials, and if necessary repair or replace any leaking used oil storage containers or tanks prior to returning them to service.[215]

The rules require generators to ensure that their used oil is transported only by transporters who have obtained an identification number and state permit. The transporter does not need to have an identification number if the used oil is reclaimed under a contractual

---

210 *Id.* § 11-279-20.

211 *Id.* § 11-279-21.

212 *Id.* § 11-279-22.

213 40 C.F.R. Part 112. Common "triggers" for applicability of the federal Spill Prevention, Control and Countermeasures regulations are: (1) if the underground storage capacity of a facility is more than 42,000 gallons of oil; (2) if the aboveground storage capacity for used oil more than 1,320 gallons; or (3) if a single aboveground container has a capacity in excess of 660 gallons.

214 Haw. Admin. R. § 11-281. *See infra* chapter 7 of this Handbook.

215 Haw. Admin. R. § 11-279-22.

agreement with specific terms allowing return to the generator for use as a lubricant, cutting oil or coolant after processing or re-refining.[216]

A generator may transport its own oil to an approved and permitted collection center if the generator uses its own vehicles and transports no more than 55 gallons at a time. Generators may also transport their own used oil to self-owned aggregation points if they use their own vehicles and transport no more than 55 gallons at a time.[217] Used oil aggregation points may also accept used oil from household do-it-yourselfers.[218] A used oil aggregation point is any site or facility that accepts, aggregates and stores used oil collected only from other used oil generation sites owned or operated by the owner of the used oil aggregation point, from which used oil is transported to the aggregation point in shipments of no more than 55 gallons at a time.[219]

10.2 USED OIL TRANSPORTER AND TRANSFER FACILITIES

Used oil transporters are persons who transport used oil, persons who collect used oil from more than one generator and transport the collected oil, and owners and operators of used oil transfer facilities. The transporter rules do not apply to on-site transportation, or to generators' transportation of their own oil to collection centers or aggregation points, as allowed by the rules pertaining to generators. The rules also exempt transportation of used oil from household do-it-yourselfers to a regulated generator, collection center, aggregation point, processor/re-refiner or burner.

Transporters may also be subject to regulation as generators, processor/re-refiners, burners and marketers. Transporters may only dispose of used oil in compliance with the rules, and must obtain a used oil permit from the Department of Health.[220] Transporters must also

216 *Id.* § 11-279-24.

217 *Id.* § 11-279-24.

218 *Id.* §§ 11-279-1, 11-279-32.

219 *Id.* § 11-279-32.

220 *Id.* § 11-279-40.

obtain an EPA identification number by submitting an EPA for 8700-12[221] or a letter containing specific information as required by rule.[222]

Used oil transporters may only deliver used oil to another transporter with an EPA identification number, a used oil processing/re-refining facility with an EPA identification number, an off-specification used oil burner facility with an EPA identification number or an on-specification used oil burner facility.[223] Transporters must meet all Department of Transportation regulations.[224] Transporters who transport used oil which falls within the federal definition of hazardous waste,[225] must also comply with federal regulations regarding the transportation of hazardous waste. Unless trucks which were previously used to transport hazardous waste are emptied as required by the hazardous waste rules prior to transporting used oil, the used oil is considered to have been mixed with hazardous waste and may be subject to regulation under the hazardous waste rules.[226]

Used oil transfer facilities are transportation related facilities including loading docks, parking areas, storage areas, and other areas where shipments of used oil are held for more than twenty-four hours but less than thirty-five days during the normal course of transportation. Facilities that store used oil for more than thirty-five days are subject to all rules applicable to processors/re-refiners.[227]

Transfer facilities may only store used oil in tanks, containers or units which are subject to regulation under the hazardous waste rules. Containers and aboveground tanks must be in

---

221 Copies of EPA form 8700-12 are available from the Department of Health at (808) 586-4226, from the federal RCRA/Superfund Hotline at 1-800-424-9346 or (703) 920-9810, or from the EPA's website, http://www.epa.gov/epaoswer/hazwaste/data/form8700/forms.htm (visited August 11, 2000).

222 *Id.* § 11-279-42.

223 *Id.* § 11-279-43.

224 49 C.F.R. Parts 171 through 180.

225 49 C.F.R. 171.8.

226 Haw. Admin. R. § 11-279-40.

227 *Id.* § 11-279-45.

good condition, not leaking, and must have secondary containment impervious to used oil. Containers, aboveground tanks and fill pipes for underground tanks must be labeled with the words "Used Oil." Upon detection of a release, the facility must stop and contain the release, clean up and manage properly the released used oil and other materials and if necessary repair or replace any leaking used oil storage containers or tanks prior to returning them to service.[228] Facilities are also subject to the federal Spill Prevention, Control, and Countermeasures rules[229] and any state or federal underground storage tank rules.[230]

Transporters must keep detailed records of all shipments accepted or delivered. These records must be maintained for three years.[231] Annual reports must be submitted to the Director.[232]

10.3 PROCESSORS AND RE-REFINERS

"Processing" means chemical or physical operations designed to produce from used oil, or to make used oil more amenable to production of fuel oils, lubricants or other used-oil derived products. Processing may include blending used oil with virgin petroleum products, blending used oils to meet fuel specification, filtration, simple distillation, chemical or physical separation and re-refining.[233] Processors/re-refiners may also be subject to regulation as generators, transporters, off-specification used oil burners, and used oil fuel marketers. Processors/re-refiners may only dispose of used oil in compliance with the rules and must obtain a used oil permit from the Department of Health.[234] Professors/re-refiners must also obtain an EPA

228 *Id.* § 11-279-45.

229 *Supra*, note 213.

230 Haw. Admin. R. § 11-281. *See infra* ch. 7 of this Handbook.

231 *Id.* § 11-279-46.

232 *Id.* § 11-279-48.

233 *Id.* § 11-279-50.

234 *Id.* § 11-279-50.

identification number by submitting an EPA form 8700-12 or a letter containing specific information required by rule.[235]

Detailed preparedness and prevention requirements apply to processing and re-refining facilities. Facilities must be maintained and operated to minimize the possibility of a fire, explosion or any unplanned release of used oil.[236] Facilities must have all required equipment such as an internal communications or alarm system, a device capable of summoning emergency assistance, fire control equipment and water at adequate volume and pressure to supply water hose systems. Equipment must be tested and maintained. Sufficient aisle space must be maintained to allow unobstructed movement of personnel and emergency equipment. Arrangements must also be made with local authorities for emergency situations. Facilities must also have a contingency plan and emergency procedures which identify an emergency coordinator.

To ensure that used oil managed at a processing/re-refining facility is not hazardous waste, the facility must determine whether the used oil managed at the facility contains greater than 1,000 ppm total halogen content. If the content is greater than 1,000 ppm, there is a rebuttable presumption that it is hazardous waste.[237] Processors/re-refiners must also have a written analysis plan describing the procedures used to comply with the analysis requirements for halogen content and other specification requirements.[238]

In addition to all storage requirements applicable to generators, processors/re-refiners must have secondary containment for containers and aboveground tanks. Special closure requirements apply to aboveground tanks which have been used to store used oil.[239]

---

235 *Id.* § 11-279-51.

236 *Id.* § 11-279-52.

237 *Id.* § 11-279-53.

238 *Id.* § 11-279-55.

239 *Id.* § 11-279-54.

Processors/re-refiners are subject to extensive recordkeeping requirements. Records must be kept of each used oil shipment accepted for processing/re-refining, as well as a log of all deliveries of used oil to burners, other processor/re-refiners or disposal facilities.[240] Operating records must be maintained, and annual and biennial reports must be submitted to the Director.

10.4 USED OIL BURNERS

A used oil burner is a facility where used oil not meeting specification requirements is burned for energy recovery. Used oil burners may also be subject to regulation as generators, transporters, processors/re-refiners and marketers. The used oil burner regulations do not apply to persons burning used oil that meets used oil fuel specifications, provided that the burner meets all requirements applicable to used oil fuel marketers.

Used oil may only be burned in industrial furnaces, boilers and hazardous waste incinerators subject to regulation under the hazardous waste rules.[241] Used oil burners must comply with many of the same standards applicable to transporters, including EPA notification, storage and tracking of used oil, and taking steps to ensure that the used oil managed at their facilities is not hazardous waste.[242] In addition to the foregoing requirements, burners must also provide special certification before accepting the first shipment of off-specification used oil from a generator, transporter or re-refiner, consisting of verification that the burner has notified the department of the location and general description of used oil management activities, and will only burn the used oil in a furnace or boiler as allowed under the rules. The burner must keep these certifications for three years.[243]

---

240 *Id.* § 11-279-56.

241 *Id.* § 11-279-61.

242 *Id.* §§ 11-279-62, 11-279-63, 11-279-64, 11-279-65.

243 *Id.* § 11-279-66.

On-specification and off-specification oil may be aggregated for]
without being subject to the processor/re-refiner rules, but on-specificati(
used oil may not be aggregated for purposes of producing on-specificatic

10.5 USED OIL FUEL MARKETERS

Used oil fuel marketers are persons who direct shipments of off-specification used oil from their facility to a used oil burner or who first claim that the used oil to be burned for energy meets specifications. Used oil fuel marketers may also be subject to the standards applicable to generators, transporters, processor/re-refiners and used oil burners.[245]

Marketers may only initiate shipments of off-specified used oil to burners who certify that they have an EPA identification number and only burn used oil in an industrial furnace or boiler, as allowed by the rules.[246]

Marketers are subject to the same notification and used oil tracking requirements applicable to transporters.[247] In addition to the foregoing requirements which parallel federal regulations, permitted marketers in Hawaii must also submit an annual report to the Director detailing the volume of or weight of the incoming used oil, the salvageable used oil recovered, and disposal.[248]

---

244 *Id.* § 11-279-61.

245 *Id.* § 11-279-70.

246 *Id.* § 11-279-71.

247 *Id.* §§ 11-279-73, 11-279-74.

248 *Id.* § 11-279-76.

CHAPTER 7

UNDERGROUND STORAGE TANKS

1.0 INTRODUCTION

There are 7,479 underground storage tank ("UST") systems registered with the State. Of this total, 2,299 are currently in use and the remainder are either temporarily out of use. Of the tanks currently in use or temporarily out of use, 2,292 are petroleum tanks, 6 are hazardous substance tanks, and of the remainder the contents are either not listed or described as "other."[1] The regulation of USTs and the clean up of related contamination are of great interest to the press, the regulated community, developers and landowners.

The 1989 Legislature enacted the Underground Storage Tank Law ("UST Law"),[2] which regulates USTs and establishes the Response Program for Petroleum Releases. The UST Law was amended during the 1992 Legislative Session for purposes of consistency and equivalency with the federal UST program.[3] The Department of Health ("Department"), Solid and Hazardous Waste Branch is responsible for the administration of the UST program. For purposes of agency organization, the UST Section of the Solid and Hazardous Waste Branch handles UST matters. A small portion of the leaking underground storage tank work is handled by the Office of Hazard Evaluation and emergency response.[4]

The Department may use revenues generated by the environmental response tax and deposited into the environmental response revolving fund to address concerns related to

---

1 State of Hawaii, Department of Health, Underground Storage Tank Program Description at 1 (12/15/99). As of 1992, the State owned or operated 100 of these USTs at nearly fifty locations. Pacific Business News, July 6, 1992 at 7.

2 Haw. Rev. Stat. ch. 342L (Michie 1999). All references to the Hawaii Revised Statutes are made to the printed version of the statutes current through the 1999 legislative session, unless otherwise noted. Where appropriate, references to acts passed during the 2000 legislative session have also been added.

3 Act approved June 18, 1992, ch. 259, 1992 Haw. Sess. Laws 669.

4 State of Hawaii, Department of Health, Underground Storage Tank Program Description at 3 (12/15/99).

underground storage tanks, including the Department's underground storage tank program and funding for the acquisition by the State of a soil remediation site and facility.[5]

2.0 RELATIONSHIP TO FEDERAL UST REGULATIONS

Underground storage tanks have been regulated by the Environmental Protection Agency ("EPA") since December 1988, when the rules prescribing technical requirements became effective.[6] The federal financial responsibility requirements were published in October 1988.

On January 28, 2000, the Department adopted state rules which implement the technical and financial responsibility requirements of the UST Law. ("UST Rules").[7] These rules were adopted as part of the Department's efforts to obtain delegation of its underground storage program from the federal government.[8] The Department submitted its request to EPA for UST program approval on February 23, 2000.[9] Until the EPA makes a final decision to grant authorization to Hawaii, persons subject to UST laws and regulations will have to comply with the authorized state requirements as well as the federal requirements.[10] In the interim, the Department is the "implementing agency" for the federal UST regulations in Hawaii.[11]

---

5 2000 Haw. Sess. Laws 245 (to be codified at Haw. Rev. Stat. § 128D-2).

6 53 Fed. Reg. 37,082 (Sept. 23, 1988).

7 Hawaii Admin. Rules, Chapter 11-281 (Weil's 2000). All references to the Hawaii Administrative Rules are current through the date of publication of this Handbook, unless otherwise noted.

8 http://www.state.hi.us/doh/eh/shwb/ust/rules.htm/ (visited July 27, 2000).

9 Letter from Steven Y.K. Chang, Chief of the Solid and Hazardous Waste Branch to Lester Kaufman, Chief of the EPA's Office of Underground Storage Tanks dated February 23, 2000.

10 The federal standards are set forth in 40 C.F.R. Parts 280 and 281.

11 State of Hawaii, Department of Health, *Technical Guidance Manual for Underground Storage Tank Closure and Release Response* (2nd Ed. March 2000).

3.0 USTs AND SUBSTANCES COVERED

The UST Law and UST Rules define the persons, tanks and substances subject to regulation by the Department. For the most part, the UST Law and UST Rules are similar to the federal law and rules.

3.1 WHO IS COVERED BY UST PROVISIONS

Owners of USTs are required to register USTs with the Department.[12] An "owner" is defined as follows: (1) in the case of a particular UST or tank system in use or brought into use on or after November 8, 1984, any person who owns a UST;[13] and (2) in the case of a UST in use before November 8, 1984, but no longer in use after that date, any person who owned such a tank or tank system immediately before the discontinuation of its use.[14] The term "person" is broadly defined to include partnerships, corporations, commercial entities, and also includes public entities, such as county, state and federal government agencies.[15] An "operator" is any person in control of, or having responsibility for, the daily operation of a UST.[16] Owners and operators of USTs are responsible for the UST tank performance standards and record maintenance.[17] Owners and operators also are responsible for fulfilling the financial responsibility requirements, and notifying the Department and taking response action in the event of a release from an UST.[18]

---

12 Haw. Rev. Stat. § 342L-30, Haw. Admin. Rules § 11-281-03.

13 The Hawaii Administrative Rules defines an owner of a UST system brought into use on or before November 8, 1984 simply as "any person who owns an UST or tank system." The federal rules further qualify a pre-1984 owner as "any person who owns as UST system used for storage, using or dispensing of regulated substances."

14 *Id.* § 342L-1, Haw. Admin. Rules § 11-281-03.

15 The Hawaii Administrative Rules include the following within the definition of a "person": estates, government corporations, partnerships, associations, consortiums, joint ventures, commercial entities and "any other legal entity."

16 Haw. Admin. Rules § 11-281-03.

17 *Id.*

18 *Id.* §§ 342L-35 to –36, Haw. Admin. R. 11-281-61, *et seq.*

3.2 LENDER LIABILITY

The EPA's final rule on lender liability with respect to petroleum underground storage tanks took effect on December 6, 1995. This rule limits the liability of lenders that hold a security interest in a petroleum UST or a facility or property on which a petroleum UST is located. The rule also applies to secured lenders that acquire title to a petroleum UST or a facility or property on which a petroleum UST is located through foreclosure proceedings. Secured lenders, which may be lending institutions or other security interest holders, may be exempted from federal requirements for UST cleanup and financial responsibility if they follow the conditions specified in the rule.[19]

The lender liability rule protects a person who holds an indicia of ownership primarily to protect a security interest in a petroleum UST or facility or property on which a petroleum UST is located, who does not participate in management of the UST, and who does not engage in the business of petroleum production, refining or marketing. Provided that the holder of the security interest satisfies these requirements, the holder will not be considered an owner or operator of a petroleum UST or facility or property on which a petroleum UST or UST system is located for the purpose of complying with federal UST regulations. In addition, to qualify for this protection the holder may not be in control of and may not have responsibility for daily operation of the UST.[20]

The term "participation in management" is defined as exercising decision making control over the operational aspects of the UST, or exercising responsibility for the overall management of the enterprise encompassing day-to-day management of the enterprise, or operational aspects of the enterprise that relate to the use, storage, filling or dispensing of petroleum contained in a UST.[21]

It is unknown whether Hawaii courts will follow the EPA lender liability rule in determining the liability of secured lenders under the UST Law. The Hawaii UST Law and UST

19 *See* 60 Fed. Reg. 46,692 (Sept. 7, 1995).

20 *Id.*

21 *Id.*

Rules currently have no lender liability protection. In order to adopt such rules, the Department would need statutory authority.

3.3 DEFINITION OF UST

The definition of an underground storage tank includes all tanks or combinations of tanks which contain regulated substances and which have ten percent or more of their volume beneath the surface of the ground.[22] In calculating the portion of the UST system beneath the ground, one must include the piping associated with dispensing, measuring and pumping equipment as well as the tank itself.

Several types of USTs are exempted from state regulation by definition. These exemptions are identical to those under federal law. The exemptions include farm and residential tanks with capacities of 1,100 gallons or less which store motor fuel for noncommercial purposes.[23] Tanks which store heating oil for consumptive use on the premises where the oil is stored also are exempted. "Heating oil" is petroleum that is No. 1, No. 2, No. 4-light, No. 4-heavy, No. 5-light, No. 5-heavy, and No. 6 technical grades of fuel oil; other residual fuel oils (including Navy Special Fuel Oil and Bunker C); and other fuels when used as substitutes for one of these fuel oils. Heating oil is typically used in the operation of heating equipment, boilers or furnaces.[24] This exemption is applicable to tanks which store fuel for use in emergency generators located on site.

Tanks which serve as septic tanks, surface impoundments, or stormwater or wastewater collection systems are exempted, as are storage tanks located in basements, tunnels or shafts, so long as the tank is located above the surface of the floor.[25] The exempted tanks, and any associated leaks, releases and response action, are not subject to regulation by the Department

---

22 Haw. Rev. Stat. § 342L-1, Haw. Admin. Rules § 11-281-03.

23 *Id.* In contrast to the federal rules, Hawaii's UST Rules require that farm tanks be used only for farm-related purposes.

24 40 C.F.R. § 280.12 and Haw. Admin. Rules § 11-281-03.

25 Haw. Rev. Stat. § 342L-1, and Haw. Admin. Rules § 11-281-03.

under the UST Law and UST Rules. Releases from exempted tanks may, however, be subject to other laws.[26]

3.4 REGULATED SUBSTANCES

The UST Law and UST Rules regulate elements, compounds, mixtures, solutions or substances that, when released into the environment, may present substantial danger to human health or welfare, or the environment.[27] In addition, all substances listed pursuant to CERCLA[28] Section 101(14)[29] are regulated under the UST Law and UST Rules,[30] excluding substances regulated as hazardous wastes under the Resource Conservation and Recovery Act, Subtitle C.[31] Petroleum, which includes crude oil and all liquid fractions at the temperature of 60° F. and at pressure of one atmosphere, is also a regulated substance. Other substances regulated by the UST Law and UST Rules may be designated by the Department.

4.0 UST PERMITTING

The Department is authorized to implement a permitting program for USTs through rules.[32] Permits are required for the installation, operation and transfer of ownership of USTs. A person wishing to accept transfer of ownership of a UST must submit an application to the Director of Health ("Director") in which the applicant accepts the obligations of the UST permit. The Director must approve the transfer if the applicant proves to the Director that the applicant is able to comply with the terms of the permit.

---

26 *See infra* ch. 9 of this Handbook.

27 Haw. Rev. Stat. § 342L-1 and Haw. Admin. Rules § 11-281-03. Hawaii's definition of "regulated substance" is much broader than the federal definition. *See* 40 C.F.R. § 280-12.

28 Comprehensive Environmental Response, Compensation and Liability Act, 42 U.S.C. § 9601 *et seq.*

29 *See* 40 C.F.R. Part 302.

30 Haw. Rev. Stat. § 342L-1.

31 42 U.S.C. §6901 *et seq. See supra* ch. 6 of this Handbook.

32 Haw. Rev. Stat. §§ 342L-4, -31.

No person may install or operate an UST after January 28, 2000 without first obtaining a permit from the Department.[33] Applications must be submitted on the application form specified by the Department.[34] A fee of $150 must accompany the application. The application must include general information regarding involved parties, including the landowner, UST owner, UST operator, the location of the UST and a description of the UST. The application must include the age, size and uses of the UST as well as other information required by the application form. Applications must be signed by the owner and operator of the UST and constitute an acknowledgement that the applicant assumes responsibility for installation and operation of the UST in compliance with the UST Rules and the conditions of the permit.[35]

Permits will only be approved when the Department is satisfied that the technical, financial and other requirements of the UST Rules can be met and that the installation and operation of the UST will be done in a manner that is protective of human health and the environment.[36] Permits are issued for a period of five years, and an application may be renewed for an additional five years.[37] Renewal applications must be received 180 days prior to permit expiration, must be submitted on the Department's renewal application form, and accompanied by a $150 renewal fee.[38]

Once an initial permit application is received, the UST must be installed within one year. Failure to complete installation within the year results in automatic permit expiration. At least seven days prior to actual installation, the owner or operator must inform the Department of the

---

33 Haw. Admin. Rules § 11-281-23.

34 The form entitled "Application for an Underground Storage Tank Permit" (Rev. 6/99) is attached as Appendix II to Chapter 11-281 of the Hawaii Administrative Rules and is also available from the Department.

35 Haw. Admin. Rules § 11-281-24.

36 *Id.* § 11-281-23.

37 *Id.* §§ 11-281-25(a) and 11-281-26.

38 The "Application for Renewal of an Underground Storage Tank Permit" (rev. 6/99) is attached as Appendix IV to Chapter 11-281 of the Hawaii Administrative Rules, and is also available from the Department.

date and time of actual installation.[39] Thirty days following installation, the owner or operator must submit certification of installation and must update any information contained in the initial permit application which has changed since the time of submission.[40]

The Director may impose permit conditions deemed reasonably necessary to ensure compliance with the UST Rules and any other relevant state requirements. Conditions may relate to equipment, work practices or operation and may include the requirement that devices for measurement or monitoring of regulated substances be installed and maintained and that the results be reported to the Director.[41]

Permit modifications are required for repairs or changes in service, piping, type of regulated substance stored, corrosion or secondary containment.[42] Modification is also required if plans to renovate or modify the UST or tank system would cause the holder to be out of compliance with the permit.[43]

Permit modification applications must be received by the Department within thirty days following the occurrence that prompted the application. Any permit modification applications

---

39 Haw. Admin. Rules § 11-281-25.

40 The "Certification of Underground Storage Tank Installation" (rev. 6/99) is attached as Appendix III to Chapter 11-281 of the Hawaii Administrative Rules. To update information contained in the original application, the owner or operator must complete Part IV of the certification form.

41 Haw. Admin. Rules § 11-281-28.

42 Haw. Admin. Rules § 11-281-29.

43 Permit modification is not required for changes in product dispensing method, financial responsibility mechanism, leak detection method, spill and overfill prevention method and temporary and permanent closures. However, written notice of these changes must be given to the Department within thirty days following implementation of the change. Notice of permanent closures must be received by Department thirty days before closure begins. Haw. Admin. Rules § 11-281-29(b) and (f).

for change in service must be received by the Department thirty days *before* the applicant begins the change in service.[44] Applications must be on the Department forms.[45]

The Director has established fees for registration and permitting ranging from $25 to $200. The fees are intended to cover the cost of issuance, implementation, and enforcement of UST permits and variances. The fees also are intended to cover costs associated with review, evaluation and approval of plans submitted for release response activities.[46] Fees should be made payable to the State of Hawaii and are nonrefundable.[47]

Permits are not transferable unless the transfer is approved by the Department. Any request for transfer approval to a new owner must be made by the new owner. Requests for transfer approval to a new operator must be made by the owner. Transfer applications must be submitted thirty days prior to the proposed effective date of the transfer on the Department forms.[48]

Permits, including application documents, must be kept at the location of the UST or tank system for which the permit was issued and must be made available for inspection upon request. Defacing, altering, forging, counterfeiting or falsifying any permit or variance is prohibited.[49]

The Department may revoke or suspend a permit if there is a release or threatened release of regulated substances which poses an imminent and substantial risk to human health or the environment. Permits may also be revoked or suspended if the permittee violates a condition of

---

44 Haw. Admin. Rules § 11-281-29(e).

45 Permit modification applications must be submitted on the form entitled, "Application for an Underground Storage Tank Permit" attached as Appendix II to Hawaii Administrative Rules Chapter 11-281.

46 *Id.* § 342L-14.

47 Haw. Admin. Rules § 11-281-35.

48 Transfer applications must be submitted on the form entitled, "Application or Transfer of an Underground Storage Tank Permit," dated June, 1999 which is attached to Chapter 11-281 of the Hawaii Administrative Rules as Appendix V.

49 Haw. Admin. Rules § 11-281-24.

the permit or if the permit was obtained by a misrepresentation, or failure to disclose all relevant facts.[50]

4.1 VARIANCES

Provisions of Hawaii's UST law which are more stringent than the federal rules may be varied by the Department only when the variance results in an equivalent degree of human health and environmental protection and does not present a greater danger to health or the environment.[51]

Variance applications must be submitted on the form prescribed by the Director,[52] must be signed by the owner or operator, and accompanied by the appropriate variance fee ranging from $100 to $200.[53] Variances will not be granted unless the application shows that UST installation or operation does not present a greater danger to human health or the environment than the installation or operation that would have been allowed under the federal rules and that the UST installation or operation does not imminently or substantially endanger human health, the environment, or public safety. All variances must include conditions requiring the owner or operator to monitor for releases and report the results to the Department.[54]

The Director will notify the applicant of his or her decision to approve, approve with conditions, or deny a variance within 180 days of receiving a complete application. If no notification is made, the application is automatically deemed approved after 180 days.[55]

---

50 Haw. Admin. Rules § 11-281-30.

51 Haw. Rev. Stat. § 342L-5 and Haw. Admin. Rules §11-281-32.

52 See Appendix VI to Chapter 11-281 of the Hawaii Administrative Rules entitled "Application for an Underground Storage Tank Variance" (rev. 6/99).

53 Haw. Admin. Rules §§ 11-281-33 and -35.

54 Haw. Rev. Stat. § 342L-6(d).

55 Haw. Admin. Rules § 11-281-33(d).

A copy of the variance, including the application documents, must be maintained at the UST location. Defacing, altering, forging, counterfeiting or falsifying a variance is prohibited.[56]

Variances may be renewed for an additional five year period. Extension applications must be made at least 180 days before the expiration of the variance, and the Director must act on the application within 180 days of receipt. Extensions will only be granted if the extension applicant has met all conditions specified in the immediately preceding variance, and the scope of the extension will not be greater than the initial variance.[57]

5.0 NOTIFICATION REQUIREMENTS

Persons who acquire ownership of an UST must submit an amended notification to the Department within thirty days of acquiring ownership regardless of whether a prior owner has already notified the Department of the UST. Likewise, new operators of USTs must submit amended notification to the Department within thirty days. Notification is also required within thirty days for change in closure, service, repairs, financial responsibility, operating methods and release detection methods.[58] All of the foregoing notification requirements are unique to Hawaii, and the federal rules do not contain similar provisions.

Owners of existing USTs were required to notify the Department of the existence of the UST by December 31, 1989. Owners of USTs taken out of operation between January 1, 1974 and May 19, 1986 were required to register the UST with the Department by December 31, 1989, unless the UST was removed from the ground prior to May 8, 1986. Owners of USTs which were taken out of operation prior to January 1, 1974 are not subject to notification requirements.

---

56 *Id.* § 11-281-34.

57 Haw. Rev. Stat. § 342-L-6(e).

58 Haw. Rev. Stat. 342L-30 and Haw. Admin. R. § 11-281-21.

Owners and operators must submit notification to the Department on the Department's UST notification form.[59] The form requests information regarding age, type, location, uses of the tank, installation, release detection, spill and overfill protection, closure, and financial responsibility, as well as a facility map. Persons who sell tanks intended for use as an UST must notify the purchaser of the tank of the UST Law notification requirements.[60] Failure to comply with notification requirements may result in administrative and civil penalties for each day of violation.[61]

6.0 CONSTRUCTION AND MONITORING REQUIREMENTS

The Department has adopted rules for new UST construction standards for release prevention, corrosion protection and materials compatibility.[62] These rules were adopted on January 28, 2000.[63] Federal rules also apply to the design, construction, installation and notification requirements regarding USTs.[64]

Hazardous substance USTs and tank systems installed after December 22, 1998 and petroleum USTs and tank systems installed after January 28, 2000 must meet the requirements of Subchapter 2 of Hawaii's UST rules in order to prevent releases due to structural failure, corrosion, or spills and overfills.[65]

USTs must be properly designed, constructed and installed. Any underground portion of the tank that routinely contains product and any piping that routinely contains regulated

---

59 The "Notification for Underground Storage Tanks" (rev. 6/99) is attached as Appendix I to Chapter 11-281 of the Hawaii Administrative Rules and is also available from the Department.

60 Haw. Rev. Stat. § 342L-30(g).

61 *Id.* § 342L-30.

62 *Id.* § 342L-32.

63 Haw. Admin. Rules § 11-281-11 et seq.

64 *See* 40 C.F.R. Part 280, Subpart B.

65 Haw. Admin. Rules § 11-281-11. Petroleum USTs or tank systems installed between December 28, 1998 and January 28, 2000 must meet the requirements of subchapter 2 with the exception of the secondary containment requirements.

substances and is in contact with the ground must be protected from corrosion in accordance with the specifications developed by nationally recognized associations or independent testing laboratories as specified in the UST Rules.[66] USTs that do not meet the rule-required specifications may be used if the construction and corrosion protection is no less protective of human health and the environment than are the rule-required specifications.

Owners and operators must utilize spill prevention and overfill equipment associated with product transfer. Spill prevention equipment must prevent release of product to the environment when the transfer hose is detached from the fill pipe. Overfill prevention equipment must automatically terminate flow into the UST when the UST is more than 95 percent full, alert the transfer operator by restricting flow or triggering a high-level alarm when the UST is more than 90 percent full, and must have flow restriction, alarms or automatic shutoff so that none of the fittings located on top of the UST are exposed to product due to overfilling. Alarms must be clearly labeled and located where they can be seen by the delivery person. Spill and overfill prevention equipment is not required if the UST is filled by transfers of 25 gallons or less at one time or if alternative equipment is deemed equally protective of human health and the environment by the Department.[67]

USTs and piping must be installed in accordance with a code of practice developed by a nationally recognized association or independent testing laboratory and in accordance with the manufacturer's instructions. Owners and operators must ensure compliance with installation requirements and certify compliance by submitting a notification or certification to the Department.[68]

Secondary containment must be designed, constructed and installed such that any regulated substance releases are contained until they are detected and removed, and so that

---

66 Haw. Admin. Rules § 11-281-12 and 13.

67 *Id.* § 11-281-14.

68 The owner or operator must submit either the "Notification for Underground Storage Tanks," dated June 1999 or the "Certification of Underground Storage Tank Installation," dated June 1999 which are attached as Appendices I and III, respectively, to Chapter 11-281 of the Hawaii Administrative Rules.

release of any regulated substances to the environment is prevented. Hazardous substance USTs installed after December 22, 1998 are required to have monthly release detection monitoring, Double-walled USTs must contain a release from any portion of the inner UST within the outer wall and detect a failure of the inner and outer walls. External liners must entirely contain a release from the largest UST within the external liner boundary, prevent precipitation or groundwater intrusion from interfering with the ability to contain or detect a release and completely surround the UST and prevent lateral and vertical migration of regulated substances in the event of a release. Underground piping must be equipped with secondary containment and pressurized piping must be equipped with an automatic line leak detector.

Owners and operators of new or existing USTs must provide a method of release detection. The method must be able to detect a release from any portion of the UST or connected underground piping which routinely contains product. The release detection must be installed, calibrated, operated and maintained in accordance with the manufacturer's instructions. Routine maintenance and service checks on the release detection system must be performed every twelve months or a timeframe specified by the manufacturer, whichever is more frequent.[69]

USTs must be monitored at least once every thirty days, and pressurized underground piping must have an automatic line leak detector or a line tightness test every twelve months. Underground suction piping must have a line tightness test every three years or use a monthly monitoring method. Release detection for USTs may be monitored through inventory control methods, manual tank gauging methods, tank tightness testing, automatic tank gauging, vapor monitoring, ground water monitoring, interstitial monitoring between the tank system and a secondary barrier immediately around or beneath it or other methods of release detection approved by the Director. Release detection for piping may be monitored using line leak detectors, line tightness testing or applicable tank methods.[70]

---

69 Haw. Admin. Rules § 11-281-51.

70 *Id.* § 11-281-52, 53.

USTs and tank systems which existed prior to January 28, 2000 must immediately comply with all performance standards, tank requirements, piping requirements, spill and overfill prevention equipment, and installation requirements. Existing steel USTs must be upgraded to meet rule-required specifications, and all existing UST metal piping that routinely contains regulated substances and is in contact with the ground must be cathodically protected.[71]

7.0 UST OPERATION REQUIREMENTS

The Department has adopted standards of performance for release detection, inventory control, tank tightness testing systems and other methods to identify releases from USTs. These rules were adopted on January 28, 2000.[72] Federal UST operating requirements also apply.[73]

Rules regarding UST operating requirements mandate that owners and operators ensure that releases due to spilling or overfilling do not occur. Transfer of product to the UST must be monitored constantly, and owners and operators must ensure that the volume of transferred product does not exceed the available space in the UST.[74] Any spills or overfills which occur must be reported, investigated and cleaned up as required by the UST Rules.[75]

Corrosion protection systems must ensure that releases due to corrosion are prevented for as long as the UST or tank system is used. Corrosion protection systems must be operated and maintained to continuously provide corrosion protection to metal components of the UST system which are in contact with the ground and routinely contain regulated substances.

Cathodic protection systems must be inspected for proper operation by a qualified cathodic protection tester who will examine frequency within six months of installation and at

71 *Id.* § 11-281-18.

72 *Id.* § 11-281-41 *et seq.*

73 *See* 40 C.F.R. Part 280, Subparts C, D.

74 Haw. Admin. Rules § 11-281-41.

75 *Id.* § 11-281-64.

least every three years thereafter. The Department recommends that inspection criteria developed by the National Association of Corrosion Engineers Standard RP0285-85 be followed. USTs with impressed current cathodic protection systems must be inspected every sixty days to ensure the equipment is operating properly. Records of the operation of the cathodic protection system demonstrating compliance with performance standards must be maintained.[76]

UST systems must be made of, lined with, or compatible with the substance stored in the UST.[77]

Owners and operators of UST systems must ensure that any repairs will prevent releases due to structural failure or corrosion for the life of the UST. Repairs must be conducted in accordance with a code of practice developed by a nationally recognized association or an independent testing laboratory.

8.0 FINANCIAL RESPONSIBILITY REQUIREMENTS

The Department has adopted financial responsibility requirements for UST owners and operators.[78] Owners and operators of USTs are required to provide evidence of financial responsibility for any response action and for liability to third parties for personal injury and property damage caused by accidental releases from operating a UST. The Department may establish certain categories of USTs and require different amounts of coverage.[79] Evidence of financial responsibility may be established by a number of methods, including insurance, guarantee, letter of credit, surety bond and self-insurance. The deadline for establishing proof of financial responsibility under the applicable federal rules was January 1, 1994.[80]

---

76 *Id.* § 11-281-42.

77 *Id.* § 11-281-43.

78 *Id.* § 11-281-91.

79 Haw. Rev. Stat. § 342L-36(a) - (f).

80 *See* 40 C.F.R. Part 280, Subpart H.

Claims for damages arising from conduct for which the financial assurance is provided may be asserted directly against the provider of financial assurance if the UST owner or operator is in bankruptcy, or if jurisdiction over the owner or operator cannot be obtained in state or federal court. The total liability of the provider of financial assurance is limited to the aggregate amount of financial assurance provided to the owner or operator. Liability of the provider of financial assurance to the owner or operator is not limited by the UST Law, but is subject to federal, state and common law. Liability under the UST Law does not diminish liability under other federal or state environmental statutes.

The financial responsibility requirements apply to all owners and operators of petroleum USTs or tank systems subject to the Hawaii Administrative Rules. State and federal government entities are exempt from the financial responsibility requirements.[81]

Either an owner or an operator is required to demonstrate financial responsibility for release response or for compensating third parties for bodily injury and property damage resulting from releases. However, both the owner and operator are liable in the event of noncompliance, and the amounts of financial responsibility assurances do not limit the owner's or operator's liability.

An owner or operator must submit documentation of financial responsibility within 30 days of a reportable release from an UST, or when notifying the Director of the installation of an UST or tank system. The Director may also require evidence of financial assurance at any time.[82]

For USTs located at petroleum marketing facilities or USTs which handle more than an average of 10,000 gallons of petroleum per month, owners and operators must demonstrate financial responsibility for $1,000,000 per occurrence. For all other petroleum USTs, the owner or operator must demonstrate financial responsibility for $500,000 per occurrence. Owners of

---

81 Haw. Admin. Rules § 11-281-91.

82 *Id.* § 11-281-110.

between one and one hundred petroleum USTs must also demonstrate responsibility for an annual aggregate amount of $1,000,000, and owners of more than one hundred petroleum USTs must demonstrate responsibility for an aggregate amount of $2,000,000. Whenever additional petroleum USTs are acquired or installed, owners and operators must review the amount of aggregate assurance they have provided.[83]

Owners or operators may demonstrate financial responsibility by passing a financial test of self-insurance, obtaining a guarantee, obtaining liability insurance from a qualified insurer or risk retention group, obtaining a surety bond, obtaining an irrevocable standby letter or credit, establishing a trust fund or by establishing a standby trust fund.[84] A local government which is an owner or operator may establish financial responsibility by meeting a local government bond rating test, passing a financial test, obtaining a guarantee or establishing a dedicated fund account.[85]

Financial assurance mechanisms may be substituted by an owner or operator if the owner or operator maintains an effective assurance mechanism or combination of mechanisms that at all times meet the requirements of the UST rules. Only after obtaining alternate financial assurance may an owner or operator cancel an established financial assurance mechanism.[86] Financial assurance providers may only cancel or fail to renew by providing written notice of termination by certified mail to the owner or operator. After notice is received, the financial assurance mechanisms may not be cancelled by the provider for 120 or 60 days, depending on the type of assurance provided. Owners and operators are required to obtain alternate coverage within 60 days after receipt of a notice of termination if a provider of financial responsibility cancels or fails to renew for any reason other than incapacity. If the owner or operator fails to obtain alternate coverage, they must submit written notice to the Director.[87] The Director may

---

83 *Id.* § 11-281-94.

84 *Id.* §§11-281-96 through 11-281-102.

85 *Id.* §§11-281-103 through 11-281-107.

86 *Id.* §11-281-108.

87 *Id.* §11-281-109.

then require the financial assurance provider to place a stipulated amount of funds into a standby trust, and may draw upon that standby trust fund if a release has occurred and the owner or operator does not comply or if certification is provided showing that a third party has made a claim.[88]

An owner or operator must submit forms documenting current evidence of financial responsibility if the owner or operator fails to obtain alternative coverage within thirty days of a financial assurance provider filing bankruptcy, suspension or revocation of the authority of a provider to issue a financial assurance mechanism, failure of a guarantor to meet a financial assurance test, or any other incapacity of a provider of financial assurance.[89] If an owner or operator provides assurance by meeting a financial test and is no longer able to meet the requirements of the financial test, they must either obtain alternate assurance within 150 days or notify the Director of such failure within 10 days.[90]

Owners and operators must maintain records documenting evidence of financial assurance mechanisms until the UST or tank system has been properly and permanently closed. If a release response action is required, financial responsibility is not released until the release response action is complete and the UST or tank system has been properly and permanently closed.[91] Records must be kept at the site of the owner's or operator's place of work.

If the Department determines that methods to satisfy the financial requirements are not generally available for certain classes of USTs, the Department may suspend enforcement of the financial responsibility requirements. The Department may do so, however, only if the State is taking steps to establish a fund for response action and compensation, or if steps are being taken

---

88 *Id.* §11-281-112.

89 *Id.* § 11-281-110.

90 *Id.* § 11-281-96(g).

91 *Id.* §§ 11-281-111 and 11-281-113.

to form a risk retention group for that class of tanks. The initial suspension may be instituted for a maximum of 180 days, and may be extended under certain conditions.[92]

9.0 REPORTING REQUIREMENTS

The Department has adopted rules for establishment and maintenance of UST records,[93] the reporting of confirmed or suspected releases, and actions taken in response to such releases.[94] These reporting requirements are documented in the Department's Technical Guidance Manual for Underground Storage Tank Closure and Release Response ("Technical Guidance Manual").[95] Reporting of releases, spills and overfills is also required by the federal rules.[96]

Owners and operators must keep and maintain records of the following information for the life of a UST: documentation of operation of corrosion protection equipment; documentation of repairs; records of compliance with release detection requirements; records of compliance with change-in-service requirements; permits or variances; proof of current financial assurance mechanisms; and, if corrosion protection is not used, a corrosion expert's analysis of site corrosion potential. The foregoing records must be kept at a location where they can be made immediately available for inspection.

Permanent closure records, including the results of site assessments, must be kept for at least three years following closure either at the site or at a readily available alternative site.[97] Release detection records must include: all written performance claims; sampling, testing or monitoring results; written documentation of calibration, maintenance and repair of release

---

92 Haw. Rev. Stat. § 342L-36(g).

93 Haw. Rev. Stat. § 342L-7.5, Haw. Admin. Rules § 281-45.

94 Haw. Rev. Stat. § 342L-35, Haw. Admin. Rules §§ 11-281-61 through 80.1.

95 State of Hawaii, Department of Health, *Technical Guidance Manual for Underground Storage Tank Closure and Release Response* (2nd Ed. March 2000).

96 40 C.F.R. subparts E and F.

97 Haw. Admin. Rules § 11-281-45.

detection equipment; records of release detection, the most recent line tightness test, and test results of the automatic line leak detectors; operating manuals and documentation of site assessments.[98]

Owners and operators must submit notification to the Department of releases, spills and overfills, and confirmed releases. When a release detection method indicates that a release may have occurred, the owner or operator must follow procedures for release reporting.

Releases and suspected releases of regulated substances from a UST must be reported to the Department within twenty-four hours.[99] Reporting requirements are triggered by the discovery of released substances, unusual UST operating conditions or indication of a release from a release detection monitoring method.[100] Spills and overfills of petroleum in excess of twenty-five gallons or a hazardous substance in the amount equal to or greater than the CERCLA reportable quantity[101] must also be reported to the Department within twenty-four hours. The initial report to Department should be made by telephone. In response to this report, the Department will send a packet of guidance materials on UST releases. The packet will include a "Confirmed Release Notification" form which must be completed and submitted to Department within seven days of the release.

Unless a release response inspection is initiated immediately, owners and operators must investigate and confirm all suspected releases of regulated substances within seven days following discovery of the suspected release. The investigation must include system test, such as tightness test, and a site assessment to measure for the presence of a release where contamination is most likely to be present. If a system test indicates a release, the UST must be repaired, replaced or upgraded, and a release response action must begin. Likewise, if a site assessment

---

98 *Id.* § 11-281-54.

99 *Id.* § 11-281-61. The telephone number of the UST Section is (808) 586-4226. Alternatively, releases can be reported to the Hazard Evaluation or Emergency Response office at (808) 586-4249. After hours reports may be made to the Hawaii State Hospital at (808) 247-2191.

100 Haw. Admin. R. § 11-281-61.

101 40 C.F.R. part 302.

indicates a release, release response action must also begin. If the investigation determines that a release has not occurred, the results of the investigation must be reported to the Department within thirty days.

Spills and overfills must be contained and immediately cleaned up in a matter that is protective of human health and the environment. A release response action should begin immediately if a petroleum spill exceeds twenty-five gallons or causes a sheen on nearby surface waters, or if a hazardous substance spills in amounts exceeding the reportable quantity for that substance. If a spill of less than twenty-five gallons of petroleum or non-reportable quantities of a hazardous substance can be contained and cleanup completed in twenty-four hours, no notification is required. Otherwise, the Department should be notified, and cleanup must continue. A written report documenting the actions taken in response to the spill or overfill must be submitted to the Department within ninety days.[102]

10.0 RESPONSE ACTION

The Department has established requirements for investigating suspected releases and for taking response actions with regard to a confirmed UST release.[103] Releases which occur after December 22, 1988 are also subject to the federal UST response action requirements.

Once a release from a UST is confirmed, owners and operators must take immediate action to contain the released substances and report the release to the Department by telephone or fax. Hazards relating to vapor, fire and explosions must be identified and mitigated.[104] Owners and operators must take necessary actions to prevent any further release of the regulated substance into the environment, and must remove as much of the UST contents as possible. Steps should also be taken to minimize the spread of contamination. Within seven days of release confirmation, owners and operators must submit a written notice of confirmation to the department including the source of the release, the method of discovery and confirmation, the

102 Haw. Admin. Rules § 11-281-64.

103 Haw. Rev. Stat. § 342L-35, Haw. Admin. Rules § 11-281-62 through 80.1.

104 Haw. Admin. Rules § 11-281-72, 40 C.F.R. § 280.61.

estimated quantity of substance released, the type of substance released, immediate hazards, the impact of the release, migration pathways and actions taken.[105]

If required by the Department, the owner and operator must post signs around the perimeter of the site informing passerby of potential hazards. The signs may only be removed when the Department determines that no further release response action is necessary or the posting of signs is no longer appropriate.[106]

The initial abatement must be completed within ninety days or sooner if directed by the Department and must include not only continued removal of as much of the UST contents as necessary to prevent further release to the environment but also a visual inspection for evidence of aboveground of exposed below ground releases. Necessary actions to minimize the spread of contamination and to prevent further migration of the release substance must be continued. The owner and operator must also continue to monitor and mitigate any safety hazards such as fire, explosion and vapors that have migrated from the UST excavation zone and entered subsurface structures such as sewers or basements. Hazards posed by contaminated soil and debris excavated or exposed must be remedied. An investigation must be undertaken to determine the possible presence of free product and to begin free product removal if necessary. Contaminated soil must be removed or remediated as necessary to prevent the spread of free product. An assessment of the release should be conducted by measuring for the presence of a release where contamination is most likely.[107] Free product removal must also be initiated as soon as practicable, but no later than ninety days following confirmation of a release.[108]

Along with conducting a release response, owners and operators must assemble necessary information about the characteristics of the site and the nature of the release in order to adequately assess the impact, or potential impact, the release has on human health and the

---

105 Haw. Admin. Rules § 11-281-72.

106 *Id.* § 11-281-73.

107 *Id.* § 11-281-74.

108 *Id.* § 11-281-76.

environment. Data must be collected regarding the nature and quantity of the estimated release, surrounding populations, water quality, use and approximate locations of wells potentially affected by the release, subsurface soil conditions, locations of subsurface sewers, climatological data and land use. Information must also be assembled regarding the results of the site assessment, and results of the free product investigations. This initial site characterization must be complete within ninety days of confirmation of the release.[109]

Owners and operators must conduct investigations of the release, the release site and the surrounding area possibly affected by the release. The extent and location of contaminated soil and the presence and concentrations of dissolved product contamination in ground water must be determined.[110]

Owners and operators must remediate contaminated soil and water to residual levels which meet Tier 1 Action levels established by the Hawaii Administrative Rules or site-specific action levels as approved by the Department. If the Department determines that cleanup activities are not carried out in accordance with the Hawaii Administrative Rules, or are not achieving cleanup levels protective of human health and the environment, the Department may impose modifications to cleanup activities by written notice to the owner and operator.

Within ninety days following release confirmation, the owner and operator must notify members of the public directly affected by a release of the proposed response to the release. The notification must be made by letter in a format provided by the Department, along with a factsheet including information regarding the UST, the release, the measures taken to assess the release and a summary of the proposed response to the release. The factsheet must be updated on a quarterly basis and sent to all members of the public.[111]

---

109 *Id.* § 11-281-75.

110 *Id.* § 11-281-77.

111 *Id.* § 11-281-78.1.

The Department may require submission of a written corrective action plan by the owner or operator within thirty days of the Department's request. The plan must demonstrate that implementation of the plan will be safe and will adequately protect human health and the environment. When determining whether the plan will be approved, the Department will consider the physical and chemical characteristics of the regulated substance, the hydrogeologic characteristics of the facility and surrounding area, the potential effects of residual contamination on nearby surface and groundwater, an exposure assessment, and any other information assembled in compliance with release response requirements.

The corrective action plan must be implemented, as modified or approved by the Department, and owners and operators must monitor, evaluate and report quarterly to the Department regarding the results of implementing the corrective action plan. Cleanup may begin before approval of the corrective action plan if the Department is notified and cleanup actions are consistent with the site cleanup criteria specified by the Hawaii Administrative Rules. When implementing cleanup measures before approval of a corrective action plan, owners and operators must comply with any conditions imposed by the Department and must also incorporate the self-initiated cleanup measures in the corrective action plan.[112]

Public participation will be allowed when the Department has made a tentative decision regarding a proposed corrective action plan or when the Department considers termination of a plan where cleanup levels established by the plan have not been achieved. Owners and operators must pay for all costs of public participation activities. The Department will issue a letter providing information to the public regarding the UST, the release, the Department's tentative decision concerning the proposed corrective action plan and an announcement that an informal meeting will be held. The general public will also be notified by publication of similar information in a local newspaper. Public comments must be submitted within thirty days after notice or at the end of the public hearing, whichever is later. A public meeting will be held only if there is sufficient interest as indicated by written request to the Department.

---

112 *Id.* § 11-281-79.

Ninety days after confirmation of a release, owners and operators must submit a written report to the Department describing all release actions and a plan for future release response actions. Beginning 180 days following release confirmation, owners and operators must submit written quarterly progress reports which describe all response actions,and a plan for future release response actions, confirmed release notification as required by the Hawaii Administrative Rules. Quarterly progress reports are not required if response actions have met Tier 1 Action Levels or site specific action levels set by the Department and a final quarterly report has been submitted.[113]

The Department's Technical Guidance Manual for Underground Storage Tank Closure and Release Response ("Technical Guidance Manual")[114] offers four cleanup options for owners and operators to demonstrate that their sites meet cleanup standards for contaminated soil and groundwater to levels that are protective of human health and the environment.

The first option is for the owner or operator to demonstrate that soil and/or groundwater contaminant concentrations, as determined by an acceptable site characterization effort, are less than Department's Tier 1 Action levels following the Department's guidance for risk-based corrective action and decision making at sites with contaminated soil and groundwater ("RBCA Guidance").[115] The Tier 1 action levels are keyed to the underground injection control line (UIC line)[116] and the "Aquifer Identification and Classification" technical report series published by the Water Resources Research Center at the University of Hawaii. Aquifer systems mauka (inland) of the UIC line are considered to be current or potential sources of drinking water, whereas aquifer systems makai (oceanward) of the UIC line are not. Release sites mauka of the UIC line are therefore subject to more stringent Tier 1 action levels which are more protective of drinking water standards.

---

113 *Id.* § 11-281-80.1.

114 *Technical Guidance Manual, supra,* note 95.

115 State of Hawaii, Department of Health, *Risk-Based Corrective Action and Decision Making at Sites With Contaminated Soil and Groundwater* (Vol. 1, Dec. 1995, revised June 1996).

116 For further discussion of UIC lines, *see infra* ch.4, § 8.0 of this Handbook.

Under the second option, the owner or operator may demonstrate that soil concentration efforts, as determined by an acceptable site characterization effort, are less than site specific Tier 2 action levels developed following the RBCA Guidance. Under Tier 2, a facility uses modeling to evaluate groundwater protection and direct exposure concerns on a controlled, but more site-specific basis. This minimizes the high costs and general lengthy review time associated with formal risk assessments.

The third option entails a risk assessment component and the use of sophisticated risk assessment analysis. This may include the use or more complex statistical analysis, contaminant analysis, fate analysis, transport analysis, direct and indirect exposure models and exposure pathway evaluations. Tier 3 evaluations usually involve collection of additional site information and completion of more extensive modeling efforts than is required for either a Tier 1 or Tier 2 evaluation.

The fourth option for demonstrating compliance is to prepare both an exposure pathway assessment report which demonstrates that no exposure pathways exist, and an exposure prevention management plan that ensures protectiveness by maintaining the absence of exposure pathways.

The Hawaii Federal District Court has ruled that the Technical Guidance Manual is a guidance document and as such does not rise to the level of a rule which has been promulgated under the Administrative Procedures Act.[117] The Manual does not create rights enforceable by any party. The Department may decide to follow the guidance provided in the Manual or act a variance with it, based on the particular facts of any given situation.[118]

---

117 *Isono v. Shell*, Civil No. U.S.D.C. 92-00558 HMF (D. Haw., Jury trial Sept. 30, 1993) (Noncompliance with guidance document not construed to establish breach of a lease covenant requiring compliance with all rules and laws).

118 *Technical Guidance Manual, supra,* note 95.

Releases from USTs permanently closed[119] or taken out-of-service before December 22, 1988 are exempt from federal response action requirements under 40 C.F.R. Part 280, Subpart F. "Permanent closure" requires the removal of all accumulated liquids and sludges. The UST must then be removed from the ground or filled with an inert solid material. Under the state UST Rules, however, the Department may direct the owner and operator of a UST which was closed before December 22, 1988 to assess the excavation zone and complete closure according to the federal rules, if releases from the UST may, in the judgment of the Department, pose a threat to human health and the environment.[120]

Loans are available to businesses that are replacing, upgrading, closing, taking remedial action related to, or cleaning up UST releases. The Hawaii Capital Loan Program was established in 1991 and funded by a $250 registration fee charged on all tanks between 1991 and 1993. The fund currently has close to $2 million and the program will end when current funds are expended. The loans, which have a low interest rate and attractive terms, are administered by the Department of Business, Economic Development and Tourism. The loans are available to small businesses and preference is given to those who meet certain criteria such as creating job potential, stimulating exports, displacing imports, using local resources or by-products, and centering on Pacific Basin activities.[121]

11.0 CLOSURE REQUIREMENTS

The Department has adopted rules for change in service, temporary closure and permanent closure of USTs.[122] Federal rules also apply to closure of USTs and out-of-service UST systems.[123] A UST may be closed temporarily or permanently. Each method of closure must be completed according to certain technical requirements.

---

119 40 C.F.R. § 280.71(b).

120 *Id.* § 280.73.

121 State of Hawaii, Department of Health, Underground Storage Tank Program Description at 7 (12/15/99).

122 Haw. Rev. Stat. § 342L-37, Haw. Admin. Rules § 11-281-81 through 86.

123 40 C.F.R. Part 280, Subpart G.

A UST is considered temporarily closed if owners and operators do not deposit regulated substances into the tank or dispense regulated substances from the tank for twelve months or less. Temporary closure of a UST is permitted for a maximum of twelve months. If the UST is closed for less than three months, corrosion protection and spill detection must be continued. If the UST is empty, however, the spill detection requirements do not apply. A UST is considered empty when no more than one inch of residue or 0.3 percent (by weight) of residue remains in the UST system. If the UST is closed for three months or longer, two additional requirements must be met: the vent lines must be kept open and functioning, and all other lines and pumps must be capped and secured.[124]

If a UST is temporarily closed for twelve months or more, the UST must be upgraded to the new performance standards for corrosion protection and release detection, or it must be permanently closed. Upgrading to meet spill and overfill equipment requirements is not required, unless after December 22, 1998 the UST is filled by transfers of more than twenty-five gallons at a time. Substandard USTs must be closed within the twelve month period unless the Department grants an extension. Before applying for a temporary closure extension, the owners and operators must complete a site assessment.[125]

Permanent closure of a UST requires pre-closure notification to the Department and to the County Fire Department. Notice of closure must be submitted to the Department at least thirty days before beginning permanent closure activities. The preclosure notification must provide the name and address of the facility; identify the person in charge of the facility and in charge of overall coordination of closure activity, consultants, contractors, and contact persons; and describe the UST system to be closed and the scheduled date for closure activities to begin. Department approval of closure activities is not required. Owners and operators must also notify

124 Haw. Admin. Rules § 11-281-81 and 40 C.F.R. § 280.70. Note that this definition of "temporary closure" is unique to the Hawaii rules.

125 *Id.*

the Department of the exact dates that closure activities will occur at least seven days prior to a permanent closure action.[126]

To be permanently closed, the UST must be empty of all liquids and accumulated sludges. The UST then must be removed from the ground or filled with a solid inert material. A site assessment area beneath and around the UST must be completed to determine whether contamination exists. The site assessment must measure for the presence of a release of a regulated substance where contamination is most likely to be present. In selecting sample types, sample locations and measurement methods, the site assessment must consider the closure method, nature of the stowed substance, the types of backfill and surrounding soil, the depth and flow of groundwater, and other appropriate factors. If a regulated substance release is discovered, the owner or operator must undertake a release response.[127]

A UST may undergo a change in service to store a non-regulated substance. The UST must be emptied prior to the change in service. The Department must be notified at least thirty days before beginning the change and again seven days prior to change in service activities. A site assessment of the area beneath and around the UST must be completed after Department notification, but before the change in service, to determine whether a release of regulated substances has occurred. If a site assessment reveals a release of a regulated substance, response action must be implemented.[128] UST systems permanently closed prior to the effective date of the federal technical rules are generally exempt from the reporting and response action requirements.

When permanent closure or change in service activities take place, the owner or operator must submit a revised written notification, to the Department, whether or not the UST was brought into service before or after January 28, 2000. For USTs which have received a Department permit, the owner or operator must submit special permit notifications.[129]

---

126 *Id.* § 11-281-82.

127 *Id.* § 11-281-83.

128 *Id.* §§ 11-281-82 and -83.

129 *Id.* § 11-281-84.

For USTs removed before December 22, 1988, or which have been left in place but have not been in operation sine December 22, 1998, a site assessment must be prepared and a release response undertaken if contaminated soil, contaminated groundwater, or free product as a vapor or liquid is discovered by any means in or around the UST location. Upon discovery of contamination, owners and operators must comply with suspected release reporting, investigation and confirmation requirements.[130]

Records which demonstrate compliance with closure or change-in-service requirements must be maintained by the owner and operator. Records of compliance, including site assessment results must be maintained for a minimum of three years after closure or change in service. The records may be maintained in one of three ways: by the owners and operators who took the UST out of service, by the current owners of the UST site, or by mailing the records to the Department if the records cannot be maintained at the facility.[131]

12.0 DEPARTMENT RESPONSE TO PETROLEUM RELEASES

The Department is authorized to respond to releases from petroleum USTs as necessary to protect human health and the environment.[132] The Department may use moneys from the Leaking Underground Storage Tank Fund to complete response action at UST sites under certain conditions.

12.1 LUST FUND

The Leaking Underground Storage Tank Fund ("LUST Fund") was established by the Department for the purpose of funding response actions taken by the Department in response to petroleum releases from USTs.[133] The LUST Fund is financed with moneys from federal grants,

---

130 *Id.*

131 *Id.* § 280.74.

132 Haw. Rev. Stat. ch. 342L, part III.

133 *Id.* § 342L-51.

legislative appropriations and other sources. LUST Fund moneys may be expended by the Department for response actions permitted under the UST Law, as described in the next section.

12.2 RESPONSE ACTION

The Department may take response action under the Department Response Program for petroleum releases under conditions which vary depending on whether the release occurred before or after the January 28, 2000 adoption of state rules for response action.

The Department may respond to a suspected or confirmed UST petroleum release which occurred prior to January 28, 2000 as necessary to protect human health or the environment. The Department must assign priority to response actions in those cases in which the Department cannot identify a solvent owner or operator of the UST or the Department believes, upon cause, that the owner or operator will not or cannot properly undertake response action. In lieu of taking response action, the Department may issue an emergency order for response action to the owner or operator and provide for a hearing before the Director within twenty-four hours.

For petroleum releases which occur after January 28, 2000, the Department may respond, consistent with the rules, as necessary to protect human health or the environment. The Department may do so, however, only under certain conditions: no person who is an owner or operator of the UST and capable of conducting the response action and completing the response action can be found within ninety days; prompt action by the Department is required to protect human health or the environment; the anticipated costs of the response action exceed the financial responsibility coverage requirements of the Department, and LUST Fund moneys are required to complete effective response action; or in instances where the owner or operator has failed to comply with an order issued under RCRA or under the UST Law in response to suspected or confirmed releases.[134] The Department must assign priority to UST release sites which create the greatest threat to human health or the environment. As part of a response action, the Department may provide alternative household water supplies and may relocate residents on a temporary or permanent basis.

134 *Id.* § 342L-52.

Under the Department Response Program for petroleum releases, the Department may complete an exposure assessment with the response action. The Department may not, however, delay response action in order to complete an exposure assessment where response action is required to abate immediate hazards or reduce exposure.[135]

In cases where the owner or operator has failed to maintain evidence of financial responsibility in accordance with federal and state law, moneys from the LUST Fund may be used to complete response action only if necessary to protect human health. If LUST Fund moneys are used by the Department, the Department must seek cost recovery for all sums expended.[136] Funding for hazardous substance and petroleum LUST cleanups can also be obtained by the State from the Environmental Response Revolving Fund ("ERRF"). The ERRF currently has about $5 million and would normally fund high priority sites as determined and administered by the Office of Hazard Evaluation and Emergency Response. All costs incurred by the ERRF are recoverable from responsible parties.[137]

The Voluntary Response Program encourages prospective developers, lenders and purchasers to voluntarily clean up properties by facilitating and streamlining the cleanup process. By participating in the VRP for a UST release response and paying the required fee, the prospective purchaser would be able to have the State oversee the work, assure that the site is cleaned up to the State's satisfaction, receive an official no further action letter, and potentially receive relief from future liability.[138]

---

135 *Id.*

136 *Id.*

137 State of Hawaii, Department of Health, Underground Storage Tank Program Description at 7 (Draft 12/15/99).

138 For further discussion of the Voluntary Response Program, *see infra* ch. 8 of this Handbook, section 12.0.

12.3 COST RECOVERY

All costs incurred by the Department for response or enforcement action relating to a UST petroleum release are recoverable from the UST owner or operator. The standard of liability in Section 311 of the Federal Water Pollution Control Act[139] applies in actions for cost recovery.[140] Under this standard, owners and operators are liable for actual costs incurred by the Department, except where the discharge was caused solely by an act of God, an act of war, an omission of a third party, or a combination thereof. In seeking cost recovery, the Department may consider the amount of financial responsibility that the UST owner or operator is required to maintain. Moneys collected by the Department in cost recovery actions are deposited into the LUST Fund.[141]

Liability to the Department for a UST release may not be transferred from the owner or operator to any other person. Insurance agreements, indemnity agreements, hold harmless agreements, subrogation rights and guarantee rights, however, are all valid and enforceable with respect to liability between the owner, operator and third parties.[142]

13.0 ENFORCEMENT MECHANISMS

The Department, county health authorities and the county police departments are authorized to enforce the UST Law, rules and any orders issued by the Department.[143] The Director or any authorized representative of the Department is authorized to request information relating to the USTs, enter facilities to ensure compliance with the UST Law, inspect and obtain samples of regulated substances in USTs, examine records, and conduct monitoring of USTs and their surrounding environment.[144]

---

139 33 U.S.C. § 1321(f)(2).

140 Haw. Rev. Stat. § 342L-53.

141 *Id.*

142 *Id.*

143 *Id.* § 342L-18.

144 *Id.* § 342L-7.

The Department's procedures for ensuring adequate compliance and enforcement are documented in an inspector's manual and an enforcement manual. The inspector's manual describes all of the procedures that lead up to an enforcement action, including selecting an inspection site, conducting an inspection, conducting a record review and writing an inspection report.[145] The enforcement manual describes how to determine an appropriate enforcement action and the process for various enforcement activities.[146]

The Department's goal is to inspect each facility every two years. The majority of inspections are operation inspections. Generally, the first operation inspection at a site is an outreach and education inspection. Violations are noted, but usually no enforcement action is issued. If violations are found in a subsequent inspection, enforcement is pursued. LUST inspections are conducted on an as needed basis. For complaints, the Department conducts a site visit or inspection where one is warranted.[147] The Department does not routinely inspect a reported suspected release because the owner or operator is responsible for confirming whether or not there was a release. However, there may be instances where an inspection is appropriate or the Department may discover a suspected release while conducting an operations inspection. Inspections at a confirmed release site will vary greatly due to the circumstances of the release.[148]

Records and information obtained under this section will be available to the public unless protected as confidential under the Hawaii Uniform Information Practices Act.[149] Improper disclosure of information is punishable by a fine and imprisonment. The person submitting the information to the Department bears the burden of showing that the information is entitled to

---

145 State of Hawaii, Department of Health, *The UST/LUST Inspector's Manual* (Draft 2, October 1998).

146 State of Hawaii, Department of Health, *The UST/LUST Enforcement Manual* (Draft 1, September 1998).

147 State of Hawaii, Department of Health, *Demonstration of Procedures for Adequate Enforcement* at 6 (Draft 12/15/99).

148 *Id.* at 7.

149 *Id.* ch. 92F.

protection under the Act.[150] The Director's authority extends over owners and operators of USTs and over any person involved in response actions relating to releases from USTs. The 1992 amendments to the UST Law expanded the authority of the Department to obtain information and data, and to inspect and require monitoring or testing activities from any person involved in a response action to a release. Previously, only the UST owner and operator were subject to these provisions.[151]

The Department may pursue an informal enforcement response by issuing either a warning letter or a request for information letter. The Department issues a warning letter for less serious violations for which a field citation is not appropriate. The warning letter is a standard format which identifies the alleged violations, outlines a schedule for compliance, and indicates that failure to comply may result in the issuance of a Notice of Violation or initiation of a civil action, either of which may include penalties. A request for information letter may be issued as the result of a complaint, before or after an inspection, and after review of records submitted by a facility. The standard form letter requests information and advises that failure to provide the information may result in the assessment of penalties.[152]

The Director may issue a Notice of Violation to any person who is violating the UST Law, the rules, or a permit issued by the Department. If the person continues the violation, the Director must issue a Notice of Violation and require the violator to submit a schedule for compliance. The Director must issue a cease and desist order against all activities in violation of the UST Law, rules or a permit, and may impose penalties. Orders issued by the Director become final in twenty days unless the person named in the order makes a written request for a hearing before the Director. If a hearing is requested, any penalty imposed becomes final and payable upon completion of the hearing and issuance of a final order confirming the penalty. Penalties are deposited to the credit of the LUST Fund.

---

150 *Id.* § 342L-15.

151 *Id.* § 342L-7.

152 State of Hawaii, Department of Health, *Demonstration of Procedures for Adequate Enforcement* at 11 (Draft 12/15/99).

If the Director finds violation of an order or accepted schedule, the Director may issue an order assessing an administrative penalty or requiring compliance. The Director may bring suit in state circuit court for appropriate relief, including an injunction. The Director may also obtain an order to suspend, modify or revoke a permit.[153]

Hearings for violations under the UST Program are conducted as contested cases under Hawaii Administrative Procedure Act.[154] If a penalty imposed in the hearing is not paid to the Department within sixty days after it becomes due, a civil action may be instituted to recover the penalty.[155]

In the event of imminent peril to public health and safety and the environment due to a release from a UST or by an action taken in response to a release from a UST, the Governor or the Director, may without hearing, issue a cease and desist order to stop the release and related activities.[156] The Governor or the Director may also seek injunctive relief through a civil action in circuit court. Injunctive relief may be sought to prevent or stop any violation of the UST Law or any variance, and to impose and collect civil and administrative penalties.[157]

13.1 FIELD CITATIONS

Any authorized Department employee may issue a field citation to an owner or operator of an UST. The notice of citation will identify the UST Law or Rules which have been violated, briefly describe the violation, and set forth the settlement amount. By signing the settlement agreement, the owner or operator agrees not to challenge the citation and waives the right to a contested case hearing.[158]

---

153 *Id.* § 342L-8.

154 *Id.* ch. 91. *See infra* ch. 13 of this Handbook.

155 *Id.* § 342L-8.

156 *Id.* § 342L-9.

157 *Id.* § 342L-12.

158 Haw. Admin. Rules §§ 11-281-121, -123, -124 and -125.

In order to settle the notice of citation, any settlement must be paid within thirty days. If the settlement amount is not paid, the field citation is automatically withdrawn and the Department may proceed with a formal enforcement action. The Department may grant an additional thirty day extension for payment of the settlement amount, provided that a written extension request is submitted, there is a satisfactory demonstration that the extension is necessitated by factors beyond the control of the owner or operator, and if the Department believes that compliance will be achieved within the extension period.[159]

All field citation penalty amounts are established by the Hawaii Administrative Rules and range from $50 to $300 per violation.[160]

13.2 ADMINISTRATIVE PENALTIES

The Director is authorized to impose, by order, administrative penalties up to the amount of $25,000 per UST for each violation of the UST Law, rules, or condition of a variance or permit. The Director may also impose administrative penalties for failure to comply with an order issued by the Department. Each day of violation and each individual UST are considered separate offenses.[161] In addition, the failure to comply with an order within the time specified is subject to a $25,000 fine for each day of noncompliance.

In imposing an administrative penalty, the Director must consider the nature and history of the violation, prior violations, the economic benefit resulting from the violation, corrective action, and good faith efforts to comply. The UST Law places the burden on the violator to show that he or she is unable to pay the proposed penalty.[162] An aggrieved party may appeal the Director's order in state circuit court as provided in the Hawaii Administrative Procedure Act.[163] To stay a cease and desist order, the court must issue a specific order to that effect.

---

159 *Id.* at § 11-281-26.

160 Appendix VIII to Chapter 11-281 of the Hawaii Administrative Rules.

161 *Id.* §§ 342L-10 to -11.

162 *Id.* § 342L-11.

163 *Id.* § 342L-13. *See infra* ch. 13 of this Handbook.

13.3 CIVIL PENALTIES

The Director may commence a civil action to impose and collect civil penalties, to collect administrative penalties, or to obtain other relief. All penalties which may be imposed on an administrative basis may also be imposed through a civil action for violation of the UST Law, rules or a condition of a permit or variance. Penalties are deposited to the LUST Fund.[164] Each violation for each individual UST is subject to a $25,000 penalty per day of violation. Failure to comply with an order issued by the Department is subject to a $25,000 penalty per day per UST. In addition, any person who denies, hampers or obstructs the Department in inspecting or entering a facility the Department is authorized to enter, or fails to provide information to the Department as required, is subject to a $500 per day penalty.[165] Any person who has an interest that is adversely affected or may be adversely affected may intervene in any civil action to enforce the UST Law.[166] An aggrieved party may appeal an order of the Director as provided in the Hawaii Administrative Procedure Act.[167]

The Department has adopted an administrative and civil penalty policy ("Policy") for its UST program.[168] The Policy's goal is to provide a logical system for quantifying the gravity of violations and the economic benefit gained from noncompliance. The policy is intended solely as guidance and the Department may decide to act at variance with the guidance based on analysis of specific factual circumstances.

A penalty calculation begins with economic benefit component. The economic benefit component represents the economic advantage that a violator has gained by delaying capital and

---

164 *Id.* § 342L-8(g).

165 *Id.* § 342L-10.

166 *Id.* § 342L-12.5.

167 *See infra* ch. 13 of this Handbook.

168 State of Hawaii, Department of Health, *Underground Storage Tank Program, Administrative and Civil Penalty Policy* (September 1998).

or non-depreciable costs and by avoiding operational and maintenance costs associated with compliance. The economic benefit is determined by adding avoided costs and delayed costs.[169]

The gravity-based penalty component serves to deter potential violators by ensuring that they are economically disadvantaged relative to owners or operators of compliant facilities. The matrix value of the component is derived from the potential for harm caused by the violation and the deviation from regulatory requirements. The matrix assigns values of $50 to $1500. The matrix value is then subject to violator specific adjustments based on the opportunity of compliance, and compliance history.[170]

The Policy allows enforcement personnel to make a further adjustment to the matrix value based on the nature and history of the violation, and in particular, the potential site-specific impacts which could be caused by the violation. The calculation is made using an environmental sensitivity multiplier which takes into account the adverse environmental effects, given the sensitivity of the local area to damage posed by a potential or actual release.[171]

The final matrix value adjustment is determined by the days of noncompliance multiplier.[172] The economic benefit component is then added to the gravity based component to form the initial penalty target figure.

During settlement discussions, the penalty may be further adjusted based on other factors, and the violator's ability to pay will be considered at this point. The Department will always assume that the violator is able to pay, unless the violator demonstrates otherwise. In cases where the violator fails to demonstrate inability to pay, by providing tax returns or other documentation of this claim, the Department will determine whether the violator is unwilling to

---

169 *Id.* at 1-6.

170 *Id.* at 7-14.

171 *Id.* at 14-15.

172 *Id.* at 16.

pay, in which case no adjustments to the initial penalty target will be made. Where inability to pay has been demonstrated to the Department's satisfaction, the Department may consider an installment plan with interest, a delayed payment schedule with interest, an in-kind mitigation activity, an environmental auditing program, or reduction of up to eighty percent of the gravity-based penalty component.[173]

14.0 REPORT SUBMITTAL GUIDELINES

All site assessment, site characterization, and remediation activities for UST releases and closures must be documented in reports submitted to the Department.[174] The state and federal UST rules state the times at which reports must be submitted.[175] The Department's UST rules and the Technical Guidance Manual contain guidance for report submittal.[176] Owners and operators are encouraged to follow the Technical Guidance Manual, which contain guidelines and a checklist for report submittals. The Manual also specifies the required content of the reports and provides technical sampling and analysis methodology.

15.0 DIRECTORY OF UST SERVICE PROVIDERS

The 1992 amendments to the UST Law require the Director to develop and maintain a directory of UST service providers.[177] The directory, which is available to the public, lists service providers engaged in installation, retrofitting, repairing, testing, and monitoring of USTs. Service providers who conduct assessments of UST sites for contamination, prepare and analyze samples, or conduct remediation or corrective action are also included in the directory. The directory is intended to provide information on the service providers relating to their training, work experience and financial liability coverage.

---

173 *Id.* at 17-18.

174 UST reports should be submitted to: UST Section, Solid and Hazardous Waste Branch, Department of Health.

175 40 C.F.R. Part 280, Subpart F.

176 *Technical Guidance Manual, supra* note 95.

177 Haw. Rev. Stat. § 342L-23.

CHAPTER 8

HAWAII ENVIRONMENTAL RESPONSE LAW
AND
HAWAII EMERGENCY PLANNING AND COMMUNITY RIGHT-TO-KNOW ACT

1.0 INTRODUCTION

In 1988, the Hawaii Legislature enacted the Environmental Emergency Response Law[1] to serve as the Hawaii version of the federal "Superfund" program. The statute was renamed the "Environmental Response Law" and the scope of the program was greatly expanded in amendments passed in 1990.[2] The Hawaii Department of Health ("Department") administers the ERL.

The ERL authorizes the Director of Health ("Director") to perform cleanups of releases or threatened releases of hazardous substances, order private parties to perform cleanups, and recover costs incurred for cleanups performed by the State.[3] The Hazard Evaluation and Emergency Response ("HEER") office addresses all aspects of releases of hazardous substances into the environment. The mission of the HEER office is to protect human health, public welfare, and the environment and to provide state leadership, support and partnership in preventing, planning for, responding to, eliminating and enforcing environmental laws related to releases or threats of releases of hazardous substances, pollutants or contaminants. The HEER On-Scene Coordinators are the primary state responders to all major incidences of chemical or oil releases into the environment and are available twenty-four hours a day. Their duty is to

---

1 Act approved June 1, 1988, ch. 148, 1988 Haw. Sess. Laws 248, codified at Haw. Rev. Stat. ch. 128D (Michie 1999). All references to ch. 128D and other chapters of the Hawaii Revised Statutes have been made to the printed version of the statutes current through the 1999 legislative session, unless otherwise noted. Where appropriate, references to acts passed during the 2000 legislative session have also been added.

2 Act approved June 26, 1990, ch. 298, 1990 Haw. Sess. Laws 654. The 1990 amendments left the statute unenforceable due to its unworkable definitions. *See generally*, David Kimo Frankel, Recent Developments, *An Analysis of Hawaii's Superfund Bill*, 1990, 13 U. Haw. L. Rev. 301 (Summer 1991).

3 Haw. Rev. Stat. § 128D-4.

oil releases into the environment and are available twenty-four hours a day. Their duty is to minimize the impact of releases on human health and the environment. Once a release is contained, HEER directs short-term or long-term remediation.[4]

To implement the response requirements of the ERL, HEER solicited the qualifications of several environmental companies, and after an exhaustive search selected two companies in 1998. A time-critical emergency environmental response contract was awarded to the Pacific Environmental Corporation (PENCO) and the non-emergency environmental response contract was awarded to Ogden Environmental and Emergency Services, Incorporated. Both contracts were extended in 1999.[5]

The ERL provides for judicial apportionment of response costs between liable parties, concurrent judicial review of cleanup orders, and innocent land purchaser protection. The ERL imposes affirmative reporting requirements for certain releases of hazardous substances. The ERL also provides civil and criminal penalties for failure to report releases as required, for knowing releases of hazardous substances, and for failure to obey an order issued by the Director.

In August 1995, the Department adopted administrative rules for the ERL, known as the State Contingency Plan, which provide technical guidance for implementation of ERL policies and requirements.[6]

---

4 Hawaii State Department of Health, *Strategic Plan for Hawaii's Environmental Protection Programs* at 55, 60 (January 1999).

5 Hawaii Department of Health, *Report to the Twentieth Legislature in Compliance With Hawaii Revised Statutes Chapters 128D and 128E on the Activities of the Department of Health Environmental Health Administration Office of Hazard Evaluation and Emergency Response and Use of the Environmental Response Revolving Fund* at 9 (2000).

6 Haw. Admin. Rules, tit. 11, ch. 451 (Weil's 2000). All references to the Hawaii Administrative Rules are current through the date of publication of this Handbook, unless otherwise noted.

2.0 RELATIONSHIP TO THE FEDERAL SUPERFUND PROGRAM

The ERL is essentially the Hawaii version of the federal Comprehensive Environmental Response, Compensation, and Liability Act ("CERCLA" or "Superfund").[7] One important purpose of the ERL is to provide enforcement authority to the Department to respond to releases of hazardous substances which may not be subject to response by the federal Environmental Protection Agency ("EPA") or the State under CERCLA or any other state or federal environmental law. For example, the ERL allows the Department to respond to certain releases of petroleum products which are not subject to CERCLA, the Water Pollution Control Law, the Resource Conservation and Recovery Act or the underground storage tank program.[8]

The ERL provisions are similar to CERCLA in many respects, including the release reporting requirements, standard of liability, response authority, recovery of costs and *de minimis* settlements. In furthering cooperation with the EPA, the ERL provides funding for the State's share of CERCLA cleanups.[9] Rules guiding implementation of the ERL are found in the State Contingency Plan.[10]

3.0 STATE CONTINGENCY PLAN

In August 1995, the Department adopted the State Contingency Plan ("SCP"). The SCP identifies the hazardous substances, pollutants, or contaminants it regulates, designates reportable quantities used in determining when notification of appropriate organizations is required, and establishes the notification requirements to be followed in the event of a release. The SCP also establishes the methods for collecting preliminary data and evaluating the actual or potential hazard posed by a release. Criteria for listing and prioritizing sites for response actions, descriptions of response actions, and associated public participation activities also are provided by the SCP.

---

7 42 U.S.C. §§ 9601-9675.

8 In 1993, the University of Hawaii completed a study of the impacts of a major oil spill in Hawaii. The report concluded that a major oil spill would cost the state approximately $7.6 billion. *See* Hawaii State Department of Health, *Strategic Plan for Hawaii's Environmental Protection Programs* at 57 (January 1999).

9 Haw. Rev. Stat. § 128D-4(c)(2).

10 Haw. Admin. Rules, tit. 11, ch. 451.

The SCP describes activities that persons other than the Department may undertake in response to a release, and the requirements for recovery of costs for those actions. The SCP also spells out the authority the Department may exercise when determining the need for response action.[11] The SCP applies to both marine and land-based spills.[12]

The SCP provides the technical criteria for site assessment ranking of priority sites. In establishing these criteria, the Department considered the degree of hazard present at the site, whether the site creates an imminent and substantial danger, and whether the response actions are effective and reasonable. In ranking priority sites, the Department established a minimum hazard threshold for sites to qualify for the listing, evaluated the potential hazard of sites and considered the results of deferral of remedial action. HEER notifies potentially responsible parties by letter of the priority ranking of their sites. During fiscal year 1999, HEER completed the screening of forty-five sites and assigned the following priorities: eight medium priority. twenty low priority and seventeen "no further action" sites.[13]

In addition to establishing technical criteria and a priority ranking, the Department categorized sites subject to the ERL and maintains a list describing each site's status with regard to liable persons and site characterization.[14] This listing, which is available to the public, is intended to keep the community apprised of the status of ERL sites.

4.0 DEFINITION OF REGULATED SUBSTANCES

The ERL addresses releases and threats of releases of hazardous substances, pollutants, and contaminants. The Department treats hazardous substances differently from pollutants and contaminants with regard to liability, release reporting and cost recovery.

---

11 *Id.* § 11-451-1(a)(1)-(13).

12 State of Hawaii, Department of Health, Response to Comments on Proposed State Contingency Plan at 4 (1995).

13 *Report to the Twentieth Legislature*, supra note 5 at 12.

14 Haw. Rev. Stat. § 128D-7(a) - (c).

The ERL definition of "hazardous substances" includes all substances designated under the Clean Water Act, Sections 307(a) and 311(b)(2)(A); CERCLA, Section 102; the Solid Waste Disposal Act, Section 3001; the Clean Air Act, Section 112; and the Toxic Substances Control Act, Section 7.[15] The ERL also expressly lists oil and trichloropropane as hazardous substances.[16] Oil is defined as "oil of any kind or in any form, including, but not limited to, petroleum, fuel oil, sludge, oil refuse, oil mixed with wastes, crude oil or any fraction or residue."[17] In addition to these enumerated hazardous substances, the Director may designate any other substance as a hazardous substance through rules.

Unlike hazardous substances, pollutants and contaminants are not defined by a specific list of substances. Instead, substances are classified as pollutants and contaminants under a risk-based definition.[18] The ERL definition of pollutants and contaminants is substantively identical to the CERCLA definition except that CERCLA excludes certain petroleum products, crude oil and gas, whereas Hawaii does not.[19]

5.0 RESPONSIBLE PARTIES AND DEFENSES

The ERL places responsibility for the cleanup of releases or threatened releases of hazardous substances on liable persons. Liability is strict, joint and several, and unlimited in dollar amount. There is only one statutory exemption from this liability scheme. Liability of any person for a release of heavy fuel oil from a tank barge carrying heavy fuel oil inter-island is limited to $700,000,000.[20] This limitation on liability applies only to releases which are subject to the Federal Oil Pollution Act of 1990[21] and which are releases from tank barges which carry oil and are not equipped with a means of self-propulsion.

---

15 *Id.* § 128D-1. *See* 40 C.F.R. Part 302 for the list of hazardous substances subject to CERCLA.

16 *Compare* CERCLA § 101(14), 42 U.S.C. § 9601(14), the last sentence of which expressly excludes petroleum products.

17 Haw. Rev. Stat. § 128D-1. This definition is based on the definition of "oil" found in the Clean Water Act.

18 Haw. Rev. Stat. § 128D-1.

19 *See* CERCLA § 101(33), 42 U.S.C. § 9601(33).

20 Haw. Rev. Stat. § 128D-6.5.

21 33 U.S.C. § 2700 *et seq.*

The provision which defines "liable persons" in the ERL[22] is essentially identical to the provision defining "liable persons" in CERCLA.[23] Persons held strictly liable under the ERL are:

(1) The owner or operator or both of a facility or vessel;

(2) Any person who at the time of disposal of any hazardous substance owned or operated any facility at which such hazardous substances were disposed of;

(3) Any person who by contract, agreement, or otherwise arranged for disposal or treatment, or arranged with the transporter for transport for disposal or treatment, of hazardous substances owned or possessed by such person, by any other party or entity, at any facility or on any vessel owned or operated by another party or entity and containing such hazardous substances; and

(4) Any person who accepts or accepted any hazardous substances for transport to disposal or treatment facilities or sites selected by such person, from which there is a release, or a threatened release, which causes the incurrence of response costs of a hazardous substance.

For purposes of imposing liability, virtually every legal entity is considered a "person."[24] The definition of "person" specifically includes government entities. Thus, the State, state agencies, the counties, and county agencies are subject to ERL liability in the same manner as a private party.[25]

Defenses to liability under the ERL are few and limited in their application. Liable persons may utilize the following defenses to liability for releases, threats of releases and any resulting damage:

---

22 Haw. Rev. Stat. § 128D-6(a).

23 CERCLA § 107, 42 U.S.C. § 9607(a).

24 Haw. Rev. Stat. § 128D-1.

25 The State of Hawaii faces significant potential liability as an "owner." The State owns almost 1.5 million acres of land, approximately one-third of the land area of the State. Although most of the land is unusable, a significant percentage is developed. David Callies, Regulating Paradise 153 (1984).

(1) Any unanticipated grave natural disaster or other natural phenomenon of an exceptional, inevitable, and irresistible character, the effect of which could not have been prevented or avoided by the exercise of due care or foresight;

(2) An act of war;

(3) An act or omission of a third party other than an employee or agent of the defendant, or than one whose act or omission occurs in connection with a contractual relationship, existing directly or indirectly, with the defendant, if the defendant establishes by a preponderance of the evidence that the defendant exercised due care with respect to the hazardous substance concerned, taking into consideration the characteristics of such hazardous substance, in light of all relevant facts and circumstances; and the defendant took precautions against foreseeable acts or omissions of any such third party and the consequences that could foreseeably result from such act or omission;[26] or

(4) Any combination of the foregoing paragraphs.[27]

Liability is limited to releases or threatened releases of hazardous substances only.[28] Although the State may respond to a release or threatened release of a pollutant or contaminant,[29] no liability may be imposed for such releases or threatened releases. Furthermore, the following activities are not "releases" giving rise to ERL liability: a release from the normal application of fertilizer; the legal application of a pesticide product registered under the Federal Insecticide, Fungicide and Rodenticide Act ("FIFRA");[30] a release from a sewage system conducting only domestic wastewater; and releases permitted by the federal, state, or local government, or other legal authority.[31] The ERL also exempts from liability motor vehicle, aircraft and watercraft exhaust emissions, and releases in the workplace for purpose of bringing a claim against the employer.[32]

---

26 Application of the "third party" defense requires the act or omission of an unrelated third party, such as may be found in "midnight dumping."

27 Haw. Rev. Stat. § 128D-6(c).

28 *Id.* §§ 128D-5(a), -6, -8(a).

29 *Id.* § 128D-4(a).

30 7 U.S.C. § 136 *et seq.*

31 Haw. Rev. Stat. § 128D-1, *see* definition of "release."

32 *Id.*

5.1 LENDERS AND INNOCENT LAND PURCHASERS

The ERL imposes strict liability on the owner of a facility for damages and response costs caused by a release or threatened release of a hazardous substance at the facility.[33] The definition of "owner," however, specifically excludes:

> a person who, without participating in the management of the vessel or facility, holds indicia of ownership primarily to protect its security interest in the vessel of security.[34]

This definition of "owner" is designed to protect secured lenders who hold a security interest in a property, but make no decisions regarding the hazardous substance and do not cause or contribute to the release or threatened release. Until such time as the Department adopts rules pertaining to lenders, the provisions of the Asset Conservation, Lender Liability and Deposit Insurance Protection Act of 1996[35] apply to the actions of lenders after 1997. This federal act expanded CERCLA's secured creditor exemption.

The ERL's secured lender exemption is similar to CERCLA definition of "owner operator," which protects secured lenders from liability so long as the lender does not participate in the management of the facility.[36] If a person is a lender who holds indicia of ownership primarily to protect a security interest, without participating in the management of a vessel or facility, that person is exempt from liability if they sell or otherwise divest themselves of the vessel of facility at the earliest practicable, commercially reasonable time.

Separate and apart from the security interest exemption, lenders who acquire property incident to a foreclosure may defend against liability for response costs by establishing that they are "innocent landowners." The innocent landowner provision also applies to owners of a facility who, at the time of purchase, did not know of or have any reason to know of any

---

33 *Id.* § 128D-6(a)(1).

34 *Id.* § 128D-1.

35 CERCLA § 101, 42 U.S.C. §9601(20)(E).

36 CERCLA § 101, 42 U.S.C. § 9601(20)(A).

hazardous substances disposed of at the facility.[37] As in CERCLA,[38] a party may defend against liability by arguing it did not know and had no reason to know that hazardous substances had been released or disposed of on the property. Before claiming this defense, the party must show it undertook an "appropriate inquiry" at the time of acquisition, including inquiry into previous ownership and uses of the property. The ERL provides the following factors a court is to consider in determining whether "appropriate inquiry" was taken:

(1) specialized knowledge or experience on part of the defendant;

(2) relationship of the purchase price to the value of the property if uncontaminated;

(3) commonly known or reasonably ascertainable information about the property;

(4) the obviousness of the presence or likely presence of contamination at the property; and

(5) the ability to detect such contamination by appropriate inspection.[39]

The "innocent land purchaser" defense must be established by a preponderance of the evidence. At this time, Hawaii courts have not addressed this defense to ERL liability.

6.0 PROGRAM FUNDING

The ERL program is funded through the environmental response revolving fund ("Fund").[40] Moneys for the Fund are appropriated by the Legislature and obtained from settlements, awards, judgments, interest recovered through compliance proceedings, and response costs recovered by the attorney general.[41] Civil penalties collected under the ERL and other state environmental statutes[42] are deposited into the Fund.[43] Moneys generated by the

37 Haw. Rev. Stat. § 128D-6(d)(1).

38 CERCLA § 101(35)(A), 42 U.S.C. § 9601(35)(A).

39 Haw. Rev. Stat. § 128D-6(d).

40 *Id.* § 128D-2.

41 *Id.* § 128D-5(b).

42 *Id.* § 128D-8(d). *See* Haw. Rev. Stat. §§ 342B-11.5, 342D-39, 342F-11.5, 342H-10.5, 342J-10.5, and 342N-9.5.

43 Haw. Rev. Stat. § 128D-2(a).

environmental response tax also supply the Fund.[44] When the total balance of the Fund exceeds $20,000,000, the Department must notify the Department of Taxation which must then discontinue the imposition of the environmental response tax, unless and until the total balance of the Fund declines to less than $3,000,000, at which time the tax will be reinstated.[45]

7.0 ROLE OF REVOLVING RESPONSE FUND IN SITE CLEANUP

The Director is authorized to take any response action consistent with the State Contingency Plan to protect the public health, welfare or environment.[46] In doing so, moneys from the Fund may be utilized by the Director to perform removal or remedial actions in response to a release or threatened release of a hazardous substance, pollutant or contaminant.[47] The Fund also may be utilized for restoration, rehabilitation, replacement or acquisition of natural resources that were damaged or destroyed due to a release.[48]

The Fund may be utilized for costs of response to releases from the legal application of pesticides under FIFRA.[49] Although the State may respond to the lawful release of a pesticide, liability for the accompanying response costs does not extend to private parties. The State may also respond with Fund moneys to releases from activities permitted by the EPA or the Department. For example, the State may conduct a removal or remedial action in response to a discharge made under an NPDES permit,[50] if the site presents an imminent and substantial danger to human health, welfare or the environment. The State cannot, however, recover costs incurred in conducting the removal or remedial action from private parties if the discharges

---

44 *Id.* § 243-3.5.

45 *Id.* § 128D-2(a).

46 *Id.* § 128D-4(a).

47 *Id.* § 128D-4(c)(1).

48 *Id.* § 128D-4(c)(3).

49 *Id.* § 128D-4(c)(4). For discussion of FIFRA and the Hawaii Pesticides Law, *See infra* ch. 11 of this Handbook.

50 *See infra* ch. 3 of this Handbook for discussion of the NPDES permitting program under the Hawaii Water Pollution Control Law.

resulted from the legal application of a pesticide product under FIFRA or were permitted by a federal, state of local permitting authority.[51] Finally, the ERL authorizes payment, from the Fund, of the State's share of CERCLA[52] response costs for response actions conducted under CERCLA authority.[53] Revenues generated by the environmental response tax and deposited into the Fund are to be used for oil spill prevention and remediation, direct support of county used oil recycling programs, drinking water concerns, and support for underground storage tank programs. In the year 2000, the Legislature expanded the use of Fund money to included support for environmental and natural resource protection programs, including, but not limited to energy conservation and alternative energy development, and to address concerns related to air quality, global warming, clean water, polluted runoff, and solid and hazardous waste.[54]

8.0 LIABLE PARTY CLEANUP PARTICIPATION

Once the Director identifies a party as a liable person,[55] the Director may issue an administrative order directing that person to take action in response to a release or threatened release of a hazardous substance.[56] In the event that a release or threatened release creates a substantial endangerment to the public health, welfare or the environment, the Director may issue orders as necessary without a hearing. The issuance of these emergency orders is not limited to liable persons: the Director may issue an emergency order to anyone, including someone who is not involved with the release.[57]

A potentially liable person may respond to a release or threatened release of a hazardous substance without receiving an order from the Director. This type of voluntary response may happen in instances where the release occurs at the party's facility, or where a potentially liable

---

51 Haw. Rev. Stat. § 128D-5.

52 42 U.S.C. § 9604(c)(3).

53 Haw. Rev. Stat. §§ 128D-4(c)(2), -4(c)(5).

54 2000 Haw. Sess. Laws 245 (to be codified at Haw Rev. Stat. § 128D-2).

55 *Id.* § 128D-6(a). *See supra* § 4.0 of this Chapter.

56 *Id.* § 128D-4(a)(1).

57 *Id.* § 128D-4(a)(2).

person has the technical information regarding the released substance readily available, or is best equipped to respond to the release. In the event the party who conducted the response is not liable, the party may seek reimbursement from the State and contribution or indemnity from liable persons for costs incurred in the voluntary response cleanup.[58]

In 1995, the Department designated the Honolulu Harbor project as a state superfund site for an area-wide study involving multiple potentially responsible parties ("PRPs"). Information was requested from various land owners and operators. A core work group of PRPs was formed and has hired a consultant to consolidate the environmental data and conduct an investigation under a voluntary agreement with the Department.[59] At present, the Department is still working on identifying PRPs, along with a plan of action that will address both long term and present releases.[60]

9.0 REPORTABLE QUANTITIES AND REPORTING REQUIREMENTS

The State Contingency Plan ("SCP") establishes reportable quantities for designated hazardous substances, unlisted hazardous substances, trichloropropane and oil.[61] The SCP requires reporting of releases of hazardous substances, but does not require reporting of releases of pollutants or contaminants. Reportable quantities for listed hazardous substances[62] are contained in (1) the federal list of extremely hazardous substances for emergency planning and notification,[63] and (2) the list of CERCLA hazardous substances.[64]

58 *Id.* § 128D-18(d). *See infra* §§ 10.2 and 10.3 of this Chapter.

59 Hawaii State Department of Health, *Strategic Plan for Hawaii's Environmental Protection Programs* at 58 (January 1999).

60 Interview with Curtis Martin, Office of Hazard Evaluation and Emergency Response, Department of Health (July 28, 2000)

61 *See* Haw. Admin. Rules § 11-451-5 for designated hazardous substances.

62 Haw. Admin. Rules § 11-451-5.

63 40 C.F.R. Part 355, Appendices A and B.

64 As found in 40 C.F.R. Part 302, Table 302.4. Note that oil and trichloropropane, which are not designated as hazardous substances under CERCLA and are not listed in 40 C.F.R. Part 302, are hazardous substances under the ERL. For trichloropropane, the reportable quantity is ten pounds.

Unlisted hazardous substances have the reportable quantity of one hundred pounds, unless the substances exhibit toxicity characteristics. Unlisted hazardous substances which exhibit toxicity characteristics[65] have the reportable quantities identified in the listed CERCLA hazardous substances, for the particular hazardous substance exhibiting the toxicity characteristic. If the unlisted hazardous substance exhibits toxicity characteristics on the basis of more than one hazardous substance, the reportable quantity is the lowest of the reportable quantities identified in the listed CERCLA hazardous substances. If the unlisted hazardous substance exhibits toxicity characteristics and ignitability, corrosivity, reactivity, or toxicity, the reportable quantity is the lowest of the applicable reportable quantities. The reportable quantities are based on the weight of the entire amount of material released, not merely the weight of the hazardous substance component.[66]

The SCP defines a reportable quantity for oil four ways.[67] First, a reportable quantity is any amount of oil which when released into the environment causes a sheen to appear. "Sheen" is defined "an iridescent appearance of any petroleum on the surface of any surface water, ground water, or any navigable water of the State which is caused by the release of such petroleum."[68] The SCP employs substantially the same definition of "navigable water" as the EPA regulations governing discharge of oil[69] and the EPA regulations governing the determination of reportable quantities for hazardous substances.[70] Second, a reportable quantity of oil is any free product that appears on groundwater. "Groundwater" is defined by the SCP as any water in a saturated zone or stratum beneath the surface of land or water.[71] Third, a release of oil greater than twenty-five gallons is reportable. Finally, a release of less than twenty-five

---

65 Toxicity characteristics are tested for by the TCLP 1311 method, which measures the potential of a substance to leach into the surrounding environment.

66 Haw. Admin. Rules § 11-451-6(c)(2).

67 The reportable quantity for oil designated in the SCP conforms to that identified by the federal regulations for the underground storage tank program. *See* 40 C.F.R. § 280.53. Under the SCP, the definition of oil includes sludge and oil mixed with waste. Haw. Admin. Rules § 11-451-3(a).

68 Haw. Admin. Rules § 11-451-3(a).

69 40 C.F.R. Part 110.1.

70 40 C.F.R. Part 117.1 *et seq.*

71 Haw. Admin. Rules § 11-451-3(a).

gallons of oil that is not contained and remedied within seventy-two hours also must be reported.[72]

9.1 NOTIFICATION OF RELEASES

Notification requirements in the SCP set forth the notification process to be followed when a hazardous substance release meets or exceeds the reportable quantity. The purpose of the notification process is to assure that appropriate organizations are notified of releases of hazardous substances that present or may present a substantial danger to the public health or welfare, the environment, or natural resources.[73]

Notification is required for releases of both listed and unlisted hazardous substances. For listed hazardous substances, a release in any twenty-four hour period of a quantity equal to or exceeding the reportable quantity criteria must be reported.[74] For unlisted hazardous substances, a release in any twenty-four hour period of a quantity equal to or exceeding the reportable quantity must be reported.[75] The ERL provides no "grace period." All releases must be reported immediately to the Department.

Only releases occurring on or after August 17, 1995, the effective date of the SCP, are subject to the notification requirements. The applicable date is that of the release of the hazardous substance, not the date of the discovery of the release.[76] Any person in charge of a facility or vessel may provide notification to the Department by telephone or in person.

---

72 *Id.* § 11-451-6(b)(5).

73 *Id.* § 11-451-7(a).

74 *See id.* § 11-451-7(b).

75 *See id.* § 11-451-6(c).

76 State of Hawaii, Department of Health, Response to Comments on Proposed State Contingency Plan, at 38 (1995).

Notification must be given to both the Department and all affected local emergency planning committees ("LEPC").[77] A minimum of one LEPC is established in each county.[78] The LEPC is to prepare and implement local emergency response plan.[79] The plan is to include the identification of facilities, the routes likely to be used for the transportation of hazardous substances, the methods and procedures for response to any hazardous substance release, designation of a community emergency coordinator, and public notification procedures.[80]

Verbal notification to the Department must include the trade and chemical name of the hazardous substance and the chemical abstract service registry number, if available. The notification must include the approximate quantity of hazardous substance released, the reportable quantity or the basis for notification, the location of the release, a brief description of the release, when the person in charge learned of the release, the source of the release, and the caller's name, address, and telephone number.

The notification must include the owner and operator's name, address, and telephone number, as well as the name and telephone number of a contact person, measures taken in response to the release, the names of federal, state or local government agencies that have been notified, possible health risks associated with the release, and any other relevant information.[81]

Written notice, including all of the above information, must be given to the Department no later than thirty days after the initial discovery of the release.[82] Written but not verbal notification is required for a release of oil of less than twenty-five gallons in any twenty-four hour period that is not contained and remedied within seventy-two hours.[83]

---

77 Haw. Rev. Stat. § 451-7(c).

78 *Id.* § 128E-5(a).

79 *Id.* § 128E-5(f).

80 For discussion of the Hawaii Emergency Planning and Community Right-to-Know Act and the role of the LEPC, *see infra* § 16 of this Chapter.

81 Haw. Admin. Rules § 11-451-7(d).

82 *Id.* § 11-451-7(e).

83 *Id.* § 11-451-7(b)(1)-(e).

Releases of mixtures or solutions containing a hazardous substance are subject to the notification requirements only where a component hazardous substance is released in a quantity equal to or greater than its reportable quantity. This provision applies only where the person in charge of the facility or vessel knows the exact concentrations of all the hazardous substance components present in the mixture or solution. If the exact concentration of all the hazardous substance components is not known, reporting is required.[84] Continuous releases are to be reported to the Director, not to the EPA or the National Response Center.[85]

Certain categories of releases are exempt from SCP notification requirements. These include releases of hazardous substances emanating from bituminous pavement, landscaping materials, or building materials in good repair. Also exempt are sheens resulting from discharges of oil from a properly functioning vessel engine, and discharges or emissions from a point source regulated under a valid permit, such as an air pollution control or NPDES permit.[86]

Under the dual regulation of CERCLA and the ERL, a release of a reportable quantity of a hazardous substance must be reported within a twenty-four hour period to both the National Response Center as well as the Hawaii State Emergency Response Commission ("HSERC"), and the affected LEPC. The National Response Center may be contacted at (800) 424-8802; the HSERC, which is the Hawaii State Department of Health, at (808) 586-4249 (business hours), (808) 247-2191 (after hours), or 911 (24 hours).

The LEPC for each county may be contacted as follows: Hawaii, (808) 961-8215 (business hours), (808) 935-3311 (after hours); Kauai, (808) 241-6336 (business hours), (808) 241-6711 (after hours); Maui, (808) 243-7561 (business hours), 911 (after hours); City & County of Honolulu, (808) 523-4121 (business hours), 911 (after hours). The State phone system may be accessed toll-free from outer islands by dialing (800) 468-4644.

---

84 *Id.* § 11-451-7(f).

85 *Id.* § 11-451-7(g).

86 *Id.* § 11-451-7(i); *see* Haw. Rev. Stat. 128D-1, definition of "release," for exceptions.

Any person who fails to report a hazardous substance release to the Department immediately, as required, is subject to a civil penalty up to $10,000 per day or prosecution for a criminal misdemeanor. Information that is reported under this section cannot be used in any criminal case, except in a prosecution for perjury or for giving a false statement.[87]

10.0 CLEANUP PROCESS

The actual cleanup process may be divided into two types of responses: removal actions and remedial actions. Removal actions serve as the first step in the cleanup and include an evaluation, possible cleanup and disposal of the released substances. Removal actions are intended to prevent, minimize and mitigate damage to the public health and environment.[88] These actions are immediate responses to alleviate the damaging effects of the release.

A release or threat of release of a hazardous substance may require cleanup of the affected media: surface water, groundwater, soil or air. Some releases may affect only one media; others may affect two or more.

The SCP establishes comprehensive procedural requirements the Department is to follow, or require others to follow, when responding to a release or threat of a release of a hazardous substance, pollutant, or contaminant that may pose a substantial endangerment to public health or welfare, the environment, or natural resources.[89] All response actions, including assessment and investigation activities, must at a minimum comply with applicable requirements.[90]

---

87 Haw. Rev. Stat. § 128D-3(c). *See infra* §§ 15.1 and 15.2 of this Chapter.

88 *Id.* § 128D-1.

89 Haw. Admin. Rules § 11-451-8(a).

90 *Id.* § 11-451-8(e). *See id.* § 11-451-3 for definition of "applicable requirements."

In 1997, the HEER office revised its Technical Guidance Manual for implementation of the SCP.[91] The Technical Guidance Manual explains response action procedures recommended by HEER and is intended to assist consultants, landowners and facility operators with site cleanups.

Response actions are to be implemented as soon as site data and information allow.[92] The Department may provide potentially responsible parties with notice of their potential liability in soliciting cooperation for response actions,[93] and provide oversight for actions taken by potentially responsible parties to ensure that response actions are consistent with the SCP.[94] The Department is committed to recovering any cost incurred and payable from the Fund in accordance with the ERL.[95]

Unlike the federal Superfund law, the ERL does not allow the Department to waive any applicable federal, state or local laws in conducting cleanups. Under the SCP, however, no state or county permit may be required for the portion of any removal or remedial action carried out in full compliance with the ERL.[96] Nonetheless, as a policy matter the Department encourages potentially responsible parties to obtain permits for response actions where doing so would not significantly delay implementation of the response action.[97]

---

91 State of Hawaii, Department of Health, Hazard Evaluation & Emergency Response, *Technical Guidance Manual for the Implementation of the Hawaii State Contingency Plan* (October 1997). The Technical Guidance Manual is available on the Department's website, http://www.hawaii.gov/health/eh/heer/index.html (visited August 12, 2000). The Department is currently working on revisions to the Technical Guidance Manual, and expects to finalize them by the end of year 2000. Interview with Curtis Martin, Office of Hazard Evaluation and Emergency Response, Department of Health (July 28, 2000).

92 Haw. Admin. Rules § 11-451-8(f).

93 *Id.* § 11-451-8(d).

94 *Id.* § 11-451-8(i).

95 *Id.* § 11-451-8(c).

96 *Id.* § 11-451-3.

97 State of Hawaii, Department of Health, Response to Comments on Proposed State Contingency Plan at 9 (1995).

If appropriate, the Department may post, or require to be posted, signs informing persons of the potential presence of hazardous substances at the site.[98] The signs must bear the legend "Notice-Hazardous Substances, Pollutants, or Contaminants May be Present – Unauthorized Personnel Keep Out," along with a designated point of contact and their phone number. The signs must be legible from a distance of at least twenty-five feet.[99]

The Department must prepare a draft response action memorandum containing its preliminary remedy selection decision.[100] The memorandum must be made available as part of the administrative record. At its discretion, the Department may open a public comment period regarding the memorandum of not less than thirty days, which may be followed by a public meeting.[101] New information fundamentally changing the basic features of the remedy is to be discussed in the final response action memorandum, or, in the alternative, additional comments on the revised draft response action memorandum may be sought.[102]

10.1 INITIAL ASSESSMENTS

Initial assessments are to be conducted to collect preliminary data and evaluate the degree of hazard a release or threat of a release poses to public health or welfare, the environment, or natural resources. Such data may also guide the determination of whether a response action should be a removal action or a remedial action.[103] Assessment activities may include site inspections, the review of existing information, and field sampling analysis, the results of which may be compiled in a report containing a description of the pathways of migration of hazardous substances and a recommendation as to whether further action is warranted.[104]

98 Haw. Admin. Rules § 11-451-8(h).

99 Response to Comments, *supra* footnote 97 at 75.

100 Haw. Admin. Rules § 11-451-15(h).

101 *Id.* § 11-451-15(i).

102 *Id.* § 11-451-15(j).

103 *Id.* § 11-451-11.

104 *Id.* § 11-451-11(b).

The Director may consider a number of factors in determining whether a response action should be a removal action or a remedial action. These factors include the immediacy of the threat, implementation time, cost, community interest, the degree of risk based on actual or potential exposure, threat of release from storage containers, weather conditions, and threat of fire or explosion.[105]

10.2 REMOVAL ACTIONS

If the Department determines a removal action may be appropriate, the Department is to review, or require to be reviewed, all existing site assessments.[106] The purpose of a removal action is to address all immediate threats, permanently and completely address the threat posed by the entire site, contribute to the efficient performance of any anticipated remedial action, and consider presumptive response actions identified under the SCP.[107] Presumptive response actions are those actions where contamination may be treated, contained, or disposed of in a manner which has proved successful at similar sites with similar contamination.[108] The Department is required under the SCP to complete a removal action report documenting the decision selecting a removal action.[109] Under the SCP, only the most qualified technologies that apply to the media or source of contamination should be considered for a removal action.[110]

Public participation in removal actions conducted by the Department using Fund moneys may be undertaken if the Department determines cost of the removal action may exceed $25,000, such participation is in the public interest, or significant concern has been or is likely to be expressed. Upon such a determination, the Department is to publish a notice of availability of the public record in the newspaper and provide a public comment period of not less than thirty

---

105 *Id.* § 11-451-12(b).

106 *Id.* § 11-451-13(a).

107 *Id.* § 11-451-13(c).

108 *Id.* § 11-451-15(d).

109 *Id.* § 11-451-13(d).

110 *Id.* § 11-451-13(a).

days.[111] Public participation in removal actions conducted by potentially responsible parties must likewise consist of a notice of the availability of the public record and a thirty-day comment period.[112]

10.3 REMEDIAL INVESTIGATIONS AND ACTIONS

The SCP describes the methods, procedures, and criteria the Department must follow or require to be followed in developing and conducting a remedial investigation. Remedial investigations are designed to define and evaluate the nature and magnitude of the threat of the release, including the release's source and probable direction of migration.[113] If the Department determines it lacks sufficient information, it may require supplemental remedial investigations to aid in its selection of the appropriate remedial action.[114]

The SCP articulates a number of tasks to be performed as part of tailoring the remedial investigation so that its scope, timing, and detail match the complexity of the facility or vessel problems being addressed. These tasks include identifying likely remedial actions and potentially applicable technologies, preparing site-specific health and safety rules and sampling and analysis rules, and identifying potentially responsible parties.[115]

A remedial investigation may be terminated upon the Department's determination that there is no release, the source of the release is not subject to the ERL, the release presents no threat, the type of release does not warrant a response, or the remedial investigation is completed.[116] The SCP provides guidelines for data collection and evaluation, including field investigations.[117]

---

111 *Id.* § 11-451-13(f).

112 *Id.* § 11-451-13(g).

113 *Id.* § 11-451-14(a).

114 *Id.* § 11-451-14(b).

115 *Id.*

116 *Id.* § 11-451-14(e).

117 *Id.* § 11-451-14(d).

Remedial actions may be taken instead of or in addition to removal actions. Remedial actions are intended to provide a permanent correction to the release and to any damage which resulted from the release. They are to prevent or minimize migration of the released substances in soil and water, and may include the onsite treatment of the released substances, provision of alternative water supplies and establishment of a monitoring program. Permanent relocation of residents and businesses in the affected area is another remedial action option provided by the ERL, if such action is necessary to protect the public health or if relocation is more cost-effective than offsite disposition of the released substances.[118] The methods and criteria for conducting removal and remedial actions are included in the SCP.[119]

The SCP calls for the development of remedial action alternatives that protect the environment through waste recycling and through eliminating, reducing or controlling risks posed by a site.[120] In developing alternatives, the Department may establish acceptable cleanup levels by considering applicable requirements, assessment results, or the specific cleanup standards identified in the SCP for systemic toxicants and for known or suspected carcinogens.[121] The SCP does not, however, establish specific cleanup levels. Remedial action alternatives are to be evaluated with regard to effectiveness, implementability, and cost.[122]

10.4 SITE LISTING AND NO FURTHER ACTION DETERMINATIONS

The SCP sets forth detailed criteria for the listing and prioritization of facilities or vessels for the list of sites subject to the ERL and SCP maintained and revised by the Department. These criteria include actual or probable releases to groundwater, surface water, air, or soil; the existence of uncontrolled substances, such as leaking containers; and the danger of fire or

---

118 Haw. Rev. Stat. § 128D-1, *see* definition of "remedial action."

119 *Id.* § 128D-7(a).

120 Haw. Admin. Rules § 11-451-15(b).

121 *Id.*

122 *Id.* § 11-451-15(g).

explosion.[123] Based on these and other related criteria, the Department will designate sites as either high, medium, or low priority.[124]

The SCP describes the circumstances under which a facility or vessel is entitled to a "no further action" determination by the Department. Under the SCP, this determination is warranted when "no further response appears appropriate based on all of the information that may then reasonably be obtained."[125] In making this determination, the Department is to consider whether the facility or vessel meets the minimum hazard threshold criteria,[126] or whether response actions have sufficiently addressed the release or threat of release.[127] Such facilities will be deleted from the list of sites, but are eligible for re-listing if additional response actions are warranted.[128]

10.5 ORDER FROM DEPARTMENT

The Director may take action consistent with the SCP to protect public health, welfare or the environment in the event of a release or substantial threat of release of a hazardous substance, pollutant or contaminant. In taking action related to a hazardous substance release, the Director may issue an administrative order to liable persons requiring response action. In the event that the Director determines that the release or threat of release presents an imminent and substantial threat to human health, welfare or the environment, the Director may issue orders without a prior hearing to persons unrelated to the release or threat of release.[129] This broad authority is intended to assist the State in responding to those actual releases or threatened releases which pose a danger to the community where the liable person cannot be identified, is unavailable or cannot participate in response actions. This broad authority also gives the State access to qualified technical personnel whose services the State may not otherwise be able to obtain.

---

123 *Id.* § 11-451-9(b).

124 *Id.* § 11-451-9(d).

125 *Id.* § 11-451-10(a).

126 *See id.* § 11-451-9(b)(2).

127 *Id.* § 11-451-10(a).

128 *Id.* § 11-451-10(c).

129 Haw. Rev. Stat. § 128D-4(a).

Recently, the ERL has been amended to allow the Department to hire toxicologists and ecological risk assessors, and to pay for those positions out of the environmental response revolving fund.[130] The HEER office toxicologists and epidemiologists serve as the DOH's environmental health experts on poisons and pathogens. They assess risks to human health and assist in providing guidelines and procedures for public health advisories or for the elimination of these risks from the environment.

11.0 COST ALLOCATION AND RECOVERY

State funds or private funds may be expended to conduct a response action under the ERL, and response costs may be borne by the State, by private parties or both. These response costs may be recovered by the state and may be the subject of an apportionment or contribution action by a private party.

Costs incurred for response actions conducted by the State may be recovered by the State from liable persons.[131] Costs incurred for response actions conducted by liable persons may be allocated among all liable persons through judicial apportionment and contribution procedures. Persons whose liability is minimal in comparison to the other liable persons may settle their claims with the State through procedures provided for *de minimis* settlements.

Persons may seek reimbursement from the State either while the action is being conducted or after it is completed. The State may be petitioned for reimbursement through concurrent judicial review during the response action if the person is in compliance with the Department's orders. After the response action is completed, persons who have incurred response costs may petition the State for reimbursement through an administrative review procedure.

---

130 *Id.* § 128D-2.5, 12.6.

131 *Id.* § 128D-5.

11.1 COST RECOVERY

The State is authorized to recover costs incurred in responding to releases or threatened releases of hazardous substances. In fiscal year 1999, cost recovery efforts resulted in the State's collection of $945,635.[132] The State also may recover costs incurred for the restoration, rehabilitation, replacement or acquisition of natural resources which were damaged due to a release of a hazardous substance, pollutant or contaminant.[133] Damage to natural resources which occurred wholly before July 1990 is exempted from cost recovery.[134] During fiscal year 1999, natural resource damage assessment became a major area of focus for the Department.[135]

The State, through the Attorney General, must initiate an action for recovery of response costs within six years of the completion of all response actions. Actions for the recovery of natural resources damages must be instituted within three years of the date the loss was discovered and related to the release.[136]

The State may expend moneys in the Fund to conduct response actions, but may not recover those costs incurred in responding to releases of pollutants and contaminants or in responding to hazardous substance releases allowed by federal, state or local permit, or other legal authority. Costs incurred by the State for responses to releases due to the legal application of a pesticide product in accordance with FIFRA are not recoverable.[137] With these statutory limitations, the State, although not restricted from responding to any releases of hazardous substances, pollutants or contaminants, is limited in the types of response costs it can recover from liable persons. These cost recovery limitations are intended to protect persons from

132 *Report to the Twentieth Legislature, supra* note 5 at 9.

133 Federal and state trustees are designated to recover natural resource damages. The Director of Health and the chairperson of the State Board of Land and Natural Resources were designated as co-trustees under the Oil Pollution Act of 1990. Primary trustees also include the Department of the Interior (including the Fish and Wildlife Service, the National Park Service, and the Bureau of Land Management), the National Oceanic and Atmospheric Administration within the Department of Commerce, and the Department of Agriculture's Forest Service.

134 Haw. Rev. Stat. § 128D-5(a).

135 *Report to the Twentieth Legislature, supra*, note 5 at 9.

136 Haw. Rev. Stat. § 128D-5(d).

137 *Id.* § 128D-5(a).

liability for response costs incurred by the State in connection with releases due to the legal uses of certain chemicals and releases due to legal discharges pursuant to a valid permit.

11.2 REIMBURSEMENT

Any person who has incurred response costs in compliance with an order from the Director may petition the State for reimbursement from the Fund. The administrative review of orders must be requested by petition within sixty days after the completion of an order. The petitioner must have complied with the Director's order to be entitled to petition for a hearing and reimbursement of response costs.[138] A contested case hearing in accordance with the Hawaii Administrative Procedure Act[139] must be commenced within thirty days of receipt of the petition, and the petition must be granted or denied by the hearing officer within thirty days of the hearing.[140]

In order to prevail at the administrative hearing and receive reimbursement from the State for response costs, the petitioner must show by clear and convincing evidence that the petitioner is not a liable party and that the costs of compliance incurred by the petitioner were reasonable.[141] This burden of proof is unprecedented in administrative actions, and a party may wish to consider judicial review instead.[142] If the petitioner demonstrates that the Director's order or portion of the order requiring a selected response was arbitrary and capricious, the petitioner will be reimbursed for all response costs which are found to be arbitrary and capricious.[143] Additional reimbursement may be awarded to the petitioner, including costs, attorneys' fees and other expenses.[144]

---

138 *Id.* § 128D-19(a).

139 Haw. Rev. Stat. ch. 91. *See infra* ch. 13 of this Handbook.

140 Haw. Rev. Stat. § 128D-19(b).

141 *Id.* § 128D-19(c).

142 *See infra* ch. 13 of this Handbook.

143 Haw. Rev. Stat. § 128D-19(d).

144 *Id.* § 128D-19(e).

11.3 APPORTIONMENT AND CONTRIBUTION

The 1991 amendments to the ERL added provisions for contribution, indemnity and apportionment of costs incurred for private party response actions among liable persons.[145] Private party response actions are those taken at sites where the Department provides no oversight or where the response action is not carried out pursuant to a consent agreement or order issued by the Department.[146] Liable persons may file a claim to seek contribution or indemnity any time after the party seeking contribution has incurred response costs.[147] Although liability to the State is joint and several, liable persons may seek judicial apportionment of response costs and judicial resolution of claims for indemnity or contribution amongst themselves.

The response action must be consistent with the SCP for liability to arise under the ERL.[148] Response actions are deemed consistent with the SCP in the absence of material or substantial deviations from SCP provisions when evaluated as a whole, or where carried out in compliance with the terms of an order or consent agreement.[149]

In an apportionment action, all recoverable costs shall be apportioned by the court among the liable persons. If a portion of the costs cannot be allocated to a person, an orphan share is created for the designation of all unallocated costs. The orphan share is then apportioned and paid by the remaining solvent liable parties. Once the apportionment of recoverable costs is complete, each liable party is responsible for payment of its allocated share and also for a proportion of the orphan share, if one has been created.[150]

For an example of the apportionment of response costs, including an orphan share, consider the following scenario. The total response costs are $100,000, and four persons are liable in equal proportion (i.e., 25% each). One liable person is bankrupt and cannot pay its

---

145 *Id.* § 128D-18.

146 Haw. Admin. Rules § 11-451-18(d).

147 Haw. Rev. Stat. § 128D-18(d).

148 Haw. Admin. Rules § 11-451-18(b). *See also* Haw. Rev. Stat. § 128D-6.

149 Haw. Admin. Rules § 11-451-18.

150 Haw. Rev. Stat. § 128D-18(f).

share. The $25,000 share of the insolvent party is placed into an orphan share for which the remaining solvent persons are responsible. Because the remaining persons are equally liable, the orphan share is divided equally among the three remaining persons. Each person is responsible for one-third (33%) of the $25,000 orphan share, or $8,333.33. The total liability of each liable person, A, B and C, after apportionment is $25,000 plus the orphan share portion of $8,333.33. A, B and C are each therefore liable for the payment of $33,333.33. This method of apportionment ensures that the three solvent liable persons are responsible for the entire response costs of $100,000.

The ERL provides guidelines for the court to consider in an apportionment action. These guidelines include consideration of the volume and toxicity of the hazardous substances at the site, the degree of the liable person's involvement in the response action, compliance with permits, and cooperation with government officials.[151] In the event a party cannot establish by a preponderance of the evidence that it is liable for only a portion of the response costs by a preponderance of the evidence, the court may use equitable principles to apportion costs among the liable persons.[152] These equitable principles may be applied in cases where the wastes or releases are so intermingled that they cannot be separated for purposes of apportionment.

Any party who has incurred response costs may also seek contribution or indemnity from another liable person. As in apportionment, the court may use equitable principles to allocate costs among liable persons.[153]

11.4 *DE MINIMIS* SETTLEMENTS

The *de minimis* settlement provision provides a mechanism by which a potentially liable person can reach settlement with the State where the person is responsible for only a minor portion of the response costs at the facility.[154] The Director may reach settlement with any of the

151 *Id.* § 128D-18(g).

152 *Id.* § 128D-18(h).

153 *Id.* § 128D-18(d).

154 *Id.* § 128D-20.

potentially responsible parties, regardless of whether they qualify for *de minimis* status. In order for a person to be eligible for a *de minimis* settlement, however, the Director must determine that one of the following two conditions are met:

1. The amount and toxicity of the party's hazardous substances are minimal compared to the other hazardous substances at the facility; or
2. The party is the owner of the property and did not conduct or permit any activity involving hazardous substances, or contribute to the release of the hazardous substance.[155]

The settlement agreement may include a covenant not to sue if the covenant would not be inconsistent with the public interest. The Director is obligated to reach settlement and execute a covenant not to sue as soon as possible once the necessary information on the release, the site and the response action is available. The settlement agreement may be entered as a consent decree or as part of an administrative order, with the state courts having jurisdiction to enforce the settlement agreement.[156]

Any party that has settled with the State is not liable for later claims made for contribution or indemnity for the same matter to the extent the matter was addressed in the settlement. The potential liability of the non-settling parties remains, unless it is explicitly discharged in the settlement agreement. If settlement is reached, the total liability of the non-settling parties to the State is reduced by the settlement amount.[157] The SCP and ERL require the maintenance of a list of *de minimis* settlements completed under this section.[158]

12.0 VOLUNTARY RESPONSE

The Voluntary Response Program ("VRP") was created on July 7, 1997 by amendments to Hawaii's ERL, and was further revised by amendments in 1998. The purpose of the VRP is to streamline the cleanup process in a way that will encourage prospective developers, lenders and

---

155 *Id.* § 128D-20(a).

156 *Id.* § 128D-20(b) - (d).

157 *Id.* § 128D-20(e).

158 *Id.* § 128D-7(c). *See also* Haw. Admin. Rules § 11-451-9.

purchasers to voluntarily cleanup property. In order to obtain an exemption from liability, parties may implement a voluntary response action. The exemption from future liability will run with the land and apply to all future owners of the property, but will not exempt anyone who was liable under the ERL prior to conducting the voluntary response action.[159] However, a voluntary response is still subject to all other requirements of the remedial process.[160] Voluntary response actions may not be pursued at sites where the EPA or the United States Coast Guard is already proceeding under various federal statutes. Additionally, if the Director determines that a site poses an imminent and substantial threat to human health, the environment or natural resources, a voluntary response my be disallowed.[161]

Since the inception of the VRP in 1997, there have been only ten applications to participate in the program. Of these applications, eight are either in process through the voluntary response program or have finished the response process completely.[162]

Applications to proceed with voluntary response actions must include information regarding the requesting party, the property owners and the property location. The application must also include site information, including its occupational history and any known or suspected contamination. The requesting party must also provide the Department with any and all reports and data pertaining to environmental investigations or response actions on the property. Within sixty days of initial approval of an application, the requesting party and the Department must negotiate an agreement for conducting the voluntary response action. If the Department denies an application, there is no right of appeal.[163] If an application is denied because it is incomplete or inaccurate, the requesting party will receive a notice and may cure the

---

159 Haw. Rev. Stat. § 128D-39.

160 *Id.* § 128D-31

161 *Id.* § 128D-32.

162 Interview with Curtis Martin, Office of Hazard Evaluation and Emergency Response, Department of Health (July 31, 2000).

163 *Id.* § 128D-34

deficiency. If the application is denied a second time, the Director may require an additional processing fee for any subsequent submittal.[164]

When the Department receives an application to implement a voluntary response action along with the $1,000 application processing fee, the Department will post a sign at the site within ten days that will notify the public of their opportunity to comment. A notice of the voluntary response action will also be published the Office of Environmental Quality Control's bulletin, The Environmental Notice. The public comment period will run concurrently with and will not delay the application process.[165] If an application is denied because it is incomplete or inaccurate, the requesting party will receive a notice and may cure the deficiency. If the application is denied a second time, the Director may require an additional processing fee for any subsequent submittal.[166]

If a voluntary response is approved, the Department will continue to be involved, and will charge oversight costs of $100 per hour for staff time plus oversight costs.[167] Upon approval of a voluntary response application, the Department may require an initial deposit of up to $5,000 to pay for these oversight costs. If oversight costs are not paid, the Department may pursue an enforcement action.[168] Likewise, the Director may terminate a voluntary response agreement when there is an imminent and substantial threat to public health, the environment or natural resources, where the requesting party is not acting in good faith or fails to comply with the terms of the agreement or when the draft remedial action is inadequate.[169]

Once a voluntary response action is satisfactorily completed, the requesting party will receive a letter of completion from the Director. This letter will be noted on the property deed and will also be sent to the county agency that issues building permits. The letter will address

---

164 *Id.* § 128D-35.

165 *Id.* § 128D-34.

166 *Id.* § 128D-35.

167 *Id.* § 128D-37.

168 *Id.* § 128D-36.

169 *Id.* § 128D-41.

the specific hazardous substances, pollutants, contaminants, media and land that were addressed in the response action. If contamination is left on site, the letter of completion will identify land use restrictions and any required management plan.[170]

Prospective purchasers who wish to qualify for an exemption from liability must enter into a voluntary response agreement with the Department prior to becoming the owner or operator or the property. Prospective purchasers and parties who purchase property from an owner who has conducted a voluntary response action will not be liable to the Department for the specific hazardous substances, pollutants, contaminants, media and land area encompassed by the letter of completion. Parties exempt from future liability to the Department are also exempt for claims for contribution or indemnity regarding matters addressed in the response action.[171]

Liability remains for other laws or requirements or to other parties. Likewise, parties will remain liable if the letter of completion is acquired by fraud, misrepresentation or failure to disclose material information or if transactions were made for the purpose of avoiding liability.[172]

Home Depot U.S.A., Inc. was the first company to participate in the VRP and has been working with the Department to address contamination at a new store in Iwilei.[173] The project addressed petroleum-related contamination in soil and groundwater.[174] The selected remedy included installation of a vapor control system over the entire site and groundwater

---

170 *Id.* § 128D-39.

171 *Id.*

172 *Id.*

173 http://www.state.hi.us/doh/eh/heer/vrp.html (visited August 12, 2000).

174 Department of Health, Communications Office Press Release, Feb. 3, 1999.

monitoring.[175] This project was completed and received a letter of completion in September 1999.[176]

13.0 ADMINISTRATIVE RECORDS

The SCP provides guidelines for the establishment and content of administrative records.[177] For response action selection, the administrative record may contain data and analysis information, technical literature, documents made available to the public, decision documents, orders, and an index.[178] Privileged or confidential documents containing information which forms the basis for the selection of a response action are to be summarized into a statement disclosing the non-confidential information. If the information cannot be summarized in a disclosable manner, it is to be placed in the confidential portion of the administrative record file, and listed in the index to the record.[179]

Separate administrative records shall be established for documents considered by the Director in issuing an order pursuant to section 128D-17 of the ERL.[180] The administrative record for the selection of a remedial action or removal action will be made available for public inspection when the draft response action memorandum is complete. Interested persons are allowed to make comments which become part of the administrative record.[181] Once the decision document selecting the response action has been finalized, the Department may add documents to the administrative record, hold additional public comment periods, and consider additional public comments if the comments contain significant information which substantially supports the need to significantly alter the response action.[182]

---

175 Department of Health, Hazard Evaluation and Emergency Response Office, Response Action Memorandum (June 18, 1999).

176 Department of Health, Communications Office Press Release, September 17, 1999.

177 Haw. Admin. Rules § 11-451-19.

178 *Id.* § 11-451-19(b).

179 *Id.*

180 *Id.* § 11-451-19(d).

181 *Id.* §§ 11-451-20, 11-451-21.

182 *Id.* § 11-451-22.

14.0 JUDICIAL REVIEW

Any person who receives and complies with an order issued by the State under the ERL may seek concurrent judicial review of the order.[183] However, injunctive relief may not be sought, and continuing compliance with the order is required during the judicial review process. The person receiving the order may supplement the administrative record for thirty days, and the Director may hold a hearing to hear testimony and receive other evidence.[184] The court's review of the matter is limited to the administrative record. The court will hear oral arguments and accept written briefs, if so requested by any party.

The Director's determination that the party is a liable person is reviewed by the court under the "arbitrary and capricious" standard. If the court determines that the petitioner is not subject to liability under the ERL, the Director's order will be vacated, and the person will be reimbursed from the Fund or from the State. Reimbursed costs include witnesses' and attorneys' fees.

The court also applies the arbitrary and capricious standard of review to the technical aspects of the order, such as the nature and scope of the remedy. If upon review the court finds the order arbitrary and capricious, contesting persons are given thirty days to find technical modifications to the order mutually agreeable to the Department. If the liable persons and the Department are unable to agree, then a technical panel is appointed to complete binding resolution of the issues. Each party may elect a qualified technical panel member,[185] who together select a third panel member. The ERL requires that each technical panel member have expertise in the physical, chemical, biological or health sciences. The technical panel should resolve the outstanding technical issues of the order and submit the resolution to the court for entry of an order.

---

183 Haw. Rev. Stat. § 128D-17(a).

184 Hawaii Admin. Rules § 11-451-23, Haw. Rev. Stat. § 128D-17(b).

185 Haw. Rev. Stat. § 128D-17(g).

A party also may seek judicial review of petition for administrative review which has been denied in whole or in part. This review of the petition denial shall be conducted according the Hawaii Administrative Procedure Act.[186] The court may award reimbursement to the petitioner from the Fund or from the State. Other fees and costs may be reimbursed, including reasonable attorneys' fees, if appropriate.

15.0 ENFORCEMENT MECHANISMS

Several mechanisms are available to the State to enforce the ERL. The State may impose civil and criminal penalties for violations of the ERL, the SCP, or orders which have been issued by the Director. The State also may seek injunctive relief to prevent violation of the ERL, the administrative rules or any order.[187]

The Department may enter any site or any facilities, vessels, or properties adjacent to a site to conduct further response actions, where entry is necessary to determine the need for response.[188] The Department may designate as its representative, solely for the purpose of access, one or more potentially responsible parties who have agreed to conduct a response action.[189] If consent to enter is not granted, or is conditioned, the Department may issue an order directing compliance with the request for access.[190] The SCP describes the required contents of such orders.[191] Force shall not be used to compel compliance with an order, nor may an order be used for any criminal investigations.[192]

186 *Id.* § 128D-17(k). *See infra* ch. 13 of this Handbook.

187 *Id.* §§ 128D-8, 128D-9, 128D-10.

188 Haw. Admin. Rules § 11-451-24(a).

189 *Id.* § 11-451-24(d).

190 *Id.*

191 *Id.* § 11-451-24(g).

192 *Id.* § 11-451-24(i).

15.1 CIVIL PENALTIES

Civil penalties may be imposed by the State for a number of different violations. Civil penalties are provided for failing to report a release of a hazardous substance, knowingly releasing of a hazardous substance, and failing to comply with any provision of the ERL, any order issued by the State or any rule which has been adopted under the ERL.[193]

Any person who fails to report the release of a hazardous substance immediately upon knowledge of the release is subject to a maximum $10,000 civil penalty per day of failure to report.[194] Any person who knowingly releases a hazardous substance in an amount above the reportable quantity is subject to a civil penalty up to a maximum of $100,000 per day of violation.[195] Both of these violations are also subject to criminal prosecution.

Civil penalties also may be imposed for failure to comply with an order issued by the Director. A person who is liable for a release or threat of release and who fails to provide response action as required in an order may be liable for punitive damages. Liability for punitive damages claimed by the State may amount to three times the costs paid from the Fund due to the liable person's inaction. Punitive damages may be imposed in addition to any response costs which may be recovered by the State.[196]

Additionally, any person who willfully, knowingly or recklessly violates or fails to comply with any provision of the ERL, any administrative rule, or an order issued by the Director is subject to civil penalty of up to $50,000 per day, per violation.[197] These penalties may be recovered by the State through a civil action in the state circuit court. A person acts "knowingly" with respect (a) to his or her conduct, when he or she is aware that his or her conduct is of that nature; (b) to attendant circumstances, when he or she is aware that such

---

193 Haw. Rev. Stat. § 128D-8.

194 *Id.* § 128D-3(c).

195 *Id.* § 128D-10.

196 *Id.* § 128D-8(a).

197 *Id.* § 128D-8(b).

circumstances exist; and (c) to a result of his or her conduct, when he or she is aware that it is practically certain that his of her conduct will cause such a result.[198]

15.2 CRIMINAL PENALTIES

In addition to civil penalties, certain violations of the ERL carry criminal penalties. Criminal penalties may be imposed for failure to report a reportable release of a hazardous substance[199] and for knowingly releasing a hazardous substance in an amount above the reportable quantity.[200]

Any person who fails to report a hazardous substance release to the Department immediately upon knowledge of the release is subject to prosecution for a criminal misdemeanor.[201] Conviction carries a maximum sentence of one year[202] and a maximum fine of $2,000.[203]

Anyone who knowingly releases a hazardous substance in an amount above the reportable quantity is subject to prosecution for a class C felony.[204] The maximum sentence that may be imposed for a class C felony is five years.[205] A fine of up to $10,000 may also be imposed on a person convicted of a class C felony.[206] Releases that occur in accordance with an appropriate permit do not constitute a "knowing release."

As with civil penalties, a person acts "knowingly" with respect (a) to his or her conduct, when he or she is aware that his or her conduct is of that nature; (b) to attendant circumstances,

---

198 *Id.* § 702-206(2).

199 *Id.* § 128D-3(c).

200 *Id.* § 128D-10.

201 *Id.* § 128D-3(c).

202 *Id.* § 706-663.

203 *Id.* § 706-640(1) (d).

204 *Id.* § 128D-10.

205 *Id.* § 706-660(2).

206 *Id.* § 706-640(1) (c).

when he or she is aware that such circumstances exist; and (c) to a result of his or her conduct, when he or she is aware that it is practically certain that his or her conduct will cause such a result.

The criminal penalties for failure to report and for knowing release of a hazardous substance took effect upon the State's adoption of the SCP in August, 1995.[207] Criminal penalties may not be imposed on certain employees. Actions which may be criminal under the ERL and which an employee has taken within the scope of his or her employment will not subject the employee to criminal prosecution if the employee is not a supervisor or manager.[208] This provision is intended to protect those employees who cause a release, but have acted pursuant to direction from management.

The HEER office works with the Environmental Crimes Task Force co-chaired by the Assistant U.S. Attorney, the State Attorney General's Office and the resident EPA Criminal Investigation Special Agent. Criminal activity of interest usually involves the intentional release of hazardous substances or their storage and transportation in a manner contrary to law in an effort to eliminate disposal costs. In 1999, the Task Force's work resulted in the first indictment and conviction of an individual under the Class C felony provision of the ERL for the intentional release and non-reporting of diesel fuel at Maalaea Harbor, Maui.[209]

16.0 CITIZEN SUITS

The 1991 amendments to the ERL added a citizen suit provision, similar to the CERCLA citizen suit provision, which took effect June 1993.[210] The citizen suit provision permits civil suits to be filed in circuit court against any person who is alleged to be in violation of a rule, requirement or order effective under the ERL. The Director also may be sued for his or her

---

207 *Id.* § 128D-7(e).

208 *Id.* § 128D-15.

209 *Report to the Twentieth Legislature, supra* note 5 at 23.

210 *Id.* § 128D-21. *See CERCLA § 310,* 42 U.S.C. § 9659.

failure to perform any nondiscretionary act or duty.[211] The State may intervene in any citizen suit in which it has not been named a party.[212]

Certain requirements must be met before a citizen suit can be brought. Sixty days prior to filing the suit, notice must be given to the Director and to the alleged violator. The method of notice is to be determined by rule. A citizen suit may not be instituted if the Director has issued a notice letter to the violator concerning the violation or if the Director has undertaken a response action, including investigation, in connection with the alleged violation.[213] The costs of litigating a citizen suit may be awarded to the substantially prevailing party at the court's discretion in the course of issuing a final order.[214] As in the Air Pollution Control Law and the Water Pollution Control Law,[215] the citizen suit provision provides an enforcement tool to address violations of the ERL which have not been addressed by the Department.

17.0 HAWAII EMERGENCY PLANNING AND COMMUNITY RIGHT-TO-KNOW ACT

The 1993 Legislature enacted the Hawaii Emergency Planning and Community Right-To-Know Act, also called HEPCRA.[216] HEPCRA is largely modeled upon the federal Emergency Planning and Community Right-To-Know Act of 1986, which is commonly referred to as EPCRA.[217] Both HEPCRA and EPCRA establish reporting requirements applicable to certain facilities and emergency notification requirements for releases of certain chemicals. HEPCRA creates the Hawaii State Emergency Response Commission as well as the Local Emergency Planning Committees to implement the program. The purpose of HEPCRA is to set

---

211 Haw. Rev. Stat. § 128D-21(a)(2).

212 *Id.* § 128D-21(f).

213 *Id.* § 128D-21(c)(2).

214 *Id.* § 128D-21(e).

215 *See supra* chs. 2 and 3 of this Handbook.

216 Act approved June 21, 1993, ch. 300, part 1, 1993 Haw. Sess. Laws 673 (codified at Haw. Rev. Stat. ch. 128E).

217 42 U.S.C. § 11001 *et seq.*

up a framework to prepare for responses to releases of hazardous substances at three levels: the facility, local (county) government and state government.

17.1 HAWAII STATE EMERGENCY RESPONSE COMMISSION

The Hawaii State Emergency Response Commission ("HSERC") is established within the Department of Health ("Department") by HEPCRA.[218] The HSERC consists of agency directors, representatives of each county and the University of Hawaii, as well as other persons appointed by the governor. The HSERC is tasked with the development of a State Contingency Plan for the implementation of HEPCRA, development of a State Chemical Inventory Form and development of a public information, education and participation program for facility owners and the public.[219] The HSERC is also authorized to adopt rules and to appoint hearing officers to conduct public hearing and informational meetings.[220] From a policy perspective, the HEER Office is vested with the mandate to provide statewide leadership in preparing for and responding to hazardous substance releases and supports the HSERC.[221]

17.2 LOCAL EMERGENCY PLANNING COMMITTEE

HEPCRA designates each county as an emergency planning district.[222] HEPCRA requires that at least one local emergency planning committee ("LEPC") be established in each county.[223] The LEPC and its contact person has been established for each county as follows:[224]

---

218 Haw. Rev. Stat. § 128E-2.

219 *Id.* § 128E-2(g).

220 *Id.* § 128E-3.

221 State of Hawaii, Department of Health, *Strategic Plan for Hawaii's Environmental Protection Programs* at 65 (January 1999).

222 Haw. Rev. Stat. § 128E-4. One exception is Kalawao County on the Island of Molokai, which is designated to be the responsibility of the Department.

223 Haw. Rev. Stat. § 128E-5(a).

224 Department of Health, Hazard Evaluation and Emergency Response Office, Hazardous Substance Release Notification and Inventory Guideline (undated, effective Nov. 1995).

County of Hawaii:	Jay Sasan Industrial Safety Officer 25 Aupuni Street Hilo, HI 96720 961-8215 935-3311 (after hours) 961-8248 (fax)
City and County of Honolulu:	Leland Nakai Oahu Civil Defense 650 S. King Street Honolulu, HI 96813 523-4121 911 (after hours) 524-3439 (fax)
County of Kauai:	Clifford Ikeda Kauai Civil Defense 4396 Rice Street, Room 107 Lihue, HI 96766 241-6336 241-6711 (after hours) 241-6335 (fax)
County of Maui:	Joseph Blackburn, Captain Maui Fire Department 200 Dairy Road Kahului, HI 96732 243-7561 911 (after hours) 242-4479 (fax)

The LEPC members are appointed by the HSERC and consist of members in firefighting, law enforcement, first aid, civil defense and emergency management areas. The LEPC members also include state and county officials, news media personnel, community groups and members from the regulated community.[225] The mayor of each county completes a list of recommended persons which is then considered by the HSERC. The HSERC is authorized to make appointments to the LEPC.

---

225 Haw. Rev. Stat. § 128E-5(c).

Each LEPC is tasked with the preparation of a local emergency response plan, implementation and annual review and update of the plan.[226] The plan must include several components specified by HEPCRA. At a minimum, the plan must identify the following: each facility which is subject to HEPCRA, procedures to be followed in responding to a release of an extremely hazardous substance, community and facility emergency coordinators, procedures to ensure effective, prompt and reliable notification of a release to all necessary persons and the public, and methods to determine when a release has occurred and the likely affected population.[227] In addition, the plan must also detail emergency facilities and equipment, training programs, evacuation plans, and methods and schedules for exercising the emergency plan.[228]

The LEPC is charged with completing several other duties. The LEPC is authorized to request information to from facilities and is required to submit the local emergency response plan to the HSERC. The LEPC is also to report alleged violations of HEPCRA to the HSERC upon request, handle funds allocated to implementation of HEPCRA, to prepare reports and recommendations as requested by HSERC and to evaluate the need for resources, if necessary. Finally, the LEPC is charged with primary responsibility for receiving, managing and processing hazardous chemical information forms and requests for public information, data and trade secrets.[229]

17.3 REPORTING REQUIREMENTS

The owner or operator of a facility which is required to make available a Material Safety Data Sheet ("MSDS") for each of its hazardous substances is also required to comply with reporting requirements under HEPCRA. Reporting is required for hazardous substances present at the facility in the amount of 10,000 pounds or more, and for extremely hazardous substances present in the amount of 500 pounds or more, or present at the threshold planning quantity,

---

226 *Id.* § 128E-5(f)(2).

227 *Id.* § 128E-5(f)(2)(A)-(E).

228 *Id.* § 128E-5(f)(2)(F)-(I).

229 *Id.* § 128E-5(f)(3)-(9).

whichever is less. The owner or operator of each facility must complete and submit a chemical list by March 1 of each year along with facility diagrams, location area maps, and emergency response plans required by state or federal law. If requested, an MSDS must be submitted within thirty days of the request. In addition, a Chemical Inventory Form,[230] facility diagrams and location area maps are to be submitted by March 1 of each year along with facility diagrams and location area maps and emergency response plans required by state and federal law. A filing fee of $100 must also be submitted with each Chemical Inventory Form to the HSERC by March 1 of each year.[231] All submissions are to be submitted to the HSERC, the appropriate LEPC and the local fire department, upon request.[232]

HEPCRA incorporates certain federal reporting requirements. Pursuant to HEPCRA requirements, each owner or operator of a facility is required to prepare and submit the toxic chemical release form by July 1 of each year.[233]

In the event a release of an extremely hazardous substance occurs from the facility in an amount at or above the reportable quantity, owners and operators are required to immediately notify the HSERC and LEPC.[234] The notification must be made immediately after the release by telephone, radio or in person.[235] A release, which results in exposure to persons solely within the site on which the facility is located, is exempt from the notification requirement.[236] Reportable releases which occur during transportation of a substance should be reported by telephone to

---

230 The federal EPCRA Tier II list is to be used until a State form is developed.

231 Haw. Rev. Stat. § 128E-9. In fiscal year 1998, HEER collected $62,800 in Tier II reporting fees which it deposited into the environmental response revolving fund. See Twentieth Report to the Legislature, supra note 5 at 16.

232 *Id.* § 128E-6(a)(2).

233 *Id.* § 128E-6(a)(3). *See also* EPCRA, § 323, 42 U.S.C. § 11043.

234 *Id.* § 128E-6(a)(4). *See* ch. 9 of this Handbook for release reporting requirements.

235 EPCRA § 304(b), 42 U.S.C. § 11004(b).

236 *Id.* § 11004(a)(4).

911.[237] The HSERC is authorized to adopt rules which establish the contents of hazardous substance release reports.[238]

17.4 PENALTIES

Civil and criminal penalties are provided in HEPCRA. Violation of the emergency planning, reporting or notification requirements of HEPCRA is subject to a fine of $1,000 to a maximum of $25,000 for each violation, each day. Knowing failure to report a release of a hazardous or extremely hazardous substance is subject to criminal prosecution for a misdemeanor and fines in the amount of $1,000 to $25,000 or both. The same criminal fines and prosecution for a misdemeanor may be sought for intentionally obstructing a representative of the Department, a hazardous materials response team or an LEPC member attempting to perform his or her duties under HEPCRA.[239]

The HSERC is authorized to enforce HEPCRA and the rules. The HSERC may cause a notice of violation to be served upon alleged violators, issue orders, set a hearing for the appearance of the alleged violator, and impose civil penalties by written notice.[240]

---

237 *Id.* § 11004(b)(1).

238 Haw. Rev. Stat. § 128E-7. As of the printing of this Handbook, rules regarding the content of hazardous substance release reports have not been adopted.

239 *Id.* § 128E-11.

240 *Id.* § 128E-12.

CHAPTER 9

RELEASE REPORTING PROVISIONS

1.0 INTRODUCTION

Oil and chemical spills have the potential to pollute Hawaii's ocean, streams and groundwater. During fiscal year 1999, the Office of Hazard Evaluation and Emergency Response received 567 notifications of chemical or oil spills and responded to 265 of them. This was a seven percent increase over the 530 spill notifications reported in fiscal year 1998.[1] The Environmental Council's goal is to reduce the number of spills to 200 in the year 2000.[2]

Several of the Hawaii environmental statutes and rules contain provisions which impose an affirmative obligation to report releases of hazardous substances or pollutants to the State Department of Health. A person who fails to report a release as required is subject to civil sanctions or criminal penalties, or both.

The following chapters of the Hawaii Revised Statutes require the reporting of releases of regulated substances:

- Water Pollution Law, Haw. Rev. Stat. § 342D-51.
- Underground Storage Tank Law, Haw. Rev. Stat. § 342L-34.
- Environmental Response Law, Haw. Rev. Stat. § 128D-3.
- Hawaii Emergency Planning and Community Right-to-Know Act, Haw. Rev. Stat. § 128E-6.

---

1 Hawaii Department of Health, *Report to the Twentieth Legislature in Compliance With Hawaii Revised Statutes Chapters 128D and 128E on the Activities of the Department of Health Environmental Health Administration Office of Hazard Evaluation and Emergency Response and Use of the Environmental Response Revolving Fund* at 2 (2000).

2 State of Hawaii, The Environmental Council, *1999 Annual Report of the Environmental Council* at 24 (1999).

In addition, the newly enacted Hawaii Radiation Control Rules contain reporting requirements.[3]

This Chapter discusses each of the release reporting requirements under Hawaii law in turn. In addition, each release reporting provision is discussed in the chapter of this Handbook which addresses the particular statute.

The release reporting requirements under each statute differ in the released substances that are subject to reporting, the released quantities that are subject to reporting and the time within which the release must be reported. Some releases may be subject to a reporting requirement under more than one statute. Some releases may be subject to federal, state and local law, and therefore must be reported to the Environmental Protection Agency, Hawaii Department of Health and the local emergency planning committee.

2.0 RELATIONSHIP TO FEDERAL REPORTING STATUTES

The reporting obligations under Hawaii law are very similar to those under federal law. Under federal programs which have been delegated to the State, releases are reported solely to the State. However, certain releases are also subject to federal reporting requirements.

3.0 RELEASE REPORTING OF POLLUTANT DISCHARGES INTO HAWAII WATERS

The Water Pollution Law requires notification to the Director of Health ("Director") of unlawful discharges of water pollutants into state waters.[4] An unlawful discharge is one which is not in compliance with the Water Pollution Law or the rules, or is one which exceeds permit or variance conditions or limitations. A discharge into a publicly owned treatment works or sewage system not in compliance with the applicable pretreatment standard or a pretreatment permit

---

[3] Haw Admin. R., Title 11, Chapter 54 (Weil's 2000). All references to the Hawaii Administrative Rules are current through the date of publication of this Handbook, unless otherwise noted.

[4] Haw. Rev. Stat. §§ 342D-50 to -51 (Michie 1999). All references to the Hawaii Revised Statutes are made to the printed version of the statutes current through the 1999 legislative session, unless otherwise noted. Where appropriate, references to acts passed during the 2000 legislative session have also been added.

condition is also unlawful. Any person who causes an unlawful discharge has an affirmative duty to report the discharge to the Director within twenty-four hours.[5]

A "person" who may be subject to liability includes individuals, corporate organizations, trusts, federal, state and local agencies and other legal entities. "State waters" is defined to include all fresh, brackish and salt water in, around and within the State, including drainage ditches and groundwater. The term "water pollutants" broadly includes all dredged spoil, solid refuse, incinerator residue, sewage, garbage, sewage sludge, munitions, chemical waste, biological materials, radioactive materials, heat, wrecked or discarded equipment, rock, sand, soil, sediment, cellar dirt and industrial, municipal and agricultural discharge.[6] The potential scope of liability for unlawful discharges under this statute is very broad as it may include virtually any substance.

The person who has caused the unlawful discharge and fails to report the unlawful discharge as required to the Director within twenty-four hours is subject to civil penalties. The maximum penalty which may be imposed for failure to report an unlawful discharge is $25,000 per day.[7]

The telephone number for reporting releases to the Department under the Water Pollution Law is (808) 586-4309.

4.0 RELEASE REPORTING FOR UNDERGROUND STORAGE TANKS

The Department of Health adopted regulations for the reporting of releases from underground storage tanks ("USTs") in January 2000.[8] Federal release reporting requirements

---

5 *Id.* § 342D-51. A valid permit issued pursuant to the Water Pollution Law which specifies another reporting time takes precedence over the general twenty-four hour reporting time. *Id.*

6 *Id.* § 342D-1.

7 *Id.* § 342D-30(a).

8 *Id.* § 342L-34 and Hawaii Admin. Rules Chapter 281.

also apply to owners and operators of UST systems.[9] Reporting of releases must be made to the Department of Health ("Department"), within twenty-four hours.[10]

The substances regulated under the UST program and subject to reporting requirements are petroleum products, including used oil, diesel, gasoline and fuel oil, and all substances listed pursuant to CERCLA § 101(14).[11] Hazardous wastes regulated under RCRA Subtitle C are exempted from reporting requirements under the UST program.[12] Certain tanks are also exempt from UST regulations, including reporting requirements.[13]

All owners and operators of USTs are responsible for reporting releases and suspected releases of regulated substances. Owners and operators of USTs must report to the Department within twenty-four hours if any of the following occur:

(1) evidence of released regulated substances are discovered at the site or in the surrounding area such as the presence of free product or vapors in soils, basements, sewer and utility lines, and nearby surface water;

(2) unusual operating conditions of the UST are observed by the owners or operators, including the erratic behavior of product dispensing equipment, unexplained water in the tank or sudden loss of product from the tank unless a component of the UST is found to be defective but not leaking and is immediately repaired or replaced; or

(3) release detection equipment indicates that a release may have occurred.[14]

If the release detection monitoring equipment is found to be defective, and is immediately repaired or replaced, and additional monitoring does not confirm the initial result, or if the second month of inventory control data does not confirm the suspected release, the suspected release need not be reported to the Department.

---

9 Haw. Admin. Rules § 11-281-61 and 40 C.F.R. § 280.50.

10 *See infra* ch. 7, § 9.0 of this Handbook.

11 40 C.F.R. Part 302.

12 *See* definition of "regulated substances" in Haw. Admin. Rules § 11-281-03.

13 Haw. Admin. Rules § 11-281-01. *See also* 42 U.S.C. § 6991(l)(A)-(I) and 40 C.F.R. § 280.10(b).

14 Haw. Admin. Rules § 11-281-61. *Cf.* 40 C.F.R. § 280.50.

After the suspected release is initially reported to the Department, the UST owners and operators must investigate and confirm all suspected releases within a seven day period.[15] If the substance released is a hazardous substance at or above its reportable quantity, and the reportable quantity is released within a twenty-four hour period, the release must be reported both to the National Response Center at (800) 424-8802 pursuant to CERCLA, and to the Department at (808) 586-4249, (808) 247-2191 or 911, pursuant to the Environmental Response Law and State Contingency Plan.[16]

Spills and overfills of petroleum in an amount greater than twenty-five gallons or that cause a sheen on nearby surface water must be reported to the Department within twenty-four hours by the owner and operator of the UST. All petroleum and hazardous substance spills, even those in an amount less than the reportable quantity, must be contained and cleaned up. If the cleanup cannot be completed within twenty-four hours, the spill or overfill must be immediately reported to the Department regardless of the amount of the spill or overfill.[17]

Persons who fail to report a release from a UST as required are subject to civil penalties up to the amount of $25,000 per UST for each day of continued noncompliance.[18]

The telephone number for reporting petroleum releases to the Department under the UST Law is (808) 586-4228.

5.0 REPORTING REQUIREMENTS FOR RELEASES OF HAZARDOUS SUBSTANCES.

The Environmental Response Law ("ERL")[19] regulates the release of hazardous substances into the environment. The reporting requirements under the ERL are the same as the reporting requirements under CERCLA for CERCLA-listed hazardous substances. In addition,

---

15 Haw. Admin. Rules § 11-281-63.

16 *See infra* ch. 8 of this Handbook.

17 Haw. Admin. Rules § 11-451-6 and 40 C.F.R. § 280.53(a)(1).

18 Haw. Rev. Stat. § 342L-10(a).

19 *Id.* ch. 128D. *See infra* ch. 8 of this Handbook.

the State Contingency Plan ("SCP")[20] establishes the reportable quantities for two additional hazardous substances listed by the ERL: oil and trichloropropane, and for unlisted hazardous substances. All releases of hazardous substances in an amount equal to or greater than the reportable quantity which occur within a twenty-four hour period must be immediately reported to the Director.

The SCP establishes reportable quantities for designated hazardous substances, unlisted hazardous substances, trichloropropane and oil.[21] The SCP requires reporting of releases of hazardous substances, but does not require reporting of releases of pollutants or contaminants.

Reportable quantities for listed hazardous substances[22] are those contained in (1) the listed extremely hazardous substances for emergency planning and notification,[23] (2) the listed CERCLA hazardous substances,[24] and (3) 58 Federal Register 54,840, Table 302.4.[25]

Unlisted hazardous substances, which exhibit the characteristics of ignitability, corrosivity or reactivity, have the reportable quantity of one hundred pounds.[26] The reportable quantities are based on the weight of the entire amount of material released, not merely the weight of the hazardous substance component.[27] Unlisted hazardous wastes which exhibit toxicity characteristics when tested with the TCLP test method 1311 have the reportable quantities identified in the CERCLA list for the hazardous substance exhibiting the toxicity characteristic.[28] If the unlisted hazardous waste exhibits toxicity characteristics on the basis of more than one hazardous substance, or on the basis of one or more of the other characteristics

---

20 Haw. Admin. Rules tit. 11, ch. 451.

21 *See* Haw. Admin. Rules § 11-451-5 for designated hazardous substances.

22 *See id.* § 11 -451-5.

23 40 C.F.R. Part 355, apps. A and B.

24 40 C.F.R. Part 302, Table 302.4. Note that oil and trichloropropane, which are not designated as hazardous substances under CERCLA, are not listed in 40 C.F.R. Part 302.

25 Haw. Admin. Rules § 11-451-6(b).

26 *Id.* § 11-451-6(c)(1).

27 *Id.* § 11-451-6(c)(2).

28 *Id.*

referenced in § 11-451-5(c), the reportable quantity is the lowest of the reportable quantities identified in the CERCLA list.[29] For trichloropropane, the reportable quantity is ten pounds.[30]

The SCP defines a reportable quantity for oil four ways.[31] Under the SCP, the definition of oil includes sludge and oil mixed with waste.[32] First, a reportable quantity is any amount which when released into the environment causes a sheen to appear on surface water, ground water, or any navigable water of the State. "Sheen" is defined "an iridescent appearance of any petroleum on the surface of any surface water, ground water, or any navigable water of the State which is caused by the release of such petroleum."[33] The SCP employs substantially the same definition of "navigable water" as the EPA regulations governing discharge of oil,[34] and the EPA regulations governing the determination of reportable quantities for hazardous substances.[35] Second, a reportable quantity of oil is any free product that appears on ground water. "Groundwater" is defined by the SCP as any water in a saturated zone or stratum beneath the surface of land or water.[36] Third, any release of oil in an amount greater than twenty-five gallons is reportable. Finally, a release of less than twenty-five gallons of oil that is not contained and remedied within seventy-two hours must also be reported.[37]

Notification requirements in the SCP set forth the notification process to be followed when a hazardous substance release meets or exceeds the reportable quantity. The purpose of the notification process is to assure that appropriate organizations are notified of releases of hazardous substances that present or may present a substantial danger to the public health or welfare, the environment, or natural resources.[38]

---

29 *Id.*

30 *Id.* § 11-451-6(b)(4).

31 The reportable quantity for oil designated in the SCP is similar to that identified by the federal regulations for the underground storage tank program. *See* 40 C.F.R. § 280.53.

32 Haw. Admin. Rules § 11-451-3(a).

33 *Id.*

34 40 C.F. R. Part 110.1.

35 40 C.F.R. Part 117.1.

36 Haw. Admin. Rules § 11-451-3(a).

37 *Id.* § 11-451-6(b)(5).

38 *Id.* § 11-451-7(a).

Notification is required for releases of both listed and unlisted hazardous substances. For listed hazardous substances, a release in any twenty-four hour period of a quantity equal to or exceeding the reportable quantity criteria must be reported. For unlisted hazardous substances, a release in any twenty-four hour period of a quantity equal to or exceeding the reportable quantity must be reported .[39] The ERL provides no "grace period": reportable releases must be reported immediately to the Department.

Only releases occurring on or after August 17, 1995, the effective date of the SCP, are subject to the notification requirements. The applicable date is the date of the release of the hazardous substance, not the date of the discovery of the release.[40] Any person in charge of a facility or vessel may provide notification to the Department by telephone or in person.[41]

Written notice must be given to the Department no later than thirty days after the initial discovery of the release. The written notice must be sent by certified mail or by some other means with proof of delivery.[42] Only written notification, and not verbal notification, is required for a release of oil in an amount less than twenty-five gallons within any twenty-four hour period which is not contained and remedied within seventy-two hours.[43]

Releases of mixtures or solutions containing a hazardous substance are subject to the notification requirements only where a component hazardous substance is released in a quantity equal to or greater than its reportable quantity. This provision, however, applies only where the person in charge of the facility or vessel knows the exact concentrations of all the hazardous substance components present in the mixture or solution. If the exact concentration of all the hazardous substance components is not known, reporting is required if the entire released

---

39 *Id.* § 11-451-7(b)(2).

40 State of Hawaii, Department of Health, Response to Comments on the Proposed State Contingency Plan, at 38 (1995).

41 Haw. Admin. Rules § 11-451-7(b).

42 *Id.* § 11-451-7(e).

43 *Id.* § 11-451-7(b)(1).

mixture equals or exceeds the reportable quantity of any hazardous component.[44] Continuous releases of hazardous substances which are stable in rate and quantity are to be reported to the Director, and not to the Environmental Protection Agency or the National Response Center.[45]

Certain categories of releases are exempt from SCP notification requirements. These include releases of hazardous substances emanating from bituminous pavement, landscaping materials or building materials in good repair. Also exempt from notification requirements are sheens resulting from discharges of oil from a properly functioning vessel engine, and discharges or emissions from a point source regulated under a valid permit, such as an air or NPDES permit.[46] In addition, releases which are permitted by a federal or state permit need not be reported to the Department. The definition of "release" includes all spills, leaks, placement, and discharges into the environment. For example, releases may occur from tanks, holding pits, drums, trailer trucks and tank cars. "Releases" may also include the abandonment or discarding of barrels, containers and other closed receptacles containing any hazardous substance, pollutant or contaminant. The term "release" excludes emissions from engine exhaust, nuclear materials, the normal application of fertilizer, the legal application of a registered pesticide, releases from sewage systems collecting and conducting primarily domestic wastewater, and releases permitted by federal, state or local authority.[47] These excluded activities and incidents are not "releases" and need not be reported to the Department.

The telephone number for reporting releases of hazardous substances to the Department under the ERL is (808) 586-4249 (business hours), (808) 247-2191 (after hours) or 911 (24 hours).

---

44 *Id.* § 11-451-7(f).

45 *Id.* § 11-451-7(g).

46 *Id.* § 11-451-7(i).

47 *See* definition of "release" in Haw. Rev. Stat. § 128D-1, and Haw. Admin. Rules 11-451-3(a).

6.0 REPORTING REQUIREMENTS FOR THE RELEASE OF EXTREMELY HAZARDOUS SUBSTANCES

The Hawaii Emergency Planning and Community Right-to-Know Act ("HEPCPA")[48] establishes reporting requirements for releases of extremely hazardous substances that occur from a facility.[49] HEPCRA references and adopts the reporting requirements established under the federal Emergency Planning and Community Right-to-Know Act.[50] Owners and operators of a facility are required to immediately notify the Hawaii State Emergency Response Commission ("HSERC") and the appropriate Local Emergency Planning Committee ("LEPC") if a release of an extremely hazardous substance occurs in an amount at or above the reportable quantity[51] from the facility. The notification must be made immediately after the release occurs by telephone, radio or in person.[52] Releases which result in exposure to persons solely within the site on which the facility is located are exempted from the notification requirement.[53] The HEER office serves as the HSERC and its telephone numbers for reporting releases of hazardous substances are (808) 586-4249 (business hours), (808) 247-2191 (after hours). Releases should be reported to the appropriate LEPC as follows:

City and County of Honolulu
(808) 523-4121 (business hours) 91 1 (after hours)

County of Hawaii
(808) 961-8215 (business hours)
(808) 935-3311 (after hours)

County of Maui
(808) 243-7561 (business hours)
911 (after hours)

48 Haw. Rev. Stat. ch. 128E. *See infra* ch. 8, § 16.0 of this Handbook.

49 Haw. Rev. Stat. § 128E-6.

50 *Id.* § 128E-6(a)(4).

51 *See* 40 C.F.R. Part 302.

52 42 U.S.C. § 11004(b).

53 *Id.* §1004(a)(4).

County of Kauai
(808) 241-6336 (business hours)
(808) 241-6711 (after hours)

Reportable releases which occur during transportation of a substance should be reported by telephone to 911.[54]

7.0 RADIATION RELEASE REPORTING REQUIREMENTS

The Hawaii Radiation Control Law[55] contains various release reporting requirements. Licensees must file a report with the Department within five days if any test of a sealed radioactive source indicates leakage or contamination.[56]

If any radiation sources are lost, stolen or missing, if radiation machines are missing, or if missing radioactive material exceeds a specified quantity and it appears to the licensee that an exposure to individuals in unrestricted areas could result, an immediate report must be made to the Department's Noise, Radiation and Indoor Air Quality Branch at (808) 586-4700. The telephone reporting requirement is delayed for thirty days for smaller quantities of missing material. Following an initial telephone report regarding lost, stolen or missing sources of radiation, licensees are required to make a written report to the Department within thirty days.[57]

Immediate reporting by telephone, telegram, mailgram or facsimile is also required if radiation sources cause or threaten to cause individuals to receive specified dose equivalencies or if radioactive material is released inside or outside a restricted area so that if any individuals had been present for twenty-four hours, they would have received an intake five times greater than the occupational annual limit on intake. Reporting may be delayed for twenty-four hours for lower dose equivalencies or lower multiples of the occupational annual limit on intake.[58]

---

[54] *Id.* § 11,004(b)(1).

[55] Haw. Admin. Rules, Title 11, Chapter 45. *See infra* ch. 9 of this Handbook.

[56] *Id.* § 11-45-96.

[57] *Id.* § 11-45-88.

[58] *Id.* § 11-45-89.

Licensees must submit written notification within thirty days for certain threatened or actual exposures, or for levels of radiation or concentrations of radioactive material in excess of applicable license limitations or regulatory requirements. Reports must describe the extent of individual exposure, including dose estimations, the levels of radiation and concentrations of radioactive materials, the cause, and corrective steps taken or planned to ensure against a reoccurrence. Reports also must include identification information for exposed individuals.[59]

[59] *Id.* § 11-45-90.

CHAPTER 10

ENVIRONMENTAL IMPACT STATEMENTS

1.0 INTRODUCTION

The purpose of the Hawaii Environmental Impact Statement ("EIS") Law is "to establish a system of environmental review which will ensure that environmental concerns are given appropriate consideration in decision-making along with economic and technical considerations."[1] The Hawaii EIS Law is designed to integrate environmental review with state and county planning processes.

The Hawaii EIS Law, enacted in 1974, was patterned after the federal National Environmental Policy Act.[2] The requirements of the Hawaii EIS law are found in Chapters 343 and 344 of Hawaii Revised Statutes and Title 11, Chapters 200 and 201 of the Hawaii Administrative Rules, Department of Health. The Environmental Council's Committee on Administrative Rules, in collaboration with the Office of Environmental Quality Control ("OEQC") , met throughout 1995 to discuss working drafts of proposed amendments to the rules, and the amended rules were adopted on August 31, 1996.

The OEQC administers the Hawaii EIS law and publishes a bulletin twice monthly ("The Environmental Notice") which contains information regarding proposed actions, the availability of Environmental Assessments and EISs for public review, and agency determinations.[3] The OEQC also publishes a comprehensive guide regarding its environmental review process entitled

---

1 Haw. Rev. Stat. § 343-1 (Michie 1999). All references to the Hawaii Revised Statutes are made to the printed version of the statutes current through the 1999 legislative session, unless otherwise noted. Where appropriate, references to acts passed during the 2000 legislative session have also been added.

2 42 U.S.C. §§ 4321 - 4370c.

3 Haw. Rev. Stat. § 343-3. Copies of The Environmental Notice are available on the OEQC website at http://www.state.hi.us/health/oeqc (visited August 12, 2000).

A Guidebook for the Hawaii State Environmental Review Process.[4] The Environmental Council ("Council") is the rulemaking body.[5]

2.0 RELATIONSHIP TO THE FEDERAL NEPA

Although patterned after the federal National Environmental Policy Act ("NEPA"), the Hawaii EIS Law varies from NEPA in several ways.

NEPA applies to "major Federal actions significantly affecting the quality of the human environment."[6] The Hawaii EIS Law applies to similar State actions, as well as actions which fall into specified categories. The categories include specific actions and actions in specific geographical locations.[7] Further, the Hawaii EIS Law, unlike NEPA, includes in the scope of the EIS the proposed action's effects on economic and social welfare.[8] By particularizing the subjects of inquiry, the Hawaii EIS Law calls for a broader range of information than does NEPA.[9]

Hawaii's State Environmental Policy Law,[10] Chapter 344 of the Hawaii Revised Statutes, establishes the State's environmental policy and includes guidelines State agencies must consider in program development.[11] Chapter 344 parallels NEPA Section 101, which contains the declaration of national environmental policy and considerations that underlie NEPA.[12] Hawaii

---

4 Copies of *A Guidebook for the Hawaii State Environmental review Process* (October 1997) can be obtained by contacting OEQC by telephone at (808) 586-4185 or from the OEQC web page at http://www.state.hi.us/health/oeqc (visited August 12, 2000).

5 *Id.* § 343-6.

6 42 U.S.C. § 4332(2)(c).

7 Haw. Rev. Stat. § 343-5.

8 *Id.* § 343-2.

9 *Life of the Land v. Ariyoshi*, 59 Haw. 156, 163, 577 P.2d 1116, 1121 (1978).

10 Haw. Rev. Stat. ch. 344 (1993).

11 *Id.* §§ 344-3 to -4.

12 42 U.S.C. § 4331.

Revised Statutes Section 343-5 is analogous to NEPA's key action-forcing section, Section 102(2)(c),[13] which requires the preparation of an EIS for proposals for legislation and other federal actions.

The Hawaii Supreme Court compared the Hawaii EIS Law to NEPA in *Molokai Homesteaders Cooperative Association v. Cobb.*[14] There a citizen group brought suit challenging the validity of an agreement between the Board of Land and Natural Resources of the State and a private corporation for the corporation's use of water transmission facilities on the island of Molokai. The citizen group argued the State had neglected to adopt environmental standards and guidelines as mandated by Chapter 344 prior to making the agreement. The Court found that Chapter 344 does not call for the adoption of specific guidelines covering each agency determination.[15] The Court compared Chapter 344 to NEPA § 101 and characterized it as a policy statement reflecting concerns and goals in general terms.[16] NEPA § 101 does not mandate adoption of guidelines by an agency before the agency makes decisions.

Whenever an action is subject to both federal NEPA and the Hawaii EIS Law, the applicant or applying agency is responsible for notifying the appropriate federal agency, the OEQC and any state agency with a definite interest in the action.[17] The OEQC and agencies are to "cooperate with federal agencies to the fullest extent possible to reduce duplication between federal and state requirements and the rules suggest joint EISs with concurrent public review and processing at both levels of government."[18]

When preparation of a federal EIS under NEPA has been delegated to a state or county agency, the Hawaii EIS Law applies in addition to the federal law. Where the federal EIS law

---

13 *Id.* § 4332(2)(c).

14 63 Haw. 453, 629 P.2d 1134 (1981).

15 *Id.,* 63 Haw. at 462, 629 P.2d at 1141.

16 *Id.*

17 Haw. Admin. Rules § 11-200-25 (Weil's 2000). All references to the Hawaii Administrative Rules are current through the date of publication of this Handbook, unless otherwise noted.

18 Haw. Rev. Stat. § 343-5(f); Haw. Admin. Rules § 11-200-25.

has requirements in addition to but not in conflict with the Hawaii law, the OEQC and agencies are to cooperate so that one document complies with all applicable laws.[19]

Citizen groups in Hawaii have more than once brought suit under NEPA challenging federal actions on the grounds of failure to prepare an EIS or inadequacy of the EIS prepared.[20] Hawaii courts have determined that the Army Corps of Engineers and the Trust Territories of the Pacific are subject to NEPA requirements.[21] For example, the Navy's bombing activity on the Hawaiian island of Kaho'olawe was held to be an agency action for which an annual EIS would be required.[22] The construction of the H-3 highway was challenged several times under the Hawaii EIS Law for failure to prepare an EIS,[23] submission of an inadequate EIS,[24] and failure to prepare a supplemental EIS.[25]

3.0 ACTIONS SUBJECT TO HAWAII LAW

The Hawaii EIS Law applies to certain types of actions. "Action" is defined by the Hawaii EIS statute as "any program or project to be initiated by any agency or applicant."[26] "Applicant" is defined as "any person who, pursuant to statute, ordinance, or rule, officially requests approval for a proposed action."

---

19 Haw. Admin Rules. § 11-200-25.

20 *Life of the Land v. Volpe*, 363 F. Supp. 1171 (D. Haw. 1972) (Preliminary injunction against construction of airport reef runway denied on grounds plaintiff not likely to prevail on claim that EIS was inadequate).

21 *People of Enewetak v. Laird*, 353 F. Supp. 811 (D. Haw. 1973); *Mahelona v. Hawaiian Elec. Co.*, 418 F. Supp. 1328 (D. Haw. 1976).

22 *Aluli v. Brown*, 437 F. Supp. 602 (D. Haw. 1977).

23 *Stop H-3 Ass'n v. Volpe*, 353 F. Supp. 14 (D. Haw. 1972); *amending* 349 F. Supp. 1047 (D. Haw. 1972).

24 *Stop H-3 Ass'n v. Brinegar*, 389 F. Supp. 1102 (D. Haw. 1974), *rev'd by Stop H-3 Ass'n v. Coleman*, 533 F.2d 434 (9th Cir. 1976), *cert. denied sub nom. Wright v. Stop H-3 Ass'n*, 429 U.S. 999, 97 S. Ct. 526 (1976).

25 *Stop H-3 Ass'n v. Dole*, 740 F.2d 1442 (9th Cir. 1984), *cert. denied sub nom, Yamasaki v. Stop H-3 Ass'n*, 471 U.S. 1108, 105 S. Ct. 2344 (1985).

26 Haw. Rev. Stat. § 343-2.

The Hawaii EIS Law also applies to certain classes of actions and actions located in certain specified areas. Section 343-5(a)[27] requires an Environmental Assessment for actions which:

(1) propose the use of state or county lands or the use of state or county funds. Excepted are actions using (a) funds for feasibility or planning studies an agency has not yet approved, and (b) funds to be used for the acquisition of unimproved real property, provided the agency considers environmental factors in any planning or approval process;

(2) propose any use within any land classified as conservation district by the state Land Use Commission under Hawaii Revised Statutes chapter 205;

(3) propose any use within the shoreline area as defined in Hawaii Revised Statutes § 205A-41;

(4) propose any use within a designated historic site;

(5) propose any use within the Waikiki area of Oahu, delineated as the "Waikiki Special District";

(6) propose any amendments to existing county general plans where such amendment would result in designations other than agriculture, conservation, or preservation. "County general plan" here does not refer only to a county's denominated "general plan," but more broadly, it refers to the county's planning process which finds expression in, is implemented by, and is identified with various maps, plans and other documents, however denominated.[28] Actions proposing any new county general plan or amendments to any existing county general plan generated by a county are exempt under this subsection;

(7) propose any reclassification of land classified as conservation district by the state Land Use Commission under Hawaii Revised Statutes Chapter 205; or

(8) propose the construction, expansion or modification of new or existing helicopter facilities which by way of their activities may affect any land classified as conservation district, shoreline area or historic site as defined in the statute.

---

27 Haw. Rev. Stat. § 343-5(a)(1).

28 Haw. Op. Att'y Gen. No. 85-30 at 7 (Dec. 20, 1985).

The mere "impact" of an action on a shoreline or conservation area is insignificant to trigger an Environmental Assessment if the action will not take place "within" those areas.[29]

If a private party has petitioned to utilize State land, including conservation land, the State agency may require an EIS from that private party, and the State agency may incorporate any or all of that EIS in any EIS required of the agency itself.[30] Further, once the private party's EIS has been through the notice and comment procedure, no further notice and comment need be done by the State agency on its EIS for the same action. Hawaiian homelands are interpreted as unique "state lands" with special duties attached to them, but they are "state lands" nonetheless for purposes of the Hawaii EIS Law.[31]

The Hawaii EIS Law applies to non-county initiated actions which propose amendments or changes to a county's planning documents, regardless of how those documents are titled, if those changes would result in a land use designation other than agriculture, conservation or preservation.[32] The County's development plan is an integral part and expression of the County's planning process and should be subject to environmental review.[33]

An Environmental Assessment is necessary before the Land Use Commission can reclassify conservation lands for other uses.[34] For example, an Environmental Assessment must be prepared before a boundary amendment is approved by the Land Use Commission.[35] An EIS must also be prepared for the harvesting of trees on public land.[36]

---

29 *Citizens for the Protection of the North Kohala Coastline v. County of Hawaii*, 91 Haw. 94, 105-06, 979 P. 2d 1120, 1131-32 (1999).

30 Declaratory Ruling by the Environmental Quality Commission (Nov. 30, 1977).

31 *Kepo'o v. Watson*, 87 Hawai'i 91, 97-98, 952 P.2d 379, 386-86 (1998).

32 Haw. Op. Att'y Gen. 85-30 (Dec. 20, 1985).

33 *Id.* at 10.

34 Haw. Rev. Stat. § 343-5(a)(2).

35 *Pearl Ridge Estates Community Ass'n v. Lear Siegler Properties, Inc.*, 65 Haw. 133, 135, 648 P.2d 702, 704 (1982).

36 Haw. Rev. Stat. § 183-16.5.

An Environmental Assessment is also necessary before creating underpasses under a state highway. In *Citizens for Protection of North Kohala Coastline v. County of Hawai'i*,[37] a developer's proposal to construct two underpasses under a highway for golf carts and maintenance vehicles constituted the "use of state lands" thereby triggering environmental review of the entire larger project consisting of a hotel, residential subdivision, 18-hole golf course, tennis facilities and other related site improvements and infrastructure. The Supreme Court ruled that the project was ripe for review by an Environmental Assessment, despite the developer's argument that the underpasses were a mere idea which would be the subject of a subsequent Environmental Assessment reviewed by other state agencies. The Supreme Court reached this conclusion based upon the statutory requirement that environmental review be taken at the "earliest practicable time"[38] and because environmental review at an early time would be an integral part of the decision-making process.

One issue of environmental interest in Hawaii is the development of geothermal resources, tapping volcanic power for the provision of energy. The Hawaii Legislature directed the Board of Land and Natural Resources to conduct an assessment of areas with geothermal potential for the purpose of designating geothermal resource subzones.[39] The Land Use Law declares that an EIS under the Hawaii EIS Law is not required for this assessment.[40] However, applications for use of these areas for development of geothermal resources, including the drilling of exploratory wells, are subject to the Hawaii EIS Law, where appropriate,[41] and subject to geothermal resource permits.[42]

---

37 *Citizens for Protection of North Kohala Coastline v. County of Hawai'i*, 91 Hawai'i 94, 979 P.2d 1120 (1999).

38 Haw. Rev. Stat. §343-5(c).

39 Haw. Rev. Stat. § 205-5.2(a) (1993).

40 *Id.*

41 *Id.* §§ 205-5.1(c) and -5.3.

42 In three cases, plaintiffs have appealed the granting of geothermal resource permits on grounds other than whether an EIS was prepared: *Medeiros v. Hawaii City Planning Comm'n*, 8 Haw. App. 183, 797, P.2d 59 (1990); *Pele Defense Fund v. Puna Geothermal*, 8 Haw. App. 203, 797, P.2d 69 (1990); and *Aluli v. Lewin*, 73 Haw. 56, 828 P.2d 802, *recon. denied*, 73 Haw. 625, 831 P.2d 935 (1992).

3.1 EXEMPTIONS

Certain classes of actions are generally exempted from the EIS process because they are likely to have minimal or no significant effect on the environment.[43] The Hawaii Administrative Rules[44] define these exempt classes of actions as:

(1) operation, repair or maintenance of existing structures, facilities, equipment or topographical features involving negligible or no expansion or change of use beyond that previously existing;

(2) replacement or reconstruction of existing structures and facilities, provided they have substantially the same purpose, capacity, density, height and dimensions as the structures replaced;

(3) construction, location and alteration of single, new small facilities or structures, such as (a) single family residences, (b) multi-unit structures with not more than four dwelling units, (c) stores, offices and restaurants with an occupant load of not more than twenty persons, (d) public utility extensions and accessory structures to serve such facilities or general accessory or appurtenant structures such as garages, carports, patios, swimming pools and fences;

(4) minor alterations in the conditions of land, water or vegetation;

(5) basic data collection, research, experimental management and resource evaluation activities which do not result in a serious or major disturbance to an environmental resource;

(6) construction or placement of minor structures accessory to existing facilities;

(7) interior alterations involving such things as partitions, plumbing and electrical work;

(8) demolition of structures, except those located on any designated historic site;

(9) zoning variances, except shoreline setback variances; and

(10) continued administrative activities such as purchase of supplies and personnel related actions.

---

43 Haw. Rev. Stat. § 343-6(a)(7).

44 Haw. Admin. Rules § 11-200-8(a).

Any agency may request that new exemptions be added to the above list, or that existing exemptions be deleted.[45] In addition, each agency may develop its own list of actions which fall within the exemptions.[46] These lists must be consistent with the letter and intent of the Hawaii Administrative Rules and Chapter 343. These lists are to be submitted to the Council for review and concurrence. The Governor may exempt any affected action or program from compliance with the Hawaii EIS Law in the event that the Governor declares a state of emergency.[47]

All exemptions are inapplicable, however, when the cumulative impact of planned successive actions of the same type, in the same place, over time, is significant.[48] Additionally, an action which is normally insignificant in its impact on the environment may be significant in a particularly sensitive environment and therefore subject to EIS requirements.

The Hawaii Supreme Court has stated that the definition of "significant effect" in section 343-1(8) is subjective.[49] In *McGlone v. Inaba*, citizens brought suit to enjoin the Board of Land and Natural Resources ("BLNR") from approving the construction of underground utilities on conservation land on the ground that the BLNR had not required the preparation of an EIS prior to the approval of construction.[50] In its approval of the Conservation District Use Application to construct the underground utilities, the BLNR had found that an EIS was not required since the proposed construction of a single family residence was deemed an exempt activity under the EIS rules.[51]

Plaintiff citizens, however, claimed these categorical exemptions were inapplicable. As the house site was adjacent to a wildlife sanctuary and possible habitat of the endangered

45 *Id.* § 11-200-8(c).

46 *Id.* § 11-200-8(d).

47 *Id.* § 11-200-8(f).

48 *Id.* § 11-200-8(b).

49 *McGlone v. Inaba*, 64 Haw. 27, 636 P.2d 158 (1981).

50 *Id.*, 64 Haw. at 28, 636 P.2d at 160.

51 *Id.*, 64 Haw. at 29, 636 P.2d at 161.

Hawaiian Black-necked stilt, they argued it was a case in which "an action that is normally insignificant in its impact on the environment may be significant in a particularly sensitive environment."[52] The *McGlone* court found in its review of the BLNR's actions that it could not determine whether the BLNR found the area a "particularly sensitive environment."[53] Regardless of that deficiency, the court held that it could not find the BLNR's ruling--that the proposed construction would probably not have a significant effect on the sanctuary and that no EIS was required--was clearly erroneous in view of the record. The court found ample evidence in the record to support the finding that there would be minimal and temporary effect on the sanctuary. The court added that the BLNR's approval contained conditions protecting against pollutants entering the lagoon and limiting construction to hours when the endangered stilt were not feeding, and that apparently there had been no noticeable disturbance of the birds.[54]

In 1995 the State Legislature exempted Hawaiian fishponds from the Environmental Impact Statement Law.[55] Under this law, the reconstruction, restoration, repair or use of traditional Hawaiian fishponds is exempt from the requirements of Chapter 343 provided the fishpond is not adjacent to a sandy beach; stocks only native aquatic organisms; is not used to grow cultured organisms requiring artificial feeding, aeration or pumping of water for their growth; does not add bulk chemicals to the water to control parasites or pathogens; does not hamper coastal access; does not harm threatened or endangered species; and is not used for water recreational purposes.[56] Only the traditional system of aquaculture practiced by native Hawaiians is exempt; fishponds designed or constructed in a manner other than the "loko i'a" system of ancient Hawaii are not exempt from Chapter 343.

In 1998 the State Legislature also exempted the purchase of the assets of the Waiahole water system to ensure the conservation and expansion of diversified agriculture on the island of

52 Haw. Admin. Rules § 11-200-8(b).

53 *McGlone*, 64 Haw. at 37, 636 P.2d at 165.

54 *Id.*, 64 Haw. at 38, 636 P.2d at 165-66.

55 Haw. Rev. Stat. § 183B-2.

56 *Id.*

Oahu and protect the Pearl Harbor aquifer. The legislature found that the acquisition, administration, operation, maintenance and improvement of the Waiahole water system is in the public interest and will serve the public health, safety, and welfare of the people of the State.[57]

4.0 PREPARATION OF THE ENVIRONMENTAL ASSESSMENT

The first step in the EIS process is the preparation of an Environmental Assessment ("EA") to determine whether the proposed action will require the preparation of an EIS. When an agency proposes any of the actions subject to the Hawaii EIS law, the agency prepares an EA at the earliest practicable time to determine whether an EIS must be required.[58] When a nonagency applicant proposes actions which require agency approval, the agency receiving the request for approval prepares the EA based upon information provided by the nonagency applicant.[59]

An important step in the preparation of the EA is consultation with agencies having jurisdiction or expertise in the area of the proposed action, as well as consultation with citizen groups and individuals.[60] The OEQC provides a list of agencies and groups appropriate for consultation.[61]

The applicant is to provide to the agency whatever information the agency deems necessary to facilitate the assessment process.[62] For all agency or applicant actions, the proposing or approving agency must analyze alternatives in the EA.[63]

---

57 *Id.* § 343-6.5 and 1998 Haw. Sess. Laws 111 § 2.

58 *Id.* § 343-5(b).

59 *Id.* § 343-5(c).

60 Haw. Admin. Rules §§ 11-200-9(a) and (b).

61 This list is available from the OEQC website at http://www.state.hi.us/health/oeqc/forms/gov_maillist.html (visited August 12, 2000).

62 *Id.*

63 *Id.* § 11-200-9(c).

The contents of an EA produced for either an agency or applicant-initiated action are similar. The assessment contains identification and description of (1) the applicant or proposing agency; (2) the approving agency; (3) the agencies, citizen groups, and individuals consulted in making the assessment; (4) a general description of the action's technical, economic, social, and environmental characteristics; (5) a summary description of the affected environment, including site maps; (6) a summary of impacts and alternatives considered; (7) proposed mitigation measures; (8) agency determination or, for draft EAs, an anticipated determination; (9) findings and reasons supporting the agency determination or anticipated determination; (10) agencies to be consulted in the preparation of an EIS, if an EIS is to be prepared; (11) a list of all required permits and approvals; and (12) written comments and responses to comments.[64] An EA produced for agency actions must also include an identification of potential environmental impacts, an evaluation of the potential significance of each impact, and provision for the detailed study of significant impacts.[65]

Once the Draft EA is complete it is submitted to the OEQC and notice is published in The Environmental Notice bulletin. The public review and comment period runs for thirty days from the date of publication. The applicant or proposing agency must respond in writing to all comments, incorporate comments as appropriate and append all comments and responses to the Final EA. The applicant or agency need not consider or respond to comments not received or postmarked within thirty days of publication by OEQC.[66]

Once the Final EA is complete, the agency must then issue either a "finding of no significant impact" determination ("FONSI")[67] or an environmental impact statement preparation notice. The final determination will require an EIS if the agency finds that the proposed action

---

64 *Id.* §11-260-10.

65 Haw. Admin. Rules § 11-200-9(a).

66 *Id.* § 11-200-9.1

67 In 1996, the legislature substituted the term "finding of no significant impact" for the term "negative declaration" in Hawaii's Environmental Impact Statement Law. The term "negative declaration," however, is still used synonymously by the Hawaii Administrative Rules which have not yet been amended to conform to the 1996 legislative changes to the statute.

"may have a significant effect on the environment."[68] If an EIS is required, the agency is to prescribe the information necessary in the EIS to assure adequate discussion and disclosure of environmental impacts.

If the determination is that an EIS is not required, this notice serves as a FONSI. Publication of a FONSI initiates a thirty-day review and comment period during which that determination may be challenged through litigation.[69] If the determination is not challenged within this period, the proposed action may proceed without preparation of an EIS. Very few of all proposed actions subject to the Hawaii EIS Law ultimately result in preparation of an EIS. Although 137 Draft EAs were submitted to OEQC in 1999, only 11 Final EISs were processed.[70]

4.1 DETERMINATION OF SIGNIFICANCE

To make the final determination as to whether an EIS is required, the agency must determine whether the proposed action will have a "significant effect" or "significant impact." The agency must consider "the sum of effects on the quality of the environment," and shall evaluate the overall and cumulative effects of the action. The agency must consider every phase of the proposed action, the primary and secondary expected consequences, and the cumulative as well as the short-term and long-term effects of the action.[71]

In 2000, the Legislature amended the statutory definition of "significant effect" to include any adverse affect on welfare or cultural practices of the community and State. In amending the statute, the Legislature found that native Hawaiian culture plays a vital role in preserving and advancing the unique quality of life and the "aloha spirit" in Hawaii, and that the past failure to require native Hawaiian cultural impact assessments has resulted in the loss and destruction of many important cultural resources and has interfered with the exercise of native Hawaiian

68 Haw. Rev. Stat. § 343-5(b)-(c).

69 Haw. Rev. Stat. § 343-7.

70 State of Hawaii, The Environmental Council and the Office of Environmental Quality Control, *The 1999 Environmental Report Card* at 3.

71 Haw. Admin. R. §11-200-12.

culture.[72] The Environmental Council has adopted guidelines for assessing cultural impacts.[73] Cultural impacts differ from other types of impacts assessed in environmental assessments or environmental impact statements. A cultural impact assessment includes information relating to the practices and beliefs of a particular cultural or ethnic group or groups. Such information may be obtained through scoping, community meetings, ethnographic interviews and oral histories. The OEQC publishes a list of cultural impact assessment providers who may be contracted to perform an assessment of a project's impacts on the culture of Hawaii's people.[74]

4.2 SIGNIFICANCE CRITERIA

In considering the significance of potential environmental effects, agencies are to consider the sum of the effects on the quality of the environment, and are to evaluate the overall and cumulative effects of an action.[75] In determining whether an action may have a significant effect on the environment, the agency is to consider every phase of a proposed action, the expected primary and secondary consequences, and the short-term, long-term, and cumulative effects of the action.[76]

In most instances, an action will be determined to have a significant effect on the environment if it:

(1) involves an irrevocable commitment to loss or destruction of any natural or cultural resource;

(2) curtails the range of beneficial uses of the environment;

---

72 2000 Haw. Sess. Laws 50 (to be codified at Haw. Rev. Stat. 343-2).

73 State of Hawaii, OEQC, *Guidelines for Assessing Cultural Impacts* (adopted by the Environmental Council, State of Hawaii November 19, 1997). These guidelines are available from the OEQC's website at http://www.state.hi.us/health/oeqc/guidance/cultural.htm (visited August 12, 2000).

74 State of Hawaii, OEQC, Directory of Cultural Impact Assessment Providers (August 26,1998). This directory is available from the OEQC's website at http://www.state.hi.us/health/oeqc/guidance/directory.htm (visited August 12, 2000).

75 Haw. Admin. Rules § 11-200-12(a).

76 *Id.* § 11-200-12(b).

(3) conflicts with the State's stated long-term environmental polices, goals or guidelines;

(4) substantially affects the economic or social welfare of the community or the State;

(5) substantially affects public health;

(6) involves substantial secondary impacts, such as population changes or effects on public facilities;

(7) involves a substantial degradation of environmental quality;

(8) cumulatively has considerable effect upon the environment or involves a commitment to larger actions;

(9) substantially affects a rare, threatened or endangered species or its habitat;

(10) detrimentally affects air or water quality or ambient noise levels;

(11) affects an environmentally sensitive area such as a flood plain, tsunami zone, erosion-prone area, geologically hazardous land, estuary, fresh water, or coastal waters;

(12) substantially affects scenic vistas and viewplanes identified in county or state plans or studies; or,

(13) requires substantial energy consumption.

For coastal area developments, the Hawaii Coastal Zone Management Act[77] further protects and controls land use within the shoreline area. This Act authorizes the creation of Special Management Areas in which no development can take place without a special permit. The effect on beach access and the minimization of adverse environmental impacts must be considered in the permitting process and may affect the EIS preparation.

In *Molokai Homesteaders Cooperative Association v. Cobb*,[78] the Supreme Court found that the approved action, an agreement between the State and a private corporation for use by the corporation of water transmission facilities, was one with a probable "significant effect" and was

---

77 Haw. Rev. Stat. ch. 205A; *see infra* ch. 11, § 3 of this Handbook.

78 63 Haw. 453, 629 P.2d 1134 (1981).

in fact the type of action requiring an environmental impact statement. "The use of a government pipeline, the implicit commitment of prime natural resources to a particular purpose, perhaps irrevocably, and the substantial social and economic consequences of the governmental approval of the proposal would dictate the preparation of an EIS."[79] In that particular case, however, the Supreme Court found no EIS was required because the execution of the agreement between the corporation and the State came before the effective date of the legislation, and the Hawaii EIS Law clearly was not intended to be retroactive.[80]

5.0 PREPARATION OF THE ENVIRONMENTAL IMPACT STATEMENT

The EIS is prepared in two stages, initially as a Draft EIS, available for public review and comment for a forty-five day period after publication, and then as a Final EIS submitted to the approving authority or agency. Agencies and applicants must endeavor, through a full and complete consultation process, to develop a fully acceptable EIS prior to filing the Draft EIS with the OEQC, and may not rely solely upon the review process to expose environmental concerns. The proposing agency or applicant may also hold a public scoping meeting to receive comments on the scope of a Draft EIS.[81]

The preparation of a Draft EIS begins with publication of an EIS Preparation Notice in the The Environmental Notice, thus initiating a thirty-day review and comment period.[82] The proposing agency or applicant must respond in writing and address all concerns and questions before proceeding with the preparation of the EIS.[83] The thirty-day review and comment period may be extended.[84]

---

79 *Id.*, 63 Haw. at 467, 629 P.2d at 1144.

80 *Id.*, 63 Haw. at 469, 629 P.2d at 1144-45.

81 *Id.* § 11-200-15(a).

82 Haw. Admin. R. § 11-200-15(b).

83 *Id.* § 11-200-15(d).

84 *Id.* § 11-200-15(b)-(c).

The EIS process involves identifying environmental concerns, obtaining various relevant data, conducting necessary studies, receiving public and agency input, evaluating alternatives, and proposing measures for avoiding, minimizing, rectifying or reducing adverse impacts.[85] In the preparation of an EIS, the proposing agency or applicant must assure that all appropriate agencies, citizen groups and concerned individuals (as delineated in the rules) are consulted.[86] Consultation should occur during preparation; preparers of the EIS should not depend upon the review process to expose environmental concerns.[87] The rules set out the procedures for notification of, eliciting comments from, and responding to those consulted.[88]

The EIS is to contain an explanation of the environmental consequences of the proposed action. Its contents must declare the environmental implications of the proposed action and discuss all relevant and feasible consequences of the action. The EIS also must include responsible opposing views, if any, on significant environmental issues raised by the proposal.[89]

The OEQC has adopted guidelines for assessing various impacts. There are guidelines available for assessing water well development projects,[90] and a shoreline hardening policy and accompanying assessment guidelines.[91] The OEQC also provides content guidelines for

---

85 Haw. Admin. Rules § 11-200-14.

86 *Id.* § 11-200-15(a).

87 *Id.*

88 *Id.* § 11-200-15(b)-(d).

89 *Id.* § 11-200-16.

90 State of Hawaii, OEQC, *Guidelines for Assessing Water Well Development Projects* (May 1998). These guidelines may be obtained from the OEQC's website at http://www.state.hi.us/health/oeqc/guidance/wells.html (visited August 12, 2000).

91 State of Hawaii, OEQC, *Shoreline Hardening Policy and Environmental Assessment Guidelines* (December 1998). These guidelines may be obtained from the OEQC's website at http://www.state.hi.us/health/oeqc/guidance/shoreline.htm (visited August 12, 2000).

biological surveys, ecosystem impact analysis, and mitigation measures,[92] and for sustainable building design.[93]

5.1 DRAFT EIS CONTENT REQUIREMENTS

The Draft EIS must contain a project description which includes: (1) a detailed map of the site of the proposed action as well as a related regional map, (2) a statement of objectives, (3) a general description of the proposed action's technical, economic, social and environmental characteristics, (4) any use of public funds or lands for the action, (5) the phasing and timing of the action, (6) summary technical data, including diagrams, and (7) an historical perspective.[94] This information need not be supplied in extensive detail beyond that needed for evaluation and review of the environmental impact of the proposed action.

The Draft EIS should contain any known alternatives for the action, regardless of cost.[95] These alternatives must be discussed, and it must be explained why these alternatives were rejected. The alternatives discussed may include the alternative of "no action."

The Draft EIS must contain a description of the environmental setting, including the environment in the vicinity of the action before the proposed action is begun, from both a local and regional perspective.[96] Special emphasis should be placed on environmental resources that are rare or unique to the region and site, including human-made resources of historic, archaeological, or aesthetic significance. Information about related projects, public or private, existing or planned, must be included for the purpose of determining cumulative effects.

---

92 State of Hawaii, OEQC, *Content Guidelines for Biological Surveys, Ecosystem Impact Analysis and Mitigation Measures* (undated). These guidelines may be obtained from the OEQC's website at http://www.state.hi.us/health/oeqc/guidance/biological.html (visited August 12, 2000).

93 State of Hawaii, OEQC, *Guidelines for Sustainable Building Design in Hawai`i* (adopted by the Environmental Council on October 13, 1999). These guidelines may be obtained from the OEQC's website at http://www.state.hi.us/health/oeqc/guidance/sustainable.htm (visited August 12, 2000).

94 Haw. Admin. Rules § 11-200-17(e).

95 *Id.* § 11-200-17(f).

96 *Id.* § 11-200-17(g).

Population and growth characteristics in the region must be identified and discussed. Sources of all data used for the evaluation of environmental consequences must be expressly noted.

The Draft EIS must contain a statement of the relationship of the proposed action to land use plans, policies and controls for the affected area.[97] Conformance or variance with such plans should be described and discussed. Where a conflict or inconsistency exists, the Draft EIS must contain a description of the extent or reconciliation, and the reason why the applicant has decided to proceed. The Draft EIS also should contain a list of necessary approvals required for the action by government agencies, boards or commissions, and the status of those approvals described.

The Draft EIS must also describe the probable impact of the proposed action on the environment, along with impacts of the natural or human environment on the project. The probable impact statement must consider all phases of the action and all consequences on the environment, including direct and indirect effects. Where related projects exist, the Draft EIS must also include a discussion of the interrelationships between the projects and the cumulative environmental impacts. Secondary effects of the project must also be thoroughly addressed, and estimations of any significant population and growth impacts of the project shall also be discussed. If the project will cause a direct or indirect source of pollution, all necessary data must be incorporated into the Draft EIS.[98]

The Draft EIS must address the relationship between short-term uses of the environment and the maintenance and enhancement of long-term productivity.[99] This should include a discussion of such short-term versus long-term trade-offs necessitated by the proposed action and the extent to which the action forecloses future options, narrows the range of beneficial uses of the environment, or poses long-term risks to health or safety.

---

97 *Id.* § 11-200-17(h).

98 Haw. Admin. R. § 11-200-17(i).

99 *Id.* § 11-200-17(j).

The Draft EIS must address all irreversible and irretrievable commitments of resources, including labor and material resources and natural and cultural resources, that would be involved in the proposed action.[100] Unavoidable impacts, the use of nonrenewable resources, any irreversible curtailment of the range of potential uses of the environment, or the possibility of environmental accidents should be discussed in this section. Although commitments of resources must be addressed, the Hawaii Supreme Court has held that the Hawaii EIS Law does not expressly mandate a cost-benefit analysis or quantification in monetary terms.[101]

The Draft EIS must address all probable adverse environmental effects which cannot be avoided.[102] This includes any adverse effects such as water or air pollution, urban congestion, threats to public health or other consequences adverse to the State's established environmental goals and guidelines. This section must include the rationale for proceeding with the action in the face of these unavoidable effects. If part of this rationale is that there are offsetting interests and considerations of governmental policies, then this discussion should include the extent to which alternatives to the proposed action would meet these same interests without the adverse environmental effects of the proposed plan.

The Draft EIS must consider mitigation measures proposed to minimize the environmental impact of the action.[103] There should be a description of any mitigation measures in the proposed plan which would reduce significant, unavoidable adverse impacts to insignificant levels. The basis for considering the resultant levels insignificant should be included, along with the rationale for why the proposed mitigation measures were chosen from among alternatives.

---

100 *Id.* § 11-200-17(k).

101 *Life of the Land v. Ariyoshi*, 59 Haw. 156, 577 P.2d 1116 (1978).

102 Haw. Admin. Rules § 11-200-17(l).

103 *Id.* § 11-200-17(m).

The Draft EIS must contain a summary of unresolved issues and either a discussion of how such issues will be resolved before the action is taken, or what overriding reasons there are for proceeding with the action without resolving the problems.[104]

The Draft EIS must identify the person, firm or agency preparing the EIS, as well as contain a list identifying all governmental agencies, other organizations and private individuals consulted in preparing the statement.[105] It should also contain reproductions of all substantive comments and responses made during the consultation process, as well as a list of those consulted who had no comment.[106] Finally, the Draft EIS must also contain (1) a summary sheet describing the proposed action, the impacts, proposed mitigation, alternatives, unresolved issues, compatibility with land use plans and a listing of permits and approvals, (2) a table of contents and (3) a statement of purpose and need for the action.[107]

5.2 FINAL EIS CONTENT REQUIREMENTS

After the Draft EIS has been through the forty-five day public notice and comment period, a Final EIS is prepared. The Final EIS must include the Draft EIS revised to incorporate substantive comments raised during the consultation process, along with a list of persons, organizations and public agencies commenting on the Draft EIS, and the actual or summarized comments and recommendations received on the Draft EIS.[108] The Final EIS must be formatted so that the reader can easily distinguish changes made to the text of the Draft EIS. The Final EIS must also contain the responses of the applicant or proposing agency to significant environmental points raised in the process.[109]

---

104 *Id.* § 11-200-17(n).

105 *Id.* § 11-200-17(o).

106 *Id.* § 11-200-17(p).

107 *Id.* § 11-200-17(b)-(d).

108 *Id.* § 11-200-18.

109 *Id.*

The style of the EIS should convey information in a form easily understood both by lay readers and decision makers.[110] The EIS should be a self-contained document with minimal need for cross-reference. Data and analyses may be summarized if less important.

5.3 ACCEPTABILITY

After a proposing agency or non-agency applicant has submitted a Draft EIS to the OEQC, the agency or applicant may, but is not required to, request the Council to make a recommendation regarding the acceptability or non-acceptability of the EIS.[111] If the Council decides to make a recommendation, the Council must take "prompt measures" to determine the acceptability of an agency's EIS, and in the case of a non-agency applicant the recommendation will be submitted to the applicant within thirty days. The Council's recommendation is published in the The Environmental Notice.

Acceptability of a Final EIS is based on whether it fulfills all the procedural and substantive requirements of an EIS, adequately discloses and describes all identifiable environmental impacts, and satisfactorily responds to comments received during the review period.[112] The Governor is the approving authority for actions involving State funds or lands proposed by an agency, and the Mayor is the approving authority for actions involving only county funds or land.[113] For actions proposed by applicants, the approving agency has the authority to determine the acceptability of the EIS.

An approving agency must notify the OEQC and the non-agency applicant of acceptance or nonacceptance of the Final EIS within thirty days of the official receipt.[114] Extensions are possible at the request of the applicant. If the agency fails to accept or reject the EIS within the thirty day period, the EIS is deemed accepted. The rules do not place a time limit on the

---

110 *Id.* § 11-200-19.

111 *Id.* § 11-200-23(c) and (d).

112 *Id.* § 11-200-23(b).

113 *Id.* § 11-200-23(c).

114 *Id.* § 11-200-23(c) and (d).

acceptance or nonacceptance by the OEQC, the Governor or Mayor of an EIS prepared for an agency action.

Upon acceptance or nonacceptance of the Final EIS, the approving authority or agency must file a notice with the OEQC and the proposing agency or applicant.[115] A notice of nonacceptance must contain specific findings and reasons for nonacceptance. The OEQC publishes the determination of acceptance or nonacceptance in The Environmental Notice.

A nonaccepted EIS may be revised by a proposing agency or applicant.[116] The revised EIS should document the inadequacies of the EIS, addressing the findings and reasons for nonacceptance, and discuss the revisions. The procedures for submitting a revised EIS are the same as those for a Final EIS. The revised EIS will be evaluated on the basis of whether it satisfactorily addresses the findings and reasons for non-acceptance.

An EIS may be withdrawn by sending a letter to the OEQC to notify them of the withdrawal. Any resubmittal of the EIS, however, must meet all of the requirements applicable to a new EIS such as filing, distribution, publication, review, acceptance and notification.[117]

5.4 SUPPLEMENTAL EIS

If there are any major changes to an action ~~which~~ described in an accepted EIS, such as changes in size, scope, location or timing of the action, a Supplemental EIS must be prepared and approved.[118] The accepting agency determines whether a Supplemental EIS is required.[119]

Proposing agencies or applicants must prepare a Supplemental EIS whenever the proposed action has been modified to the extent that new or different environmental impacts are

---

115 *Id.* § 11-200-23(c) and (d).

116 *Id.* § 11-200-23(e).

117 *Id.* § 11-200-23(f).

118 *Id.* § 11-200-26.

119 *Id.* § 11-200-27.

anticipated. This includes changes in scope, intensity of impacts, and mitigating measures, as well as new evidence or circumstances which have come to light. Some changes may be made to the action without submission of a Supplemental EIS, so long as the changes will not have a "significant effect," and will not result in individual or cumulative impacts not originally disclosed.[120]

The content requirements of a Supplemental EIS are the same as for the EIS. The Supplemental EIS must include a detailed description of all changes, the positive and negative aspects of these changes, and a description of the EIS process followed.[121] In addition, the Supplemental EIS may incorporate by reference unchanged material from the original EIS. The Supplemental EIS follows the same procedures as the EIS and the requirement of the thirty day consultation, filing, public notice, distribution, the forty-five day public review, comments and response, and acceptance procedures remain the same.[122] The accepting authority or approving agency determines whether the Supplemental EIS is acceptable and its determination is published in The Environmental Notice.

6.0 PUBLIC PARTICIPATION

The Hawaii EIS Law allows the public to participate in the EIS process by commenting at various stages of review. An agency may, but is not required to, solicit comments on an EA from other agencies and the public by publishing the contents of the EA in The Environmental Notice.[123] However, where a FONSI is expected on an EA, the contents of the Draft EA must be made available for public review and comment for thirty days.[124] Any comments received during this period must be answered in writing.

---

120 *Id.* § 11-200-26.

121 *Id.* § 11-200-28.

122 *Id.* § 11-200-29.

123 *Id.* § 11-200-9(c).

124 Haw. Rev. Stat. § 343-5(b)-(c).

During the consultation period after publication of an EIS Preparation Notice, members of the public have thirty days to request to become a consulted party and to make written comments regarding the environmental effects of the proposed action.[125] Written responses must be made to substantive comments.[126] The Draft EIS must contain these comments.[127]

Comments on a Draft EIS are received for forty-five days from the date of notice of availability of the Draft EIS. The proposing agency or applicant must then respond to the written comments from the public.[128] The response must include a point-by-point discussion of the validity, significance, and relevance of the comments, and a discussion as to how each comment was evaluated and considered in planning the proposed action.[129] The comments and responses must be incorporated in or appended to the Final EIS. The public also can participate in the EIS process by litigating agency decisions.[130]

7.0 ROLE OF THE ENVIRONMENTAL COUNCIL

The Hawaii EIS process is administered by the OEQC and the Council. The Council issues rules and hears appeals from agency determinations as to the adequacy of an EIS.[131] The Council is composed of fifteen members appointed by the Governor, comprising a "broad and balanced representation of educational, business, and environmentally pertinent disciplines and professions."[132] The Council is to include representatives of the humanities and the sciences, environmental interest groups, real estate and visitor industries, architectural, engineering and construction professions, and public health and planning professions.

---

125 Haw. Admin. Rules § 11-200-15(b).

126 *Id.* § 11-200-15(d).

127 *Id.* § 11-200-17(p).

128 Haw. Rev. Stat. § 343-5(b); Haw. Admin. Rules § 11-200-22(c).

129 Haw. Admin. Rules § 11-200-22(c).

130 *See infra* § 8.2 of this Chapter.

131 Haw. Rev. Stat. §§ 343-6, and 5(c).

132 *Id.* § 341-3(c).

The Council issues rules according to the rulemaking procedure set forth in the rules.[133] The Council may initiate or receive petitions for initiation of the rulemaking procedure and must publish notices for and hold public hearings on any rulemaking procedure.[134]

The Council may issue a declaratory order as to the applicability of any statutory provision, rule, or order of the Council on petition by an interested person or agency.[135] The Council may refuse to issue a declaratory ruling, or may order a hearing on the matter before issuing a declaratory hearing.[136]

The Council hears appeals from applicants when an agency has determined that an EIS is unacceptable.[137] The hearings are conducted as contested case hearings under the Hawaii Administrative Procedure Act.[138] Procedures and powers of the hearing officer for appeals to the Council are set forth in the rules.[139]

All meetings of the Council are open to the public, except when it is deemed necessary by two-thirds of the members present to hold an executive meeting.[140] No order, ruling, appointment, contract, or decision is to be finally acted upon at an executive meeting. The Council is to give notice of its meetings to the public. All materials used or produced by the Council are to be a matter of public record, except minutes of and materials used in executive meetings.[141]

---

133 Haw. Admin. Rules §§ 11-201-16 to -20.

134 *Id.* §§ 11-201-16 to -18.

135 *Id.* § 11-201-21.

136 *Id.* § 11-201-22, -23.

137 *Id.* § 11-201-26.

138 *Id.* § 11-201-28. *See infra* ch. 13 of this Handbook.

139 *Id.* §§ 11-201-28 to -30.

140 *Id.* § 11-201-3(c).

141 *Id.* § 11-201-5.

The rules limit the ability of any member, officer, employee or counsel to appear in connection with some matter before the Council.[142] Any party to a hearing before the Council may request by affidavit five days before the hearing that a Council member or hearing officer be disqualified from that hearing for personal bias or prejudice.[143] Council members or hearing officers may disqualify themselves if they feel they cannot be impartial in a given matter.

The OEQC implements the EIS process and is headed by the Director of Environmental Quality Control. The OEQC is responsible for the publication in The Environmental Notice of the notice of availability of, and determinations regarding, EAs and EISs and for distribution of the EIS for agency and public review.[144] The OEQC also develops a list of persons and agencies with jurisdiction or expertise in certain areas to act as EIS reviewers.

The Council is responsible for preparation of an annual report summarizing the progress of federal, state and county agencies in achieving the State's environmental goals and policies.[145] The annual report summarizes the documents processed by the OEQC, and discusses significant environmental developments and recommendations of the Council. The annual report is distributed by the OEQC.[146]

8.0 APPEALS

The Hawaii Administrative Procedure Act[147] provides for judicial review of contested cases by "any person aggrieved by a final decision and order in a contested case or by a preliminary ruling of the nature that deferral of review pending entry of a subsequent final

---

142 *Id.* § 11-201-6(e).

143 *Id.* § 11-201-7.

144 Haw. Rev. Stat. § 343-3; Haw. Admin. Rules § 11-200-21.

145 Haw. Rev. Stat. § 341-6.

146 *See, e.g.*, State of Hawaii, The Environmental Council and Office of Environmental Quality Control, *The 1999 Environmental Report Card.*

147 Haw. Rev. Stat. ch. 91. *See infra* ch. 13 of this Handbook.

decision would deprive appellant of adequate relief."[148] Specific details of administrative appeals and judicial review processes are provided in the Hawaii EIS Law and the rules.

8.1 ADMINISTRATIVE APPEALS

Within sixty days after the nonacceptance of an EIS by an approving agency, the applicant may appeal the nonacceptance to the Council.[149] The Council must notify the applicant of its determination on that appeal within thirty days of the receipt of the appeal. Appeals to the Council are rare. Since the Hawaii EIS law was promulgated in 1974, there has only been one appeal to the Council from an agency's decision. That appeal was withdrawn before the Council rendered its decision.[150]

The Council must provide the applicant and the agency with its specific findings and reasons for the determination, regardless of whether that determination is an affirmance or reversal of the agency's decision.[151] The agency must abide by the Council's determination. There have been few appeals to the Council from an agency's decision, apparently due in part to the relatively few EISs that have been found to be unacceptable by the reviewing agencies.[152]

8.2 JUDICIAL REVIEW

Judicial review is provided by the Hawaii EIS Law. There is no requirement that administrative remedies be exhausted before the initiation of judicial review.

An aggrieved party wishing to bring a judicial challenge based on the failure to prepare an Environmental Assessment may do so within 120 days after the proposed action is started.[153]

148 Haw. Rev. Stat. § 91-14(a).

149 Haw. Admin. Rules § 11-200-24.

150 Interview with Les Segundo, Office of Environmental Quality Control (July 28, 2000).

151 Haw. Admin Rules § 11-200-24

152 David Callies, Regulating Paradise 127 (1984).

153 Haw. Rev. Stat. § 343-7(a).

A challenge to a determination in an EA that an EIS is required must be brought within sixty days from the date of publication of the final determination in The Environmental Notice. Any challenge to a determination that an EIS is not required must be initiated within thirty days of publication in The Environmental Notice.[154] To bring a challenge on the subject of acceptance of a Final EIS, an aggrieved party may appeal within sixty days from the date of notice of the final determination.[155]

In a challenge to acceptance of a Final EIS, an "aggrieved party" may be an applicant, an affected agency, the Council, or persons who provided written comments during the consultation or review periods of the EIS process.[156] Others, by court action, may be adjudged aggrieved. To appeal an administrative decision, a person must have participated as an adversary in the hearing, whether or not the person formally intervened.[157] Any challenge to review of an EIS by a person who has provided written comments is limited to those concerns listed in the comments.[158]

The Hawaii Supreme Court has discussed the standard of judicial review which governs the court's determination on appeal of whether an EIS contains sufficient information to satisfy statutory requirements. In *Life of the Land v. Ariyoshi*,[159] a citizen group sought an injunction halting the construction of the Central Maui Water Transmission System on the ground that the environmental impact statement was inadequate and unacceptable. The court stated:

> In making such a determination a court is governed by the "rule of reason," under which an EIS need not be exhaustive to the point of discussing all possible details bearing on the proposed action but will be upheld as adequate if it has been compiled in good faith and sets forth sufficient information to enable the decision-maker to consider fully the environmental factors

---

154 *Id.* § 343-7(b).

155 *Id.* § 343-7(c); Haw. Admin. Rules § 11-200-24.

156 Haw. Rev. Stat. § 343-7(a) to (c).

157 *Jordon v. Hamada*, 62 Haw. 444, 616 P.2d 1368 (1980).

158 Haw. Rev. Stat. § 343-7(c) and *Price v. Obayashi Hawaii Corp.*, 81 Haw. 171, 183, 914 P.2d 1364, 1376 (1996).

159 59 Haw. 156, 577 P.2d 1116 (1978).

> involved and to make a reasoned decision after balancing the risks of harm to the environment against the benefits to be derived from the proposed action, as well as to make a reasoned choice between alternatives.[160]

The Court denied the group's request for an injunction, holding that the citizen group had not demonstrated a strong case for inadequacy and had not pointed out which effects should have been addressed by the EIS.[161]

In *Perry v. Planning Commission of County of Hawaii*,[162] neighboring landowners brought suit to reverse the granting of a special land use permit on several grounds, including that no EIS was filed. The permit was granted to a developer for the use of approximately sixty-five acres of land within an agricultural district on the island of Hawaii for "quarrying purposes." The Hawaii Land Use Commission had approved the permit after a public meeting, finding as a part of their conclusions that no EIS was required.[163] The Hawaii Supreme Court denied the landowners' claims on all counts, saying with regard to the EIS issue simply that the contention was without merit.[164]

However, in *Ziegler v. Hawaii DLNR*, the First Circuit Court did grant a preliminary injunction to plaintiffs to prevent the Department of Land and Natural Resources ("DLNR") from entering into an agreement with a private rancher to allow cattle grazing in a state game management area.[165] The court agreed that the DLNR should not enter into such an agreement without preparing an EIS, given that the area was a critical habitat for an endangered bird, and

160 *Life of the Land v. Ariyoshi*, 59 Haw. at 164-65, 577 P.2d at 1121, adopting *County of Suffolk v. Secretary of Interior*, 562 F.2d 1368, 1375 (2d Cir. 1977), *cert. denied*, 98 S. Ct. 1238 (1978).

161 *Id.*, 59 Haw. at 164, 577 P.2d at 1122.

162 62 Haw. 666, 619 P.2d 95 (1980).

163 *Id.*, 62 Haw. at 671-72, 619 P.2d at 101.

164 *Id.*, 62 Haw. at 686, 619 P.2d at 108.

165 *Ziegler v. Hawaii DLNR*, Civil No. 55760, unpublished Order of Preliminary Injunction (Haw. 1st Cir. Feb. 6, 1980).

the cattle would be grazing on the food and nesting plants utilized by that bird.[166] The court agreed that the DLNR's decision not to prepare an EIS was based on clearly insufficient information and was therefore "arbitrary and capricious and constituted an abuse of discretion."[167] The Supreme Court has also noted that neither Chapter 343 of the Hawaii Revised Statutes nor the administrative rules of Chapter 200 indicate a level of detail or specificity that should be included on any given subject in an EIS, and that "[t]he statute and rules were designed to give latitude to the accepting agency as to the content of the EIS."[168]

The sufficiency of an EIS is a question of law, which may be addressed through the summary judgment procedure where the only question presented is whether the EIS complies with applicable statutory mandates and there are no factual determinations to be made regarding EIS adequacy.[169]

A plaintiff must bring any judicial appeal in a timely manner. In *Waikiki Resort Hotel v. City & County of Honolulu*,[170] the plaintiff neighboring landowner objected on several grounds to grant of a permit to build a hotel apartment house in Waikiki, including that an EIS was not done. However, since the plaintiff filed his complaint 419 days after the issuance of the building permit and 329 days after work started under that permit, instead of within the 180 days required then by the Hawaii EIS Law, the court declined to consider the appeal.[171] Similarly, where plaintiffs filed an appeal to a FONSI regarding the construction of a sixth electrical generating plant, but did so more than sixty days after public notification of the negative declaration, the court held it had no jurisdiction to hear the appeal.[172]

---

166 *Ziegler v. Hawaii DLNR*, Civil No. 55760, unpublished Findings of Fact and Conclusions of Law at 6 (Haw. 1st. Cir. Jan. 29, 1980).

167 *Id.*

168 *Price v. Obayashi Hawaii Corp.*, 81 Hawai'i 171, 183, 914 P.2d 1364, 1376 (1996).

169 *Id.*, 81 Hawai'i 171, 182, 914 P.2d 1364, 1375 (1996).

170 63 Haw. 222, 624 P.2d 1353 (1981).

171 *Waikiki Resort Hotel*, 63 Haw. at 252, 624 P.2d at 1373.

172 *Waianae Coast Neighborhood Bd. v. Hawaiian Elec. Co.*, 64 Haw. 126, 637 P.2d 776 (1981).

The Hawaii EIS Law is not retroactive, and appeals may not be taken for actions which were decided before the Law went into effect. In *Hewitt v. Waikiki Shopping Plaza*,[173] the co-tenant of a roadway filed suit against co-tenants for wrongful use of street and for failure to prepare an EIS before constructing a shopping plaza. The Zoning Board of Appeals found that the proposed action would not have a significant effect on the environment and that an EIS was not required.[174] However, since the action was pending before the agency when the Hawaii EIS Law passed and was approved by the agency before the effective date of the EIS rules, the court held on appeal that the EIS requirements were not applicable to this project and in fact the Zoning Board's finding that an EIS was not required was superfluous.[175]

The standard of review following a contested case hearing is somewhat different. Following a contested case hearing, a court must apply the standards set forth in the Hawaii Administrative Procedure Act,[176] and is further guided by a presumption of validity of the agency's decision. The appellant therefore bears a heavy burden to prove that the decision is invalid because it is unjust and unreasonable in its consequences.[177]

The Supreme Court has ruled that where an administrative agency's conclusion of law is plainly erroneous and inconsistent with both the letter and intent of a statutory mandate, the agency's decision is not entitled to deference. Thus, in *Kahana Sunset Owners Ass'n v. County of Maui*,[178] the court vacated the Maui Planning Commission's decision that an environmental assessment was not required for a proposed drainage project. The Supreme Court found that the

---

173 6 Haw. App. 387, 722 P.2d 1055 (1986).

174 *Id.*, 6 Haw. App. at 392, 722 P.2d at 1059.

175 *Id. See also*, *Molokai Homesteaders Coop. Ass'n*, *supra*, 63 Haw. 453, 629 P.2d 1134 (1981).

176 Haw. Rev. Stat. § 91-14(g). *See infra* at Chapter 13.

177 *Kahana Sunset Owners Ass'n v. County of Maui*, 86 Haw. 66, 68, 947 P.2d 378, 380 (1997).

178 *Id.* 86 Haw. 710-72, 947 P.2d 383-84.

drainage project was a "completely new drainage system" serving over 300 residences and therefore did not fall within the exemption under administrative rules for "minor structures accessory to existing facilities."

CHAPTER 11

ADDITIONAL ENVIRONMENTAL LAWS

1.0 DISCLOSURES IN RESIDENTIAL REAL PROPERTY TRANSACTIONS

In 1994, the Hawaii Legislature enacted a statute to establish mandatory seller disclosures of material facts in real estate transactions. The Mandatory Disclosure Law became effective on July 1, 1995[1] and was substantially amended in 1996.[2] The Law requires disclosure of all "material facts" relating to the residential real property being offered for sale. The preamble to the Mandatory Disclosure Law expressly rejects the common law doctrine of *caveat emptor* and instead adopts the doctrine of full disclosure.

1.1 APPLICABILITY OF MANDATORY DISCLOSURE LAW

The Mandatory Disclosure Law is applicable to any sale of residential real property.[3] The term "residential real property" includes a fee simple or leasehold real property on which currently is situated either one to four dwelling units or a residential condominium or cooperative apartment, the primary use of which is occupancy as a residence.[4] The Law does not apply to commercial, industrial or otherwise nonresidential property. The Law also exempts certain transfers or dispositions of residential real property, including: sales to a co-owner, spouse, parent or child of the seller; conversions of leased land from lease to fee simple; qualified absentee owner sales and transfers by operation of law such as foreclosure, devise, descent or court order. Initial sales of new single family dwelling units and

---

1 Act approved June 22, 1994, ch. 215, 1994 Haw. Sess. Laws 517 (codified at Haw. Rev. Stat. ch. 508D).

2 Act approved June 12, 1996 Haw. Sess. Laws 161.

3 Haw Rev. Stat § 508D-2. All references to the Hawaii Revised Statutes are made to the printed version of the statutes current through the 1999 legislative session, unless otherwise noted. Where appropriate, references to acts passed during the 2000 legislative session have also been added.

4 *Id.* § 508D-1.

condominium apartments are also exempt, as well as transfers for which the seller and buyer agree in writing will not be covered under the Mandatory Disclosure Law.[5]

1.2 WRITTEN DISCLOSURE OF REAL PROPERTY STATEMENT

The seller must provide written disclosure statements to the purchaser prior to any sale of residential real property and the disclosure must be signed and dated by the seller within six months before or ten calendar days after the acceptance of a real estate purchase contract.[6]

Upon delivery of the disclosure statement to the buyer, the buyer then has fifteen days to examine the disclosure statement and decide whether to rescind the purchase contract. If the buyer elects to rescind the contract, the buyer must deliver written notification to the seller within fifteen days, and all deposits must be immediately returned to the buyer. Failure to provide notice of rescission is deemed an acceptance of the disclosure statement.[7]

Sellers must supplement their disclosure statements with any information which materially affects the value of the residential real property if that information has not been disclosed or becomes inaccurate after the original disclosure statement is provided to the buyer.[8] If a buyer receives a disclosure statement that fails to disclose a material fact or contains an inaccurate assertion which materially affects the property value, and the buyer later discovers the inaccuracy prior to closing the purchase contract, the buyer may elect to rescind the contract within fifteen days of discovering the inaccurate information or receiving an amended disclosure. If the property sale has been recorded, the buyer has no right to rescind based on the later discovered inaccurate information, but may pursue other remedies.[9]

---

5 *Id.* § 508D-3.

6 *Id.* § 508D-4.

7 *Id.* § 508D-5.

8 *Id.* § 508D-13.

9 *Id.* § 508D-6.

The Mandatory Disclosure Law requires the preparation of a written disclosure which purports to fully and accurately disclose all material facts relating to the residential real property which are within the knowledge or control of the seller, which are disclosed by documents recorded in the bureau of conveyances or which can be observed from visible, accessible areas. All past or present conditions, facts or defects which materially affect the property value must be disclosed by the seller or at seller's direction.[10]

Certain environmental conditions would most likely be considered material facts subject to the Mandatory Disclosure Law. For example, the presence of asbestos containing building materials or lead-based paint should be considered material facts subject to disclosure. In fact, the standard disclosure forms developed by the Hawaii Association of Realtors request information on a number of environmental hazards, including but not limited to asbestos, formaldehyde, radon gas, lead based paint, chemical storage tanks and contaminated soil or water.[11]

Disclosures need not include the fact that an occupant had AIDS, AIDS related complex or had tested positive for human immunodeficiency virus. Disclosures also need not include the fact that the property was the site of an occurrence that had no effect its physical environment or improvements.[12]

The Mandatory Disclosure Law requires the disclosure statement to be prepared in good faith and with due care, meaning "honesty in fact in the investigation, research, and preparation of the statement." Information in the disclosure statement may include facts based on only the seller's personal knowledge, facts provided to the seller by governmental agencies and departments, and existing reports prepared for the seller by third-party consultants, including licensed engineers, land surveyors, geologists, termite control experts,

---

10 *Id.* § 508D-1. Standard forms for sellers' real property disclosure statements have been developed and made available by the Hawaii Association of Realtors. *See* Seller's Real Property Disclosure Statement, Single Family Residence (rev. June 1996). Forms are available for condominium/co-op organizations, vacant land and other real property transactions.

11 Hawaii Association of Realtors, Seller's Real Property Disclosure Statement, Single Family Residence (rev. June 1996).

12 Haw. Rev. Stat. § 508D-8.

contractors or home inspection experts. Sellers are under no obligation to engage services for the investigation, research or preparation of a disclosure statement, and the failure to engage such services is not deemed an absence of good faith or due care.[13]

1.3 DAMAGES

When a seller negligently fails to provide a disclosure statement, the buyer may rescind the purchase or may sue for actual damages, plus the possible recovery of attorneys' fees, court costs and administrative fees.[14] Consequently, the failure to disclose environmental conditions, contamination or hazards which qualify as material facts may expose the seller to rescission of the contract, as well as fees and costs. However, when a buyer receives a disclosure statement and elects to rescind the purchase contract, the buyer is not entitled to any damages, but is instead only entitled to the immediate return of all deposits.

When the buyer elects to complete the purchase of residential real property even if the seller fails to provide a disclosure statement, the buyer has no right to rescind a real estate purchase contract despite the seller's failure.

Sellers may also be liable for unfair and deceptive acts and practices claims which could subject them to treble damages and attorneys' fees. The Hawaii Supreme Court has ruled that purchasers of a residence were "consumers" within the definition of Hawaii's consumer protection statute[15] because they committed money in a "personal investment" and were involved in conduct involving trade or commerce.[16] A plaintiff, however, proving both fraud and unfair or deceptive acts or practices violations cannot recover for fraud and punitive damages, on the one hand, and treble damages, on the other; rather, the plaintiff must elect a remedy.[17] With respect to transfers of residential real property, the Mandatory

---

13 *Id.* § 508D-9.

14 *Id.* §§ 508D-16, -20.

15 *Id.* § 480-1.

16 *Cieri v. Leticia Query Realty, Inc.*,80 Hawai'i 54, 67-69, 905 P.2d 29, 42-44 (1995).

17 Id., 80 Hawai'i at 72, 905 P.2d at 47.

Disclosure Law also imposes an affirmative duty upon the seller to disclose material facts relating to the subject property.

2.0 HAWAII ENVIRONMENTAL DISCLOSURE LAW

The Hawaii Environmental Disclosure Law ("Disclosure Law")[18] requires disclosure of financial, legal and environmental information prior to certain additional purchases of securities by a present stockholder of the same corporation. The Disclosure Law was enacted as an early warning system to protect agricultural lands and to inform the public of anticipated changes in the use of agricultural land due to changes in ownership of publicly held Hawaii corporations.[19] The sole purpose of the Disclosure Law is to create a procedure whereby the requested information is made available to the public.[20] Hawaii citizens and other stockholders of the corporation are able to review the information, which may influence the stockholders' decision to sell or retain their ownership interests in that Hawaii corporation.

For the first time in more than a decade, a corporation recently filed a Chapter 343D disclosure. Flexi-Van Leasing, Inc. which is privately held by Mr. David Murdock, submitted an environmental disclosure statement with the Office of Environmental Quality Control pertaining to his proposal to acquire Castle & Cooke, Inc.[21] The last filing of a 343D disclosure occurred in 1989 when BHP acquired PRI.[22]

The Disclosure Law requires a person who owns ten percent or more of any class of voting stock of a Hawaii corporation to file a statement with the Office of Environmental Quality Control ("OEQC") before that person purchases an additional five percent or more of the same security, or five percent or more of the assets of that Hawaii corporation.[23] The

---

18 Haw. Rev. Stat. ch. 343D.

19 *See* Act approved April 26, 1982, ch. 53, § 1, 1982 Haw. Sess. Laws 58.

20 Haw. Op. Att'y Gen. 86-16, at 3 (1986).

21 State of Hawaii, Department of Health, Office of Environmental Quality Control, The Environmental Notice at 1, June 8, 2000.

22 *Id.*

23 Haw. Rev. Stat. § 343D-3.

statement must include a detailed description of the corporation's organization and the purchaser's audited financial statements for the past five years.[24] Financial records that are submitted to the OEQC are not retained as confidential. The amount of detail provided in the disclosure to the public is within the discretion of the OEQC.[25]

The statement must include the purchaser's history of compliance or noncompliance with environmental laws and regulations and the purchaser's involvement in judicial or administrative proceedings involving environmental laws or regulations.[26] Lastly, the statement must include any intentions by the purchaser to influence the corporation to take any actions within the next five years which may require the filing of an environmental impact statement.[27] The purchaser must wait fifteen days after the delivery of the statement to the OEQC before completing the purchase of stock or assets.

The OEQC may extend the fifteen-day waiting period to forty-five days pending a hearing to determine the accuracy and completeness of the filing.[28] The OEQC is required to issue a written, public opinion within five days after the hearing is concluded. Regardless of whether a hearing is held, the OEQC may request additional relevant documents from the person submitting the filing. These documents must be produced to the OEQC within thirty days or as requested by the OEQC.[29]

The OEQC may prohibit further purchases of stock or assets if the purchaser refuses to file the required statement, refuses to produce the requested documents or fails to participate in a hearing.[30] The Attorney General may be requested to enforce the prohibition against the

---

24 *Id.* § 343D-3(1)(A)-(B).

25 Haw. Op. Att'y Gen. 86-16 (1986).

26 Haw. Rev. Stat. § 343D-3(1)(C)-(D).

27 *Id.* § 343D-3(1)(E). Environmental impact statements are discussed in ch. 10 of this Handbook.

28 *Id.* § 343D-4.

29 *Id.* § 343D-5.

30 *Id.* § 343D-6.

purchase of stock or assets. In doing so, the Attorney General may bring an action for an injunction and seek to impose a maximum civil penalty of $100,000 upon the purchaser.[31] Aggrieved persons, including the corporation which is the subject of the filing, are granted standing to bring an action for injunction, rescission, civil penalties and other relief.[32] Any person who brings a successful action under the Disclosure Law is entitled to recover reasonable attorneys' fees and costs.[33]

Purchases made by a stockholder who already owns fifty percent or more of the stock or assets, and purchases of stocks or assets of corporations which have less than one hundred stockholders of record are exempt from the Disclosure Law.[34]

3.0 HAWAII ENDANGERED SPECIES ACT

The Conservation of Aquatic Life, Wildlife, and Land Plants Act ("Conservation Act")[35] serves as the Hawaii Endangered Species Act. The Conservation Act controls activities relating to or affecting endangered species and also establishes conservation programs. The Conservation Act was enacted under the federal Endangered Species Act[36] and has been approved by the Secretary of the Interior.[37] The Conservation Act creates a cooperative agreement between the federal and state implementing agencies. The Department of Land and Natural Resources ("DLNR") is the implementing state agency for the Conservation Act.

---

31 *Id.* § 343D-10(a).

32 *Id.* § 343D-10(b).

33 *Id.* § 343D-10(c).

34 *Id.* § 343D-9.

35 Haw. Rev. Stat. ch. 195D.

36 16 U.S.C. § 1531 *et seq.*

37 *Id.* § 1535.

3.1 DETERMINATION OF ENDANGERED AND THREATENED SPECIES

The Conservation Act incorporates the listing of endangered or threatened species under the federal Endangered Species Act into its own listing.[38] Additional species indigenous to Hawaii may be listed as endangered or threatened through rulemaking upon the DLNR's own recommendation or upon the petition of three interested persons.[39] The federally listed and indigenous endangered and threatened species include reptiles, mollusks, mammals and birds.[40]

3.2 PROHIBITED ACTIVITIES

The Conservation Act prohibits the export, taking, possession, sale and transport of endangered species.[41] The definition of "taking" has been litigated extensively on the federal level and also has been addressed by the Hawaii courts. The term "taking" has been defined to include harm which results in significant environmental modification or degradation of habitat which actually injures or kills wildlife. For instance, maintaining feral goats and sheep which destroy an endangered bird's critical habitat has been considered a "taking" under the Conservation Act.[42] However, "taking" does not include destruction of habitat which is not likely to jeopardize the existence of the endangered species. For example, continued construction of the H-3 highway through the Oahu Creeper's habitat was not considered a "taking".[43] The "taking" issue is evaluated on a case by case basis after the determination of the impact of the activity on the species' habitat.

---

38 Haw. Rev. Stat. § 195D-4(a).

39 *Id.* § 195D-4(d).

40 Haw. Admin. Rules, tit. 13, ch. 124, Exhibits 1 – 4.

41 Haw. Rev. Stat. § 195D-4(e).

42 *Palilla v. Hawaii Dep't of Land and Natural Resources*, 471 F. Supp. 985 (D. Haw. 1979).

43 *Stop H-3 Ass'n v. Lewis*, 538 F. Supp. 149 (D. Haw. 1982) *aff'd in part*, 740 F.2d 1442 (9th Cir. 1984).

3.3 PERMITS

Temporary licenses to allow prohibited activities involving endangered and threatened species may be issued by the DNLR. For activities involving endangered species, licenses may be issued only for scientific purposes or to enhance propagation of the endangered species. These permits are nonassignable and may be revoked for due cause.[44]

Permits for the taking, sale, transport or export of an endangered species may only be issued by DLNR for scientific purposes or to enhance the propagation or survival of the species. Permits to possess legally obtained endangered species may be issued for educational purposes which enhance species survival.[45]

With regard to threatened wildlife, the DLNR may issue permits for collecting, processing, killing, selling or transporting the threatened wildlife only for scientific or educational purposes including cultural activities, or for activities which will enhance species survival.[46] The Board of Land and Natural Resources ("Board") may only issue a license after a two-thirds majority vote of its authorized membership and after holding a public hearing on the affected island. Public notice of a proposed license is published in the Office of Environmental Quality Control's bulletin, The Environmental Notice, and the application and proposed license will remain available for public review and comment for sixty days.[47]

Permits may be issued for keeping indigenous wildlife, introduced wild birds, game birds and game mammals in captivity for protection, treatment or propagation. Lastly, permits may be issued to control and destroy game birds and mammals, introduced wild birds and feral animals which cause or can cause substantial agricultural or aquacultural damage to crops.[48]

---

44 Haw. Rev. Stat. § 195D-4(f).

45 Haw. Admin. Rules § 13-124-4.

46 *Id.*

47 *Id.*

48 *Id.* § 13-124-7.

3.4 CONSERVATION PROGRAMS

The DLNR is required to conduct research on indigenous aquatic life, wildlife, land plans, and endangered species and their associated ecosystems. The DLNR is authorized to acquire lands or interests needed to carry out conservation programs, and may use its authority to carry out programs for the conservation, management and protection of species and ecosystems.[49]

All state agencies are required to use their authority in furtherance of conservation purposes by carrying out programs for the protection of threatened and endangered species and taking necessary action to ensure that actions authorized, funded or carried out by the agency do not jeopardize the continued existence of threatened or endangered species. The governor is also required to encourage all federal agencies to utilize their authority in furtherance of conservation efforts.[50]

In carrying out conservation programs, priority is given to the conservation and protection of those endangered species and associated ecosystems whose extinction within Hawaii would imperil or terminate their existence in the world.

The DLNR is also required to initiate amendments to the conservation district boundaries in order to include high quality native forests and the habitat of rate native species of flora and fauna.[51]

3.5 LANDOWNER CONSERVATION INCENTIVES

In order to encourage landowners to participate in conservation efforts, the Legislature has created a system of voluntary habitat conservation plans and safe harbor agreements. After approval of a habitat conservation plan, safe harbor agreement, or issuance of an incidental take license, no state agencies or departments may impose any new

---

49 Haw. Rev. Stat. § 195D-5.

50 *Id.*

51 *Id.* at § 195D-5.1.

requirement or condition on a landowner or successor in order to protect a threatened or endangered species.[52]

Persons participating in the DLNR's voluntary conservation programs may receive permission to use adjacent public lands for commercial nature tourism activities that increase public education and support for endangered species, provided that an agreed percentage of fees are donated to the DLNR's endangered species trust fund.

Any information submitted by a landowner in the course of preparing a habitat conservation plan or a safe harbor agreement will be kept confidential until notice of the proposed plan is published in The Environmental Notice. Even after publication, the precise location of any threatened or endangered species may remain confidential.[53]

The DLNR's endangered species recovery committee ("Committee") reviews all safe harbor agreements and habitat conservation plans. The Committee serves as a consultant to the Board and the DLNR on matters relating to endangered, threatened, proposed and candidate species. After review of the applications, the Committee will make recommendations, based on the best available scientific and other reliable data, regarding whether the applications should be approved, amended or rejected. In making its recommendation, the Committee must consider the cumulative impacts of the proposed action on the recovery potential of the endangered, threatened, proposed or candidate species.[54]

3.5.1 HABITAT CONSERVATION PLANS

In 1997, the Legislature authorized the DLNR to enter into a habitat conservation plan with any landowner or group of landowners. Habitat conservation planning applications must identify the geographic area, habitats or ecosystems which are the focus of the plan, the endangered, threatened, and candidate species, the actions to be undertaken to

---

52 *Id.* at § 195D-23.

53 *Id.* at § 195D-24.

54 *Id.* at § 195D-25.

protect those ecosystems, an implementation schedule, and an adequate funding source to ensure that the proposed measures are undertaken in accordance with the schedule.[55]

After a habitat conservation plan is complete, the public is notified in the Office of Environmental Quality Control's bulletin, The Environmental Notice. The proposed plan and application then remain available for public review and comment for sixty days.

After a public hearing on the affected island, and a two-thirds vote of approval from the Board's authorized membership, the Board may enter into a habitat conservation plan. Any approved plan must further conservation purposes by protecting, maintaining, restoring or enhancing identified ecosystems upon which endangered threatened or candidate species depend, that the plan will increase the likelihood of recovery of the endangered or threatened species, and that the plan satisfies all Conservation Act requirements.[56]

Once a habitat conservation plan has been approved, the participants must submit an annual report to DLNR. The annual report must include a description of activities and accomplishments, an analysis of the problems and issues encountered in meeting or failing to meet objectives, areas needing technical advice, status of funding, and management objectives or the next fiscal year.[57]

Although the DLNR has not yet received any applications for approval of habitat conservation plans, it has been working with several state agencies in connection with development in the Ewa Plain area pursuant to the East Kapolei Master Plan. Since the phase out of sugar cane production in the Ewa Plain, the ko'oloa'ula or Red Ilima, has been found along the planned route for the North-South Road between Kapolei and the H-1 Freeway. A habitat conservation plan must therefore be approved before state transportation officials can move ahead with design and construction. DLNR anticipates that the habitat

---

55 *Id.* at § 195D-21.

56 *Id.*

57 *Id.*

conservation plan will be presented to the Board of Land and Natural Resources for approval in the near future.[58]

3.5.2 SAFE HARBOR AGREEMENTS

In 1997, in order to encourage landowners to voluntarily engage in conservation efforts, the Legislature authorized the Board to enter into safe harbor agreements with landowners. A safe harbor agreement may authorize the taking of an endangered, threatened, proposed or candidate species incidental to an otherwise lawful activity in a created, restored, maintained or improved habitat.[59] The U.S. Fish and Wildlife Service also allow allows private landowners to pursue survival enhancement pursuant to safe harbor agreements[60] which comply with the terms of the federal safe harbor agreement policy.[61]

Safe harbor agreements must ensure, based on the best scientific and other reliable data, that the take would not jeopardize the continued existence of any protected species and that the take would not reduce the endangered species population below the number found on the property prior to entering into the agreement. Safe harbor agreements must propose to create, restore, maintain or improve significant amounts of habitat for a minimum of five years. The safe harbor agreement must increase the likelihood that the endangered or threatened species for which a take is authorized will recover and that any authorized take will take place only in the habitat created, restored, maintained or improved under the agreement. The safe harbor agreement must also show that the cumulative impact of the activity provides net environmental benefits and that there is an identified and adequate source of funding.[62]

The public must be notified of any proposed safe harbor agreements by publication in The Environmental Notice and the public comment period must last at least sixty days.

---

58 Interview with Randy Kennedy, Division of Forestry and Wildlife, DLNR (August 8, 2000).

59 Haw. Rev. Stat. § 195D-22.

60 50 C.F.R. §§ 17.22 and 17.32.

61 64 Fed. Reg. 32717-26 (June 17, 2000).

62 *Id.*

Following the public comment period, safe harbor agreements must be approved by two-thirds vote of the Board's authorized membership, after a public hearing on the affected island. The Board must find that the cumulative activities to be undertaken in the area covered by the agreement are environmentally beneficial.[63]

The rights and obligations created by the safe harbor agreement run with the land for the term specified in the agreement, which is recorded by the DLNR with the bureau of conveyances or the land court.

Safe harbor agreements may be repealed if any parties have breached their obligations, have failed to cure the breach in a timely manner, and the effect of the breach is to diminish the likelihood that the agreement will accomplish its goals. Safe harbor agreements may also be repealed if the specified funding sources no longer exist and have not been replaced.[64]

On January 28, 2000, the DLNR received the fist proposal from a landowner to participate in a safe harbor agreement. Under the proposed agreement, the Nene, or Hawaiian goose, would be reintroduced to Puu O'Hoku Ranch, Molokai. The proposed agreement announced the desire of the landowner and the DLNR to establish a free ranging population of 75 Nene on ranch premises and 200 Nene on Molokai. Under this Agreement, the Ranch will maintain or improve significant amounts of Nene habitat for a period of seven years, by continuing cattle ranching operations and thereby maintain open, short grass habitat, assist DLNR to establish and maintain release sites and assist DLNR to control predators around breeding and release sites.[65]

Although the Ranch has no intention of harming or taking any Nene, the proposed agreement authorizes the incidental take of all Nene introduced to the enrolled lands, and

---

63 *Id.*

64 *Id.*

65 Letter from Michael G. Buck to the Chairperson and Members of the Board of Land and Natural Resources, January 28, 2000.

their progeny, as a result of lawful activities at the Ranch. The request was approved at the Board's January 28, 2000 meeting, and notice was given to the public in The Environmental Notice dated February 8, 2000. As of the date of publication of this Handbook, the agreement is in the process of being finalized.[66]

3.6 ENFORCEMENT MECHANISMS

The DLNR and the county police officers enforce the Conservation Act. Employees and agents of the DLNR may be conferred powers to serve and execute warrants, issue citations and arrest offenders. DLNR employees are also authorized to enforce the terms and conditions of any license to enter privately owned lands, upon written notification to the affected landowner.[67]

Searches may be conducted by the DLNR agents and police officers, and documents, materials, plant and animal life found to be in violation of the Conservation Act may be seized. All seized items are forfeited to the State upon conviction of the person from whom the seizure was made. Forfeited items may be destroyed or disposed of in any manner deemed appropriate by the DLNR.[68]

Persons who violate the Conservation Act are subject to criminal fines and imprisonment for a misdemeanor. The first conviction for violation of the Conservation Act's provisions or rules is punishable by a fine of $250 to $1,000 or imprisonment for one year or both. Subsequent convictions within five years are punishable by a fine of $500 to $1,000 or imprisonment for one year or both. Additional fines for injury to protected species may be levied against the convicted person. A fine of $500 will be levied for each specimen of a threatened species which was intentionally, knowingly or recklessly killed or removed from its habitat. Similarly, a $1,000 fine will be levied for each specimen of an endangered species similarly killed or removed.[69]

---

66 Interview with Carol Terry, Division of Forestry and Wildlife, DLNR (August 7, 2000).

67 Haw. Rev. Stat. § 195D-7.

68 *Id.* § 195D-8.

69 *Id.* § 195D-9.

Any person may petition the chairperson to appoint a hearings officer for a request to enjoin any person alleged to be in violation of the Conservation Act, the conservation rules, a habitat conservation plan, safe harbor agreement or incidental take license. The request may also require the state to take action to enforce the Conservation Law any rules, plans, agreements or licenses.[70]

If, after diligent effort, the chairperson cannot resolve the matter with in a reasonable period of time not to exceed ninety days, or if the petitioner is not satisfied with the chairperson's resolution, then a contested case hearing will be held. During the contested case, the hearing officer may not impose monetary damages or criminal penalties against any violator, but may issue findings of fact and an order directing that the party be found in violation.

Any person may petition for an immediate hearing if they believe that a violation of a habitat conservation plan, safe harbor agreement or incidental take license has occurred or is likely to occur. Petitions for immediate hearings must demonstrate the efforts made to notify the landowner of the alleged violations, along with specific facts showing that the continued existence of an endangered or threatened species is likely to be jeopardized unless the alleged violation is immediately enjoined. If the chairperson finds good cause for a hearing, a hearing will be conducted within forty-eight hours after the filing of the petition. The hearing officer must order temporary injunctive relief, if he or she determines that there is a substantial likelihood that the continued existence of an endangered or threatened species will be jeopardized unless the violation is immediately enjoined.[71]

4.0 HAWAII COASTAL ZONE MANAGEMENT LAW

The Hawaii Coastal Zone Management Program ("Program") was promulgated in 1977 in response to the Federal Coastal Zone Management act of 1972 and regulates public and private uses in the coastal zone.[72] The objectives and policies of the Program are varied:

70 *Id.* § 195D-27.

71 *Id.*

72 Haw. Rev. Stat. ch. 205A.

to provide recreational resources; to protect, preserve and, where appropriate, restore historic, scenic, and coastal ecosystem resources; to provide economic uses; to reduce coastal hazards; to improve the development of a review process, communication and public participation in the management of coastal resources and hazards; to stimulate public awareness, education and participation in coastal management; to protect beaches for public use and recreation, and locate new structures inland from the shoreline setback to conserve open space and minimize loss of improvements due to erosion; and to implement the state's ocean resources management plan.[73] The Program designates special management areas in the coastal zone which are subject to special controls on development. The Program also establishes setback boundaries for development along the shoreline.

4.1 RELATIONSHIP TO THE FEDERAL COASTAL ZONE MANAGEMENT ACT

The federal Coastal Zone Management Act[74] establishes a federal program for management, development and protection of the coastal zone. The coastal states are authorized to develop and implement a state coastal zone management program, after approval by the Secretary of Commerce.[75] Hawaii received federal approval of its state Coastal Zone Management Program in the late 1970s and is eligible for grants in aid from the federal program. The Hawaii Coastal Zone Management Program designates the Office of Planning as the lead agency which administers the Program. However, each county is responsible for designation of the special management areas and for establishment of the shoreline setbacks. The Hawaii Coastal Zone Management is evaluated by the Department of Commerce, National Oceanic and Atmospheric Administration on a regular basis.[76] The evaluation of

---

73 http://www.hawaii.gov/dbedt/czm/program.html (visited July 28, 2000).

74 16 U.S.C. § 1451.

75 16 U.S.C. § 1456(b).

76 *See, e.g.,* Notice of Intent to Evaluate, 62 Fed. Reg. 54,096 (Oct. 17, 1997); 58 Fed. Reg. 68,390 (Dec. 27, 1993); 56 Fed. Reg. 63,934 (Dec. 6. 1991); 55 Fed. Reg. 52,069 (December 19, 1990) and 53 Fed. Reg. 48,285 (Nov. 30, 1988).

findings are available to the public and a notice of availability of the findings is published in the Federal Register.[77]

4.2 SPECIAL MANAGEMENT AREAS

A Special Management Area ("SMA") is a designated area of land which extends inland from the shoreline and is designated for intensive management by the counties. The SMA is established by the county planning commission or by the county council ("county authority") and includes the shoreline and coastal water related land. The SMA is a designated area inland to the extent necessary to control shorelands, the uses of which have a direct and significant impact on the coastal waters.[78] Maps which specify the SMA are kept at the Department of Land Utilization for the City and County of Honolulu. In the other counties, the maps designating the SMA are available at the county administrative offices.[79] Although the SMA originally encompassed all lands extended not less than 100 yards inland from the shoreline, in some areas the SMAs extending several miles inland to cover areas in which coastal resources are likely to be directly affected by development activities, such as Kawainui Marsh on Oahu and Waipio Valley on the Big Island.[80]

4.3 PERMITTING FOR DEVELOPMENT

Development or planned development in the SMA requires a Special Management Area Use Permit ("SMA Use Permit").[81] Development is defined broadly to include construction, demolition or alteration of the size of any structure; change in the intensity of use of water or land, including subdivision of land; grading, removing, dredging, extraction of any materials; and the placement of any solid material or waste in any phase onto the land

---

77 *See, e.g.*, Notice of Availability of Evaluation Findings, 56 Fed. Reg. 34,051 (July 25, 1991); 54 Fed. Reg. 20,175 (May 10, 1989); 53 Fed. Reg. 48,284 (Nov. 30, 1988); 52 Fed. Reg. 34,977 (September 16, 1987); and 51 Fed. Reg. 46,907 (Dec. 29, 1986).

78 *See* Haw. Op. Att'y Gen. 75-18 (1975).

79 Haw. Rev. Stat. § 205A-23.

80 http://www.hawaii.gov/dbedt/czm/sma.html (visited July 28, 2000).

81 Development within an SMA may also trigger the requirement for an environmental assessment. See Haw. Rev. Stat. 343, and Haw. Admin. Rules § 11-200-6, discussed in ch. 10, § 3.0 of this Handbook.

designated as an SMA.[82] The term "development" may also include planned development of the foregoing activities.[83]

Certain uses are exempt from the definition of development and therefore do not require a SMA Use Permit. The following uses are exempted: construction of a single family residence which is not part of a larger development; demolition or removal of structures, except designated historic sites; subdivision of land into four or fewer parcels, provided that no associated construction activities are proposed; the use of land for agriculture, aquaculture, husbandry or forestry purposes; and repairs to existing structures, utility lines and roads.[84] However, the exemption for demolition or removal of structures does not apply where the planned demolition activity is or may become part of a larger project, and where the cumulative impact of the larger project may have significant environmental impact on the SMA. In those cases, the demolition or removal activity is not exempted and may be considered "development" under the Program.[85]

SMA Use Permits are separated into three categories: emergency permits to reconstruct structures damaged by natural hazards and to prevent such harm; minor permits which authorize development valued at $125,000.00 or less; and the standard use permit which authorizes development valued at over $125,000.00.[86] Each county establishes rules which govern the SMA Use Permit application procedures.[87]

---

82 *Haw. Rev. Stat.* § 205A-22.

83 *Hui Malama Aino O Ko'olau v. Pacarro*, 4 Haw. App. 304, 666 P.2d 177 (1983).

84 Haw. Rev. Stat. § 205A-22.

85 *Hawaii's Thousand Friends v. City and County of Honolulu,* 75 Haw. 237, 858 P.2d 726 (1993) (The planned demolition of Camp Kailua was part of the overall Kailua Beach Park project and therefore the cumulative impact of the whole project must be evaluated to determine whether the proposed demolition was "development" for purpose of determining applicability of SMA Use Permit requirements). For the list of exempted uses for the City and County of Honolulu, *see* Honolulu, Haw., Rev. Ordinances § 25-1.3 (rev. April 12, 2000).

86 Haw. Rev. Stat. § 205A-22.

87 *See, e.g.* Honolulu, Haw., Rev. Ordinances, ch. 25 (rev. April 12, 2000).

The county authority must consider several guidelines in determining whether to grant a SMA Use Permit. All development in the SMA must ensure adequate public access to beaches, recreational areas and natural reserves, protect public recreation areas, historical and archeological sites, minimize adverse effects from solid and liquid waste treatment, and minimize alteration to existing vegetation and land forms. Further, the county authority may not approve a permit for development until the county authority has found that the development will not have any substantial adverse environmental effect, except if such adverse effect is minimized and clearly outweighed by public health and safety or compelling public interest.[88] The county authority is required to give Hawaiian cultural interests of participating parties "full consideration" and is obligated to "preserve and protect" native Hawaiian rights to the extent feasible when the authority issues an SMA Use Permit.[89] The county authority may impose conditions, such as the completion of an archeological survey, prior to the issuance of the Permit.[90]

If the specific findings required by the Coastal Zone Management Act are not made by the county authority in the course of the SMA Use Permit process, the permit may be overturned by a court, after reviewing the county's action on the permit. In particular, the county authority is required to make a specific finding that the proposed development will not have any substantial adverse environmental impact, unless this adverse impact is clearly outweighed by public health and safety.[91] For example, the sole finding by a county authority that the proposed development would have significant impact on the existing highway system is an insufficient basis to deny an SMA Use Permit. In this case, the county authority must determine whether the extra traffic generated by the proposed project would

---

88 Haw. Rev. Stat. § 205A-26 (1985).

89 *Public Access Shoreline Hawaii v. Hawaii County Planning Comm'n*, 79 Haw. 425, 903 P.2d 1246 (1995). The City and County of Honolulu, Department of Land Utilization requires protection of historic or cultural resources which are uncovered during project activity as part of the SMA permit process. *See* State of Hawaii, Office of Environmental Quality Control, 1994 Annual Report of the Environmental Council, at 19 (1995).

90 *Alaloa v. Planning Comm'n of Maui County,* 68 Haw. 135, 705 P.2d 1042 (1985).

91 *Mahuiki v. Planning Comm'n of Kauai*, 65 Haw. 506, 654 P.2d 874 (1982).

have a substantial adverse environmental effect on the SMA.[92] Lastly, the county must ensure that the development is consistent with the county zoning.

The county authority is required to give public notice of all SMA Use Permit applications. Notice must be given to persons whose property rights may be adversely affected and to persons who have requested notice. Notice also must be given in a newspaper of general statewide circulation. The county authority establishes the regulations governing public hearings on SMA Use Permit applications, and the county may act on permit applications by way of the public hearings.[93] Other agencies may not grant permits which authorize development unless the SMA Use Permit approval is received first.[94]

4.4 SHORELINE AND SETBACKS

The Board of Land and Natural Resources is responsible for determining all state shorelines and for handling appeals of shoreline determinations.[95] The planning department of each county establishes the shoreline setback within its borders. The shoreline setback area is the area between the shoreline and the shoreline setback line. The "shoreline" means the upper reaches of the wash of the waves at high tide, usually evidenced by the edge of vegetation growth. Where there is no vegetation in the immediate vicinity, the shoreline is the upper limit of debris left by the wash of the waves.[96] The county planning department enforces the shoreline setbacks and reviews all plans for proposed activity which will require a variance from the established setbacks.[97] In conjunction with the planning department, the county authority acts on variance applications. The county authority is required to provide public notice, and hold a public hearing prior to any action on a variance application.[98]

---

92 *Topliss v. The Planning Comm'n*, 9 Haw. App. 377, 842 P.2d 648 (1993).

93 *Sandy Beach Defense Fund v. City Council of Honolulu,* 70 Haw. 361, 773 P.2d 250 (1989)(a contested case hearing under Haw. Rev. Stat. ch. 91 is not required).

94 Haw. Rev. Stat. § 205A-29.

95 *Id.* § 205A-43.

96 Haw. Admin. Rules § 13-222-2.

97 *Id.*

98 Haw. Rev. Stat. § 205A-43.5.

4.4.1 DETERMINATION OF SHORELINE

The shoreline is determined by the Board of Land and Natural Resources ("Board") through a standard certification procedure.[99] To request a shoreline certification, an application must be filed with the state Department of Land and Natural Resources ("DLNR") in Honolulu or in the county in which the subject shoreline is located. The applicant must conduct a field survey and submit the results along with a number of maps to the DLNR.

The DLNR must be granted access to enter the property and inspect the shoreline. The State land surveyor may consult with the applicant's field surveyor and may enter the applicant's premises to verify the shoreline map. The DLNR must give public notice of the receipt of an application for shoreline certification. Interested persons may submit comments on the application for certification within fourteen days of the public notice, which is published in The Environmental Notice, a semi-monthly publication issued by the Office of Environmental Quality Control.[100] Both owners and interested persons have the right to appeal a shoreline certification or the rejection thereof within certain time periods.[101] Once the shoreline is certified by the chairperson of the Board, the shoreline certification is valid for twelve months.[102]

4.4.2 SHORELINE SETBACKS AND VARIANCES

Each county, through its planning department, is free to adopt setbacks along shorelines between twenty and forty feet inland from the shoreline.[103] Currently, most shoreline setback lines are set at forty feet from the shoreline.[104] Setbacks greater than forty feet may be established through rulemaking or by ordinance.[105] The City and County of

---

99 Haw. Admin. Rules, tit. 13, ch. 222.

100 The OEQC publishes shoreline certifications, environmental impact statement notices and other documents prepared under Haw. Rev. Stat. ch. 343 in its bimonthly publication, The Environmental Notice.

101 Haw. Admin. Rules § 13-222-26.

102 Haw. Rev. Stat. § 205A-42.

103 *Id.* § 205A-43(a).

104 http://www.hawaii.gov/dbedt/czm/setback.html (visited July 28, 2000).

105 Haw. Rev. Stat. § 205A-45.

Honolulu has adopted shoreline setbacks of forty feet but the shoreline setback may be smaller for shallow lots.[106] In addition, the City and County of Honolulu will not approve most new subdivisions unless they can accommodate a sixty-foot shoreline setback.[107] Structures and activities are generally prohibited within a setback without a variance. The term "structure" is defined broadly to include portions of buildings, pavement, road, pipe, flume, utility line, fence, groin, wall, revetment, or anything requiring a fixed location on or under the ground.[108]

The county authority is required to give public notice, including notice to the abutting neighbors, and is required to hold a public hearing on variance applications. Variances may be granted for a number of purposes, including cultivation of crops, aquaculture, landscaping, drainage, boating or water sports recreational facilities, and other improvements to facilities which are in the public interest.[109] Variances to the shoreline setbacks may be granted without a public hearing only in certain instances: to protect legal structures which are in immediate danger of shoreline erosion; to allow maintenance or repair of boating, maritime or water sport recreational facilities; where a public hearing has not been requested; and for the stabilization of shoreline erosion by the moving of sand entirely on public lands.[110]

Variances are not required for certain structures in the shoreline setback area. Structures completed prior to June 22, 1970 and structures which received a building permit, setback variance or shoreline approval prior to June 16, 1989 are not required to obtain a variance. Structures involved with existing agriculture or aquaculture in the shoreline area on June 16, 1989 and certain maintenance, repair or alteration work done on legal boating, maritime or water sports recreational facilities are also exempt from variance requirements.[111]

---

106 Honolulu, Haw., Rev. Ordinances § 23-1.4 (rev. April 12, 2000).

107 *Id.* § 23-1.7.

108 *Id.* §§ 23-1.3 and 23-1.5. The definition of "structure" adopted by the county ordinances is broader than the statutory definition. *Cf.* Haw. Rev. Stat. § 205A-41.

109 Haw Rev. Stat. § 205A-46.

110 *Id.* § 205A-43.5.

111 *Id.* § 205A-44(b).

The Coastal Zone Management Program prohibits certain activities other than construction in the shoreline area. Sand, dead coral, rocks, soil and other beach or marine sediments may not be taken within the shoreline area, unless authorized by a variance. However, each person may take one gallon of these shoreline materials per day for reasonable, personal and noncommercial use. When clearing drainage pipes, streams and canals or the shoreline for maintenance purposes, the sand must be placed on adjacent areas unless that placement would cause significant turbidity.[112] These restrictions are intended to protect sand, coral and other natural resources at the shoreline area.

4.5 ENFORCEMENT OF SETBACKS

The planning department of each county is responsible for enforcement of shoreline setbacks. Any structure or activity which is prohibited, has not received a variance under the Coastal Zone Management Act or has not complied with the conditions of a variance must be removed or corrected. No other state or county permit or approval may be considered a variance of the shoreline setback. Any unauthorized structure placed or constructed by a person which affects the shoreline area and is partially located on private property is considered to be entirely within the shoreline area for enforcement purposes.[113]

4.6 PENALTIES

Any person who fails to obtain a SMA permit as required, or violates the Coastal Zone Management Law, administrative rules or a SMA permit is subject to a civil fine of up to $10,000. In addition, a fine of up to $1,000 may be imposed per day for each day the violation continues. These penalties may be imposed for violations of a shoreline setback variance or any violation of the shoreline setback statutory provisions or rules.[114]

---

112 *Id.* § 205A-44(a).

113 *Id.* § 205A-43.6.

114 *Id.* § 205A-32(a)-(b).

The civil fines may be imposed through an administrative or judicial proceeding. If the fine is imposed administratively, the alleged violator must first be given an opportunity for a contested case hearing pursuant to the Hawaii Administrative Procedure Act.[115]

5.0 HAWAII PESTICIDES LAW

The Hawaii Pesticides Law ("Pesticides Law") governs the licensing, sale and use of pesticides within the State of Hawaii.[116] Although the Federal Insecticide, Fungicide and Rodenticide Act ("FIFRA")[117] places ultimate supervisory responsibility for uniform control of pesticides with the Environmental Protection Agency ("EPA"), the State may regulate the sale or use of pesticides which are used intra-state and may regulate the sale or use of pesticides which are not prohibited by FIFRA.[118] The State labeling and packaging requirements cannot be different than those imposed by FIFRA. States may register pesticides for limited local use to treat limited and sudden pest infestations. Stricter state regulation of pesticides is permissible, as FIFRA does not preempt more stringent state legislation.[119] Pursuant to FIFRA, the Pesticides Law regulates pesticides within Hawaii. The Hawaii Department of Agriculture ("DOA") is responsible for the administration of the Pesticides Law, which addresses three activities: the licensing, sale and use of pesticides.

5.1 LICENSING AND SALE OF PESTICIDES

The Pesticides Law requires pesticides which are received, used, sold, offered for sale or distributed within Hawaii to be licensed by the Board of Agriculture ("Board").[120] Licensing is not required for pesticides which are shipped between facilities located in Hawaii which are owned by one person.

---

115 Haw. Rev. Stat. ch. 91. *See infra* ch. 13 of this Handbook.

116 Haw. Rev. Stat. ch. 149A.

117 7 U.S.C. § 136 *et seq.*

118 *Id.* § 136v.

119 *Agricultural Chems. Assn. v. Rominger*, 500 F. Supp. 465 (E.D. Cal. 1980). *See* 7 U.S.C. § 136v.

120 Haw. Rev. Stat. § 149A-13.

The application for the license must contain a description of the pesticide, a copy of the labeling, claims made for the pesticide including directions for use and information about the licensee. The DOA may require the submission of the complete formula of the pesticide.[121] The completed application and the appropriate filing fees must be submitted to the DOA for a three-year license. The DOA may refuse to license a pesticide or may cancel the license of a pesticide if the proposed use of the pesticide would result in unreasonable adverse effects on the environment. The DOA may refuse to license a pesticide if the pesticide or its labeling does not conform to the Pesticides Law or the rules, if the licensee fails to comply with the licensing procedures or if the labeling contains false or misleading information.[122]

The DOA may cancel the license of a pesticide where its continued use would result in unreasonable adverse effects on the environment. The cancellation must be made after the DOA holds a hearing.[123] The DOA may suspend the license of a pesticide during cancellation proceedings without a hearing if it is necessary to prevent an imminent hazard. The suspension remains in effect until the matter is resolved by a hearing and the DOA issues its final order on the matter.[124] The licensee may contest any license refusal, cancellation or suspension through a contested case hearing pursuant to the Hawaii Administrative Procedure Act.[125]

5.2 LABELING AND SALE REQUIREMENTS

The labeling requirements under the Pesticides Law conform to the minimum requirements under FIFRA.[126] The labeling requirements are extremely detailed and are set

---

121 Haw. Admin. Rules § 4-66-34.

122 Haw. Rev. Stat. § 149A-14(a).

123 *Id.* § 149A-14(b).

124 *Id.* § 149A-14(c).

125 *Id.* § 149A-14(d). The Hawaii Administrative Procedure Act is set out in Haw. Rev. Stat. ch. 91. *See infra* ch. 13 of this Handbook.

126 *Id.* § 149A-15.

forth in the administrative rules.[127] In addition to the licensing requirements, sellers or distributors of pesticides must obtain an annual permit from the DOA and keep records of individual sales of licensed pesticides.[128] The records must be kept at the principal place of business and be made available to the DOA upon request. A permit for the sale of pesticides may be denied, suspended or revoked for reasonable cause. The DOA may take such action after a hearing pursuant to the Hawaii Administrative Procedure Act.[129]

By rule, the Department may require the distinct coloration of certain licensed pesticides as necessary to protect public health and the environment.[130]

5.3 SEIZURES, "STOP-SALE" AND "REMOVAL FROM SALE" ORDERS

Any pesticide which is sold, distributed or transported in violation of the Pesticides Law or rules may be seized by the State. Upon entry of a court order, the seized pesticides may be destroyed, sold or returned to the owner for relabeling or reprocessing. A "stop-sale" or "removal from sale" order may also be issued by the Chairperson of the Board or an authorized agent for violation of the Pesticides Law or rules.[131]

5.4 PESTICIDE USE

Generally, pesticides must be used and applied in a manner consistent with their labeling. However, pesticides may be applied at a concentration, frequency or dosage less than that specified on the labeling. Use of a pesticide against a pest different than that specified on the label and the mixture of a pesticide with fertilizer is permitted if that use or mixture is not prohibited by the labeling.[132] Pesticide containers must be stored, transported

---

127 *See* Haw. Admin. Rules, tit. 4, ch. 66.

128 Haw. Rev. Stat. § 149A-17. A pesticide applicator training packet is available from the University of Hawaii, Cooperative Extension Service.

129 *Id.* § 149A-18. *See infra* ch. 13 of this Handbook for discussion of the Hawaii Administrative Procedure Act.

130 2000 Haw. Sess. Laws 154 (to be codified at Haw. Rev. Stat. § 149A-16).

131 Haw. Rev. Stat. § 149A-20.

132 *Id.* § 149A-31.

and discarded in a manner which does not have unreasonable adverse effects on the environment.[133] Some pesticide waste and pesticide containers may be considered hazardous waste and subject to special handling requirements.[134]

Restricted use pesticides must be applied by a certified commercial or private pesticide applicator or under the direct supervision of a certified pesticide applicator.[135] Commercial pesticide applicators are categorized by the type, location and method of pesticide application,[136] and must be certified through an examination given by the State.[137]

Pesticides which are classified for restricted use under FIFRA are also classified as restricted use pesticides under the Pesticides Law and are listed in the administrative rules.[138] In addition, the Board may classify other pesticides for restricted use if they meet certain toxicity criteria, pose a health hazard, are anticipated to be fatal to an endangered species or are anticipated to result in significant population reductions in non-target species. Currently, approximately ninety pesticides are classified as restricted use pesticides.[139] Restricted use pesticide dealers are required to obtain a license from the DOA and maintain certain records.[140]

5.5 SPECIAL LOCAL NEED AND EXPERIMENTAL USES

A pesticide for a special local need which is not present on a nationwide or regional basis may be registered if it does not cause unreasonable adverse effects on persons or the environment. The labeling, packaging and coloration requirements for these pesticides are the same as required under FIFRA and under the Hawaii rules. Pesticides registered for special

---

133 *Id.* § 149A-31(2).

134 *See supra* ch. 6 of this Handbook.

135 Haw. Rev. Stat. § 149A-31(4).

136 Haw. Admin. Rules § 4-66-56.

137 *Id.* §§ 4-66-57 to -58.

138 *Id.* § 4-66-32(d).

139 Haw. Rev. Stat. § 149A-2; Haw. Admin. Rules § 4-66-32.

140 Haw. Admin. Rules. §§ 4-66-52 to -53.

local needs must specify "for distribution and use only within the State of Hawaii" on the label.[141] For example, in Hawaii, pesticides for special local needs may be registered for local crops such as sugar, pineapple, orchids, anthuriums or ginger. The DOA is required to report pesticide registrations for special local need to the Environmental Protection Agency ("EPA").

Experimental use permits may be issued for pesticide products which are to be tested in experimental programs to determine efficacy and potential adverse effects. In Hawaii, pesticides with experimental use permits are routinely tested on flower, fruit and vegetable crops grown locally. Experimental use permits may not be issued for products which contain ingredients which have been cancelled or suspended by the EPA.[142] Experimental use permits are subject to numerous other conditions under both FIFRA and the Pesticides Law.[143]

5.6 EXEMPTIONS

The Department may grant an exemption for experimental or research work directed toward obtaining knowledge of the characteristics and proper usage of unspecified or experimental pesticides. A written research exemption may be granted to the University of Hawaii, other state and federal agencies, or private agencies.[144]

Pesticides exempt from FIFRA § 136w(b)[145] are automatically exempt from the Hawaii Pesticide Law, provided that the product meets the terms and conditions of the EPA's exemption, and the Department has not determined by rule that the pesticide may cause unreasonable adverse effects on the environment.[146]

141 *Id.* §§ 4-66-37 to -41.

142 *Id.* §§ 4-66-45 to -46.

143 *Id.* §§ 4-66-47 to -51.

144 Haw. Rev. Stat. § 149A-37.

145 FIFRA § 25, 7 U.S.C. § 136w(b).

146 2000 Haw. Sess. Laws 154 (to be codified at Haw. Rev. Stat. § 149A-37).

5.7 CANCELLATION OR SUSPENSION OF PESTICIDE USES

In the event that the use of a pesticide is determined to have unreasonable adverse effects on the environment, the use of such pesticide may be cancelled, restricted or suspended by the Chairperson of the Board, with the approval of the Director of Health. Two situations require the DOA to determine whether unreasonable adverse effects exist from the use of a pesticide: the presence of pesticide residues in drinking water, and the use of a pesticide which is approved for special local need for which any use has been suspended or cancelled by the Environmental Protection Agency.[147]

5.8 PESTICIDE USE REVOLVING FUND

In 1996, the Legislature established a pesticide use revolving fund ("Fund"). The Fund consists of fees for licensing, registration and training. The Fund may only be expended to support licensing, certification and education, and compliance monitoring activities.[148] As of July 1, 2000 the Department may also use the Fund for development of integrated pest management strategies, which are defined as a sustainable approach to managing pests by combining biological, cultural, physical, and chemical tools in a way that minimizes economic, health, and environmental risks.[149]

The Department must submit an annual report to the Legislature disclosing all money deposited into and disbursed from the Fund. At the close of each fiscal year, unexpended money in the excess of $250,000 remaining in the Fund lapses to the state general fund.[150]

5.9 ENFORCEMENT MECHANISMS AND PENALTIES

The DOA is authorized to inspect any public or private property for pesticide use and to collect samples.[151] The first violation of the Pesticides Law may result in a warning notice

---

147 Haw. Rev. Stat. § 149A-32.5.

148 *Id.* § 149A-13.5.

149 2000 Haw. Sess. Laws 154 (to be codified at Haw. Rev. Stat. §§ 149A-2 and 149A-13.5).

150 *Id.*

151 *Id.* § 149A-36.

which cites the violation and the necessary corrective action. Administrative penalties may be assessed for violations of the Pesticides Law or the rules.

Administrative penalties for violations committed by a commercial applicator, dealer or distributor or any private person who violates licensing, transport, sale, distribution or pesticide application requirements for commercial purposes may be assessed up to $5,000 for each offense. Administrative penalties may be assessed against private pesticide applicators for violations committed after receiving a written warning from the DOA. Subsequent to receipt of a warning from DOA for the first violation, a private applicator may be assessed a maximum administrative penalty of $1,000 per offense for each violation of the Pesticides Law relating to use of pesticides while on property owned or rented by that person or that person's employer. Procedurally, administrative penalties may be assessed only after the person charged has been given notice and an opportunity for a contested case hearing[152] pursuant to the Hawaii Administrative Procedure Act.[153] The administrative penalty and any proposed action contained in the notice of finding of violation become a final order unless the persons charged make a written request for a hearing within twenty days of receipt of the notice.

In the event the Department is unable to collect an administrative penalty, collection is referred to the attorney general who recovers the amount by court action. In order to prevail in a judicial proceeding to recover an administrative penalty, the attorney general need only show that notice was given, a hearing was held or the time granted for requesting a hearing expired without such a request, an administrative penalty was imposed, and that the penalty remains unpaid.[154]

Criminal penalties may be sought by the State for knowing violations of the Pesticides Law and for improper release of information obtained under FIFRA. A registrant, commercial applicator, dealer, wholesaler or retailer who knowingly violates the Pesticides Law is subject

---

152 Haw. Rev. Stat. § 149a-41(b) as to be amended by 2000 Haw. Sess. Laws 154.

153 *Id.* § 149A-41(b). The Administrative Procedure Act is set out in Haw. Rev. Stat. ch. 91. *See infra* ch. 13 of this Handbook.

154 Haw. Rev. Stat. § 149A-41 as to be amended by 2000 Haw. Rev. Stat. § 154.

to a fine of up to $25,000 or imprisonment for up to one year for conviction of a misdemeanor or both. A private applicator may be fined up to $1,000 or imprisoned for up to a year or both for a knowing violation. Any person who fraudulently uses or reveals information acquired pursuant to FIFRA, Section 3, shall be fined up to $10,000 or imprisoned for up to three years or both upon conviction.[155]

6.0 HISTORIC PRESERVATION AND STATE BURIAL LAWS

In 1976, in response to threats to the historic and cultural heritage of the State from rapid social and economic developments, the State Legislature enacted the Historic Preservation Law.[156] Historic preservation under this law includes research, protection, restoration, rehabilitation and interpretation of structures, objects, districts, areas and sites significant to history, architecture, archaeology or culture of the State, its communities or the nation.[157]

The Historic Preservation Law is implemented through a State historic preservation officer, who is appointed by the Governor,[158] and a Hawaii Historic Places Review Board ("Review Board").[159] A ten member Review Board is established within the Department of Land and Natural Resources ("DLNR"). The Review Board members are appointed by the Governor and include members who are professionals in the fields of sociology, history, architecture and archeology, and a member who is knowledgeable in traditional Hawaiian culture and society.[160] Under the Historic Preservation Law, the DLNR is responsible for determining the depository for artifacts or other materials generated or recovered through historic preservation projects taking place on State lands. The DLNR itself may serve as the

---

155 *Id.* § 149A-41(c).

156 Act approved May 13, 1976, ch. 104, § 2, 1976 Haw. Sess. Laws 172 (codified at Haw. Rev. Stat. ch. 6E).

157 Haw. Rev. Stat. § 6E-2.

158 *Id.* § 6E-5.

159 *Id.* § 6E-5.5(a).

160 *Id.*

depository for any specimen or object of natural, historical or archaeological value, or the object or specimen may be delivered to the Bishop Museum.[161]

6.1 STATE BURIALS LAW

The DLNR's State Historic Preservation Division currently responds to two or three inadvertent burial site discoveries each week, and is involved in up to 250 burial cases annually. Since 1991, approximately 3,000 sets of Native Hawaiian skeletal remains have been reinterred.[162]

In 1990, partly in response to the removal of 1,100 Hawaiian remains from an ancient graveyard at Honokahua, Maui, the State Legislature passed the State Burials Law.[163] The State Burials Law amends the Historic Preservation Law by establishing procedures for determining the proper treatment of Hawaiian burials, and establishes penalties for violation of the Law.

The Burials Law is supplemented by administrative rules of practice and procedure ("Burials Rules") relating to burial sites and human remains which became effective September 28, 1996.[164] The Burials Rules apply to sites, other than actively maintained cemeteries, where human skeletal remains are known to be present, and appear to be over fifty years old. The Burials Rules also apply to any burial goods already removed from a site which appear to be over fifty years old.[165]

The Burials Law and Burials Rules create the Island Burial Councils ("Councils") for Hawaii, Maui/Lanai, Molokai, Oahu and Kauai/Niihau, which decide upon proper treatment of previously identified burials and assist in a statewide inventory of unmarked Hawaiian

161 *Id.* § 6E-6.

162 http://www.state.hi.us/dlnr/hpd/hpburials.htm (visited August 9, 2000).

163 Act approved July 3, 1990, ch. 306, 1990 Haw. Sess. Laws 955.

164 Haw. Admin. Rules, Title 13, Chapter 300.

165 *Id.* § 13-300-3.

burial sites.[166] The Councils have between nine and fifteen members and are comprised of at least one representative from each geographic region of the island and representatives of development and large property owner interests. Regional representatives possess an understanding of Hawaiian culture, history, customs, practices, and in particular, beliefs and practices relating to the care and protection of native Hawaiian burial sites and ancestral remains and burial goods.[167] The primary responsibility of the Councils is to determine preservation or relocation of previously identified native Hawaiian burial sites.[168]

6.2 PROCEDURAL RULEMAKING

The DLNR may adopt, amend or repeal rules implementing the Burials Law pursuant to petition or upon its own motion in compliance with the Hawaii Administrative Procedure Act.[169] Any rulemaking petition must disclose the petitioner's interest in the subject matter, draft text of the proposed rules, a designation of rules and laws affected by the petition, an explicit statement of the reasons for the petition, and any other relevant facts, views or arguments.[170] After receipt of petition and consultation with other government agencies, group representatives and Hawaiian organizations, the DLNR will either deny the petition or initiate rulemaking procedures within 180 days.

A notice of any proposed rulemaking is published in a general circulation newspaper and in each county affected by the proposed rules at least thirty days prior to the date set for any hearing. Notices will also be mailed to all persons have submitted a written request to DLNR for advance notice of rulemaking proceedings. Hearings may only be conducted on less than thirty-day notice if an agency finds an imminent peril to public health, safety or morals and states in writing the reasons for its finding. Any rules adopted pursuant to the

---

166 Haw Rev. Stat. § 6E-43.5 and Haw. Admin. Rules § 13-300-21.

167 Haw Rev. Stat. § 6E-43.5(a)-(b) and Haw. Admin. Rules § 13-300-22.

168 Haw. Admin. Rules § 13-300-24.

169 Haw. Rev. Stat. ch. 91. *See infra* ch. 13 of this Handbook.

170 Haw. Admin. Rules § 13-300-11.

abbreviated hearing procedure are considered "emergency rules" which are only effective for less than 120 days without renewal.[171]

The DLNR is required to conduct a public hearing to receive testimony and evidence, and must fully consider all written and oral submissions before taking final action in a rulemaking proceeding.[172]

6.3 BURIAL SITE IDENTIFICATION

Burial sites can be identified by oral or written testimony regarding the location and description of a burial site. The council or the DLNR will evaluate the testimony. The Council will make recommendations to DLNR whether to accept testimony presented regarding a native Hawaiian burial site. Sites will be classified as "previously identified" if they are recognized by the DLNR, as are burial sites discovered during archaeological inventory surveys that appear to be over fifty years old.

The DLNR has developed a statewide inventory of approximately 38,000 known historic properties. The inventory expands at the rate of approximately 1,000 new sites per year. Records on these properties are included in over 3,500 archaeological reports housed in DLNR's library, and the DLNR is now in the process of developing computerized inventory so it will be accessible via the State's geographic information system.[173] The DLNR is also required to develop an inventory which identifies and documents burial and reburial sites based on consultation with knowledgeable persons, inspection and documentation of the burial site. Where lineal descendants disagree with the recording of information, no information is placed in the inventory, but is instead maintained in a tax map key record so that the burial site is protected from harm. Landowners are notified by writing of burial site information pertaining to their properties.[174]

---

171 *Id.* § 13-300-12.

172 *Id.* § 13-300-13.

173 http://www.state/hi.us/dlnr/hpd/hpinvntory.htm (visited August 9, 2000).

174 Haw. Admin. Rules § 13-300-28 and 13-300-31.

Whenever the DLNR is reviewing a permit for a parcel in which a burial site is located, or where activity is known which may cause harm to a burial site, DLNR immediately notifies any known lineal descendants.[175]

The DLNR evaluates the ethnicity of all skeletal remains based upon oral or written evidence of histories, traditions, genealogies, and archaeological evidence. When archaeological evidence establishes ethnicity beyond a reasonably belief, the evaluation ends, and further oral or written information is not gathered. When the oral and written information also does not establish ethnicity, osteological evidence is used if the DLNR proposes to preserve a burial site in place.[176]

Human skeletal remains over fifty years old may not be examined without DLNR authorization to evaluate ethnicity. Any physical examinations must be conducted in a respectful manner with recognition of the sensitivities associated with deceased human beings.[177]

6.4 HANDLING OF HUMAN SKELETAL REMAINS

There is a prohibition on the private possession of human skeletal remains over fifty years old which have been knowingly removed or which originated from a Hawaii burial site. Such possession does not amount to a violation if the remains were voluntarily turned over to DLNR by September 26, 1998. The DLNR may only authorize possession of skeletal remains where possession is an ethically acceptable practice, the remains were manufactured into artifacts prehistorically, where an established lineal or cultural descendant wishes to possess the remains or authorizes possession by a third person, or where remains are being temporarily curated by a private archaeological firm until reburial occurs.[178]

175 *Id.*

176 *Id.*

177 *Id.* § 13-300-32.

178 *Id.* § 13-300-41.

Human skeletal remains reasonably believed to be Native Hawaiian may only be photographed after consultation with known lineal descendants and the appropriate council.[179]

It is unlawful to offer to sell or exchange any exhumed human skeletal remains over fifty years old or associated burial goods. Without prior written authorization from DLNR, it is also unlawful to remove such remains or goods from the jurisdiction of the State. Written applications must be made to the DLNR requesting authorization to remove items from State jurisdiction, and must include the specific reasons for removal, the written consent of lineal descendants, and a description of any lineal relationship. The application will be reviewed by the DLNR, any known lineal descendants, and either the Island Burial Council or an appropriate ethnic organization. Requests will be granted or denied within forty-five days.[180]

6.5 NOTIFICATION OF INADVERTENT DISCOVERY OF BURIAL SITES

Under the State Burials Law, at any site (other than an actively used cemetery) where human skeletal remains are discovered or known to be buried, and appear to be over fifty years old, the remains and their associated burial goods may not be moved without DLNR approval.[181] Upon accidental discovery of a burial site, all disturbing activity in the immediate area that could damage the remains or the potential historic site must cease, and the burial remains must be left in place.[182] The discovery is to be reported as soon as possible to the Historic Preservation Division of the DLNR,[183] as well as the appropriate medical examiner or coroner, and the county police.[184] If the discovery occurs on a

---

179 *Id.* § 13-300-1.

180 *Id.* § 13-300-42.

181 Haw. Rev. Stat. § 6E-43(a).

182 *Id.* § 6E-43.6(a).

183 The State Historic Preservation Division, DLNR, can be reached by phone at (808) 692-8015 or by fax at (808) 692-8020.

184 Haw. Rev. Stat. § 6E-43.6(b).

Saturday, Sunday or holiday, a report must be made to the division of conservation and resource enforcement.[185] The DLNR is to notify the appropriate Island Burial Council and the Office of Hawaiian Affairs.[186]

Once notification of inadvertent discovery has been made, DLNR assures that all activity in the immediate area of human skeletal remains ceases and that appropriate action to protect the integrity and character of the burial site from damage is undertaken. The DLNR will also assure that a representative of the medial examiner or coroner's office and a qualified archaeologist determines whether the skeletal remains are over fifty years old. DLNR will also conduct any necessary site inspection, gather information to help document the nature of the burial context, notify the regional burial council member, inform the landowners and determine whether to relocate or preserve the skeletal remains in place.[187]

6.6 JURISDICTION OVER BURIAL SITES

Inadvertent discovery of native Hawaiian skeletal remains and burial goods on land managed by the department of Hawaiian home lands is governed by applicable provisions of the Native American Graves Protection and Repatriation Act.[188] At other locations, however, if the remains are under fifty years old, they come under the county police department jurisdiction. If the coroner determines the remains are historic or prehistoric burials, fifty years old or older, however, the DLNR is to gather sufficient information, including oral tradition, to document the nature of the burial context and determine appropriate treatment of the remains.[189] DLNR will send staff to the burial site to decide whether to preserve the burial in place or relocate the remains. The DLNR will complete its evaluation within one to three working days depending upon site location and the number of skeletons present.[190]

---

185 Haw. Admin. Rules § 13-300-40. The Division of Conservation and Resource Enforcement, DLNR, can be reached by phone at (808) 587-0077.

186 Haw. Rev. Stat. § 6E-43.6(b).

187 Haw. Admin. Rules § 13-300-40.

188 *Id.* § 13-300-40(o) and 25 U.S.C. § 3001.

189 Haw. Rev. Stat. § 6E-43.6(c).

190 Haw. Admin. Rules § 13-300-1.

The DLNR is statutorily exempt from Department of Health rules pertaining to permitting requirements prior to exposure, removal, disinterment, reburial, or any other act related to human skeletal remains within DLNR jurisdiction.[191]

6.7 DETERMINATIONS TO PRESERVE IN PLACE OR RELOCATE REMAINS

The determination of whether to preserve a burial in place or relocate remains is made by the DLNR in consultation with the landowner and any known lineal or cultural descendants. If Native Hawaiian skeletal remains are involved, DLNR must consult with the appropriate Island Burial Council. Where human skeletal remains are reasonably believed to be non native Hawaiian, the DLNR makes preservation or relocation decisions after consultation with appropriate ethnic organizations.[192]

An Island Burial Council's decision to preserve in place or relocate the burial is to be guided by a number of considerations. These considerations include the site's preservation value, the concentration of skeletal remains, the burial's association with important individuals and events, and the existence of known lineal descendents.[193] The Council's determination must be rendered within forty-five days of referral by the DLNR.[194] Council determinations may be administratively appealed pursuant to the Hawaii Administrative Procedure Act.[195]

Within ninety days following the final determination to preserve in place or relocate remains, the burial site component of a preservation or mitigation plan must be approved by the DLNR.[196] When preservation in place is not possible, DLNR or the property owner will develop a plan to properly reinter the burial at another location. Intentional removal of skeletal remains or burial goods is prohibited until a relocation determination is made by

191 *Id.* § 13-300-3 (f).

192 *Id.* 13-300-40.

193 Haw. Rev. Stat. § 6E-43(b).

194 *Id.*

195 *Id.* § 6E-43(c). *See infra* ch. 13 of this Handbook.

196 Haw. Rev. Stat. § 6E-43(d) and Haw. Admin. Rules § 13-300-40(h).

DLNR. Temporary removal may be authorized by DLNR to protect remains or burial goods from imminent harm, until a determination is made.[197]

6.8 REMOVAL OF SKELETAL REMAINS OR BURIAL GOODS

Removal is to be overseen by a qualified archaeologist and a mitigation plan must be prepared by or with the concurrence of the DLNR.[198] In discoveries where land development activities are taking place, the landowner, permittee or developer is responsible for executing a mitigation plan, preservation plan or archaeological data recovery plan including relocation of remains. In the event of knowing noncompliance with the plan resulting in the direct or indirect taking, appropriation, excavation, injury, destruction or alteration of any a burial site, the landowner, permittee or developer is subject to statutory and administrative penalties.[199] In the absence of land development activities, these responsibilities fall upon the DLNR. The DLNR is responsible for verification of the successful completion of the mitigation plan.[200]

The DLNR is to determine the place of relocation after consultation with the Island Burial Council, property owners, representatives of the relevant ethnic group and any identified lineal descendents, as appropriate. Relocation of the remains must conform to Department of Health requirements and may also include traditional ceremonies, as determined by the lineal descendents. Additional expenses from special reinterment requests are to be paid by the affected descendents.[201] Project activities may resume once the necessary archaeological excavations have been completed.[202]

---

197 Haw. Admin. Rules § 13-300-40(k)

198 Haw. Rev. Stat.. § 6E-43.6(c).

199 Haw. Admin. Rules § 13-300-40(l) and (n).

200 Haw. Rev. Stat. § 6E-43.6(e).

201 *Id.* § 6E-43.6(f).

202 *Id.* § 6E-43.6(e).

6.9 BURIAL SITES ON STATE LANDS

Before the State may approve any project involving a permit, land use change or other entitlement for use which may effect a burial site, the agency or office is required to advise the DLNR and allow review of the effect of the proposed project on the burial site. The DLNR must inform the public of any such project proposal, even if it is not otherwise subject to the requirements of a public hearing or other public notification.[203] The proposed project may not begin or continue until the DLNR has given its written concurrence.

The historic preservation program provides for acquisition of burial sites in fee or in any lesser interest by gift, purchase, condemnation, devise, bequest, land exchange or other means to be held in trust by the State.[204] Burial sites located on lands or under waters owned or controlled by the State are to be held in trust for preservation or proper disposition by the lineal or cultural descendents.[205] The State may transfer burial sites under its jurisdiction only upon consulting the appropriate Island Burial Counsel.[206]

6.10 ENFORCEMENT AND PENALTIES

Under the State Burials Law, any person may maintain an action for restraining orders or injunctive relief. This relief may be sought against the State or any person, upon a showing irreparable injury, for the protection of a burial site. The Attorney General may also bring an action in the name of the State for restraining orders or injunctive relief to restrain and enjoin violations of the Law.[207]

The Historic Preservation Law makes it unlawful for any person to knowingly take, appropriate, excavate, injure, destroy or alter any burial site or its contents located on private or State lands except as permitted by the DLNR. Violators are subject to fines of not more

---

203 *Id.* § 6E-42(a).

204 *Id.* § 6E-3(11).

205 *Id.* § 6E-7(c).

206 *Id.* § 6E-7(d).

207 *Id.* § 6E-13.

than $10,000 for each separate offense. Each day of continued violation constitutes a separate offense.[208]

If the violator directly or indirectly has caused the loss of, or damage to, a burial site, the violator may be fined an additional amount determined by the court to be equivalent to the value of the loss or damaged burial site. Furthermore, equipment used by a violator for the taking, appropriation, excavation, injury, destruction, or alteration of a burial site, or for the transportation of the violator to or from the burial site, shall be subject to seizure and disposition by the State without compensation to its owner or owners.[209] Any person who knowingly violates these provisions with respect to burial sites may also be "blacklisted" and prohibited from participating in the construction of any State or County funded project for ten years.[210]

The State Burials Law also prohibits the offer for sale or exchange of any exhumed prehistoric or historic human skeletal remains or associated burial goods, or the removal of those goods or remains from the jurisdiction of the State without obtaining a permit. Each object or part of a human skeleton or burial good offered for sale, or removed from the jurisdiction, constitutes a separate offense.[211] Removal of skeletal remains and associated burial goods without a DLNR permit is punishable by a fine of up to $10,000.[212]

Violators of the State Burials Law are also subject to prosecution for the crime of desecration pursuant to Hawaii Penal Code.[213] Desecration includes the intentional damaging or physically mistreating of a place of burial in such a way that the defendant knows will outrage the sensibilities of persons likely to observe or discover his or her action.

---

208 *Id.* § 6E-11 and Haw. Admin. Rules § 13-300-43.

209 *Id.* § 6E-11(c).

210 *Id.* § 6E-11(d).

211 *Id.* § 6E-12.

212 Haw. Admin. Rules § 13-300-42(f).

213 Haw. Rev. Stat. § 711-1107. *See also id.* § 6E-11(b).

The crime of desecration is a misdemeanor under the Hawaii Penal Code and carries a potential imprisonment term of one year.[214]

6.11 APPEALS

Any person aggrieved by a council determination to preserve in place or relocate native Hawaiian skeletal remains and burial goods may submit a written petition for an appeals panel to hold a contested case proceeding. Petitions for contested case proceedings must be filed within forty-five days following receipt of written notification of a council determination.[215]

After the presiding officer determines that a contested case hearing is required, the DLNR will serve a notice of hearing on the parties no less than fifteen days prior to the hearing. Notice will also be published in general circulation newspapers of the State and within the county from which the appeal is being taken.[216] The hearing officer may admit the applicant, the landowner, known lineal descendants and persons with a substantial interest in the matter. However, the presiding officer may deny an application to be a party when the petitioner's position is substantially the same as the position of a party already admitted and where admission will not add substantially new information or will render proceedings inefficient and unmanageable.

The appeals panel presiding over the contested case hearing will consist of three members of the board of land and natural resources and three council chairpersons. The presiding officer will only vote in the event of a tie. Appeals panel members may not sit in on proceedings in which they have a pecuniary or business interest.[217]

The appeals panel will hold a prehearing conference and conduct the hearing. Witnesses, documents or records may be subpoenaed and the presiding officer will rule on

---

214 Haw. Rev. Stat. § 711-1107.

215 Haw. Admin. Rules §§ 13-300-51 and 13-300-52.

216 *Id.* § 13-300-53.

217 *Id.* §§ 13-300-55 and 13-300-62.

the admissibility of all evidence. Any motions must be made in writing, and must be accompanied by an affidavit or memorandum setting forth the grounds on which they are based. Within ninety days of the hearing, the appeals panel will render its formal written findings, conclusion and decision and order approving or denying the request to preserve or relocate the burial site.[218]

Parties aggrieved by the appeals panel decision may obtain judicial review under the Hawaii Administrative Procedure Act.[219]

7.0 RADIATION CONTROL

The Northwest Interstate Compact on Low-level Radioactive Waste Management ("Compact")[220] provides the substance of the Hawaii Radioactive Waste Management Law.[221] The Compact was enacted in 1985 to provide regional disposal sites for low-level radioactive waste pursuant to the federal Low-Level Radioactive Waste Policy Act of 1980, which requires states to provide disposal capacity for waste generated within the State by January 1986 or risk being excluded from out-of-state disposal sites.[222] The Compact establishes regulatory requirements for the packaging and transportation of the waste, and places the duties of inspection and enforcement on the party states. The states eligible to become party to the Compact are Alaska, Hawaii, Montana, Oregon, Utah, Washington and Wyoming.[223]

Facilities located in the party states may not accept low-level radioactive waste generated outside any of the party states, unless the Compact Committee approves the acceptance. The Compact Committee is comprised of one official from each party state.[224]

---

218 *Id.* §§ 13-300-56, -57, -58, -59, -60, -64.

219 Haw. Rev. Stat. ch. 91. *See infra* ch. 13 of this Handbook.

220 Authorized by the Omnibus Low-Level Radioactive Waste Interstate Compact Act of 1986, 42 U.S.C. § 2021d.

221 Haw. Rev. Stat. ch. 339K.

222 42 U.S.C. § 2021c.

223 Haw. Rev. Stat. ch. 339K, art. III.

224 *Id.* § 339K-1, arts. IV and V.

Hawaii generators of low-level radioactive waste must comply with the regulatory requirements of the Compact in order to dispose of the waste outside of Hawaii. In particular, all shipments of low-level waste must comply with the packaging and transportation requirements of the host state which is accepting the waste.[225]

Pursuant to the general, administrative, and industrial hygiene provisions for the Department, the Department is authorized to implement rules regarding sources of ionizing radiation.[226] Hawaii therefore implemented Radiation Control rules on November 12, 1999. The Rules set minimum standards for all persons and facilities who receive, possess, use, transfer, own, or acquire any source of radiation and also to all persons who provide radiation services.[227]

7.1 LICENSING

The Hawaii Radiation Control Rules establish licensing requirements for sources of radiation, the licensing of persons providing radiation services, and the licensing of persons transporting radioactive material to a carrier for transport.[228] The Rules contain a long list of radiation machines exempt from licensing requirements, including televisions and electronic equipment that produces radiation incidental to its operation at below a specified dose rate.[229] The Rules also exempt material regulated by the U.S. Nuclear Regulatory Commission.[230]

---

225 *Id.* art. III.

226 Haw Rev. Stat. §§ 321-11 and 321-71.

227 Haw. Admin. Rules § 11-45. This Handbook will not address Hawaii's occupational exposure rules, rules pertaining to industrial radiographic operations, rules regarding the use of x-rays or radionuclides in the healing arts, rules regarding health physics services and medical physics services, rules regarding wireline services operations and subsurface tracer studies, or rules regarding therapeutic radiation machines contained in Title 11, Chapter 45 of the Hawaii Administrative Rules.

228 *Id.* § 11-45-17.

229 *Id.* § 11-45-18.

230 *Id.* § 11-45-3.

Facilities which do not have a current license may not assemble or install a radiation machine. Likewise, sources of radiation may not be transferred to facilities which do not have a current license.[231]

License applications must be submitted sixty days before engaging in the following activities: acquiring or operating any radiation machine; acquiring, storing manufacturing, using or handling any radioactive material; selling, leasing or installing radiation machines; furnishing radiation machine servicing; furnishing radiation services for radioactive materials; providing health or medical physics services; or transporting or delivering radioactive material to a carrier for transport.[232]

Applications must be submitted on forms furnished by the Department and should contain information regarding the facility, the purpose of radiation use, a listing of each radiation machine and radioactive materials, the curriculum vitae and board certification for applicants for health or medical physics services, and an identification of the radiation machine installer. The application must also be accompanied by a non-refundable filing fee ranging from $30 to $100 as required by the schedule contained in the Hawaii Radiation Control Rules. The applicants' signatures constitutes their agreement to comply with the Rules. If the Director fails to act on a completed application within sixty days, the application is automatically granted.[233]

Licenses will be issued to applicants determined to meet the requirements of the Hawaii Radiation Control Rules, and licenses must be posted in a location visible to individuals utilizing the facility.

Licenses will expire biennially on the date specified by the Department, and can be renewed before the expiration date by submitting a renewal application. Renewal applicants must be in compliance with the Hawaii Radiation Control Rules, however at the Director's

---

231 *Id.* § 11-45-27.

232 *Id.* §§ 11-45-22(a) – (d).

233 *Id.* § 11-45-22.

discretion, if corrective actions are acceptable, renewal will be allowed in the event of noncompliance. The license will renew automatically if the Director fails to act on a completed renewal application within sixty days. Licenses not renewed are declared defunct.[234]

7.2 CONSTRUCTION REQUIREMENTS

Any facility utilizing sources of radiation must comply with shielding evaluation and area radiation survey requirements. Before construction or modification, the construction plans must be submitted to the Department for review and approval. Construction plans must show the location of the radiation source, the general direction of x-ray beams, the location of windows, doors and operators' booths, the structural composition, dimensions and thickness of walls, doors, partitions, floors and ceilings, room dimensions, the type of occupancy of all spaces adjacent, above and below radiation sources and, if there is an exterior wall, the distances to the closest area where it is likely that individuals may be present.

Facilities must utilize the services of a qualified medical physicist to determine shielding requirements and provide the Department with a written shielding evaluation report. Shielding evaluations are optional for dental, podiatric or other facilities as determined by the Department.[235]

To determine compliance with radiation protection standards, facilities must also have a qualified medical physicist conduct an area radiation survey within six months after beginning operations. Within thirty days of completion of the survey, the licensee must forward the radiation survey report to the Department. Subsequent radiation surveys are required if there is a change in the number of radiation sources, the spatial relationship to the radiation sources relative to walls, partitions, doors, floors or ceilings, or the workload or utilization of the radiation source.[236]

234 *Id.* § 11-45-24.

235 *Id.* § 11-45-33.

236 *Id.* § 11-45-34.

7.3 TRANSPORTATION

Persons who transport radioactive material or who deliver radioactive material to a carrier for transport must have a license.[237] Licensees who transport radioactive material outside of the confines of their premises or who deliver radioactive material to a carrier for transport must comply with the U.S. Department of Transportation regulations and assure that any special instructions needed to safely open the package are sent to the consignee. If the U.S. Department of Transportation regulations are not applicable to a shipment for any reason, licensees must nonetheless conform to the standards and requirements of those regulations as if they did apply.[238]

Before any source of radiation currently licensed by another state or the U.S. Nuclear Regulatory Commission is brought to Hawaii, the person proposing to bring the source must give written notice to the Department at least seven working days before the source is brought to Hawaii. The notice must include the type of radiation source, information about the proposed use, the exact locations where the source will be used, stored and secured, along with a copy of the license issued by either the U.S. Nuclear Regulatory Commission or another state.[239]

7.4 LABELING AND STORAGE REQUIREMENTS

The radiation symbol is the three bladed design specified by the Hawaii Radiation Control Rules.[240] The radiation symbol must be conspicuously etched or stamped on any source, source holders, or device components containing radiation sources subjected to high temperatures. Facility areas must be posted with appropriate signage denoting radiation areas, high radiation areas, very high radiation areas, airborne radioactivity areas, or the presence of radioactive materials. Caution signs need not be posted if the radiation source is present for less than eight hours, provided that the radiation sources are constantly attended and the area is subject to the licensee's control. Caution signs are also not required for hospital patient rooms

---

237 *Id.* § 11-45-22(d) and 11-45-23(e).

238 *Id.* §§ 11-45-205 and –206.

239 *Id.* §11-45-30.

240 *Id.* §§ 11-45-63 and Appendix D.

provided that the patient could be released from confinement, for certain low-level sources, and for the presence of diagnostic x-ray systems used solely for healing arts purposes.[241]

Each container of licensed material must contain a durable, clearly visible label bearing the radiation symbol and the appropriate caution warning. The label must also provide additional information regarding the licensed material. Before disposal of empty, uncontaminated containers, the radioactive material label must be removed or defaced. Radiation machines must be labeled in a conspicuous manner which cautions individuals that radiation is produced when the machine is energized.[242] The rules provide certain exemptions to labeling requirements, including exemptions based on quantity, concentration, accessibility, or other exemptions applicable to containers in transport which are packaged and labeled in accordance with U.S. Department of Transportation Regulations.[243]

Radiation sources stored in controlled or unrestricted areas must be secured from unauthorized removal or access. Radioactive material, which is not in storage or in a patient, must be maintained under constant surveillance, whether or not it is in a controlled or unrestricted area.[244]

7.5 RADIOACTIVE WASTE DISPOSAL

Radioactive material may only be disposed by transfer to an authorized recipient, by decay in storage, by release in effluents or as otherwise authorized by the Hawaii Radiation Control Rules. Incineration may only be used for disposal if approved by the Department. Disposal by release into sanitary sewerage is only permitted if the material meets requirements

241 *Id.* §§ 11-45-64 and –65.

242 *Id.* § 11-45-67.

243 *Id.* § 11-45-67.

244 *Id.* §§ 11-45-61 and 62.

for solubility, quantity, and number of radionuclides.[245] County ordinances, however, may contain their own prohibition against disposal of radioactive material.[246]

Persons who receive radioactive waste from third parties must be specifically licensed to treat the waste before disposal, to incinerate the waste, to decay the waste in storage, or to store the radioactive material before it can be transferred to an authorized disposal facility.[247]

Transfer of low-level radioactive waste to a disposal facility must be documented by shipment manifests and must meet waste generator certification standards established by the Northwest Compact in Low-Level Radioactive Waste Management.[248] Waste disposal records, including records for disposal by release into sanitary sewerage or by incineration, must be kept for three years.[249]

7.6 RECORDKEEPING

Licensees are required to maintain records showing the receipt, transfer and disposal of all sources of radiation.[250] The licensee must also keep the following records for three years: radiation protection programs, records of surveys, records for tests for leakage or contamination of a sealed source, records of prior occupational dose, records of planned special exposures, records of individual monitoring results, and records of dose to individual members of the public. Records of testing entry control devices for very high radiation areas must be retained on an indefinite basis. The licensee must maintain adequate safeguards against tampering with and loss of records.[251]

---

245 *Id.* § 11-45-70 through -73.

246 *See e.g.*, Honolulu, Haw., Rev. Ordinances, § 14-1.9(g)(12) (rev. April 12, 2000); Maui, Haw., Maui County Code § 14.21A.015(11) (February 2000).

247 Haw. Admin. Rules § 11-45-70.

248 *Id.* § 11-45-75.

249 *Id.* § 11-45-85.

250 *Id.* § 11-45-6(a).

251 *Id.* §§ 11-45-78, -79, -80, -81, -82, -83, -84, -86 and -87.

7.7 REPORTING AND NOTIFICATION REQUIREMENTS

Persons who sell, lease, transfer, lend, dispose, assemble, or install components of radiation machines must submit notification to the Department within fifteen days of such activities. The notification must identify the person receiving the machine, provide information about each radiation machine transferred, and the date of transfer or machine components.[252]

For the installation of diagnostic x-ray systems which contain certified component, a copy of the assembler's report prepared in compliance with federal standards must be submitted to the Department within fifteen days following completion of the assembly

If any test of a sealed source indicates leakage or contamination, the licensee must file a report with the Department within five days describing the equipment involved, the test results, and the corrective action taken.[253]

Licensees must submit reports of lost, stolen or missing sources of radiation. Immediate telephone reporting is required for missing radiation machines or if the missing radioactive material exceeds a specified quantity and it appears to the licensee that an exposure to individuals in unrestricted areas could result. The telephone reporting requirement is delayed for thirty days for smaller quantities of missing material.

Following an initial telephone report regarding lost, stolen or missing sources of radiation, licensees are required to make a written report to the Department within thirty days. The written report must include a description of the radiation source, the circumstances under which the loss or theft occurred, information about possible and actual exposures, actions taken to recover the material, and procedures adopted to ensure against recurrence. After the written report is filed, the licensee has a duty to report additional substantive information within thirty days of learning such information.[254]

---

252 *Id.* § 11-45-27.

253 *Id.* § 11-45-96.

254 *Id.* § 11-45-88.

Immediate reporting by telephone, telegram, mailgram or facsimile is also required if radiation sources cause or threaten to cause individuals to receive specified dose equivalencies or if radioactive material is released inside or outside a restricted area so that if any individuals had been present for twenty-four hours, they would have received an intake five times greater than the occupational annual limit on intake. Reporting may be delayed for twenty-four hours for lower dose equivalencies or lower multiples of the occupational annual limit on intake.[255]

Licensees must submit written notification within thirty days for certain threatened or actual exposures, or for levels of radiation or concentrations of radioactive material in excess of applicable license limitations or regulatory requirements. Reports must describe the extent of individual exposure, including dose estimations, the levels of radiation and concentrations of radioactive materials, the cause, and corrective steps taken or planned to ensure against a reoccurrence. Reports also must include identification information for exposed individuals.[256]

Planned special exposures must be reported in writing to the Department within thirty days and must disclose that a planned special exposure was conducted, the date, and the exceptional circumstances requiring the planned exposure, the name of the management official who authorized the planned exposure, what actions were necessary and why, what precautions were taken, what individual and collected doses were expected, and the actual doses.[257]

Licensees must submit a written notice of intent to vacate premises which may have been contaminated with radioactive materials as a result of the licensee's activities. This notification must be submitted to the Department in writing thirty days before vacating or relinquishing possession or control of the premises. If the Department deems it necessary, the licensee must decontaminate the premises in the manner specified by the Department.

---

255 *Id.* § 11-45-89.

256 *Id.* § 11-45-90.

257 *Id.* §§ 11-45-91 and –82.

7.8 INSPECTIONS

The Department is required to inspect and examine radiation facilities in order to determine their compliance with the Hawaii Radiation Control Rules. Licensees are required to afford the Department entrance to inspect sources of radiation and facilities where sources of radiation is used or stored.[258] Facilities which are not in compliance will receive written notification.[259]

Upon receipt of an inspection report, licensees must complete any required corrective action within the time specified by the Department. Extensions of time to complete corrective action must be submitted to the Department in writing before the specified completion date.[260]

7.9 ENFORCEMENT

The Director may order any alleged violators to appear before the Director and answer the allegations of noncompliance. The notice and order must comply with the Hawaii Administrative Rules.[261] The Director may also issue an order requiring immediate action to protect the public health from imminent and substantial danger, and provide an opportunity for a hearing within twenty-four hours. The Director may also institute a civil action for the enforcement of any orders.[262]

---

258 *Id.* § 11-45-6.

259 *Id.* § 11-45-4.

260 *Id.* §11-45-6(e).

261 Haw. Rev. Stat. § 91. *See infra* ch. 13 of this Handbook.

262 Haw. Admin. Rules. § 11-45-5.

CHAPTER 12

HAWAII ENVIRONMENTAL COMMON LAW

1.0 INTRODUCTION

Environmental statutes and regulations now provide detailed prohibitions and remedies to address almost every area of environmental concern. Generally, however, these statutes and regulations do not displace prohibitions and remedies available under the common law. This chapter examines several common law doctrines which may apply to matters affecting the environment.

2.0 NUISANCE

Under the doctrine of nuisance, the common law provides causes of action for environmentally damaging activities, either by way of an action for damages, or an equitable action to restrain the continuance of the wrong.

Hawaii has had numerous statutes providing for the abatement of particular activities amounting to nuisances.[1] In 1972, however, Hawaii's common nuisance law[2] was repealed, leaving no general statutory authority for abatement of such nuisances. Nevertheless, the Hawaii Intermediate Court of Appeals held that in the absence of such statutory law, the circuit courts in equity may enjoin such activities on a showing that they do in fact constitute a nuisance.[3]

In a case in which plaintiff was struck by a telephone pole floating in the waters of a public beach, the Hawaii Supreme Court defined nuisance to include:

> that which unlawfully annoys or does damage to another, anything that works hurt, inconvenience, or damage, anything which annoys or disturbs one in the free use, possession, or enjoyment of his

1 *Marsland v. Pang,* 5 Haw. App. 463, 479, 701 P.2d 175, 188 (1985).

2 Haw. Rev. Stat. Ch. 727 (repealed 1972). The common nuisance laws had enumerated various acts and activities constituting nuisance. *See Marsland, supra*, 5 Haw. App. at 480 n.16, 701 P.2d at 188 n.16.

3 *Marsland, supra*, 5 Haw. App. at 480, 701 P.2d at 190.

> property or which renders its ordinary use or physical occupation uncomfortable, and anything wrongfully done or permitted which injures or annoys another in the enjoyment of his legal rights.[4]

Hawaii's case law as to which specific activities or events constitute nuisance relative to health and the environment is sparse. In one case regarding an overhanging banyan tree, the court held that non-noxious plants are ordinarily not nuisances, but constitute a nuisance only when they actually cause or there is imminent danger of them causing harm to property other than plant life, in ways other than by casting shade or dropping leaves, flowers or fruit.[5]

The Hawaii Supreme Court has defined public nuisance as follows:

> A nuisance, to be a public nuisance, must be in a public place, or where the public frequently congregates, or where members of the public are likely to come within the range of influence; for, if the act or use of property be in a remote and unfrequented locality, it will not, unless malum in se, be a public nuisance (citation omitted)...If the nuisance affects a place where the public has a right to go, and where the members thereof frequently congregate, or where they are likely to come within its influence, it is a public nuisance.[6]

Hawaii has defined an individual's right to sue for public nuisance. In a case involving the right to use formerly public trails to the beach, the Hawaii Supreme Court held that it is not required that an individual's injury be different in kind than that of the community at large. To have standing to sue, the plaintiff need only show injury in fact, and that the concerns regarding a possible multiplicity of lawsuits are satisfied by any means, including a class action.[7]

The abatement of nuisances that may be dangerous or injurious to health is within the

---

4 *Littleton v. State*, 66 Haw. 55, 67, 656 P.2d 1336, 1344 (1982), *citing* 58 Am. Jur. 2d., Nuisances § 1 at 555 (1971).

5 *Whitesell v. Houlton*, 2 Haw. App. 365, 367-68, 632 P.2d 1077, 1079 (1981).

6 *Littleton, supra,* 66 Haw. at 67, 656 P.2d at 1344, *citing City of Burlington v. Stockwell*, 47 P. 988, 989-90 (Kan. App. 1897).

7 *Akau v. Olohana Corp.*, 65 Haw. 383, 388-89, 652 P.2d 1130, 1134 (1982).

jurisdiction of the State of Hawaii, Department of Health ("Department").[8] The statute does not, however, define such nuisances.[9] Commentary on the statute notes that this section does not authorize the Department to declare something to be a nuisance that is not a nuisance.[10]

Hawaii has detailed environmental protection laws, and these state statutes on air,[11] noise[12] and water pollution[13] also give the authority for enforcement to the Director of Health. These prohibitions against polluting activities may serve to designate the impermissible activities as nuisances for purposes of a personal suit, but this has not been tested in the Hawaii courts.

A Hawaii statute prohibits the criminal use of a noxious substance, and it imposes a misdemeanor penalty on knowingly depositing on the premises or in the vehicle of another "any . . . device, irritant or offensive smelling substance, with the intent to interfere with another's use of the premises or vehicle."[14] According to the commentary on this section, this action formerly fell under the repealed common nuisance law.

Certain agricultural activities which might otherwise be considered actionable as nuisances are protected by the Right to Farm Act.[15] This Act prohibits the declaration of any farm operation as a nuisance if the operation has been lawfully in operation, using reasonable care, for at least a year, unless some aspect of the operation has been determined previously to be injurious to the public health or safety, or the nuisance aspect of the operation has been shown to

---

8 Haw. Rev. Stat. § 322-1 (Michie 1999). All references to the Hawaii Revised Statutes made to the printed version of the statutes current through the 1999 legislative session, unless otherwise noted. Where appropriate, references to acts passed during the 2000 legislative session have also been added.

9 *Id.* Ch. 322.

10 *See Akwai v. Royal Ins. Co.*, 14 Haw. 533, 537 (1902).

11 Haw. Rev. Stat. Ch 342B.

12 *Id.* Ch.342F.

13 *Id.* Ch. 342D.

14 *Id.* § 708-828.

15 *Id.* Ch. 165.

result from injurious conducting of the activity.[16] This protection exists whether a complaint designates such claims as brought in nuisance, negligence, trespass or any other area of law or equity; however, the protection does not extend to nuisances from water pollution or flooding. For the purposes of the Right to Farm Act, nuisance is defined as any interference with reasonable use and enjoyment of land, including but not limited to smoke, odors, dust, noise or vibration.[17]

3.0 INTENTIONAL TORTS

Claims for intentional tortious conduct may be brought in connection with a release of a hazardous substance, pollutant or contaminant. In Hawaii, claims for trespass or infliction of emotional distress are possible tort theories.

3.1 TRESPASS

In some jurisdictions, claims of trespass can be brought against polluters whose pollution intrudes on another's property. However, under Hawaii law, trespass is limited to intrusions onto the property of another by a person[18] or animal.[19] Trespass by intrusion of substances or inanimate objects under another's control is not included in the statutory definition of trespass or in the case law of Hawaii.

Trespass has also been used as a basis to bring claims against the State for an alleged diversion of a stream from its State-maintained ditch reservation onto a landowner's property. *Anderson v. State*, [20] involved claims that the State diverted the Pa'iakuli Stream across privately owned land. Although the Intermediate Court of Appeals did not reach a detailed discussion of

---

16 *Id.* § 165-4.

17 *Id.* § 165-2.

18 Haw. Rev. Stat. §§ 708-813, -814, -815, which cover criminal and simple trespass, all refer to unlawful entry by a person.

19 Haw. Rev. Stat. §§ 142-63, -64, -65 refer to trespass on another's property by animals such as cattle and horses.

20 *Anderson v. State,* 88 Hawai'i 241, 965 P.2d 783 (1998).

trespass issues, it did analyze the applicable two-year statute of limitations.[21] Although Anderson knew of the diversion many years earlier, the court ruled that the stream diversion was a "continuing trespass," and thus fell within an exception to the two-year limitations period. Therefore, the court concluded that where an actor continuously diverts water over which he or she has direct control, and the diversion causes continuous and substantial damage to that persons property and the actor knows of this damage, such an act may present evidence of a continuous tort.[22]

3.2 INFLICTION OF EMOTIONAL DISTRESS

In Hawaii, no party is liable for the negligent infliction of serious emotional distress if the distress arises solely out of damage to property or material objects.[23] Any party making a claim for negligent infliction of emotional distress must therefore prove physical injury to a person.[24]

Environmentally damaging conduct may lead not only to claims for physical damage, but claims for negligent or intentional infliction of emotional distress. Courts may be reluctant to award damages for mental distress unless accompanied by physical injury. In *Rodrigues v. State*, however, a case brought under the State Tort Liability Act in which plaintiffs' home was flooded due to a blocked drainage culvert, the Hawaii court created a cause of action for mental anguish independent of any claims for physical injuries claimants personally may or may not have suffered.[25] The court created a "reasonable person" standard, holding that serious mental distress may be found when a reasonable person, normally constituted, would be unable to cope adequately with the mental stress engendered by the circumstances of the case.[26]

---

21 Haw. Rev. Stat. § 662-4.

22 *Id.*, 88 Haw. at 250, 965 P.2d at 792.

23 Haw. Rev. Stat. § 663-8.9.

24 *Calleon v. Miyagi*, 76 Haw. 310, 876 P.2d 1278 (1994).

25 *Rodrigues v. State*, 52 Haw. 156, 472 P.2d 509 (1970).

26 *Id.* 52 Haw. at 173, 472 P.2d at 520.

The *Rodrigues* court held that the general standard of proof required to support such a claim of mental distress is some guarantee of genuineness and seriousness of the claim in the circumstances of the case.[27] The plaintiff must also show his or her serious mental distress was a reasonably foreseeable consequence of the defendant's act.[28]

With *Rodrigues*, Hawaii became the first jurisdiction to eliminate the physical injury requirement for recovery for serious mental distress.[29] Hawaii also does not distinguish between mental distress suffered from witnessing injury to another and distress resulting from the destruction of one's property. Further, medical testimony concerning the plaintiff's fear or distress is not necessary in order to award a reasonable amount of damages.[30]

This principle has been applied in asbestos cases. In 1990, the federal court applied Hawaii law, citing *Rodrigues*, to find plaintiff's fear of cancer from exposure to asbestos gave rise to an independent cause of action in negligence, rather than being an element of damages in a products liability claim.[31] The federal court held, however, that Hawaii law required that plaintiff show compensable harm (i.e., some functional impairment, not just a physiological effect) underlying the emotional distress, before recovery may be had for mental anguish from fear of cancer from exposure to asbestos.[32]

4.0 NEGLIGENCE

A Hawaii appellate court applied the law of negligence, as it relates to dangerous agencies and instrumentalities, to a case involving harm done by the unannounced release of highly chlorinated water by the Board of Water Supply.[33] Although the court found chlorine, as

---

27 *Id.* 52 Haw. at 172, 472 P.2d at 519.

28 *Id.* 52 Haw. at 174, 472 P.2d at 521.

29 *Campbell v. Animal Quarantine Station*, 63 Haw. 557, 560, 632 P.2d 1066, 1068 (1981).

30 *Id.* 63 Haw. at 564, 632 P.2d at 1071.

31 *In re Hawaii Fed. Asbestos Cases*, 734 F. Supp. 1563, 1569 (D. Haw. 1990).

32 *Id.* 734 F.Supp. at 1567.

33 *Kajiya v. Department of Water Supply*, 2 Haw. App. 221, 224, 629 P.2d 635, 639 (1981).

a poisonous or dangerous chemical, to be an inherently dangerous substance, the court declined to apply the strict liability standard typically applied to high explosives.[34] Rather, in this case of first impression in Hawaii, the court adapted the "dangerous force" rule to such dangerous agencies. The court held that liability for negligence with respect to dangerous instrumentalities includes a duty to warn, provided that the persons in control of the instrumentality knew or should have known the instrumentality to be dangerous and if the danger is not obvious and apparent to those endangered.[35]

The same Hawaii court also declined to apply strict liability for hazardous activity against a sugar cane company whose burning activities, which were part of harvest operations, caused smoke to obscure the road, resulting in an automobile accident.[36] The trial court judge granted a directed verdict on the strict liability issue, after which the jury found the defendant, who had placed warning signs and flagmen in the road, not negligent.[37] The court determined that negligence *per se* occurs where an act or omission is contrary to statutory duty, or is so opposed to the dictates of common prudence that it can be said without hesitation or doubt that no careful person would have committed it.[38] The court defined negligence *per se* as it might apply to such situations, but declined to address this theory as it was not raised by the parties at trial.

The application of *res ipsa loquitur* doctrine in some jurisdictions raises a presumption of negligence, shifting the burden of proof to the defendant.[39] However, under Hawaii law, *res ipsa* merely establishes a prima facie case of negligence.[40] In a wrongful death action for the explosion of an atomic simulator in Hawaii, the Ninth Circuit Court of Appeals held nothing bars

---

34 *Id.* 2 Haw. App. at 224 n.4, 629 P.2d at 639 n.4.

35 *Id.* at 226, 629 P.2d at 640.

36 *Bloudell v. Wailuku Sugar Co.*, 4 Haw. App. 498, 501 n.6, 669 P.2d 163, 167 n.6 (1987).

37 *Id.* 4 Haw. App. at 499, 669 P.2d at 166.

38 *Id.* 4 Haw. App. at 502 n.7, 669 P.2d at 167 n.7 (citations omitted).

39 *Jenkins v. Whittaker Corp.*, 785 F.2d 720, 732 (9th Cir. 1986).

40 *Id.* 785 F.2d at 733; *Turner v. Willis*, 59 Haw. 319, 324-25, 582 P.2d 710, 714 (1978).

application of *res ipsa* to strict liability.[41] Hawaii courts have permitted recovery in strict liability based on *res ipsa*-like theories of circumstantial evidence.[42]

It is well settled in Hawaii that nonjudicial government officials do not have absolute immunity from tort suits arising out of the performance of their public functions.[43] A public official can be held liable for general, special and punitive damages if it is found that in exercising official discretion the official was motivated by malice and not by an otherwise proper purpose.[44]

While Hawaii recognizes tort liability for the violation of a statute, a statutory duty extends only to those persons for whose protection or benefit the statute was enacted, and for injuries of the character the statute was designed to protect against.[45] Generally, the required standard of conduct may be determined by reference to a statute.[46] However, compliance with established statutory and administrative standards is not necessarily conclusive on the issue of negligence.[47]

In a case with important implications for environmental torts, the Hawaii Supreme Court allowed the concept of market-share liability where a hemophiliac who tested HIV-positive after transfusions of blood products sued manufacturers of the blood products.[48] The Court compared this case to "mass" toxic tort cases in which traditional rules of negligence can no longer be

---

41 *Jenkins*, 785 F.2d at 733.

42 *Id.*

43 *Kajiya*, 2 Haw. App. at 226, 629 P.2d at 640.

44 *Id.* 2 Haw. App. at 227, 629 P.2d at 640.

45 *Namuu v. City & County of Honolulu*, 62 Haw. 358, 362, 614 P.2d 943, 946 (1980) (police not negligent for failure to apprehend escaped mental patient).

46 *Ono v. Applegate*, 62 Haw. 131, 137, 612 P.2d 533, 539 (1980) (statute prohibiting sale of alcohol to person under the influence of intoxicating liquor imposes a duty of care).

47 *Pickering v. State*, 57 Haw. 405, 408, 557 P.2d 125, 127 (1976) (highway guard rail designed in conformity with established federal standards).

48 *Smith v. Cutter Biological, Inc.*, 72 Haw. 416, 823 P.2d 717 (1991).

applied.[49] The Court, however, held that a defendant could escape such liability if the defendant could show that it had no product on the market at the time of plaintiff's injury.[50]

5.0 STRICT LIABILITY

No case law in Hawaii has imposed strict liability for environmental damage. Strict products liability is available in Hawaii if the plaintiff shows that the manufacturer is engaged in the business of selling the product, that the product contains a defect dangerous to the user or customer, and the defect is the cause of the injury.[51]

In Hawaii, state of the art evidence is not admissible in strict products liability actions for purposes of establishing whether the seller knew or reasonably should have known of the dangerousness of the product.[52] State of the art evidence refers to the ability or inability to discover the danger posed by the product at the time the product is marketed in light of the state of scientific knowledge or technology at that time.[53] Since application of strict liability does not require showing that defendant was negligent, the issue of knowledge is irrelevant in a strict products liability case.[54]

It is settled Hawaii law that adherence to government specifications by an asbestos manufacturer is not an absolute defense to liability for the harm done by the product.[55] Applying this principle, the federal district court held that the fact that a defendant manufacturer relied on government specifications for asbestos did not preclude the defendant from compliance with a Hawaii state statutory requirement to warn. Such compliance would not have violated the

---

49 *Id.* 72 Haw. at 428, 823 P.2d at 724.

50 *Id.* 72 Haw. at 439, 823 P.2d at 729.

51 *Johnson v. Raybestos-Manhattan*, 69 Haw. 287, 288, 740 P.2d 548, 549 (1987).

52 *Id.* 69 Haw. at 287, 740 P.2d at 549.

53 *Id.* 69 Haw. at 288 n.1, 740 P.2d at 549 n.1.

54 *Id.* at 288, 740 P.2d at 549.

55 *Nobriga v. Raybestos-Manhattan, Inc.*, 67 Haw. 157, 161-62, 683 P.2d 389, 392 (1984).

defendant's government contract. Accordingly, the government contract defense was not available to the manufacturer when the issue was failure to warn.[56]

The Hawaii Supreme Court has held that pure comparative negligence principles apply to strict liability claims.[57] In a case in which the plaintiff was exposed to asbestos dust and fibers while working in the defendant's shipyard, and was also a smoker, the jury found the plaintiff 51% responsible for his injuries.[58] The court held that the fact that the plaintiff's negligence was found to be greater than the manufacturer's negligence reduced, but did not defeat the plaintiff's claim.[59]

6.0 PUNITIVE DAMAGES

In Hawaii, punitive damages may be awarded when the defendant is shown by clear and convincing evidence to have acted "wantonly or oppressively or with such malice as implies a spirit of mischief or criminal indifference to civil obligations, or where there has been some willful misconduct or that entire want of care which would raise the presumption of a conscious indifference to consequences."[60] Punitive damages would be appropriate for acts which result in environmental harm under such circumstances, although this proposition is as yet untested in Hawaii courts.

The Hawaii Supreme Court has long recognized punitive damages to be recoverable in tort for negligence.[61] Punitive damages may be awarded in products liability cases, even in cases

---

56 *In re Hawaii Fed. Asbestos Cases*, 715 F. Supp. 298, 300 (D. Haw. 1988).

57 *Hao v. Owens-Illinois, Inc.*, 69 Haw. 231, 236, 738 P.2d 416, 418-19 (1987).

58 *Id.* 69 Haw. at 234, 738 P.2d at 418.

59 *Id.* 69 Haw. at 236, 738 P.2d at 419.

60 *Masaki v. General Motors Corp.*, 71 Haw. 1, 13, 780 P.2d 566, 575 (1989) *citing Kang v. Harrington*, 59 Haw. 652, 660-61, 587 P.2d 285, 291 (1978).

61 *Id.* 71 Haw. at 10, 780 P.2d at 572.

based on strict liability.[62] Even though fault is not an element of strict liability, imposition of punitive damages does require a finding of aggravated fault.[63]

The proper measure of punitive damages is based upon the "degree of malice, oppression or gross negligence which forms the basis for the award and the amount of money required to punish the defendant, considering his financial condition."[64]

7.0 REAL PROPERTY TRANSACTIONAL LIABILITY

Hawaii's Environmental Response Law imposes strict liability on the owner or operator of a facility for response costs and damage caused by the release or threatened release of hazardous substances at the facility.[65] When the facility or property is bought and sold, liability for environmental damage caused by any previous releases of hazardous substances may be transferred with the sale.[66] Provisions of the Environmental Response Law were invoked by parties to a suit arising from the removal of underground storage tanks from the Keeaumoku Superblock development in Honolulu. To date, however, Hawaii courts have not addressed the liability of property owners for past releases of hazardous substances.

7.1 STATUTORY DUTY TO DISCLOSE

The Environmental Response Law provides that a property or facility owner or operator who has knowledge of the release or threatened release of a hazardous substance on the property, and subsequently transfers ownership to a buyer without disclosing that knowledge, remains strictly liable as an owner or operator under the statute.[67]

---

62 *Id.* at 11, 780 P.2d at 573; *National Consumer Co-op Bank v. Madden*, 737 F. Supp. 1108, 1114 (D. Haw. 1990).

63 *Masaki, supra,* 71 Haw. at 11, 780 P.2d at 572.

64 *Man v. Raymark Indus.*, 728 F. Supp. 1461, 1465 (D. Haw. 1989).

65 Haw. Rev. Stat. Ch. 128D.

66 *See supra* ch. 8, § 4.0 of this Handbook.

67 Haw. Rev. Stat. § 128D-6(d).

The Environmental Response Law also contains an "innocent landowner" defense. An owner or operator of a facility or property may avoid liability under the statute if (1) the owner or operator acquired the property after the release or placement of the hazardous substance on the property, and (2) at the time the owner or operator acquired the property the owner or operator did not know or had no reason to know, after having undertaken all appropriate inquiry, that any hazardous substance was on the property.[68] These statutory provisions echo the principles of the tort of misrepresentation.

7.2 DISCLOSURE DUTIES OF SELLERS, GENERALLY

There is a general duty on the part of sellers to disclose to the buyer any concealed dangerous conditions known to the seller.[69] The Mandatory Disclosure Law is applicable to the sale of any residential real property.[70]

A seller who knows of physical problems or adverse claims against the subject property and makes representations and agrees to sell the property without informing the buyer of those problems may be guilty of fraud and misrepresentation.[71] The "knowledge" requirement for the tort of fraud may be satisfied if it is shown that the representations were made with a reckless disregard for their truth or falsity.[72]

7.3 DISCLOSURE DUTIES OF BROKERS

A real estate broker has a duty to ascertain and disclose all material facts concerning every property for which the licensee accepts the agency.[73] Similarly, agents or others

---

68 *Id.*

69 *See* Restatement (Second) of Torts §353 (1977).

70 Haw. Rev. Stat. Ch. 508D-2; *see supra* ch. 11, § 1 of this Handbook.

71 *Shaffer v. Earl Thacker Co., Ltd.*, 3 Haw. App. 81, 88, 641 P.2d 983, 988 (1982).

72 *In the Matter of Hawaii Corp.*, 567 F. Supp. 609, 630 (D. Haw. 1983).

73 Haw. Rev. Stat. § 467-14(18).

representing horizontal property regimes are prohibited from making any false or misleading statements or omissions as to the property.[74]

Seller's agents are not required to prepare disclosure statements for residential real property transactions. However, if the seller's agent becomes aware of facts inconsistent with a disclosure statement or an inspection report of a third party, the seller's agent must disclose these facts to the seller, the buyer, and their agents.[75]

8.0 LENDER LIABILITY

Hawaii's Environmental Response Law adopted federal CERCLA principles of lender liability for environmental harm associated with the property in which the lender has a secured interest.[76] Lenders who hold or held a lien or security interest which attached to a facility are not liable persons, provided the lender makes or made no decision which caused or contributed to the release or threatened release from the facility.[77] This secured lender exemption was discussed at length in EPA's former lender liability rule under CERCLA, which protected secured lenders from liability so long as the lender does not participate in the management of the facility.[78] Although a federal appellate court vacated this lender liability rule based on the EPA's lack of authority to promulgate such a rule,[79] the EPA has reaffirmed its intentions to follow this rule as

---

74 *Id.* § 514A-68.

75 Haw. Rev. Stat. § 508D-7.

76 *See* definition of "owner" in Haw. Rev. Stat. § 128D-1. For further discussion of lender liability under Hawaii Environmental Response Law and CERCLA, see the discussion in chapter 8 of this handbook, § 5.1.

77 Haw. Rev. Stat. § 128D-1; 42 U.S.C. § 9601(20)(A).

78 The EPA's lender liability rule was formerly codified at 40 C.F.R. § 300.1100 but was removed from the federal regulations in 1995. *See* 60 Fed. Reg. 33912, 33913 (June 29, 1995).

79 *Kelly v. EPA*, 15 F.3d 1100 (D.C. Cir. 1994), *reh. denied*, 25 F.3d 1088 (D.C. Cir. 1994), *cert. denied*, *American Bankers Ass'n v. Kelley*, 115 S.Ct. 900 (1995).

enforcement policy.[80] It is not known whether the Hawaii courts will choose to adopt the EPA's interpretation of the security interest exemption.

Where title or control of a property is conveyed to state or local government due to bankruptcy or foreclosure, however, the party who owned or operated the facility immediately prior to its conveyance may be liable as an owner or operator.[81]

The EPA's final rule on lender liability with respect to petroleum underground storage tanks limits the liability of lenders that hold a security interest in a petroleum UST or a facility or property on which a petroleum UST is located.[82] The rule also limits the liability of secured lenders who acquire title or deed to a petroleum UST or a facility or property on which a UST is located through foreclosure proceedings. To qualify for this protection, the interest holder must have no responsibility or control over the daily operation of the UST.[83] It is unknown whether Hawaii courts will follow the EPA lender liability rule in determining the liability of secured lenders under the UST law.

9.0 CRIMINAL LIABILITY

Criminal liability for environmental offenses is statutorily imposed. Air pollution[84] and water pollution[85] control laws, safe drinking water laws,[86] hazardous waste management laws,[87]

---

80 *See* U.S. Environmental Protection Agency, *Policy on CERCLA Enforcement Against Lenders and Government Entities that Acquire Property Involuntarily* (Memorandum, Sept. 22, 1995).

81 Haw. Rev. Stat. § 128D-1, definition of "owner" or "operator." *See supra* ch. 8 of this Handbook.

82 For further discussion of lender liability rules with regard to underground storage tanks, see the discussion in Chapter 7 of this handbook, § 3-2.

83 *See* 60 Fed. Reg. 46,692 (Sept. 7, 1995).

84 *See supra* Chapter 2, § 13.3 of this Handbook.

85 *See supra* Chapter 3, § 7.3 of this Handbook.

86 *See supra* Chapter 4, § 11.0 of this Handbook.

87 *See supra* Chapter 6, § 10.3 of this Handbook.

the Environmental Response Law,[88] the Hawaii Emergency Planning and Community Right-to-Know Act[89] and other environmental laws authorize the imposition of criminal penalties for violations. Criminal sanctions provide an additional method of enforcement against violations of these laws.

In a criminal prosecution for violation of the Hawaii Air Pollution Law, the Hawaii Supreme Court held that corporate officers are not free from personal liability where they perform or authorize the corporation's unlawful acts in violation of such pollution statutes.[90] Hawaii statutory law imposes such personal liability on any agent of a corporation having primary responsibility for discharge of a duty imposed on the corporation.[91] Personal liability may not be imposed on corporate officers who served only as an accommodation and did not participate actively in corporation's affairs.[92]

---

88 *See supra* Chapter 8, § 14.2 of this Handbook.

89 *See supra* Chapter 8, § 16.0 of this Handbook.

90 *State v. Kailua Auto Wreckers, Inc.*, 62 Haw. 222, 230-31, 615 P.2d 730, 736-37 (1980).

91 Haw. Rev. Stat. § 702-228(2).

92 *Kailua Auto Wreckers, supra,* 62 Haw. at 235, 615 P.2d at 738-39.

CHAPTER 13

ADMINISTRATIVE PROCEDURE AND JUDICIAL REVIEW

1.0 ADOPTION OF RULES AND REGULATIONS

The Hawaii Administrative Procedure Act is based on the Model State Administrative Procedure Act and is set forth in the Hawaii Revised Statutes, Chapter 91. For the enforcement of the environmental laws and rules, Chapter 91 provides proceedings less costly and less formal than civil litigation.[1] Pursuant to Chapter 91, the Department of Health ("Department") has adopted rules of practice and procedure which govern access to public records, hearings on contested cases, procedures for rulemaking and special proceedings.[2] As of the date of publication of this Handbook, the Department is in the process of revising its practice and procedure rules.[3] The stated purpose of these rules is to "secure the just, speedy, and inexpensive determination of every proceeding authorized by law."

1.1 RULEMAKING PROCEDURE

The Department may promulgate rules on its own initiative with proper statutory authority or in response to a petition submitted by an interested person.[4] An agency will adopt rules when a statute requires or permits the agency to do so. Also, any interested person may file a petition for rulemaking action. The Department must initiate public rulemaking procedures within thirty days of the filing of the petition or deny the petition in writing.[5]

---

1 Haw. Admin. Rules, tit. 11, ch. 1, part A(1) (Weil's 2000). All references to the Hawaii Administrative Rules are current through the date of publication of this Handbook, unless otherwise noted.

2 Haw. Admin. Rules, tit. 11, ch. 1, Rules of Practice and Procedure

3 Interview with Office of Planning, Policy and Program Development, Hawaii Department of Health (August 2, 2000).

4 Haw. Rev. Stat. § 91-6 (Michie 1999). All references to the Hawaii Revised Statutes made to the printed version of the statutes current through the 1999 legislative session, unless otherwise noted. Where appropriate, references to acts passed during the 2000 legislative session have also been added.

5 Haw. Admin. Rules, tit. 11, ch. 1, part (D)(6).

Prior to adopting, repealing or amending a rule, the Department must give a minimum of thirty days notice for a public hearing.[6] As of January 1, 2000, all state agencies are required to provide notice of each proposed rulemaking action on the lieutenant governor's website.[7] The Department's public notice of its rulemaking must include a general description of the subject matter and the purpose of the adoption, amendment or repeal of the rule. Alternatively, the notice must contain a statement of the substance of the proposed rule to be adopted, amended or repealed. The notice must include the statutory authority for the proposed rulemaking.[8] As a practical matter, the notice must be drafted so that the public can understand the proposal and formulate responses.[9] The department may charge up to a maximum fee of ten cents per page, plus mailing costs for paper copies of any proposed and final rules or for notices or proposed rulemaking actions.[10] The Department generally accepts requests for copies of the rule made by telephone. The place, time and date of the public hearing must be included in the notice, which is also mailed by the Department to all persons who have requested advance notice of rulemaking.

The notice must be published at least once in a newspaper of general circulation.[11] The notice must be published in a statewide paper for state agency rules and in a countywide paper for county agency rules. The Honolulu Advertiser and the Honolulu Star Bulletin usually serve as the Hawaii statewide newspapers. Several different papers may serve for county notices on the neighbor islands. The notices may be placed anywhere in the newspaper: they are not required to be in the legal section.[12] Once notice is given, the Department must allow interested persons to submit comments, arguments and data in writing or orally at the public hearing.[13] If

---

6 Haw. Rev. Stat. § 91-3(a)(1).

7 *Id.* § 91-2.6. Proposed rules are currently posted at http://swat.state.hi.us (August 11, 2000).

8 *Id. See also* Haw. Admin. Rules, tit. 11, ch. 1, part (D)(1)(b).

9 *Costa v. Sunn,* 64 Haw. 389, 642 P.2d 530 (1982). *See also State v. Rowley*, 70 Haw. 135, 764 P.2d 1233 (1988).

10 Haw. Rev. Stat. § 91-2.5.

11 Id. § 91-3(a)(1).

12 Haw. Op. Att'y Gen. 89-4 (1989).

13 Haw. Rev. Stat. § 91-3(a)(2).

the proposed rule affects the neighbor islands, interested persons residing or working on the neighbor islands must be given an opportunity to present testimony at the public hearing. This may be accomplished in two ways: a public hearing may be held on the neighbor island or participation in a public hearing on Oahu may be provided by video conference arrangements.

A sign language interpreter will be provided at the hearing by the Department upon request. Any person with a hearing impairment who desires such assistance at the public hearing must contact the Environmental Planning Office at least seventy-two hours prior to the scheduled hearing.[14]

1.2 PUBLIC HEARING

At a public hearing, the Director or his or her representative serves as the presiding officer. All interested persons must be allowed a reasonable opportunity to testify on the subject matter of the hearing. To that end, testimony may be given orally or in writing at the hearing. Generally, a sign-up sheet is provided at the entrance to the hearing location for those persons wishing to provide testimony at the hearing. The presiding officer then calls in turn each person who has signed up to testify. In addition to or in lieu of presenting testimony at the public hearing, any interested person may submit written comments to the Department after the close of the public hearing.[15] The rules specify that written comments must be submitted within five days after the close of the hearing. In practice however, written comments are accepted up to two weeks after the close of the last public hearing. The deadline for submitting written testimony to the Department is specified in the public notice and announced at the public hearing. The rules also require an original and five copies to be filed with the Department. In practice, only one copy of written testimony must be submitted after the hearing.

After consideration of all the testimony that has been submitted, the Department may make its decision at the close of the hearing or at a later date. If the decision is to be made at a

---

14 *See, e.g.*, Notice of Public Hearing, Docket No. 92-EPO-REG-2, Honolulu Advertiser (June 16, 1992).

15 Haw. Admin. Rules, tit. 11, ch. 1, part D(3).

later date, the presiding officer should announce that date at the close of the public hearing.[16] The decision and adoption of new rules generally takes a minimum of a few months. Changes may be made in a rule between the proposed original version which was presented at a public hearing and the rule as it is finally adopted. If substantial changes are made after the initial public hearing, however, another public hearing may be required.[17]

The adoption, repeal or amendment of administrative rules by the Department is subject to the Governor's approval. Likewise, actions affecting county rules are subject to approval by the county mayor, except that approval is not required for rules governing the county boards of water supply.[18]

The public notice and comment requirements may be waived by the Governor or the mayor if the rules are a condition for federal funding and if no discretion is allowed in terms of interpretation of the federal provisions which govern the rules to be promulgated. However, all such actions must be published in a statewide newspaper to give public notice.[19] If the Department has discretion to interpret the federal provisions in drafting the required rules, waiver of the notice and hearing requirement is not permitted, and if the notice and comment requirements are not satisfied, the rules will be invalidated.[20]

1.3 EMERGENCY RULES

Emergency rules may be adopted by the Department for a maximum period of 120 days without renewal. The emergency rules may be adopted upon less than thirty days notice of hearing, upon no notice of hearing or upon no hearing in the event that the Director finds an imminent threat to public health, safety or morals, or to poultry or livestock health. The Director must determine that such immediate adoption of emergency rules is necessary, and the emergency rules must be published in a general statewide paper within five days of filing the rule

16 *Id.* tit. 11, ch. 1, part D(4).

17 *Ala Moana Boat Owners' Assn. v. State,* 50 Haw. 156, 434 P.2d 516 (1967).

18 Haw. Rev. Stat. § 91-3(c).

19 *Id.* § 91-3(d).

20 *Burk v. Sunn*, 68 Haw. 80, 705 P.2d 17 (1985).

with the Lieutenant Governor. The emergency rules may be renewed or extended by the Department through the normal rulemaking procedure.[21]

1.4 VALIDITY OF RULES

Administrative rules adopted by the standard rulemaking procedure must be approved by the Governor to become effective. Upon approval of the rules by the Governor, the Department must file certified copies of the rules with the Lieutenant Governor. Generally, the rules take effect ten days after filing, unless another date is specified.[22] Copies of the rules are available from the Director's office and are maintained at the Office of the Lieutenant Governor, State Library, State Archives and the University of Hawaii.[23] A small fee may be charged to cover mailing and reproduction.[24]

Procedural challenges to the rulemaking process have been limited by law.[25] Any challenge to the validity of the adoption, amendment or repeal of a rule must be made within three years after the effective date of the rule. This limitations period also applies to actions for declaratory judgment on the validity of rules which are based on noncompliance with statutory procedural requirements. Rules which are not promulgated in accordance with the Hawaii Administrative Procedure Act are invalid and unenforceable.[26]

The adoption, amendment or repeal of a rule cannot be invalidated solely for the Department's failure to mail copies of the proposed rule or advanced notice of rulemaking. The

---

21 Haw. Rev. Stat. § 91-4(b)(2).

22 *Id.* § 91-4(b).

23 *Id.* § 93-3. *See also*, Haw. Op. Att'y Gen. 85-15 (1985).

24 Haw. Rev. Stat. § 91-5.

25 *Id.* § 91-3(e).

26 *Burk v. Sunn,* 68 Haw. 80, 705 P.2d 17 (1985). *See also State v. Rowley*, 70 Haw. 135, 764 P.2d 1253 (1988) (Public notice of rulemaking did not include sufficient information).

Department's failure to mail must have been inadvertent to support this statutory defense in an action or the defense will fail.[27]

2.0 DECLARATORY JUDGMENTS AND RULINGS

Any interested person may get an administrative declaration on the validity of the Department's rules, or petition the Department for a declaratory order as to the applicability of a rule, statute or order to that person.[28] Generally, a formal hearing is not held on a petition for declaratory ruling. However, the petitioner or a party in interest may request a hearing by submitting a request which addresses the need for a hearing and an affidavit which establishes the supporting facts. After review of the petition, the Director may hold a hearing, but is not required to do so. In addition to declaratory orders issued in response to a petition, the Department may on its own motion issue a declaratory ruling to terminate a controversy.[29]

Any interested person may furthermore seek a judicial declaration on the validity of rules. The state circuit courts are granted jurisdiction over actions seeking judicial determination of the validity of rules. Filing a petition for an administrative declaratory ruling is not a prerequisite to filing the judicial action.[30] In addition to issuing a declaratory judgment, the court may grant affirmative, ancillary relief.[31] For instance, the court may reinstate the "old" rules and grant damages pursuant to the old rules.

A state rule may be challenged in federal court on the ground that it is unconstitutional. Before the federal court will accept the case, however, there must be a judicial declaration in state circuit court on the constitutionality of the rule.[32]

---

27 Haw. Rev. Stat. § 91-3(e).

28 *Id.* § 91-8.

29 Haw. Admin. Rules, tit. 11, ch. 1, part E(1).

30 Haw. Rev. Stat. § 91-7.

31 *See Costa v. Sunn*, 5 Haw. App. 419, 697 P.2d 43 (1985); *Jacober v. Sunn*, 6 Haw. App. 160, 715 P.2d 813 (1986).

32 *Cunningham v. Civil Service Comm'n*, 252 F. Supp. 223 (D. Haw. 1966).

3.0 CONTESTED CASES

Contested cases are proceedings which determine the rights, duties and privileges of specific parties.[33] A contested case proceeding provides the forum for resolution of permit applications and violations of environmental laws. A contested case must be required by law. For example, the Hawaii Supreme Court has held that because the Honolulu City Council is exempt from the Hawaii Administrative Procedure Act, and no other law requires it to hold hearings on special management area ("SMA") permit applications under the Coastal Zone Management Act, such hearings are not contested cases because they are not required by law.[34] Where the proceedings are required by law, and the parties' rights, duties and privileges are at issue, hearings for SMA permits are contested case proceedings.[35] Likewise, the Supreme Court has also ruled that although water use permit applications involving the use of water in a designated water management area trigger contested case hearing provisions, the designation of a water management area triggers only the statutorily-designated requirements of the Water Code[36] because the Legislature designated a statutory process which is specific to designation of a water management area.[37]

The Hawaii Attorney General's office ("AG") represents the Department in contested cases. The Department refers violations of environmental laws to the AG for enforcement through administrative, civil and criminal proceedings. Under the Hawaii Administrative Procedure Act, in matters involving a violation of Hawaii environmental laws, a Notice of Violation ("NOV") issued by the Department usually initiates a contested case.[38] NOVs are

---

33 Haw. Rev. Stat. §91-1(5). A public hearing may serve as a contested case in certain situations. *See infra* § 4.0 of this Chapter.

34 *Sandy Beach Defense Fund v. City Council of Honolulu*, 70 Haw. 361, 773 P.2d 250 (1989).

35 *See, e.g., Mahuiki v. Planning Comm'n*, 65 Haw. 506, 654 P.2d 874; *Pub. Access Shoreline Hawaii v. City Planning Comm'n*, 79 Haw. 425, 903 P.2d 1246 (1995).

36 Haw. Rev. Stat. Ch 174C.

37 *Ko'olau Agricultural Co., Ltd. v. Comm'n on Water Resource Management*, 83 Haw. 484, 496, 927 P.2d 1367, 1379 (1996).

38 Haw. Rev. Stat. § 91-9. *See also* Haw. Admin. Rules, tit. 11, ch. 1, part C, which has been superseded in part by Haw. Rev. Stat. § 91-9.

issued by the Department through the AG for violations of most environmental statutes, rules and permit conditions. One exception to the Chapter 91 contested case procedure is provided in the Environmental Response Law, where special administrative review procedures apply.[39]

The NOV must include information regarding the time and location for the hearing, legal authority for the hearing, the statute and rules involved, and the issues and facts alleged by the Department. The NOV must indicate that the party has the right to retain counsel for representation in the contested case. Contested cases may be modified or resolved by stipulation, settlement or a consent order which is executed before the hearing. Parties to a contested case may waive any procedural requirements provided by the Hawaii Administrative Procedure Act.

All parties to the contested case hearing must be given written notice of the hearing at least fifteen days before the hearing by registered or certified mail, return receipt requested. If such service by mail is refused or cannot be made,[40] the Department must publish the notice of hearing at least twice in a newspaper of a general statewide circulation.[41] The Department is required to make a reasonable and diligent inquiry to ascertain the address of each party. At the present time, the newspapers used for general statewide circulation are the Honolulu Advertiser and the Honolulu Star Bulletin.

3.1 CONTESTED CASE PROCEDURE

A basic tenet of the contested case procedure is that all parties have the opportunity to present evidence and argument on all issues involved.[42] The rules do not provide for the exchange of evidence or witness lists prior to the hearing. However, a prehearing conference or a prehearing exchange, such as those provided in federal environmental administrative procedure,[43] may be requested by a party through the presiding officer. This exchange provides an

---

39 *See infra* ch. 8, § 11.2 of this Handbook.

40 Haw. Rev. Stat. § 91-9.5(b).

41 *Id. See also Chock v. Bitterman*, 5 Haw. App. 59, 678 P.2d 576 (1985).

42 Haw. Rev. Stat. § 91-9.

43 *See* Consolidated Rules of Practice, 40 C.F.R. Part 22. Provisions for a prehearing conference are set forth at 40 C.F.R. § 22.19.

opportunity to assess the evidence related to the case and to prepare for the hearing.

The Director may act as the presiding officer of a contested case hearing. The Director may appoint a representative to conduct the hearing and to make recommendations, including findings of fact and conclusions of law, to the Director. The presiding officer is authorized to administer oaths, subpoena witnesses and documents, examine witnesses and certify official acts. The presiding officer may perform any other duty required to conduct the hearing properly. The Director is ultimately responsible for rendering a decision in the matter and issuing any further orders as needed.[44]

In a contested case hearing, which is generally informal, an individual may represent him or herself. For organized business entities, a member of a partnership may represent the partnership, and an officer or employee may represent a corporation, trust or association.[45] Both individuals and organized business entities may be represented by counsel.

The Hawaii Rules of Evidence[46] do not apply in a contested case hearing. The typical objections to admission of evidence such as hearsay, best evidence rule and similar evidentiary restrictions are not applicable in contested case hearings. The Hawaii Administrative Procedure Act requires the Department to admit any and all evidence, limited only by considerations of materiality, relevancy and repetition.[47] The presiding officer may disallow repetitious testimony and may disallow rebuttal testimony which does not involve any new argument or evidence.[48] If the contested case decision receives judicial review, mere admission of irrelevant or incompetent evidence will not be considered reversible error on appeal.[49]

---

44 Haw. Admin. Rules, tit. 11, ch. 1, part C.

45 Haw. Rev. Stat. § 91-9(b)(5).

46 *Id.* ch. 626.

47 *Cazimero v. Kohala Sugar Co.*, 54 Haw. 479, 510 P.2d 89 (1973); *Chock v. Bitterman*, 5 Haw. App. 59, 678 P.2d 576 (1984).

48 *Outdoor Circle v. Harold K.L. Castle Trust Estate*, 4 Haw. App. 633, 675 P.2d 784 (1983); *In Re* Haw. Elec. Co., 67 Haw. 425, 690 P.2d 274 (1984).

49 *Shorba v. Board of Educ.*, 59 Haw. 380, 524 P.2d 84 (1984); *Chock v. Bitterman*, 5 Haw. App. 59, 678 P.2d 576 (1984).

The standard for the receipt of documents into evidence is similarly relaxed. If an original document is not readily available, copies of documents may be received instead, provided the parties are given an opportunity to compare the original and the copy, if so requested. The Department and the presiding officer may take notice of judicially recognizable facts and generally recognizable technical or scientific facts that are within its specialty. Parties must be given notice of those facts and must be given an opportunity to contest those facts. All parties have the right to conduct cross examination of the witnesses and to present rebuttal evidence. The rules of privilege recognized by Hawaii law are applicable in contested cased hearings.[50]

The party who initiates the contested case hearing carries the burden for both production of evidence and for persuasion of the presiding officer, who serves as the fact finder. The standard of proof required in a contested case hearing is a preponderance of the evidence.[51] In cases involving an NOV issued by the Department, the Department must prove all elements of the violation in order to prevail in the case.

In hearings and other instances where the presiding officer has not heard and examined all the evidence, but is ready to render a decision that will be adverse to the private parties, the presiding officer must issue a proposed decision upon the parties and offer the parties an opportunity to file exceptions and present arguments.[52] All orders and decisions that are adverse to a party must be placed in writing or placed on the record. The decision must be accompanied by findings of fact and conclusions of law. The presiding officer must make his or her findings reasonably clear,[53] but a separate ruling on each proposed finding is not required.[54] The presiding officer may incorporate its ruling and its findings in the decision,[55] but merely

---

50 *See* Haw. R. Evid. 501-513. *See also Town v. Land Use Comm'n*, 55 Haw. 538, 524 P.2d 84 (1974).

51 Haw. Rev. Stat. § 91-10.

52 *Id.* § 91-11.

53 *In Re Haw. Telephone Co.*, 54 Haw. 663, 513 P.2d 1376 (1973).

54 *Mitchell v. BWK Joint Venture*, 57 Haw. 535, 560 P.2d 1292 (1977).

55 *In Re Terminal Transp., Inc.*, 54 Haw. 134, 504 P.2d 1214 (1972).

summarizing testimony that was presented at the hearing is not adequate for findings of fact.[56] The presiding officer's findings must be supported by substantial, probative and reliable evidence, but the presiding officer's decision need not be supported by all the evidence submitted.[57] Finally, a certified copy of the decision and order, along with the findings and conclusions, must be mailed or personally delivered to the party or the party's attorney of record.[58]

3.2 ADMINISTRATIVE RECORD

An administrative record is established for all agency decisions. The administrative record for rulemaking generally includes the public notice, written testimony and data, transcript of the public hearing and the report of the hearing officer. The administrative record for a contested case hearing is established by statute and must include the following items: all pleadings, motions, evidence received or considered, offers of proof and rulings, proposed findings and exceptions, report of the officer who presided at the hearing and the staff memoranda which were submitted to the Department in connection with the case. These items comprise the administrative record to which the Director or the presiding officer is limited in making his or her decision in a contested case.[59] Administrative agencies may not consult sources outside the record when acting in an adjudicatory capacity.[60]

4.0 JUDICIAL REVIEW OF CONTESTED CASES

The Hawaii Administrative Procedures Act provides the basis for the circuit court's appellate jurisdiction over agency decisions, allowing "any person aggrieved by a final decision

---

56 *Mitchell v. BWK Joint Venture,* 57 Haw. 535, 560 P.2d 1292 (1977).

57 *Protect Ala Wai Skyline v. Land Use & Controls Comm.*, 6 Haw. App. 540, 735 P.2d 950 (1987).

58 Haw. Rev. Stat. § 91-12; Haw. Admin. Rules, tit. 11, ch. 1, part C(10).

59 Haw. Rev. Stat. § 91-9(e), (g).

60 *Mauna Kea Power Co. v. Board of Land & Natural Resources*, 76 Haw. 259, 874 P.2d 1084 (1994).

and order in a contested case" to seek judicial review.[61] Without participation in a contested case hearing, a party cannot be "aggrieved" within the meaning of the Hawaii Administrative Procedure Act and, therefore has no right to appeal under the Act.[62] The Hawaii Supreme Court has stated that unless a state statute or agency rule mandates a hearing prior to the agency's decision, the circuit court does not have subject matter jurisdiction for purposes of judicial review, unless the agency has violated constitutional due process requirements.[63] For example, a contested case is required for an administrative agency's denial of a proposed property use when property interests are implicated.[64] Administrative hearings held prior to the Department's decision to grant permits for geothermal wells and a power plant were "contested cases" because they were required by due process.[65]

Any person who is aggrieved by a final decision and order rendered in a contested case hearing may seek judicial review of the adverse decision and order. The Hawaii Supreme Court has reviewed and considered each of the following six factors in its determination of whether judicial review of an agency decision is proper: (1) the party was an "aggrieved person" able to show his or her interests were injured or were likely to be injured; (2) the agency decision was final, leaving the claimant with no other recourse than the courts; (3) an agency hearing took place; (4) the hearing was required by statute, rule or the state constitution; (5) the claimant was involved as an adversary in the administrative proceedings; and (6) in participating in the contested case the claimant followed applicable agency rules.[66] Participation as amicus in a

---

61 Haw. Admin Rules § 91-14(a). *See also, Curtis v. Board of Appeals, County of Hawaii*, 90 Hawai'i 384, 394, 978 P.2d 822, 832 (1999).

62 *Alejado v. City & County of Honolulu*, 89 Hawai'i 221, 226, 971 P.2d 310, 315 (1999).; *Pele Defense Fund v. Puna Geothermal Venture,* 77 Hawai'i 64, 70, 881 P.2d 1210, 1217 (1994).

63 *Bush v. Hawaiian Homes Comm'n*, 76 Haw. 128, 870 P.2d 1272 (1994).

64 *Pele Defense Fund v. Puna Geothermal*, 77 Haw. 64, 881 P.2d 1210 (1994).

65 *Id.*

66 *See* Robert Wachter, An Analysis of Standing and Jurisdiction Prerequisites for Direct Appeal of Agency Actions to the Circuit Court Under the Hawaii Administrative Procedure Act After Bush v. Hawaiian Homes Commission and Pele Defense Fund v. Puna Geothermal Venture, 17 U. Haw. L. Rev. 375, 389 (1995).

proceeding is sufficient involvement in the proceeding to qualify as an "aggrieved person."[67] An unincorporated association qualified as a "person aggrieved" by the Hawaii County Council's decision to grant a SMA minor permit application, even though the association did not participate in the contested case.[68] For purposes of judicial review, denial of a motion for reconsideration is a "final" order,[69] as is a decision not to process a permit application.[70] The fact that a party has not formally intervened in the contested case is not necessarily dispositive of whether the party was involved in the proceedings.[71] Environmental and aesthetic interests are adequate to invoke and support judicial intervention.[72] The Hawaii Supreme Court has upheld the relaxed standing requirements for litigants in environmental issues.[73] The Court also found that native Hawaiian subsistence, cultural and religious practices are interests sufficiently distinguishable from those of the general public to grant standing for judicial intervention.[74]

A public hearing which is conducted pursuant to public notice may be considered a contested case, and the decision is reviewable by the circuit court.[75] However, a public hearing is not considered a contested case for purposes of judicial review where the agency has adopted rules of practice and procedure for conducting contested case hearings.[76] The Department has

---

67 *Ariyoshi v. Haw. Public Employment Relations Bd.*, 5 Haw. App. 533, 704 P.2d 917 (1985). *See also City & County of Honolulu v. Public Util. Comm'n,* 53 Haw. 431, 495 P.2d 1180 (1972).

68 *Kona Old Haw. Trails Group v. Lyman*, 69 Haw. 81, 734 P.2d 161 (1987).

69 *McPherson v. City & County Zoning Bd. of Appeals*, 67 Haw. 603, 699 P.2d 26 (1985); *Mitchell v. BWK Joint Venture*, 57 Haw. 535, 560 P.2d 1292 (1977).

70 *GATRI v. Blane*, 88 Haw. 108, 962 P.2d 367 (1998).

71 *Puna Geothermal, supra,* 77 Haw. 64, 881 P.2d 1210 (1994).

72 *Life of the Land v. Land Use Comm'n*, 63 Haw. 166, 623 P.2d 431 (1981).

73 *Puna Geothermal, supra,* 77 Haw. 64, 881 P.2d 1210 (1994). *Cf. United Public Workers, Local 646 v. Brown*, 80 Haw. 376, 910 P.2d 147 (Haw. App. 1996) (holding that allegations of only the possibility of injury, but not concrete injury, were insufficient to establish standing as an aggrieved person).

74 *Pub. Access Shoreline Hawaii v. City Planning Comm'n*, 79 Haw. 425, 903 P.2d 1246 (1995).

75 *In Re App. of Haw. Elec. Co.*, 56 Haw. 260, 264, 535 P.2d 1102 (1975).

76 *Simpson v. Dept. of Land & Natural Resources*, 8 Haw. App. 16, 791 P.2d 1267 (1990).

established such rules of practice and procedure which apply to contested case hearings.[77] Consequently, a public hearing held by the Department would not be subject to judicial review as a "contested case."

Judicial review may be sought for preliminary rulings where deferred review of the final order would deprive the appellant of adequate relief.[78] Judicial review must be sought in the circuit court within thirty days after receipt of the certified copy of the decision and order.[79] The thirty day period commences the day after the agency mails its final decision and order, and the period may be extended by as much as two days by virtue of the agency's effecting service by mail.[80] The Supreme Court dismissed an agricultural firm's appeal of the Commission on Water Resource Management's designation of certain aquifers as groundwater management areas because the notice of appeal was not timely filed.[81]

The reviewing court may order a stay of the Department's enforcement of a decision or the confirmation of any fine if the following criteria are met:

1. The appellant is likely to prevail on the merits of the appeal;
2. The appellant will suffer irreparable damage if the stay is not granted;
3. The public will not suffer irreparable harm from the stay; and
4. The stay will serve the public interest.[82]

The Department must transmit, at its own cost, the administrative record of the contested case on appeal to the reviewing court within twenty days after the record of appeal is

---

77 Haw. Admin. Rules, tit 11, ch. 1.

78 *See generally*, Boyce R. Brown & Anthony Blankley, Standing to Challenge Administrative Action in the Federal and Hawaiian Courts, 8 Haw. Bar J. 37 (July 1971).

79 Haw. Rev. Stat. § 91-14(b).

80 *Price v. Zoning Bd. of App. of Honolulu*, 77 Haw. 168, 883 P.2d 629 (1994).

81 *Ko'olau Agr. Co., Ltd. v. Comm'n on Water Resource Management*, 76 Haw. 37, 868 P.2d 455 (1994).

82 Haw. Rev. Stat. § 91-14.

determined.[83] If new evidence is discovered after the decision but before the appeal, the new evidence may be submitted. The reviewing court, upon request to present additional evidence which is material to the case, may allow the additional evidence to be taken before the Department prior to the judicial review. The Department may review the additional evidence and may then modify its findings, decision and order. Any modifications made by the Department together with the new additional evidence, must be filed with the reviewing court to become part of the record.[84]

4.1 STANDARDS OF REVIEW

The reviewing court sits without a jury, and its review is usually limited to the administrative record. The court will review the issues that were properly raised in the administrative hearing. In addition to reviewing the agency decision, the court may hear constitutional challenges to the statute at the same time.[85] In cases where alleged irregularities have occurred in the contested case hearing which are not reflected in the record, the reviewing court may go beyond the record and receive testimony. In addition, if any party requests that written briefs be submitted and oral agreements be heard, the court shall accommodate the request. After review of the administrative record, the court may affirm the Director's decision, remand the case to the Department for further proceeding, modify or reverse the Director's decision if the appellant's rights have been prejudiced.[86]

The Hawaii Administrative Procedure Act sets forth six standards of review to be applied by the court reviewing the agency's decision. In order for the court to revise or modify an agency decision, it must find that an appellant's substantial rights may have been prejudiced by an agency under one of the six subsections of the statute.[87] Errors of law are reviewed *de novo* by

---

83 *Id.* § 91-14(d). *See also* Haw. Op. Att'y Gen. 64-4 (1964).

84 Haw. Rev. Stat. § 91-14(e).

85 *Id.* § 91-14(f); *HOH v. Motor Vehicle Indus. Licensing Bd.*, 69 Haw. 135, 736 P.2d 1271 (1987).

86 Haw. Rev. Stat. § 91-14(g). For discussion of the appellate standards of review, *see generally,* Michael J. Yoshii, Appellate Standards of Review in Hawaii, 7 U. Haw. L. Rev. 273, 285 (Summer 1985).

87 *In re Hawaiian Elec. Co.*, 81 Haw. 459, 918 P.2d 561 (1996).

the reviewing court.[88] The interpretation of a statute, ordinance or charter is a question of law, reviewable *de novo*.[89] The court is free to interpret and apply the law without restraint.

The clearly erroneous standard applies to the review of factual findings made by the Department or the presiding officer.[90] Under the clearly erroneous standard, a court will not disturb an agency's determination unless, after examining the record, it is left with a definite and firm conviction that a mistake was committed.[91] As a general rule, an agency's decision within its sphere of expertise is given a presumption of validity, and one who seeks to overturn the agency's decision bears the burden of making a convincing showing that it is invalid because it is unjust and unreasonable in its consequences.[92]

The question of whether a determination is a conclusion of law or a finding of fact is a question of law for the reviewing court. Findings of fact must be sufficient so that the reviewing court can trace the steps by which the agency reached its decision.[93]

In review of decisions containing mixed fact and law, the court must determine whether the decision "was affected by other error of law."[94] Mixed questions of fact and law are reviewed under the clearly erroneous standard because such a conclusion is contingent upon the facts and circumstances of he specific case.[95] Where the Department interprets its own rules, the court will generally defer to the administrative decision if the agency's or presiding officer's ruling is

---

88 Haw. Rev. Stat. § 91-14(g)(1)-(4). *See also Dole Haw. Div. Castle & Cooke, Inc. v. Ramil*, 71 Haw. 419, 424, 794 P.2d 1115 (1990).

89 *Korean Buddhist Dae Won Sa Temple of Hawaii v. Sullivan*; 87 Hawai'i 217, 229, 953 P.2d 1315, 1327 (1998).

90 Haw. Rev. Stat. § 91-14(g)(5*); Protect Ala Wai Skyline v. Land Use & Control Comm.*, 6 Haw. App. 540, 735 P.2d 950 (1987).

91 *Windward Marine Resort, Inc. v. Sullivan,* 86 Hawai'i 171, 182, 948 P.2d 592, 603 (1997).

92 *Topliss v. Planning Comm'n*, 9 Haw. App. 377, 842 P.2d 648 (1993).

93 *Kilauea Neighborhood Ass'n v. Land Use Comm.*, 7 Haw. App. 227, 751 P.2d 1031 (1988).

94 Haw. Rev. Stat. § 91-14(g)(4); *Camara v. Agsalud*, 67 Haw. 212, 685 P.2d 794 (1984).

95 *Windward Marine Resort, Inc. v. Sullivan,* 86 Hawai'i 171, 182, 948 P.2d 592, 603 (1997).

consistent with the Legislative purpose of the statute.[96] Accordingly, the court should not substitute its judgment for the agency's judgment.[97] Finally, for administrative decisions which are discretionary with the agency, the "arbitrary or capricious" standard of review is applied by the reviewing court.[98]

4.2 APPEALS

The final judgment of a circuit court reviewing a decision by the Department may be appealed to the Hawaii Supreme Court.[99] Where the circuit court has overturned an agency's decision with respect to implementation of legislation, the agency may appeal as an aggrieved party.[100]

The Hawaii Supreme Court and the Hawaii Intermediate Court of Appeals serve as the appellate courts. The standard of review applied by the appellate court in reviewing the circuit court's review of the agency decision is the *de novo* or "right/wrong" standard.[101] Under the "right/wrong" standard, a "secondary appeal" is completed whereby the appellate court reviews the administrative record directly, without deferring to the circuit court's decision. The appellate court applies the same standards of review provided by statute and applied by the circuit court.[102] An agency's findings of fact are reviewed under the clearly erroneous standard. An agency's conclusions of law are reviewed freely under the *de novo* standard. Finally, in mixed questions

---

96 *Camara v. Agsalud*, 67 Haw. at 215, 685 P.2d at 797; *Topliss v. Planning Comm'n*, 9 Haw. App. at 391 n. 1F, 842 P.2d at 657 n. 11 (1993).

97 *Dole Haw. Div. of Castle & Cooke, Inc. v. Ramil*, 71 Haw. 419, 794 P.2d 1115 (1990).

98 Haw. Rev. Stat. § 91-14(g)(6).

99 Haw. Rev. Stat. § 91-15. For jurisdictional and procedural matters involving the Hawaii appellate courts, *see* Haw. Rev. Stat. ch. 602.

100 *Fasi v. Haw. Pub. Employee Relations Bd.*, 60 Haw. 436, 591 P.2d 113 (1979).

101 *Outdoor Circle v. Harold K. L. Castle Trust Estate*, 4 Haw. App. 633, 675 P.2d 784 (1983). *See also* *Chock v. Bitterman*, 5 Haw. App. 59, 678 P.2d 576 (1984).

102 *Outdoor Circle*, *supra*, 4 Haw. App. 633, 675 P.2d 784 (1983). The appellate court applies the standards set forth in Haw. Rev. Stat. § 91-14(g).

of fact and law, the court will defer to the agency's experience and expertise.[103]

5.0 PUBLIC RECORDS

The Uniform Information Practices Act (Modified) provides the statutory framework for disclosure of public records.[104] All rules, final decisions, orders and written statements of policy are public records which are made available to the public upon request. Permit applications, permit files, inspection reports and related documents also are available to the public for review. In addition, the results of environmental tests must be made available by the Department for public inspection and duplication.[105] For example, the discharge monitoring reports completed under the NPDES program, Water Pollution Statute, are available to the public for review. As a matter of procedure, the records must be requested by submission of a public record form to the Department in the Branch from which the document is requested. The public document form is available from the Department and may be submitted in person or by mail. After the public record form is submitted to the appropriate Branch, the Branch must approve the request, usually through the manager of the Branch. The requested materials are then made available to the requester. The Department must provide a place for review of the documents and assist with arrangements for duplication of the documents. The materials may be mailed out to the requestor for a fee.

Access to public records may be limited or denied in certain instances.[106] The records need not be disclosed if they pertain to prosecution or defense of an action to which the State or Department is a party and if the records would not be discoverable. Some records are protected by federal law and may not be available for public inspection. For example, some documents may not be available to the public for national security reasons.

---

103 *Dole Haw. Div. of Castle & Cooke, Inc. v. Ramil,* 71 Haw. 419, 424, 794 P.2d 1115, 1118 (1990).

104 Haw. Rev. Stat. § 92F. *See also* Haw. Admin. Rules, tit. 11, ch. 1, part B, which has been superseded in part by Haw. Rev. Stat.ch. 92F.

105 Haw. Rev. Stat. § 92F-12(a)(6).

106 *Id.* § 92F-13.

A person who is aggrieved by denial of access to a government record may bring an action against the Department to compel disclosure,[107] and must notify the Office of Information Practices in writing at the time of filing.[108] The action must be brought within two years in state circuit court, who shall review the matter freely, under the *de novo* standard. In such actions, the Department has the burden of proof to show that the nondisclosure was justified. If the Department cannot establish justification for nondisclosure of the records and loses the action, the Department will be assessed the plaintiff's litigation fees.

107 *Id.* § 92F-15.

108 *Id.* § 92F-15.3.

CHAPTER 14
WATER USE

1.0 THE STATE WATER CODE

The Legislature enacted State Water Code[1] ("Water Code") in 1987, finding that the water resources in Hawaii were in need of management and regulation because of shortages of water and a decline in ground water levels. The Water Code was also enacted because there was a great deal of concern regarding the status of water rights.[2] The Water Code recognizes that Hawaii waters are held for the benefit of Hawaii citizens, who are beneficiaries and have a right to have the waters protected for their use.[3] All state waters are subject to regulation under the Water Code.[4]

Under the Water Code, state waters include any and all water on or beneath the surface of the ground, including natural or artificial watercourses, lakes, ponds, or diffused surface water and water percolating, standing or flowing beneath the ground. The streams encompassed by the Water Code include any river, creek, slough or natural watercourse in which water usually flows in a defined bed or channel. However, it is not necessary that the stream flow be uniform or uninterrupted, and the fact that some parts of the bed or channel have been dredged or improved does not prevent the watercourse from being a stream.[5]

The Water Code should be liberally interpreted to obtain maximum beneficial use of waters of the State for purposes such as domestic uses, aquaculture, irrigation and other agricultural uses, power development and commercial and industrial uses. The Water Code should also be liberally interpreted to protect and improve the water quality of the state, to

---

1 Haw. Rev. Stat. Chapter 174C.

2 1987 Haw. Sess. Laws 45, § 1.

3 Haw. Rev. Stat. § 174C-2.

4 *Id.* § 174C-4.

5 *Id.* § 174C-3.

prevent discharges without necessary treatment or other corrective action, and should be applied in a manner which conforms with county land use planning. At the same time, adequate protection should be made for the protection of traditional and customary Hawaiian rights, the protection and procreation of fish and wildlife, the maintenance of proper ecological balance and scenic beauty, the preservation and enhancement of water for municipal uses, public recreation, public water supply, agriculture and navigation.[6]

The Water Code does not abridge or deny the traditional and customary rights of ahupua'a tenants who are descendants of the native Hawaiians who inhabited the Hawaiian Islands prior to 1778. Traditional and customary rights include the cultivation and propagation of taro on one's own kuleana, the gathering of hihiwai, opae, o'opu, limu, thatch, ti leaf, aho cord, and medicinal plans for subsistence, cultural and religious purposes.[7]

The Department of Land and Natural Resources ("DLNR"), through the Commission on Water Resource Management ("CWRM") administers the Water Code. The CWRM is empowered to designate water management areas, establish an instream use protection program,[8] acquire real property, identify areas of salt water intrusion, and to coordinate programs for the development, conservation, control and regulation of water resources.[9] The CWRM must designate an area as a water management area before it may fulfill its obligation to "protect, control, and regulate the use of Hawaii's water resources for the benefit of its people.[10]

---

6 *Id.* § 174C-2.

7 *Id.* § 174C-101.

8 "Instream uses" mean beneficial uses of stream water for significant purposes which are located in the stream and achieved by leaving the water in the stream. Examples of instream uses include maintenance of fish and wildlife habitats, outdoor recreational activities, maintenance of ecosystems, aesthetic values such as waterfalls and scenic waterways, navigation, instream hydropower generation, maintenance of water quality, the conveyance of irrigation and domestic water supplies to downstream diversion points, and the protection of traditional and customary Hawaiian rights. Haw. Rev. Stat. 174C-3.

9 Haw. Rev. Stat. §§ 174C-5 and 174C-14; Haw. Admin. Rules §§ 13-167-3, 13-167-33.

10 *Ko'Olau Agricultural Co. v. Commission on Water Resource Mgt.*, 83 Haw. 484, 927 P.2d 1367 (1996).

The CWRM consists of six members, four of whom are appointed by the Governor, subject to confirmation by the senate. The Board of Land and Natural Resources chairperson serves as the CWRM chairperson, and the Director of health serves as an ex officio voting member.[11] The deputy to the CWRM chairperson is the administrative head of the commission staff and acts under the direction of CWRM to administer and implement the Water Code, rules, and other directives.[12]

In 1988, the CWRM adopted rules to administer the Water Code,[13] including rules of practice and procedure, rules pertaining to: water use, wells, stream diversion works, the protection of instream water use, the Hawaii Water Plan, and the designation and regulation of water management areas.[14] These rules have not been amended since their adoption.

2.0 THE HAWAII WATER PLAN

Recognizing that there is a need for a program of comprehensive water resources planning to address the problems of supply and conservation of water, the Water Code uses the Hawaii Water Plan as the guide for developing and implementing policies.[15] Formerly known as the "state water use and protection plan," the Hawaii Water Plan consists of four parts: (1) a water resource protection plan; (2) a water use and development county, setting forth land use allocations; (3) a state water projects plan; and (4) a water quality plan prepared by the Department of Health.[16] The initial Hawaii Water Plan prepared by various state and county agencies was formally adopted by the CWRM in 1990. Further updates in 1992 were deferred pending additional refinement of plan components. In February 2000, the CWRM proposed a

---

11 Haw. Rev. Stat. § 174C-7; Haw. Admin. Rules § 13-167-7.

12 Haw. Rev. Stat. § 174C-6; Haw. Admin. Rules § 13-167-8.

13 Haw. Rev. Stat. § 174C-8.

14 Haw. Admin. Rules, Title 13, chs. 167, 168, 169, 170 and 171.

15 Haw. Rev. Stat. § 174C-2(b).

16 Haw. Rev. Stat. § 174C-31; Haw. Admin. Rules § 13-170-2.

framework for updating the Hawaii Water Plan to provide focus and additional guidance to each agency responsible for updating specific plan components.[17]

The Hawaii Water Plan directs itself to the achievement of objectives such as the attainment of maximum reasonable-beneficial water use,[18] proper conservation and development of State waters, water control for public purposes such as navigation, drainage, sanitation and flood control, the attainment of adequate water quality and the implementation of water resources policies.[19] The CWRM views the Water Plan as a "living document" which over several plan iterations will result in a truly comprehensive water resource plan. The CWRM realizes that water resource planning is an ongoing process requiring a dynamic framework which results in planning documents that provide alternative strategies addressing future uncertainties.[20]

The Hawaii Water Plan divides the counties into sections conforming as nearly as practicable to hydrological units. For each section, the Plan describes and inventories water resources and systems, presently exercised uses, unused water quantity and potential threats to water resources.[21] The Hawaii Water Plan establishes instream use[22] and protection programs as well as sustainable yield for each hydrologic unit. The "sustainable yield" is the maximum rate at which water may be withdrawn from a water source without impairing the utility or quality of

---

17 State of Hawaii, Department of Land and Natural Resources, Commission on Water Resource Management, *Statewide Framework for Updating the Hawaii Water Plan* at p. 1-2 (February 2000).

18 "Reasonable-beneficial use" means the use of water in such a quantity as is necessary for economic and efficient utilization. The use must be for a purpose and in a manner which is both reasonable and consistent with the state and county land use plans and the public interest. *See* Haw. Rev. Stat. § 174C-3. For a further discussion of "reasonable-beneficial use" *see*, Douglas W. MacDougal, *Private Hopes and Public Values in the "Reasonable Beneficial Use" of Hawai'i's Water: Is Balance Possible?*, 18 U. Haw. L. Rev. 1 (1996).

19 Haw. Rev. Stat. § 174C-31(g); Haw. Admin. Rules § 13-170-2.

20 *Statewide Framework, supra* note 17 at p. 1-2 and 2-1.

21 Haw. Rev. Stat. § 174C-31(h); Haw. Admin. Rules § 13-170-2.

22 *Supra*, note 8.

water source.[23] The instream uses and sustainable yields are then protected by permit conditions under the Water Code's various permitting programs.[24]

The CWRM may use the Hawaii Water Plan to designate certain uses as undesirable based on the nature of the activity, and may also designate uses in connection with a particular water supply source which would result in an enhancement or improvement of water resources for that area. The CWRM is also empowered to add to the Hawaii Water Plan any other information, directions or objectives it feels necessary for county guidance in the administration and enforcement of the Water Code.[25] However, amendments which affect any county may not be adopted without first giving ninety days notice and holding a public hearing.

The CWRM realizes that it faces complexities in addressing water resource planning, including growing competition in designated groundwater management areas for available potable water resources in the aquifers, major changes occurring in the agricultural industry, including the demise of sugar production, and growing public awareness of proposals requiring water resources development projects which result in increased public involvement in the overall strategies for water resource development. The future revisions of the Hawaii Water Plan also face the declining availability of existing and inexpensive water resources, and resulting increased development costs which will make use of alternative water sources such as reclaimed and desalinated water more desirable.[26]

2.1 THE WATER RESOURCE PROTECTION AND WATER QUALITY PLANS

The CWRM recognizes that the water quality plan and the water resource protection plan are the two plan components that are critical to determining water usage and determining strategies for developing water resources.[27] The water resource protection and water quality

23 Haw. Rev. Stat. § 174C-3.

24 *Id.* §§ 174C-31(i) and (j).

25 *Id.* §§ 174C-31(l), (m) and (n).

26 *Statewide Framework, supra* note 17 at pp. 2-2 through 2-3.

27 *Statewide Framework, supra* note 17 at p. 2-5.

plans are developed after study and inventory of existing water resources and the means of conserving and augmenting such resources. In preparing the plan, the CWRM reviews existing and contemplated needs and uses, and studies their effect on the environment, procreation of fish and wildlife, and water quality. The CWRM also studies the quantity and quality of water needed for and existing and contemplated uses, including irrigation, power development, geothermal power and municipal uses. The CWRM identifies rivers or streams which may be placed within a "wild and scenic rivers system" to be preserved and protected. Finally the CWRM studies related matters such as drainage, reclamation, flood hazards, floodplain zoning, dam safety, and selection of reservoir sites, as they relate to the protection, conservation, quantity and quality of water.[28]

The water resource protection plan includes the nature of water resources, hydrological units and their characteristics, existing and contemplated uses, programs to conserve, augment and protect water resources and other necessary elements. The water resource protection plan is then used by the CWRM in connection with the Department of Health to formulate an integrated coordinated program, known as the water resource protection and water quality plan, for the protection, conservation and management of the waters in each county.[29]

Each county prepares a water use and development plan, and appropriate state agencies prepare the state water projects plan. The state water projects plan provides a framework for planning and implementation of water development programs to meet projected water demands for state projects.

2.2 AGRICULTURAL WATER USE PLAN

The Department of Agriculture prepares a plan for agricultural use and development, which is updated and modified as necessary. The plan includes a master irrigation inventory plan which documents irrigation water systems, identifies the extent of needed rehabilitation, subsidizes the cost of repair and maintenance, establishes criteria to prioritize rehabilitation,

28 *Id.* §§ 174C-31(c); Haw. Admin. Rules §§ 13-170-20, 13-170-21.

29 *Id.* § 174C-31(d).

develops a five-year plan for system repair and sets up a long-range plan for system management.[30] The CWRM coordinates the incorporation of the agricultural water use and development plan into the state water projects plan.

2.3 COUNTY WATER USE AND DEVELOPMENT PLANS

The County water use and development plans address the status of water and related land development. The county plans inventory existing water uses for domestic, municipal and industrial users, agriculture, aquaculture, hydropower development, drainage, reuse, reclamation, recharge, and resulting problems and constraints. The county plans look to future land uses and related water needs, and include regional plans for water development.[31] Each county must update and modify its plans as necessary to maintain consistency with its zoning and land use policies.

2.4 WATER QUALITY PLAN

The Department of Health is required to administer the Hawaii water quality control program, and in 1999 the Legislature required the Department of Health to formulate a state water quality plan for existing and potential sources of drinking water. The Water Quality Plan has become part of the Hawaii Water Plan, and like the Hawaii Water Plan it is periodically reviewed and revised.[32] Further amendments of the water quality plan are awaiting the results of the Department of Health's source water assessment program, currently scheduled for completion in December 2001.[33]

---

30 *Id.* § 174C-31(e).

31 *Id.* § 174C-31(f); Haw. Admin. Rules §§ 13-170-30 through –32.

32 Haw. Rev. Stat. §§ 174C-66, 174C-68; Haw. Admin. Rules §§ 13-170-50 through -55.

33 For further discussion of the Department of Health's source water assessment program, *see infra* ch. 4, § 2.1 of this Handbook.

3.0 DECLARATION AND CERTIFICATION OF WATER USE

Persons making use of State waters from a well or stream diversion works, were required to file a water use declaration within one year of the effective date of the water rules, or by May 27, 1989.[34] Once a declaration was filed, and the CWRM determined that the use was reasonable and beneficial, the CWRM issued certificates describing the use. The usage confirmed by the certificate is recognized by the CWRM, subject to verification and updating, in resolving claims relating to existing water rights and uses including appurtenant rights, riparian and correlative use. Persons adversely affected by either a certification, or a refusal to certify a use, may require the CWRM to hold a hearing.[35]

When certified uses of water are terminated, the certificate holder must file a report with the CWRM.[36]

4.0 INSTREAM USE PROTECTION PROGRAM

The CWRM has established and administers a statewide instream use[37] protection program to protect, enhance and reestablish beneficial instream uses of water. The program establishes instream flow standard on a stream-by-stream basis whenever necessary, establishes interim instream flow standards, requires baseline research and hydrologic investigation on stream systems, identifies and documents significant instream uses and existing stream water development, monitors flow standards and establishes a permit system to regulate the alteration of any stream channel alteration.[38]

Each instream flow standard describes the flows necessary to protect the public interest in the particular stream. Flows are expressed in terms of variable flows of water necessary to

---

34 Haw. Rev. Stat. § 174C-26; Haw. Admin. Rules § 13-168-5.

35 Haw. Rev. Stat. § 174C-27; Haw. Admin. Rules § 13-168-6.

36 Haw. Admin. Rules § 13-168-6(c).

37 *Supra*, note 8.

38 Haw. Rev. Stat. § 174C-71; Haw. Admin. Rules § 13-169-20 through – 23.

adequately protect fishery, wildlife, recreational, aesthetic, scenic, or other beneficial instream uses in light of existing and potential water developments.

4.1 PROCEDURE FOR ESTABLISHING INSTREAM FLOW STANDARDS

Instream flow standards are the quantity or flow of water or depth of water required at a specific stream system location at certain specified times of the year to protect fishery, wildlife, recreational, aesthetic, scenic, and other beneficial instream uses.[39] The CWRM may act on its own motion and determine that public interest requires the establishment of instream flow standards. After giving notice of its intention to set instream flow standards, a stream investigation is conducted in consultation with other county, state and federal agencies. The CWRM is required to give notice and hold a hearing on any proposed instream flow standards.[40] As of the date of publication of this Handbook, no instream flow standards have been adopted, and the DLNR is in the process of revising its procedural rules regarding the stream designation process.[41]

4.2 PROCEDURE FOR ESTABLISHING INTERIM INSTREAM FLOW STANDARDS

An interim instream flow standard is a temporary instream flow standard of immediate applicability which is adopted by the CWRM without the need for a public hearing, and terminating upon the establishment of an instream flow standard.[42] Interim instream flow standards were adopted for East Maui, Kauai, Hawaii and Molokai in October 1988, for West Maui and Leeward Oahu in December 1988 and for Windward Oahu in May 1992.[43]

Pending the establishment of instream flow standards for areas not yet designated, persons with proper standing may petition the CWRM to adopt interim instream flow standards

---

39 Haw. Rev. Stat. § 174C-3.

40 Haw. Rev. Stat. § 174C-71; Haw. Admin. Rules § 13-169-30 through -36.

41 Interview with Roy Hardy, Commission on Water Resource Management, August 14, 2000.

42 Haw. Rev. Stat. § 174C-3.

43 Haw. Admin. Rules §§ 13-169-44, 13-169-45, 13-169-46, 13-169-47, 13-169-48, 13-169-49, and 13-169-49.1.

in order to protect the public interest. In considering the petition, the CWRM will weigh the importance of the present or potential instream values with the importance of the present or potential uses of water for noninstream purposes. The CWRM will also weigh the economic impact of restricting use.[44] The CWRM will act upon petitions for interim instream flow standards within 180 days, and the any interim instream flow standards may be adopted on a stream-by-stream basis or may consist of a general instream flow standard applicable to all streams within a specified area.[45]

All interim instream flow standards terminate automatically upon the establishment of an instream flow standard for the stream.[46]

5.0 DESIGNATIONS OF WATER MANAGEMENT AREAS

The CWRM may designate water management areas after conducting scientific investigations and research, and making a reasonable determination that existing or proposed withdrawals or diversions of water may threaten water resources in an area. The CWRM may also designate water management areas without conducting scientific investigations for any area in which serious disputes regarding water use is occurring. Designation establishes administrative control over withdrawals and diversions of ground and surface waters in the area to ensure reasonable-beneficial use[47] of water resources in the public interest.[48]

Designated ground water areas established under the former Ground Water Use Act,[49] including all of Oahu's north shore and leeward areas, except for the Waianae area, continued as

44 Haw. Rev. Stat. § 174C-71; Haw. Admin. Rules § 13-169-40.

45 Haw. Rev. Stat. § 174C-71; Haw. Admin. Rules § 13-169-40 through .

46 Haw. Admin. Rules § 13-169-43.

47 *Supra* note 18.

48 Haw. Rev. Stat. § 174C-41; Haw. Admin. Rules §§ 13-167-3, 13-171-3.

49 The Ground Water Use Act was formerly codified at Haw. Rev. Stat. ch. 177 and was repealed in 1987. *See* 1987 Haw. Sess. 45.

water management areas after adoption of the Water Code.[50] On July 15, 1992, the CWRM also designated five Windward O'ahu aquifers, specifically the Kawailoa, Ko'olauloa, Kahana, Ko'olaupoko, and Waimanalo aquifers, as water management areas. In 1992, the CWRM also designated the entire island of Molokai as a groundwater management area.

The designation process may be initiated by the CWRM chairperson or upon written petition. Within sixty days of receiving a petition, the chairperson will make a recommendation for or against the proposed designation, after consultation with the appropriate county council, county mayor and county water board.

The CWRM must consider several criteria in making a decision whether to designate a special management area for groundwater. The CWRM will examine: whether increased use may cause maximum withdrawal rates to reach ninety percent of the sustainable yield of the proposed groundwater management area; whether there is actual or threatened water quality degradation; whether regulation is necessary to preserve water for future needs; whether the existing withdrawals are endangering the groundwater due to upcoming or encroachment of salt water; whether well chloride content materially reduces the value of existing uses; whether excessive preventable waste is occurring; and whether there are serious disputes regarding the use of ground water resources. The CWRM will also look at whether approved government projects may result in one of the foregoing conditions.[51]

The CWRM will consider other surface water criteria in designating areas for water use regulation, including whether there are serious disputes regarding the use of surface water, and whether stream water diversion is reducing the streams' capacity to assimilate pollutants. The CWRM will also examine whether regulation is necessary to preserve the surface water supply for future needs, including whether diversions or declining surface water levels may detrimentally affect existing instream uses or prior existing offstream uses.[52]

---

50 Haw. Rev. Stat. § 174C-41.

51 Haw Rev. Stat. § 174C-44; Haw. Admin. Rules § 13-171-7.

52 Haw. Rev. Stat. § 174C-45; Haw. Admin. Rules § 13-171-8.

Once a designation recommendation has been accepted by CWRM, the Commission gives public notice and holds a public hearing. The public notice, which describes the land area to be designated as well as the nature and purpose of the public hearing, is given once each week for three successive weeks.[53] The CWRM may conduct scientific investigations necessary for it to make a designation decision. The chairperson may also require water users to report on the amount of water being withdrawn as well as the manner and extent of the beneficial use.[54]

After a public hearing has been completed, the chairperson makes a recommendation for decision to the CWRM, and the Commission will render its decision within ninety days. If the CWRM decides to designate a water management area, it must publish public notice. After public notice has been given, the CWRM's decision is final unless judicially appealed within thirty days of publication.[55] Third parties are not entitled to contested case hearings on designation decisions because no procedural due process is involved. It is only at the permitting stage that applicants' property interests are potentially affected and the contested case hearing procedures of the Hawaii Administrative Procedure Act[56] are required to satisfy due process.[57]

The CWRM chairperson or a person with proper standing may initiate procedures to modify or rescind boundaries of existing water management areas. The same procedures will be followed as for designation of water management areas.[58]

---

53 Haw. Rev. Stat. § 184C-42; Haw. Admin. Rules § 13-171-5.

54 Haw. Rev. Stat. § 174C-43; Haw. Admin. Rules § 13-171-6.

55 Haw. Rev. Stat. § 174C-46. *See also*, *Ko'Olau Agricultural Co. v. Commission on Water Resource Mgt.*, 83 Haw. 484, 927 P.2d 1367 (1996).

56 Haw. Rev. Stat. ch. 91. *See infra* ch. 13 of this Handbook.

57 *Ko'Olau Agricultural Co. v. Commission on Water Resource Mgt.*, 83 Haw. 484, 927 P.2d 1367 (1996).

58 Haw. Admin. Rules § 174C-47; Haw. Admin. Rules § 13-171-2.

5.1 PETITIONS FOR RESERVATIONS OF WATER IN WATER MANAGEMENT AREAS

The CWRM, by rule, may reserve water in such locations and quantities and for such seasons of the year as in its judgment may be necessary. Within water management areas, the commission may adopt reservations for purposes which are consistent with the public interest, including the provision of water for current and foreseeable development and use of Hawaiian Home Lands. Proceedings for the establishment of a reservation of water resources within a water management area may be initiated either by recommendation from the CWRM chairperson or upon written petition to the CWRM by any interested person with proper standing.[59]

The CWRM will not allocate reserved water from water management areas except upon application for a water use permit by the parties for whom the water was reserved. All reservations are subject to periodic review and revision in light of changed conditions.[60]

6.0 DECLARATION OF WATER SHORTAGE

The CWRM may declare, by rule, that a water shortage exists within a water management area. This declaration may be made when insufficient water is available to meet permit system requirements or when conditions require a temporary reduction in use to protect resources from serious harm. The CWRM must be of the opinion that usage has caused or may cause within the foreseeable future withdrawals that exceed recharge; that there are declining water levels or heads; that there is deterioration of water quality due to increasing chloride content; that there is excessive preventable water waste, or that there is any other situation in which further water development would endanger the aquifer of existing sources of supply. When a declaration is made, the CWRM publishes weekly notice of the declaration in a newspaper of general circulation until the declaration is rescinded.[61]

The CWRM has formulated a plan for implementation during periods of water shortage. The plan adopts a system of permit classification according to source of water supply, method of

---

59 Haw. Rev. Stat. § 174C-49(d); Haw. Admin. Rules § 13-171-60.

60 Haw Admin. Rules § 13-171-60.

61 Haw. Rev. Stat. § 174C-62; Haw. Admin. Rules §§ 13-171-41, § 13-171-43.

extraction or diversion, or any use of water. The CWRM may use the plan to impose restrictions on certain permit classes, and will notify permittees by mail of any changed permit conditions, permit suspensions or other water use restrictions.[62]

7.0 DECLARATION OF WATER EMERGENCY

The CWRM may declare a water emergency if an emergency condition arises due to a water shortage in an area, whether or not it is in a water management area. An "emergency" means the absence of a sufficient quantity and quality of water in any area whether designated or not which threatens the public health, safety and welfare.[63] The CWRM may issue an emergency declaration if it finds that the restrictions imposed through permit classifications during a declared water shortage are insufficient to protect public health, safety or welfare, or the health of animals, fish, or aquatic life, or are otherwise insufficient to protect a public water supply or recreational, municipal, agricultural or other reasonable uses. Once a water emergency is declared, the CWRM may issue orders requiring actions such as apportioning, rotating, limiting or prohibiting the use of water resources in an area.[64]

The CWRM will publish weekly notice of a water emergency declaration in the newspaper, and will also notify registered users and permittees by mail. Any party subject to an emergency order may challenge the order, but must immediately comply with its terms, whether it is challenged or not.[65]

The water emergency declaration may be rescinded by the CWRM when conditions no longer require a temporary reduction in total water use within the emergency area.[66]

---

62 Haw. Rev. Stat. § 174C-62; Haw. Admin. Rules § 13-171-42.

63 Haw. Rev. Stat. § 174C-3.

64 Haw. Rev. Stat. § 174C-62; Haw. Admin. Rules § 13-171-51.

65 Haw. Admin. Rules §§ 13-171-51, 13-171-52.

66 Haw. Admin. Rules § 13-171-53.

8.0 PERMITS

8.1 WATER USE PERMITS

Water use permits are required for the withdrawal, diversion, impoundment, or consumptive use of water in any designated water management area. Permits are not required for domestic water consumption by individual users, or for the use of catchment systems.[67] Permit applications must show that the proposed water use can be accommodated, is reasonable-beneficial,[68] and will not interfere with either existing uses or the rights of the Department of Hawaiian Home Lands. The applicant must also show that the use is consistent with state and county general plans and land use designations, as well as county land use plans and policies. The CWRM may deny the issuance of a water use permit until the applicant registers all wells owned or operated by the applicant.[69]

Permit applications must include information regarding the source and quantity of water requested, the use of water, the location of the use, the location of the well or point of diversion, and must be accompanied by a non-refundable $25 filing fee.[70] Application forms are available from the DLNR website.[71] In order to obtain a permit, the applicant must establish that the proposed use can be accommodated with the available water source, is reasonable-beneficial, will not interfere with existing legal uses, is consistent with the public interest, state and county general plans, land use designations, and with county land use plans and policies.[72]

After receiving an application, the CWRM publishes notice in a general circulation newspaper once a week for two consecutive weeks. Notification is also sent to the mayor and water board of the affected county, and to any person who has submitted a written request for notification of pending applications affecting a particular designated area.[73] Within sixty days of

---

67 Haw. Rev. Stat. § 174C-49; Haw. Admin. Rules § 13-171-11.

68 *Supra*, note 18.

69 Haw. Rev. Stat. § 174C-83.

70 Haw. Rev. Stat. § 174C-51; Haw. Admin. Rules § 13-171-12.

71 http://www.state.hi.us/dlnr/cwrm/forms.htm (visited August 13, 2000).

72 Haw Admin. Rules § 13-171-13.

73 Haw. Rev. Stat. § 174C-52; Haw. Admin. Rules § 13-171-17.

receiving notice of a permit application, the county must inform the CWRM whether the proposed use is inconsistent with county land use plans and policies.[74]

Within ten days after the public notice, written objections to the proposed permit may be filed. The CWRM will only consider objections filed by persons who have a property interest in any land within the hydrologic unit or who will be directly and immediately affected by the proposed water use.[75] A hydrologic unit is a surface drainage area or ground water basin or a combination of the two.[76] Within ten days after an objection is filed, any other party may file a brief in support of the proposed permit.

If the CWRM receives two conflicting water use applications, the CWRM will first seek to allocate water in a manner accommodating both applications. If mutual sharing is not possible, then the CWRM will approve the allocation which best serves the public interest.[77]

The CWRM will act on an application within ninety days if no hearing is required, or within one hundred and eighty days of an application requiring a hearing.[78] Permits are valid until revoked or until the designation of the water management area is rescinded.[79] The CWRM will conduct a comprehensive study of all issued permits at least once every twenty years to determine whether the permittee has complied with all permit conditions. The study results are documented in a formal report to the Legislature.[80]

---

74 Haw. Rev. Stat. § 174C-49(b); Haw. Admin. Rules § 13-171-13(b).

75 Haw. Rev. Stat. § 174C-53(b); Haw. Admin. Rules §§ 13-171-18, 13-171-19.

76 Haw. Rev. Stat. § 174C-3.

77 Haw. Rev. Stat. § 174C-54; Haw. Admin. Rules § 13-171-16.

78 *Id.* § 174C-53 (c); Haw. Admin. Rules § 13-171-19.

79 *Id.* § 174C-55; Haw. Admin. Rules § 13-171-21.

80 *Id.* § 174C-56; Haw. Admin. Rules §13-171-22.

Permits may only be transferred if the permits' conditions of use remain the same and if the CWRM is informed of the transfer within ninety days. Failure to inform the CWRM invalidates the transfer and constitutes a ground for revocation.[81]

8.1.1 PERMIT MODIFICATION

Any changes to a water use permit must be made by application, whether or not the change is material, whether the place of use is changed, or whether a greater quantity of use is sought. Permit modification applications are procedurally treated as initial permit applications. The CWRM may approve modifications without a hearing, however, if the permittee demonstrates that a change in conditions has resulted in the permit becoming inadequate, or that the proposed modification would result in a more efficient water use.[82]

8.1.2 PERMIT REVOCATION

Permits may be cancelled, permanently and in whole with the written consent of the permittee. The CWRM may revoke permits without the permittee's consent if after a hearing, it determines that materially false statements were made in an application or in any report or statement of fact required by the CWRM. Permits may also be revoked for any willful violation of permit conditions, or any violation of the Water Code. Permits may also be revoked if there is partial or total nonuse for a continuous period of four years or more, unless the reason for nonuse was conservation, was due to extreme hardship caused by factors beyond the user's control.[83]

8.2 STREAM CHANNEL ALTERATION PERMITS

The CWRM has recognized the need to protect stream channels from alteration whenever practicable to provide for fishery, wildlife, recreational, aesthetic, scenic and other beneficial instream uses. Permits are therefore required prior to undertaking any stream channel alteration. However, routing streambed and drainageway maintenance activities and maintenance of existing facilities are exempt from these permit requirements.[84]

---

81 *Id.* § 174C-59; Haw. Admin. Rules § 13-171-25.

82 *Id.* § 174C-57; Haw. Admin. Rules § 13-171-23.

83 Haw. Rev. Stat. 174C-58; Haw. Admin. Rules § 13-171-24.

84 Haw. Rev. Stat. §174C-71(3).

Stream channel alteration permit applications must provide a location and description of the proposed stream channel alteration, an assessment of the impact of channel alteration upon the stream environment, and relevant maps, plans and drawings. A nonrefundable filing fee of $25 must accompany permit applications. The CWRM will consider the adverse effect of channel alterations upon the quantity and quality of stream water or stream ecology, whether there will be an substantial and material interference with existing instream or noninstream uses or with previously permitted channel alterations. Where instream flow standards have been established, channel alteration permits will not be granted if they diminish the quantity or quality of stream water below the minimum standards. The CWRM will act on an application within ninety days and permits are valid for two years, unless otherwise specified in the permit.[85]

The CWRM may revoke a permit based upon material false statements in the application, or in any report or statement of fact. Permits may also be revoked based upon violation of the administrative rules or permit conditions. The CWRM will give written notice to the permit holder of any facts or conditions which warrant a proceeding to revoke a permit, and will provide the permit holder an opportunity for a hearing.[86]

Stream channel alteration as well as the repair or restoration of structures damaged by a sudden and unforeseen event may proceed without a permit on an emergency basis if necessary to prevent or minimize loss of life or damage to property. Measures taken must be limited to the minimum amount necessary to remove immediate threats to health and safety, and structures must be repaired or restored to a minimum facility of the same general type. Within one day after initiation of emergency work, the DLNR must be notified of the nature and circumstances so that the DLNR can issue an emergency authorization. Within thirty days after notification, a written report must be submitted to DLNR describing the nature and extent of the emergency work performed.[87]

---

85 Haw. Admin. Rules § 13-169-50 through -53.

86 Haw. Admin. Rules § 13-169-54.

87 Haw. Admin. Rules § 13-169-55.

8.3 STREAM DIVERSION WORKS PERMITS

Stream diversion works are any artificial or natural structure placed with in stream for the purpose of diverting stream water. Owners or operators of any stream diversion works were required to register with the CWRM by May 27, 1989.[88] The construction or alteration of a stream diversion works is prohibited without a permit. Normal maintenance is excluded from permitting requirements.[89]

The application for a stream diversion works permit is available from the CWRM and must describe the work location, provide engineering drawings and detailed construction specifications along with a description the general purpose of the proposed work, and must be accompanied by a non-refundable filing fee of $25. The CWRM will act on an application for a stream diversion permit within ninety days of receipt, and will issue the permit if the proposed construction complies with all laws, rules and standards. The CWRM will consider any adverse effect on the quantity and quality of stream water or stream ecology, and any substantial and material interference with instream or noninstream uses or previously permitted diversion works. The CWRM will not grant any permit for a stream in which instream flow standards or interim instream flow standards have been established if the diversions will diminish the quantity or quality of water below the minimum standards. Permits will be issued for a two-year period, unless otherwise specified in the permit.[90]

Upon completion of the construction or alteration of any stream diversion work, the permittee must file a written statement of completion with the CWRM. The report must describe the nature and extent of work performed, along with relevant maps and diagrams.[91]

The owners or operators of stream diversion works from which water is being used must use an approved meter of other device to measure the total water usage on a monthly basis. The owner must report the total water usage on a monthly basis to the CWRM, using the CWRM's

---

88 Haw. Rev. Stat. § 174C-91, 174C-92; Haw. Admin. Rules § 13-168-31.

89 Haw. Rev. Stat. § 174C-93.

90 Haw. Rev. Stat. § 174C-93; Haw. Admin. Rules § 13-168-32.

91 Haw. Rev. Stat. § 174C-94; Haw. Admin. Rules § 13-168-33.

report form.[92] The CWRM may require the reporting of other information such as type of use, salinity, and water level. It may also lessen, modify or exempt these requirements for owners or operators of small, individual stream diversion works on a case-by-case basis.[93]

The DLNR has free access to all stream diversion works at any reasonable time to inspect them, obtain data, and investigate any matter. The DLNR, however, will first make a reasonable effort to notify the owner or operator of the diversion works to obtain his or her consent and assistance.[94]

Permits are also required before the removal or abandonment of any stream diversion work.[95]

9.0 WELLS

The CWRM requires registration of existing wells, permits for well construction and pump installation, well completion reports, and has also developed well construction and installation standards. "Wells" are defined by the Water Code to include any artificial excavation or opening into the ground, or an artificial enlargement of a natural opening by which groundwater is drawn or can be made useable to supply reasonable and beneficial uses. The commission does not require a permit for temporary test borings. However, test borings related to underground storage tanks and environmental monitoring or remediation must meet the requirements of the State Department of Health. Test borings which are permanent in nature for long-term monitoring of water levels and chlorides are considered monitoring wells which

---

92 Monthly and annual ground water use report forms are available from the DLNR's website at http://www.state.hi.us/dlnr/cwrm/forms.htm (visited August 13, 2000).

93 Haw. Admin. Rules § 13-168-7.

94 Haw. Admin. Rules § 13-168-34.

95 Haw. Rev. Stat. § 174C-95; Haw. Admin. Rules § 13-168-35.

require a well construction permit from the commission.[96] The owners or operators of wells in existence as of May 27, 1988 were required to register their wells by May 27, 1989.[97]

Authorized DLNR representatives have free access to all wells and their appurtenances at any reasonable time to inspect, test, obtain data, or investigate any matter. The DLNR will first, however, make a reasonable effort to notify the owner or operator of the well and obtain his or her consent and assistance.[98]

The CWRM has adopted minimum standards for well construction and pump installation.[99] If any standard is violated, resulting in the waste or contamination of groundwater, the CWRM will notify the landowner and give them a reasonable time to correct the defect. If the landowner fails to act, the CWRM may correct the defect itself and charge the landowner for the cost of correction. The costs constitute a lien on the land until paid, and the CWRM may foreclose on the lien in any court of competent jurisdiction and recover reasonable attorneys' fees for doing so.[100]

9.1 WELL CONSTRUCTION AND PUMP INSTALLATION PERMITS

The construction of wells, the installation of pumps, and the installation of pumping equipment are prohibited without a permit. No permit is required for the replacement of pumps equal to or less than existing pump capacity, unless deemed otherwise by the COWRM chairperson.[101] Permit applications are required statewide, whether or not in a water management area. Applications are submitted either by the well driller or the pump installation

96 State of Hawaii, Department of Land and Natural Resources, Commission on Water Resource Management, Hawaii *Well Construction and Pump Installation Standards* at 1-3 (January 1997). These standards are available from the DLNR website at http://www.state.hi.us/dlnr/cwrm/forms.htm (visited August 13, 2000).

97 Haw. Rev. Stat. § 184C-83; Haw. Admin. Rules § 13-168-11.

98 Haw. Admin. Rules § 13-168-15.

99 *Well Construction and Pump Installation Standards, supra* note 96.

100 Haw. Rev. Stat. § 174C-86; Haw. Admin. Rules 13-168-14.

101 Commission on Water Resource Management, Water Resource Bulletin (February 2000).

contractor, and must be accompanied by a $25 filing fee.[102] Applications are available from the Department's website.[103]

Well construction and pump installation permits will only be issued if the proposed construction complies with applicable laws, rules and minimum standards adopted by the commission. Permit applications are also reviewed by the Department of Health to determine compliance with Department of Health rules and standards, including the appropriateness of the well location.[104] Permits for new wells or wells without a previous pumping test will require a pumping test to measure the time, pumping rate, drawdown, and chloride content. Aquifer pump test report forms are available from the DLNR's website.[105] The CWRM will act on applications within ninety days of receipt. Well construction and pump installation permits are valid for two years, unless otherwise specified in the permit.[106]

After receiving a permit, the holder may change the well location only with approval from the commission. The application to change the well location must describe the new well, and the manner of sealing or plugging any partially constructed wells under the original permits. The CWRM will issue a permit for a changed location, after review by the Department of Health, if it determines that the new location will serve the same use as the original, will draw upon the same water supply, will comply with the law, and that the incomplete and abandoned well will be sealed or plugged in a manner which prevents waste of water, damage to the water supply and which protects the public from harm. Applicants whose requests for modification are rejected may, within thirty days, submit a written petition for a hearing before the commission.[107]

---

102 Haw. Rev. Stat. § 174C-84; Haw. Admin. Rules § 13-168-12.

103 http://www.state.hi.us/dlnr/cwrm/forms.htm (visited August 13, 2000).

104 Haw. Rev. Stat. § 174C-84.

105 http://www.state.hi.us/dlnr/cwrm/forms.htm (visited August 13, 2000).

106 Haw. Admin. Rules § 13-168-12.

107 Haw. Rev. Stat. § 174C-84; Haw. Admin. Rules § 13-168-12.

The CWRM may modify, suspend or revoke a permit, after notice and hearing, on the grounds of material misstatement or misrepresentation in the permit application, failure to comply with permit provisions, willful disregard of any CWRM rules, or material change of circumstances or conditions.[108]

9.2 WELL COMPLETION REPORTS

The well driller and pump installation contractor must file written reports with the CWRM within thirty days after completing the well. The report must contain information such as a characterization of the different strata penetrated, the location of water-bearing strata, and must describe the casing, drilled hole, the well seal, flow, and pressure as well as a chemical analysis of a water sample drawn from the well.[109] Well completion report forms are available from the DLNR website.[110]

9.3 REPORTING REQUIREMENTS

The owners or operators of wells from which water is being used must use an approved meter or other device to measure the total water usage on a monthly basis. The owner must report the total water usage on a monthly basis to the CWRM. The CWRM may require the reporting of other information such as type of use, salinity, and water level. It may also lessen, modify or exempt these requirements for owners or operators of small, individual wells on a case-by-case basis.[111]

9.4 ABANDONMENT

Before a well is abandoned, the owner must file a well abandonment report which includes the reason for abandonment and a description of the work to be performed. When the well is abandoned, the owner must re-case, cement, plug back, cap, or otherwise repair the well or fill and seal the well in a manner approved by the CWRM, and may not commence the required remedial work until a permit is issued. Within thirty days after completion of work, the

---

108 Haw. Admin. Rules § 13-168-12.

109 Haw. Rev. Stat. § 174C-85; Haw. Admin. Rules § 13-168-14.

110 http://www.state.hi.us/dlnr/cwrm/forms.htm (visited August 13, 2000).

111 Haw. Admin. Rules § 13-168-7.

owner must file a well abandonment report describing the well driller who performed the work, the reason for abandonment, and a complete description of work performed.[112] Well abandonment report forms are available from the Department's website.[113]

10.0 ENFORCEMENT

The CWRM may enforce its rules and orders by suit for injunction or damages. Persons who violate the Water Code are subject to fines not exceeding $1,000. For continuing offenses, each day is considered a separate violation.[114]

11.0 CWRM RULEMAKING PROCEEDINGS

The CWRM must hold a public hearing whenever it proposes to issue, amend or repeal a rule pursuant to petition or upon its own motion. A notice of the proposed rulemaking is published at least once in a newspaper of general circulation, twenty days prior to the date set for public hearing. The notice must describe the substance of the proposed rulemaking, and reference the authority for the proposal.[115] As of March 1, 1999, public notices are published weekly in the Hawaii State and County Public Notices distributed on Oahu as an insert in the Midweek and also on the internet.[116]

Petitions for the adoption, amendment or repeal of rules may be filed with the CWRM, and must set forth the applicable test of the rule, the nature of the petitioner's interest and the reasons for the petition. The CWRM must deny the petition or initiate public rulemaking procedures within thirty days following the petition filing.[117]

---

112 Haw. Rev. Stat. § 174C-87; Haw. Admin. Rules § 13-168-16.

113 http://www.state.hi.us/dlnr/cwrm/forms.htm (visited August 13, 2000).

114 Haw. Rev. Stat. § 174C-15; Haw. Admin. Rules §§ 13-167-10, 13-168-3, 13-169-3.

115 Haw. Admin. Rules §§ 13-167-41, 13-167-42.

116 http://www.midweek.com/hscpn/index.html (visited August 13, 2000).

117 Haw. Admin. Rules § 13-167-46.

The CWRM chairperson or a designated representative will preside over the hearings, which must be conducted in such a way as to afford interested persons a reasonable opportunity to be heard on matters relevant to the issues involved. Interested persons may offer evidence and give sworn testimony. Witnesses are subject to questioning by the presiding officer or by the commission's representative, but cross-examination by private parties is not allowed unless expressly permitted by the presiding officer. Written protests, comments or recommendations in support or opposition to the proposed rulemaking may be filed with the commission within fifteen days of the public hearing.[118]

The commission may adopt, amend or repeal a rule as part of emergency rulemaking if the commission finds an imminent peril to public health, safety or morals. The CWRM may proceed without prior notice or hearing, or on an abbreviated notice and hearing. Any emergency rules adopted pursuant to this process may not be effective for more than 120 days without renewal.[119]

The CWRM may issue a declaratory ruling regarding the applicability of the Water Code, any rule or order of the commission, or any question of law or fact within its jurisdiction. The petitioner may request, or the CWRM may order hearings on such petitions, and conduct such hearings in accordance with the Hawaii Administrative Procedure Act.[120]

12.0 DISPUTE RESOLUTION

The CWRM has adopted procedural rules for the processing of citizen complaints, including the right of appeal to the commission. If any person files a complaint with the CWRM regarding the waste, polluting, diversion, withdrawal, impoundment, or consumptive use of waters without a permit, the Commission will investigate, take appropriate action and notify the complainant of its actions. Complaints related to water quality must be filed with the Department of Health.[121]

---

118 Haw. Admin. Rules § 13-167-44.

119 Haw. Admin. Rules § 13-167-45.

120 Haw. Admin. Rules § 13-167-81. For further discussion of the Hawaii Administrative Procedure Act, Haw. Rev. Stat. ch. 91, *see infra* ch. 13 of this Handbook.

121 Haw. Rev. Stat. § 174C-13; Haw. Admin. Rules § 13-167-82.

The CWRM has jurisdiction to hear disputes regarding water resource protection, water permits, constitutionally protected water interests, or where there is insufficient water to meet competing needs, whether or not the area has been designated as a water management area. The CWRM may also accept cases or controversies referred by a court or questions certified to it by a court.[122] The attorney general or representative of the attorney general's office is counsel to the commission and advises and represents the commission on all legal matters.[123]

All proceedings before the CWRM are conducted pursuant to the Hawaii Administrative Procedure Act, and the CWRM may hold proceedings, and subpoena witnesses and evidence. Documents such as pleadings, applications, submittals, petitions, reports, maps, exemptions, briefs and memoranda must be filed with the Commission chairperson at the commission office in Honolulu.[124]

The CWRM chairperson appoints hearing officers to reach preliminary decisions on matters concerning the Water Code, or the commission may refer such matters to the hearing officers by rule or otherwise. Where there is insufficient water to meet competing needs, the CWRM will adjudicate disputes, but in order to facilitate dispute resolution, the CWRM may employ mediation methods.[125]

12.1 CONTESTED CASE HEARINGS

Contested case hearings are proceedings in which the legal rights, duties or privileges of specific parties are required by law to be determined after an opportunity for an agency hearing. Any person may appear before the CWRM on his or her own behalf, as a partner of a partnership, as an officer of employee of a corporation, or may be represented by counsel.[126]

---

122 Haw. Rev. Stat. § 174C-10; Haw. Admin. Rules § 13-167-23.

123 Haw. Admin. R. § 13-167-29.

124 Haw. Rev. Stat. §§ 174C-9, 174C-60; Haw. Admin. Rules §§ 13-167-22, 13-167-25. For further discussion of the Hawaii Administrative Procedure Act, Haw. Rev. Stat. ch. 91, *see infra* ch. 13 of this Handbook

125 Haw. Rev. Stat. § 174C-11; Haw. Admin. R. § 13-167-24.

126 Haw. Admin. Rules §§ 13-167-2, 13-167-21; 13-167-51.

Contested case hearings may be initiated upon CWRM request or upon written petition from any government agency or interested person. If the CWRM determines that a contested case hearing is required, a notice of hearing will be served on all parties at least fifteen days before the hearing date, and will also be published in the newspaper.[127]

The parties to a contested case hearing may include the petitioner, all government agencies whose jurisdiction includes the land or water in question, and other parties who can show a substantial interest in the matter. The presiding officer may hold pre-hearing conferences, request briefing and appoint a mediator to seek a solution to the dispute.[128]

Contested case hearings are conducted in accordance with the Hawaii Administrative Procedure Act.[129] The presiding officer may administer oaths, compel witnesses' attendance, issue subpoenas, receive relevant evidence, and rule on objections. A verbatim record of the evidence will be recorded unless waived by all parties. The commission members may examine and cross-examine witnesses. Parties also have the right to cross examine witnesses and to submit rebuttal evidence, subject to the presiding officer's limitation. To avoid unnecessary or repetitive evidence, the presiding officer may limit the number of witnesses, the extent of direct or cross examination, or the time for testimony upon a particular issue subject to law.[130]

After evidence is taken, the proceeding is submitted for decision by the CWRM. The hearing officer must file a report with a summary of the evidence, as well as proposed findings of facts and conclusions of law which the commission may adopt, reject or modify. Within ninety days after the hearing, the commission will render its decision in writing accompanied by separate findings of fact and conclusions of law.[131]

---

127 Haw. Admin. Rules §§ 13-167-62, 13-167-53.

128 Haw. Admin. Rules §§ 13-167-54, 13-167-55, 13-167-83 through -92.

129 Haw. Rev. Stat. ch. 91. *See infra* ch. 13 of this Handbook.

130 Haw. Admin. Rules § 13-167-56, 13-167-57.

131 Haw. Admin. Rules § 13-167-63.

13.0 JUDICIAL REVIEW

Judicial review of the CWRM rules and orders is governed by the Hawaii Administrative Procedure Act and trial de novo is not allowed on review of CWRM actions.[132] Appeals from contested case proceedings may be made pursuant to the Hawaii Administrative Procedure Act, and the court may reverse or modify the CWRM's findings if they are contrary to the clear preponderance of the evidence. Any contested case hearing must be appealed directly to the Hawaii Supreme Court.[133] The CWRM's designation of a water management area, however, is not judicially reviewable because the CWRM has exclusive jurisdiction and final authority in this area.[134]

14.0 COMMON LAW WATER RIGHTS

Hawaii has a bifurcated system of water rights. In designated water management areas, the Water Code's permitting provisions prevail, but the common law governs water rights in non-designated areas. The Hawaii Supreme Court has held that the CWRM has "no authority to regulate water use through permitting in an undesignated area."[135]

14.1 APPURTENANT RIGHTS

The Water Code preserves appurtenant rights, and permits for water use based on existing appurtenant rights must be issued upon application.[136] The appurtenant rights of kuleana and taro lands, however, are not diminished or extinguished by a failure to apply for or receive a

---

132 Haw. Rev. Stat. § 174C-12; Haw. Admin. Rules § 13-167-32.

133 Haw. Admin. Rules § 13-167-65.

134 *Ko'Olau Agricultural Co. v. Commission on Water Resource Mgt.*, 83 Haw. 484, 492-93, 927 P.2d 1367, 1375-76 (1996).

135 *Ko'Olau Agricultural Co.*, 83 Haw. at 491, 927 P.2d at 1374.

136 Haw. Rev. Stat. § 174C-63; Haw. Admin. Rules § 13-171-27.

permit under the Water Code.[137] The quantity of appurtenant water rights is recognized in Hawaii as "the quantum of water utilized at the time of the Mahele."[138]

Notwithstanding common law, the CWRM may allow a water use permittee to transport and use surface or ground water outside the watershed from which it is taken if the CWRM determines that the use is consistent with the public interest, and general plans and land use policies.[139]

14.2 RIPARIAN RIGHTS

Riparian rights are the rights of a landowner on the bank of a watercourse relating to the use and ownership of stream water. The Kuleana act recognizes that the people have a right to drinking water, running water, and that the springs of water and running water shall be free to all, on all lands granted in fee simple.[140] The Hawaii Supreme Court has thus treated the Kuleana Act as a codification of riparian rights,[141] and recognized that landowners have a right to use water flowing on their land without prejudicing others' riparian rights to the natural flow of the water course.[142] Thus, the "reasonableness" of use, originally a riparian concept, is now embodied in the Water Code. Riparian owners cannot sue to prohibit another's reasonable use, unless the riparian owners can demonstrate actual harm to their own reasonable use.[143]

14.3 CORRELATIVE RIGHTS

The Hawaii Supreme Court has held that Hawaii's artesian waters are subject to the doctrine of correlative rights. The rule of "correlative rights" establishes that all owners of lands under which lies an artesian basin have rights to the waters of that basin. Each landowner may use water from the basin as long as he or she does not injure the rights of others. In times when

---

137 Haw. Rev. Stat. § 174C-101(c).

138 *Reppun v. Board of Water Supply*, 65 Haw. 531, 551-52, 656 P.2d 57, 70-71 (1982).

139 Haw. Rev. Stat. § 174C-49; Haw. Admin. Rules § 13-171-13(c).

140 Haw. Rev. Stat. § 7-1.

141 *McBryde Sugar Co. v. Robinson*, 54 Haw. 174, 504 P.2d 1330 (1973).

142 *McBryde*, 54 Haw. at 191-97, 504 P.2d 1341-44.

143 *Reppun v. Board of Water Supply*, 65 Haw. at 552-53, 656 P.2d at 71-72.

there is insufficient water for all, each landowner is limited to a reasonable share of the water. Under the rule of correlative rights, a diversion of water to lands other than that of origin might, perhaps, be permitted under some circumstances and not under others. Also under the rule of correlative rights certain larger uses, as for industrial purposes, might not be permitted even on the land of origin under some circumstances while being permitted under others.[144]

14.4 PRESCRIPTIVE RIGHTS

The Hawaii courts have recognized that prescriptive rights may exist if there is an adverse and continuous use of water for twenty years. Thus if an ancient use of spring and stream water for a taro lo'i was diverted from the lo'I for twenty years or more, the lo'i would no longer have any ancient right to that water.[145] With prescriptive rights, a person entitled to divert a given quantity of water could change the point of diversion, the place of use, the mode of use, and the objects of use at pleasure if the rights of others were not injuriously affected by the change.[146]

---

144 *City Mill Co. v. Honolulu Sewer & Water Commission*, 30 Haw. 912 (Hawai'i Terr. 1929)

145 *Pioneer Mill v. Kumuliilii*, 10 Haw. 174 (1895) (Pioneer Mill had a prescriptive right to use waters of Kauaula Stream); *Lonoaea v. Wailuku Sugar Co.*, 9 Haw. 651 (1895) (finding sufficient evidence to sustain a sugar company's prescriptive right to use water by day); *Davis v. Afong*, 5 Haw. 216 (1884) (defentant's use of water for taro were subject to the plaintiff's prescriptive right in spring water).

146 *Lonoaea v. Wailuku Sugar Co.*, 9 Haw. at 671-72.

Government Institutes Mini-Catalog

PC #		ENVIRONMENTAL TITLES	Pub Date	Price
629		ABCs of Environmental Regulation: Understanding the Fed Regs	1998	$65
627		ABCs of Environmental Science	1998	$49
672		Book of Lists for Regulated Hazardous Substances, 9th Edition	1999	$95
579		Brownfields Redevelopment	1998	$95
4100		CFR Chemical Lists on CD ROM, 1999-2000 Edition	1999	$150
4089		Chemical Data for Workplace Sampling & Analysis, Single User Disk	1997	$159
512		Clean Water Handbook, 2nd Edition	1996	$115
581		EH&S Auditing Made Easy	1997	$95
673		E H & S CFR Training Requirements, 4th Edition	1999	$99
4082		EMMI-Envl Monitoring Methods Index for Windows-Network	1997	$537
4082		EMMI-Envl Monitoring Methods Index for Windows-Single User	1997	$179
525		Environmental Audits, 7th Edition	1996	$95
548		Environmental Engineering and Science: An Introduction	1997	$95
643		Environmental Guide to the Internet, 4th Edition	1998	$75
650		Environmental Law Handbook, 15th Edition	1999	$89
353		EH&S Dictionary: Official Regulatory Terms, 7th Edition	2000	$95
652		Environmental Statutes, 2000 Edition	2000	$105
4097		OSHA CFRs Made Easy (29 CFRs)/CD ROM	1998	$159
4102		1999 Title 21 Food & Drug CFRs on CD ROM-Single User	1999	$325
4099		Environmental Statutes on CD ROM for Windows-Single User	1999	$169
570		ESAs Made Easy	1996	$75
689		Fundamentals of Site Remediation	2000	$85
515		Industrial Environmental Management: A Practical Approach	1996	$95
588		International Environmental Auditing	1998	$179
510		ISO 14000: Understanding Environmental Standards	1996	$85
551		ISO 14001: An Executive Report	1996	$75
518		Lead Regulation Handbook	1996	$95
554		Property Rights: Understanding Government Takings	1997	$95
582		Recycling & Waste Mgmt Guide to the Internet	1997	$65
615		Risk Management Planning Handbook	1998	$105
603		Superfund Manual, 6th Edition	1997	$129
566		TSCA Handbook, 3rd Edition	1997	$115
534		Wetland Mitigation: Mitigation Banking and Other Strategies	1997	$95

PC #	SAFETY and HEALTH TITLES	Pub Date	Price
547	Construction Safety Handbook	1996	$95
553	Cumulative Trauma Disorders	1997	$75
663	Forklift Safety, 2nd Edition	1999	$85
539	Fundamentals of Occupational Safety & Health	1996	$65
612	HAZWOPER Incident Command	1998	$75
535	Making Sense of OSHA Compliance	1997	$75
589	Managing Fatigue in Transportation, *ATA Conference*	1997	$75
558	PPE Made Easy	1998	$95
598	Project Mgmt for E H & S Professionals	1997	$85
552	Safety & Health in Agriculture, Forestry and Fisheries	1997	$155
669	Safety & Health on the Internet, 3rd Edition	1999	$75
597	Safety Is A People Business	1997	$65
668	Safety Made Easy, 2nd	1999	$75
590	Your Company Safety and Health Manual	1997	$95

Government Institutes
4 Research Place, Suite 200 • Rockville, MD 20850-3226
Tel. (301) 921-2323 • FAX (301) 921-0264
E-mail: giinfo@govinst.com • www.govinst.com

Please call our Customer Service Department at (301) 921-2323 for a free publications catalog.

CFRs are now available online. Call the Publishing Department at (301) 921-2355 for information.

Government Institutes Order Form

4 Research Place, Suite 200 • Rockville, MD 20850-3226
Tel (301) 921-2323 • Fax (301) 921-0264
www.govinst.com • E-mail: giinfo@govinst.com

4 EASY WAYS TO ORDER

1. Phone: **(301) 921-2323**
Have your credit card ready when you call.

2. Fax: **(301) 921-0264**
Fax this completed order form with your company purchase order or credit card information.

3. Mail: **Government Institutes Division**
ABS Group Inc.
P.O. Box 846304
Dallas, TX 75284-6304 USA
Mail this completed order form with a check, company purchase order, or credit card information.

4. Online: www.govinst.com

PAYMENT OPTIONS

❑ **Check** *(payable in US dollars to* ***ABS Group Inc. Government Institutes Division****)*

❑ **Purchase Order** *(This order form must be attached to your company P.O. Note: All International orders must be prepaid.)*

❑ **Credit Card** ☐ VISA ☐ MasterCard ☐ American Express

Exp. ___ /___

Credit Card No. ______________________

Signature ______________________

(Government Institutes' Federal I.D.# is 13-2695912)

CUSTOMER INFORMATION

Ship To: (Please attach your purchase order)

Name ______________________

GI Account # *(7 digits on mailing label)* ______________________

Company/Institution ______________________

Address ______________________
(Please supply street address for UPS shipping)

____

City ____________ State/Province ____________

Zip/Postal Code ____________ Country ____________

Tel ( )______________________

Fax ( )______________________

E-mail Address ______________________

Bill To: (If different from ship-to address)

Name ______________________

Title/Position ______________________

Company/Institution ______________________

Address ______________________
(Please supply street address for UPS shipping)

____

City ____________ State/Province ____________

Zip/Postal Code ____________ Country ____________

Tel ( )______________________

Fax ( )______________________

E-mail Address ______________________

Qty.	Product Code	Title	Price

Subtotal ________
MD Residents add 5% Sales Tax ________
Shipping and Handling (see box below) ________
Total Payment Enclosed ________

15 DAY MONEY-BACK GUARANTEE

If you're not completely satisfied with any product, return it undamaged within 15 days for a full and immediate refund on the price of the product.

All prices and publication dates are subject to change. Please call for current prices and availability.

Shipping and Handling

Within U.S:
1-4 products: $6/product
5 or more: $4/product

Outside U.S:
Add $15 for each item (Global)

Sales Tax

Maryland 5%
Texas 8.25%
Virginia 4.5%

SOURCE CODE: BP 02